Read On,
Write On

Read On, Write On

RAYNA KLINE
GEORGIA-MAE GALLIVAN
STANLEY SPICER

Clark College

Random House, New York

ISBN: 0–394–30326–1

Library of Congress Catalog Card Number: 70–127645

Manufactured in the United States of America. Composed
by Cherry Hill Composition. Printed and bound by Halliday
Lithograph Corp., West Hanover, Mass.

First Edition
98765

Foreword

Our desks, like yours, are piled high with a season's offerings of composition texts. Faced with writing a foreword for still another English text, we are at least partly inclined to apologize for office pollution. But although it does add a bit to the professional ecological problem, we think that *Read On, Write On* is not just another "new" text. We think it really is new.

This collection meets a long-felt need in two very important ways. First, the reading selections are just right: adult in topic and tone, yet clear and direct enough that even inexperienced readers can cope successfully with them. They are short—sometimes a paragraph, sometimes a page, seldom more than three or four pages—and for many freshmen the mere length of an essay can be a considerable hurdle. The articles are notably free of strange vocabulary, unsupported abstractions, and exotic and convoluted sentence structure. Ease in reading, however, does not mean that the selections are simple-minded. The editors have deliberately chosen material that most educated Americans do ordinarily read: such widely different writers as Eldridge Cleaver, Mark Twain, and Brig. Gen. (Ret.) S. L. A. Marshall; such widely different sources as *Playboy,* the American Bar Association's advice column, the *President's Report on Civil Disorders,* and the Sunday Supplement. The adult subject matter will stimulate discussion on issues about which students ought to be concerned, and the clarity of the writing will bring those issues within the reach of every student. The ideas are often forceful and sophisticated, but the language is clear and straightforward.

Second, we like this book because it is primarily designed to teach writing. Most of the readers piled high on our desks are essentially just that: readers. Whether they are organized rhetorically or topically, the student is told to admire the selections and sometimes to explain why he should admire them or to argue with the stands they take; he is rarely offered selections which can serve as models for the kind of writing he himself is expected to produce over the weekend. The gap between what he is given to read and what he is expected to write is often enormous, so enormous that we should not be surprised when perceptive students are discouraged, frightened, often immobilized—or, indeed, angered, hostile, and mobilized. Although the articles in this text cannot guarantee a peaceful year on your campus, they have been chosen not just because teachers like and admire them, but because students can understand and emulate them. This ease in understanding frees students to consider the ideas presented and respond to them, to analyze how the effect was achieved, rather than spend most of the fifty-minute hour trying to figure out what an essay "means." As they read this text, students learn to produce good writing, not just to analyze "best" writing. The gap between what they talk about and what they write has been sufficiently narrowed that most students will find they can bridge it rather comfortably.

Kline, Gallivan, and Spicer are remarkably thorough and imaginative in providing additional help for students. (1) Brief comments printed in the margin alongside the first article in each group show just what is happening and how the writer makes it happen. (2) Discussion questions guide students toward sensible discoveries, rather than trick them into answering "wrong." (3) There is enough topical continuity that students can see the same subject —the problem of poverty, for instance—handled in different ways for different purposes and can thus learn something about varying their own writing to suit their purposes and their audience. (4) The brief and simple definitions of unfamiliar words given at the beginning of each selection keep inexperienced readers from stumbling over vocabulary. (5) And the generous list of theme topics offers a stimulating set of suggestions rather than an artificially limited choice.

But even though this text is primarily aimed toward helping students, it helps teachers too. Each section moves from shorter and easier to longer and more difficult readings, so that the teacher who wants to correlate the level of difficulty with the ability of his class can do so. The *second* table of contents—Write On: Advice for Writers—makes it simple to find topics treated in the advisory sections of each chapter.

In short, we think this text does break new ground. It's not just another collection of readings. It differs from readers that concentrate on controversial issues to the exclusion of student writing; from those that arouse awareness and encourage self-examination to the exclusion of the practical writing harsh reality often demands; and from those which, even though rhetorically arranged, present essays so complex that any consideration of student writing is almost automatically excluded.

Read On, Write On began as a companion volume for *Plain English Please*. The teachers who put it together believed, with many other teachers across the country, that *Plain English Please* would work better if students could see, from published articles, that professional writers actually do write in the way we recommend. We were so pleased with the selections Kline, Gallivan, and Spicer had made, that we have, with their permission, included a few of these articles in the alternate version of our text, *Plain English Rhetoric and Reader*. We have, however, reprinted only a small sample of the variety that appears here. Used with *Plain English Please*, second edition, *Read On, Write On* should provide a thorough and integrated course.

Despite the fact that we regard this reader as a kind of godchild, and despite a natural prejudice toward seeing our own book sell, it seems quite clear that *Read On, Write On* can probably be used effectively with almost any "how-to-write" text. Indeed it can even be used by itself, and probably will be. Each section of readings is preceded by a short introduction that discusses, swiftly and thoroughly, the writing problems involved in that section, and the straightforward, nontechnical language in which these introductions are written should give almost any student the guidance he needs to read right on, to write right on.

So our initial temptation to apologize for office pollution is more than offset by an impulse to shout "Hurrah!" But because nearly every publisher is already shouting "Hurrah!" for nearly every book that comes out, we'll simply say that *Read On, Write On* seems to us a text that will work. We think your students will agree.

Gregory Cowan
Elisabeth McPherson

An Acknowledgment

We want to thank *Plain English Please* for providing the incentive and inspiration that caused us to begin the task of putting together this way out, conservative, relevant, traditional, prescriptive, permissive, issue-oriented, language-oriented, rhetoric-based, discussion-centered, based-on-time-tested-principles-of-organization-and-sound-logic, designed-to-teach-by-example-rather-than-precept, innovative, behavioristic, provocative, and Mildly Comforting Reader. We considered several subtitles:

The From-Sailing-to-Brainwashing Reader

The Slightly Distraught Reader

The Do-Your-Own-Thing Reader

The Otherwise-Your-Teacher-Would-Have-to-Xerox-It Reader

and, eventually,

The Let's-Get-This-Damned-Thing-Over-With Reader

but then abandoned them all in the fear that they might be misleading.

The usual kudos to neglected families, friends, pets, and gurus.

Rayna Kline

Georgia-Mae Gallivan

Stanley Spicer

viii

I Read On: Readings for Writers

II Write On: Advice for Writers

These general topics (with the exception of the Writing Exercises and Writing Topics, which are specific) are covered in the discussion listed on the pages below.

Read On, Write On

"I have deep perceptive thoughts, but I can't get them into sentences."

Drawing by Robert Censoni. Copyright 1969 Saturday Review, Inc.

readings on directions 1

GIVING
DIRECTIONS

At one time or another, most people have to give directions for making
something or doing something, and very often these directions have to be
written. Whether the directions cover something as simple as how to make a
flaky piecrust, or something as complicated as how to win friends and
influence people, all good written directions have several things in common.
They say clearly what the directions will cover. They stick to the point,
leaving out details and comments that have nothing to do with the topic.
They are carefully organized so that the reader can follow them without
wasting time, materials, or energy.

Some kinds of directions start by attracting the reader's interest so he will
want to read on; some of them conclude by reassuring the reader that if
he has done what he was told to do, his project cannot fail. But whether the
directions begin with a come-on and end with some comfort, or whether
they simply plunge into how-to-do-it and end when the job is done, all of
them consider the needs of their readers. The language they use and the
amount of information they give are chosen to fit the background and
ability of the audience they are written for.

A completely straightforward essay giving directions is obviously more
useful than a wonderfully amusing essay that doesn't get to the point.
However, just because directions serve a particular purpose, they don't have
to be dull. As you will see from some of the following selections, writers
frequently succeed in being amusing as well as instructive. It goes without
saying, though, that the entertaining parts are additional. Amusing comments
in directions are like the prize in a Crackerjack box, something extra put in
to make the main thing more attractive, but no substitute for the main thing.

Consider, for instance, the following selection, which gives common
sense directions on a serious matter and yet includes a playful comment
here and there to hold the reader's interest.

Capsizing

catastrophe: a sudden and very serious accident
humiliating: very embarrassing
hull: the hollow, lower part of a boat, on which everything else is
supported
gunwale: the upper rim of the hull
boom: a pole that holds the bottom of a sail and swings to let the sail
change direction
melodramatic: exaggerated; over-dramatized

[1] Very few boat owners live to an advanced age without having capsized a couple of times. Since it is bound to happen to you sooner or later, it may just as well happen sooner so that you can realize that it is no catastrophe and that you can handle yourself and your boat properly when both of you are in the water. In fact, a deliberate capsize early in your boating career will build up your confidence and get rid of your fears. Capsizing can be humiliating at times, but it is not dangerous unless you lose your head.

Introduction is startling

Main idea

[2] In a capsize, your ability to swim great distances is much less important than your ability to handle yourself sensibly in the water. Since capsizes usually come as a surprise, your first reaction is apt to be an instinctive intake of breath. If this intake happens under water, your efficiency for the rest of the day is likely to suffer. Your first rule, then, is to stop breathing as the boat goes over and to resume it only after your head is above water.

Two paragraphs give general advice which would apply to any capsize

May be summed up in two "unbreakable rules"
The first rule

[3] The only other unbreakable rule is never to abandon the boat. The shore always looks closer than it is, and the idea of swimming ashore to summon aid can be very appealing to one's heroic instincts, but almost every fatality after a capsize is caused by someone's deciding to abandon the boat and swim for shore. If you hang onto the boat (and

Linking phrase, "the only other unbreakable rule . . ."
The second rule

From *Your First Boat*, by David Klein. Copyright, 1953, by Wilfred Funk, Inc. By permission of the publishers.

you can do so fairly comfortably even if the boat has turned turtle), you may get hungry and scared and run out of conversation, but you are certain to be picked up sooner or later. Getting picked up from an overturned boat may not do much for your ego but it does wonders for your life expectancy.

[4] There are a number of things you can do in a capsize to remedy the situation. If you turn over in a canoe, you can shake out most of the water by rocking the canoe rhythmically, crawl in carefully, bail out the rest of the water, and get underway once more. If your canoe is in good condition, this technique is quite easy, and if you practice it a couple of times by capsizing deliberately, you should have no trouble in any situation. Boy scouts can go through the entire process in four minutes, but nobody will be holding a stop watch on you and the important thing is not to tire yourself out.

> Now, advice for *particular* situations
> For a canoe

[5] In an outboard boat, the motor usually makes the capsized hull very awkward to handle and sometimes will drag it almost completely under water. If the motor is submerged anyhow, you won't make matters any worse by rigging a line to it, detaching it from the boat, and letting it sink to the bottom. Then you can right the hull, bail it, and recover the motor. Finally you can row home.

> For an outboard motor

[6] To right a capsized sailboat you first have to get sail off her. Once you do, you can usually right her by standing on the centerboard and placing both hands on the gunwale. If this doesn't work, swing the boom into a vertical position so that it acts as a lever and then pull down on the main sheet so that the boom forces the boat up-right. Then get in and bail fast enough to gain on the water coming in through the centerboard trunk.

> For a sailboat

[7] Righting a capsized boat without assistance and continuing on your way is a very satisfying thing to do and a rather pleasing thing to mention casually to your friends. But the process can be very tiring, and when you are in the water you will do well to conserve your strength. Unless you are fairly certain that you can do the job successfully, you will be much wiser to sit on the bottom of the boat and devote your energies to attracting somebody's attention. A police whistle or an army signaling mirror

> Conclusion returns to good *general* advice, no matter what kind of boat

are useful gadgets to hang around your neck if the weather looks threatening. The code signal for SOS ($\cdots - - - \cdots$) may seem somewhat melodramatic for use when your outboard tips over, but it will usually bring somebody to help you.

DISCUSSION

1. Make a one-sentence summary of the most important idea in each paragraph; check with your classmates to see how closely their choices agree with yours. Do you think these sentence summaries are the *plan* from which the writer started? If you think they are not the plan, map out a simple plan on which the article must have been based.

2. In your own words, state what these directions are intended to cover. What is the most important single piece of advice the writer gives? Where do you find the sentence that comes closest to stating this advice? Why has the writer placed it there instead of somewhere else in the article?

3. If the seven sentences you have written give all the necessary information, why has the writer included the rest of what he says? Consider especially the second sentence in paragraph 1, the two middle sentences in paragraph 2, the last sentence in paragraph 3, and the first sentence in paragraph 7. How would the tone of the article be changed if these sentences were left out?

4. Do you think these directions are clear enough that you could follow them if your boat tipped over? Can you think of anything you would need to know or do that has been left out?

How Do You Paint A Room?

amateur: someone who doesn't do it for a living; opposite of professional

ambitiously: attempting a great deal

lap: one layer lying slightly over another layer

baseboard: the board around the foot of a wall

molding: frame around a panel or picture

[1] You don't have to be a professional painter to re-paint your own home with some skill, but whether you are a weekend amateur or a professional, it is important to study the thing you are going to paint before you ever pick up the brush. There's more to it than just spreading paint around, and where you start painting can make a considerable difference in the results.

[2] If you are ambitiously redoing a whole room, it is obvious that you should start with the ceiling to reduce the chances of splatters and drips on fresh paint. Start in a corner, and whether you're using a brush or a roller, paint a strip completely across the ceiling the shorter way. Paint each strip only as wide as you can reach comfortably, probably two feet, never more than three feet wide. To prevent lap marks, paint the entire ceiling without stopping and as rapidly as you can.

[3] Next, paint the walls, which are easier. Simply start at the top corner of a wall and finish one wall at a time, again being careful to avoid lap marks. When the walls are finished, do the baseboard and window trim. Paint the doors last.

[4] Start refinishing a door by first painting the door frame. Then paint the door's edges and on each immediately wipe off with a rag any overlapping dribbles of wet paint. If it's a plain, flat door, next paint the front and back. If it's a panelled door, you can't just start at the top. Instead, paint the panels and their moldings, again wiping off any overlap. Then paint the crosswise strips, and finish with the strips that go up and down. (You may see a professional just start in at the top of a panelled door and paint everything on the way down. He can do this because he can apply paint fast enough so that he's always lapping into fresh paint.)

[5] Whenever possible, start at the top and work down, whether you're painting a wall, a chair, or a boat. The job will go easier and the results will be much more satisfactory.

DISCUSSION

1. What is the main idea of this article? Find the sentence in the first paragraph that comes closest to stating it.

2. Is the main idea repeated in the last paragraph? If so, is it more general or more specific than the sentence in the first paragraph?

3. In a word or two, tell what paragraphs 2, 3 and 4 are about.

4. Is the job completed in paragraph 4? If so, why does the writer add paragraph 5?

5. Which sentence in paragraph 4 ties it to paragraph 1? How does this sentence in paragraph 4 show that the writer has kept in mind who his readers are?

Introductions and Conclusions

Good introductions tell the reader what the directions will cover and suggest
reasons for following each step. Most of them also contain clues about the
readers the article was designed for. All the introductions given below tell
you both what you will learn and why you might want to learn it:

> A good knife will last a lifetime with proper care. But to fulfill its purpose it
> must be kept sharp. Most kitchen accidents happen because a knife is too dull,
> not because it's too sharp. There is no need to keep your knife like a razor, but
> a bit of conscientious care and sharpening will give it the proper edge and
> make it a kitchen tool that is a pleasure to use. (From "How to Teach Your
> Husband Knife Sharpening," *Sunset,* November 1964.)

WHAT: how to sharpen a kitchen knife
WHY: for safety and pleasure
READERS: the general public—anybody who works in a kitchen.

> A few good pictures make all the difference between a drab, dull wall and a
> tasteful, exciting room. Even though you can't afford Picassos, you can trans-
> form your own living room for less than ten dollars and an evening's work.
> All you need are two or three poster prints from an art supply store, three or
> four yards of contrasting burlap from the yard goods department, two or
> three sheets of wallboard from a lumber dealer, and the imagination to
> combine them. (From Jay F. Rosenberg, *The Impoverished Students'
> Book of Cookery, Drinkery, and Housekeepery.*)

WHAT: how to mount poster prints
WHY: to improve the living room without spending much money
READERS: the general public—everybody who needs a new picture

> Forming your own band is a gas if you can find the right guys; if you get
> the wrong ones, it's worse than a risk, it's a disaster. To find four or five
> guys who can turn out really groovy music together, here's what you need
> to do.

WHAT: how to form a dance band
WHY: for fun
READERS: teenagers interested in popular music. (Notice that this writer
is trying to appeal to high school students by using the kind of language he
thinks they use, but the attempt fails. Such words as "gas," "guys," and
"groovy" may put off more readers than they attract. Slang rapidly dates the
article, even though it was written only three or four years ago. To reasonably
hip readers, the writer's clumsy attempt sounds strained and phony; to reasonably straight readers, the slang sounds simply silly. The choice of "gas"
rather than the more formal "exciting and entertaining" does tell us, however,
something about the readers the writer is expecting.)

> My wife Patti makes these yeast breads for us and most of our friends. The
> project originated as an effort to save money. This was a reasonable expecta-

tion, homemade bread costing roughly half per loaf what storeboughten bread costs. This would have worked out just fine, except for the fact that the homemade bread tastes *so* good that we eat three times as much of it as we did of the storeboughten type. This, therefore, is not a recipe for people who want to save money. It is a recipe for people who want to eat three times as much bread in the future as they are eating at present—and enjoy it all much more. (From Jay. F. Rosenberg, *The Impoverished Students' Book of Cookery, Drinkery, and Housekeepery.*)

WHAT: how to make yeast breads
WHY: because they taste good
AUDIENCE: the bread-eating public—almost everybody, you might first think, but actually the introduction gives some clues that tell us the readers are a smaller group, either close acquaintances or readers who are being treated like acquaintances. "My wife Patti," "these yeast breads," "storeboughten bread," "just fine," all give the introduction a tone of informality and intimacy.

Introductions prepare the reader for the directions he will be given; conclusions let him know they are completed. Some final paragraphs go back to the main idea that has been stated in the introduction; some emphasize one of the reasons for doing the job; and some reassure the reader about how easily he can accomplish whatever he's being told how to do. In *Capsizing,* for instance, the first paragraph says, "Capsizing can be humiliating at times, but it is not dangerous unless you lose your head"; the last paragraph suggests that one way of losing your head is to waste your strength by righting the capsized boat instead of sitting quietly and trying to get help. In *How Do You Paint A Room?* the introduction says ". . . where you start painting can make a considerable difference in the results"; the conclusion makes "where you start" more definite by saying ". . . start at the top and work down, whether you're painting a wall, a chair, or a boat," and it also reassures the reader by telling him that if he does start at the top, "the job will go easier and the results will be much more satisfactory."

Notice, however, that neither of these writers simply repeats what he has said before. Instead, both of them keep the idea but change the words. The reader is reminded that the promise of the introduction has been kept, but he is not bored by exact repetition. Good conclusions keep the tone of the original too. If the article begins with informal language, it should end the same way.

Writing Exercise

Write a conclusion for each of the four introductions discussed on pages 10 through 11. Make sure that your conclusion rephrases either the main idea or the reason for doing the job; let your last sentence reassure the reader.

Rubbings

archaeologists: men who study the way prehistoric people lived
bas-relief: a shallow carving in which the figures stand out only slightly from the background (like faces on coins)
deteriorating: wearing out or crumbling away
commemorative: put up in memory of a person or an event
incised: cut down from the surface (like cut glass or cut crystal)
recipient: person who receives something

[1] Remember when, as a child you covered a penny with paper and rubbed a pencil back and forth across the surface to reproduce the likeness of Abraham Lincoln? Attractive rubbings to decorate the home may be made in much the same way and are not much more difficult to do. The inexpensive materials are easily available; all you will need is some paper, a marker, a whisk broom, a soft nail brush, and masking tape.

"Remember when" opening is catchy and also explains the process. Introduction gives a reason for attempting the project and encourages the reader. It also lists the materials needed to do the job

[2] The technique of taking rubbings has long been used by achaeologists, scholars, and artists to record bas-reliefs in danger of deteriorating. Such reproductions make wonderful gifts, for they can be tailor-made to suit the interests of the persons to whom they are given. For a history lover, a rubbing of a historical marker would make a perfect gift. For a friend who is moving away, you might make a rubbing of some familiar landmark to serve as a reminder to him.

Second paragraph gives another reason

[3] There are many places where you will find suitable subjects. Part of the fun is finding them in unexpected spots. The ideal relief is not too deep or sculptural, with the raised surface flat and smooth. Good examples can usually be found among historical markers, cornerstones, manhole covers, gravestones, low reliefs on buildings, and commemorative plaques, to suggest just a few. It doesn't harm the original to make a rubbing, but stay on your paper.

Where to look for suitable subjects

Adapted from *Gifts You Can Make,* a Sunset book.

12

And if the object to be rubbed is on private property, be sure to get the owner's permission.

[4] Once you have located your subject, you can easily assemble your materials. Smooth-textured, lightweight papers produce the cleanest prints. The paper should be strong, yet thin enough to make good contact with the object being rubbed. White poster paper was used by the writer to reproduce a Mexican stone carving. You may also use newsprint (which eventually turns yellow), rice paper, lightweight bond, tissue paper, and shelf paper, all with good results.

Kinds of paper suitable for the job

[5] Markers with a wax base are best. Shoe finishing wax may be bought in a one-pound block from shoe repair shops and broken into manageable pieces. You may also use Conté crayon, litho crayon, ordinary wax crayon, and medium grade lumberman's marking pencil (available at building supply dealers). Charcoal and graphite are too soft and pile up on the surface of the paper. Use the side of the crayon to get a flat, smooth marking surface. Conté crayon should be sprayed with artist's fixative when you are finished; the other markers will not smear as easily.

Markers, suitable, and unsuitable

[6] To make the rubbing, first brush the carved or incised stone free of dirt with your whisk broom. Cut the desired length of paper and tape it in place over the stone to prevent shifting.

Preparing the subject

[7] Using the soft nail brush, go over the surface of the paper, easing it into the depressions of the stone in order to locate the design outlines. When this is done, you are ready to begin rubbing with your marker. Go over the entire surface of the stone. Be careful to stay within the desired boundary lines and to keep the tone even.

Making the rubbing

[8] This project combines fun with the satisfaction of making a gift that is out of the ordinary and thoughtfully chosen to suit the taste of the recipient.

Conclusion restates a reason for doing the job

DISCUSSION

1. What are the two reasons for making rubbings? Why does the writer give a separate paragraph to each reason? Why does the list of materials appear where it does?

2. Where does the introduction end? In what paragraph does the writer stop encouraging readers to try the project and begin giving information useful to people who have decided to do it?

3. Skillful writers sometimes encourage the reader beyond the introduction. In this article the writer weaves his encouragement into the whole article. Find words, phrases, or sentences which encourage the reader.

4. What is the main point of each paragraph from 2 through 7? Each of these paragraphs develops a point already mentioned in the first paragraph. Find the word or phrase in paragraph 1 which hints at each of these points.

5. The list of necessary materials given in the first paragraph includes five things. Why does the writer go into considerable detail about two of them and not discuss the other three at all?

6. The conclusion to this article is a single sentence. Does it seem satisfactory to you? Why or why not? If you think it is unsatisfactory, what would you add?

The Impoverished Students' Guide to Instant Decorating

I hypothesize: it's my theory
non-impoverished: people with plenty of money
impoverished: usually, reduced to poverty; in this article, poor enough to be very careful of how money is spent
surly: sulky and bad tempered
calculate: figure out
multifunctional: having many uses
receptacle: a container, something to hold things
blemished: marred or damaged
tapestry: a cloth wall hanging, often an embroidered design

[1] There are two of you—both chunky peanut butter eaters—and you've gotten yourselves a four-room, partially-furnished apartment for about $80 per month. It is one week before classes. You walk in, set down your 27 boxes full of books and clothing, and look around. You begin whimpering softly, because:

Pages 38–39 from *The Impoverished Students' Book of Cookery, Drinkery, and Housekeepery,* by Jay F. Rosenberg are reprinted by permission of the publisher, Reed College Alumni Association and the author. Distributed by Doubleday & Co. Copyright © 1965 by Jay F. Rosenberg.

1. There are one table, 3 chairs, 2 small desks, 2 beds, 1 sofa, and 5 ugly lamps in the place.
2. There are plastic curtains up in the kitchen.
3. The floors are covered with flowered linoleum.
4. And the walls are all painted LANDLADY GREEN.

[2] Begin by resigning yourself to living with the lamps. No one has *ever* designed an attractive lamp! I hypothesize that it can't be done, but I would be delighted to be proved wrong.

[3] Take down and hide the plastic curtains which are up in the kitchen. Better none at all than those.

[4] Sweep out, dust, and scrub down the entire place. It's probably the only time during the school year that you'll (a) have time to do it, or (b) feel up to doing it.

[5] The next step is to go shopping. You will have to make two stops. The first stop is at Goodwill, the Salvation Army, Union Gospel Mission, Saint Vincent dePaul, or some other place where non-impoverished non-students have contributed lots of objects suitable for furnishing an Impoverished Student's Apartment to be resold to Impoverished Students at ridiculously low prices. Stock up on such items as armchairs, kitchen chairs (which serve nicely as desk chairs), double beds (if you like that sort of thing), rocking chairs, and lots of attractive old bedspreads. Be sure to buy *lots* of attractive old bedspreads. Buy all the attractive old bedspreads in the place. Visit several such institutions if you can't find enough attractive old bedspreads at one of them. You'll need *lots* of attractive old bedspreads. Do *not* stock up on bookcases or larger desks, even though you may (should) need them. Arrange to have all the heavy large items delivered in about two days. Take the attractive old bedspreads with you. Before you make your second stop, you are going to have to do some planning. Return to the apartment with your bedspreads.

[6] When you arrive at the apartment, cover every last one of those ugly radiators with an attractive old bedspread. Cut some of the bedspreads in half, so you won't use them all for this job. You'll need more later. Now you will find it easier to think.

[7] Decision I: Provided your landlady will allow you to paint the walls, are you going to paint the walls? If so, decide on colors and measure areas to be covered.

[8] Decision II: What are you going to do about the floors?
  a. Live with them?
  b. Buy some carpets?
  c. (With your landlady's permission), paint the linoleum? If you are going to paint the linoleum, paint it black. Calculate the footage to be covered.

[9] Be sure to get permission to paint anything. Some landladies get positively surly if you don't ask them first. Again, some agree to pay for all or some of the paint if you do ask them first. So ask them.

[10] Decision III: How many running feet of bookcase are you going to need? You are going to construct a brick-and-board bookcase. Hence you

must calculate the number of bricks and boards. The only proper bookcase for an Impoverished Student is one constructed out of bricks and boards. For one thing, they are *cheap*. For another, they are *sturdy*. For yet another, they are *multifunctional*. Be sure that at least one cinderblock occurs in your bookcase —the pigeonholes make excellent receptacles for notes, letters (both incoming and outgoing), receipts, bills, and suchlike.

[11] You are now ready to complete your shopping. Go to a Builders' Supply Store. This will be a hardware store with an attached small lumber and brick yard. Buy from the friendly man:

1. Whatever paints and painting supplies you need,
2. Whatever bookcase supplies you need, and
3. Two *large, flat doors.*

You can get doors which are dented or blemished on one side far cheaper than you can get first-quality doors. Dented, blemished doors will do for our purposes.

[12] Return home.

[13] Get all the painting you're going to do over with before your furnitures are delivered. Set up the bookcases and unpack the books. Beginning to look better? Place the doors, one each, on top of your pitifully inadequate desks, good side up. Now you have nice, big, adequate desks!

[14] Take that trunk or footlocker, throw an attractive old bedspread over it, and put it in front of the sofa. Put your tea service on it. Behold! One coffee table.

[15] If the sofa itself isn't exactly a prize, throw an attractive old bedspread over it.

[16] Hang some attractive old bedspreads over the windows for curtains.

[17] Throw an attractive old bedspread over the table as a tablecloth.

[18] Start thinking about what you're going to put on the walls. Most every college campus produces in the course of the year a colorful variety of interesting and attractive posters announcing coming events. Collect them and put them up on the walls with masking tape. (Note: use *masking* tape, please, as it won't pull the paint or wallpaper loose when you go to remove the posters.)

[19] If you've got a large bloodstain on one wall that you want to cover up, drive two anchor bolts in near the ceiling, stretch a wire between them, and hang an attractive old bedspread over it to form an Instant Tapestry Hanging.

[20] Now that you've run out of bricks, boards, doors, and paint, collapse on the davenport with a peanut butter sandwich and figure out for yourself what to do with the rest of those attractive old bedspreads.

DISCUSSION

1. Is the main idea stated in the first paragraph? Does the first paragraph list materials needed for the job? If not, how can you tell from reading the first paragraph what the job will be?

2. Does the first paragraph give reasons for doing the job? If not, how can you tell what the reasons are?

3. Why does the writer keep repeating the phrase "attractive old bed-spread"? Is it because he can't think of any other way to say it? Would the essay be more effective if he sometimes said "pretty old counterpane" or "good-looking used bedspread"? Why or why not?

4. Notice that the writer uses many short paragraphs. For instance, paragraphs 12, 15, 16, and 17 are only one sentence long. Do you think some of the short paragraphs should be combined? If so, which ones and why? If you think they should be left as they are, justify your decision by pointing out why the short paragraphs are effective.

5. Does this article, like *Rubbings,* scatter encouragement throughout the paper? If you think it does, find the encouraging words or phrases or statements. How does the tone of the article affect the reader's attitude about being poor?

6. What method does the writer use to conclude? Summary? Encouragement? Repeating an important point? Something else? How can you tell whether the writer is aware that he has not said everything there is to say about redecorating a furnished apartment?

7. Does the conclusion fit the introduction? In answering this question, try to consider restated ideas, suitable tone, and original setting.

8. Rewrite the first paragraph of this essay in general terms. You might begin with something like, "Many furnished apartments available to students . . . " When you have finished your paragraph, discuss with your classmates which beginning is more effective in gaining the reader's interest, and why.

Preparing for an Essay Exam

constitute: form
principle: a general truth or law
contemporaries: people alive during the same period of time
successors: people who continue a movement or study started by someone else
pertinent: related to the subject

"Preparing for an Essay Exam" from *Successful Study: A Guide to Good Grades,* by James C. Coleman and Frieda Bornston Libaw is reprinted by permission of Scott, Foresman and Company. Copyright © 1960 by Scott, Foresman and Company.

[1] Suppose it is now Wednesday evening and on Friday you are to have a test based on the lectures and reading for half a term. During that period you studied a great deal of material, memorizing some of it and becoming familiar with much more. If you have read regularly and listened carefully to what went on in class, you have already done your original learning. You don't have to scramble now to put several weeks' work into a few days; instead, you have time to go carefully through the material, looking for points you need to study a little more thoroughly and checking those areas you feel are most important.

[2] Underlined passages and marginal notes in your text, lecture notes, and reading notes will help you in this final review. If you've used the summary method of note-taking, you will want to read quickly through the summary sections of your notebook. But rereading your notes and underlined passages doesn't constitute a thorough review.

[3] A more active approach involves checking over the material and testing yourself on it. Here are some general suggestions you may find helpful in organizing your review:

1. Answer any questions that have occurred to you. Your text may list questions at the end of chapters. Be sure to answer each one.

2. State the general principles of historians or philosophers, the aims of artists or writers, or the scientific principles which underlie the material you have covered.

3. Prepare evidence that will make such abstract statements concrete. Be able to state how certain laws were applied, to name the works in which certain theories were first expressed, etc.

4. Explore the relationships between a man's work or ideas and those of his contemporaries and successors. Know the place of a prominent figure in a general movement.

5. Make comparisons among the men, books, theories, and events that are important to the material being studied.

6. Define basic terms. For instance, give the definition of the "oxidation-reduction method" or the "Industrial Revolution."

[4] You may use all these suggestions for one test and only one or two for another, depending on the nature of the tests. The important thing is that you ask yourself pertinent questions and answer them without consulting your book. When you can do this, you know that you're already fairly well prepared for the test.

DISCUSSION

1. The first paragraph says, ". . . you have time to go carefully through the material." Another way to say it would be, "Go carefully through the material." Since most directions tell the reader, "do this, do that," why

do you suppose this author chooses another phrasing? What is there about the nature of his subject and his readers that makes his wording more effective than the standard "directions" wording?

2. How does the first paragraph make clear that the paper will not be about the general topic, "how to study," but will instead be limited to one specific kind of studying, "preparing for an exam"? In other words, how does the writer use his first paragraph to limit his topic?

3. Notice that in the middle of the article, the writer shifts back to the conventional "do this—do that" wording. Find the sentence that prepares the reader for that shift.

4. After changing to the standard wording for directions, does the writer stick to it through the rest of the paper, or does he make another shift? If you think he shifts again, show where and explain why he shifts.

5. Does the writer use either the introduction or the conclusion to encourage the readers? If you think he does, find the parts in both the first and last paragraphs that seem encouraging.

6. Does the conclusion restate the main idea? Emphasize the most important point? Summarize everything that has been said? Reassure the reader? Find the parts of the conclusion that support your answer. What is there in the conclusion that makes this article sound finished?

Organization and Transitions

The organization—the order in which the writer presents his material and the relationship of one part of what he says to the other parts—will depend on what the directions are for. If the job requires special equipment, the writer may have to talk about what is needed, where to get it, and how much it will cost. If the materials are not important, or if they are less important than getting ready to do the job, the writer may begin with the preparation. Either way, however, he is likely to finish the preliminaries before he talks about the actual process.

Since most directions deal with the steps in a process, they follow a common-sense order that stresses the need to do first things first. Most recipes, for example, begin with the ingredients, and, if the food is to be baked, suggest that the cook should preheat the oven before she mixes the ingredients. In the following recipe for a fancy dish for special guests, notice the emphasis on proper order. Notice also that although the recipe itemizes four ingredients that will be needed, it does not mention butter, onion, or chili powder because the writer assumes that these items are already available in everybody's kitchen. In telling the readers what equipment is needed for the job, the writer usually can omit ordinary things most readers will have.

CHALUPAS OR
A SORT OF CHICKEN STROGANOFF

This recipe was stolen from Sanborn's Palace of Tiles in Mexico City. Four people's worth is prepared as follows. Take:

18 frozen or canned or fresh tortillas
2 large jars of boned chicken
4–5 cans of peeled mild green chili peppers
2 pints of sour cream

Get the miserable job of de-seeding and slicing the chili peppers *out of the way first.* The peppers should be sliced into strips (along the grain). *Then, and only then,* sauté the tortillas, previously cut into 1½-inch by 1-inch strips, in butter and a cut-up small onion. *When the tortillas are all hotted up* and brown, fling in the chicken, chili peppers, and sour cream. Season lavishly with chili powder and somewhat less lavishly with cayenne pepper. Simmer the entire mixture at low heat for about 30 minutes, mushing together and tasting periodically. Serve this hot with a plain lettuce salad. The recipe really does feed only four—they eat a lot of it! [Italics added] (From Jay F. Rosenberg, *The Impoverished Students' Book of Cookery, Drinkery and Housekeepery,* p. 23.)

In directions more complicated than a simple recipe, the writer is likely to build his paragraphs around a series of steps, one leading to the next, linked together by words or phrases connecting the steps. These words or phrases are called transitions.

First of all, turn on the ignition switch . . .
Then, check the battery condition . . .
If there is current in the battery, check the cables . . .
Next, try the starter again . . .

Notice that some of these transition words are simply a guide to the order; link transitions let the reader know that he has finished one step and is ready for the next. One of them, however (If there is current in the battery . . .), works by reminding the reader of something he has already been told. Other such echo transitions begin with words such as when, after, while, etc. But whether the transitions are numbering words or reminders, they almost always have to do with time, because the order in a set of directions must be the order in which the reader will perform the task.

Writing Exercises

1. Make a brief outline of the order the writer has followed in either *How Do You Paint A Room?* or *Preparing for an Essay Exam.* It isn't necessary to make a formal outline; just jot down the main thing covered in each paragraph.

2. Find the transitions that have been used in these two articles, and then go back and mark the transitions in *Capsizing*. Distinguish between *link* and *echo* transitions.

3. Here are two sets of directions using numbers instead of transitions. Rewrite one of them in essay form, adding your own introduction and conclusion.

    a. How to make sculpture pincurls

        1. Wet hair thoroughly; part and comb flat and smooth against head, like a cap. Part off as much hair as you want for a pincurl (the larger the strand the looser the curl).

        2. Hold strand slightly up and out. Comb smooth, free of tangles, so all hair fibers stay together. Keep strand smooth and wet. DO NOT twist.

        3. Press left finger firmly against scalp, creating a hollow at the base of the tress. Draw strand forward with comb and right thumb—molding and stretching it into a pointed end.

        4. Remove finger from scalp. Now use both hands and carefully roll pointed end into a small circle. Continue rolling circle smoothly, upward toward scalp, forming curl. Do not twist.

        5. Curl now fits neatly into hollow at scalp. Fasten with clip over curl. (Instructions with Toni permanent, courtesy of the Toni Company, a division of the Gillette Company.)

In your introduction, you might explain why sculpture pincurls are more satisfactory than other methods of hair-setting; you might list the equipment needed or emphasize that this kind of set can be done at home with nothing except hair-clips and a comb; or you might discuss occasions on which girls would be particularly anxious to set their hair carefully.

As you explain this process, substitute smooth transitions for the numerals used in the original, making sure that you use echo transitions at least twice.

The conclusion need not be more than a sentence or two, mentioning again whatever you think is the most important point.

    b. How to light a Coleman lantern

        1. Be sure fuel valve is tightly closed by turning valve wheel to right. Remove filler plug and fill tank with fresh, clean, untreated gasoline. Do not tip lantern while filling. Always let it set flat on its base. Fill tank, then replace filler plug and tighten firmly with fingers.

        2. See that fuel valve is closed. Then open air check valve inside of pump barrel by turning pump plunger two full turns to left. Place ball of thumb over small hole in end of pump plunger and pump 20 to 30 strokes of air into tank. Now, turn pump plunger to right until tight.

        3. Rotate several times the gas tip cleaning lever which extends from under the lantern frame. This forces the point of the

cleaning needle in and out of the opening in the gas tip at
the end of the generator to dislodge any particles of carbon
which may have collected in the opening. The lever should
be left pointing down.

4. Have a match ready to light. Now, <u>open the fuel valve
   one-fourth</u> <u>turn</u> <u>only</u>. Light the match, insert it through the
   lighter opening and hold it under the mantle. A few seconds
   time may elapse before you will hear the mixture of gas
   and air feeding into the mantle but at that time the mantle
   will light instantly. The light may flicker somewhat for a few
   seconds but as soon as the mantle burns bright, open the valve
   as far as possible. Unless you open the valve all the way
   after the lantern has been properly instant-lighted, air pressure
   will continue to escape through the valve and generator.
   (Adapted from directions accompanying Coleman Lantern
   No. 200A, courtesy of the Coleman Company, Inc.)

In your introduction, suggest reasons why a reader might want to own
a Coleman lantern. In what kinds of situations might it be useful? You
might go on to tell the reader what he will need to keep on hand in the way
of fuel or anything else that does not come with the lantern.

As you take him through the necessary steps in lighting the lantern,
substitute smooth transitions for the numerals used in the original, making
sure that you use reminder transitions at least twice.

The conclusion should sum up whatever you think are the most important
things the reader must remember.

Pitching a Tent in a Wilderness Camp

suspend: hang down from
treelets: small trees
felled: cut down
hummocks: small mounds of dirt
projections: things sticking out from the surface
crotched sapling: a young tree with a fork in it
apex: the top point of a triangle
isosceles triangle: a triangle with two equal sides

Adapted from *The Forest*, by Stewart Edward White, reprinted by permission of Crocker-Citizens
National Bank. Copyright 1903, 1931 by Doubleday & Co., Inc.

[1] Finding the right place to camp and pitching your tent carefully can make all the difference between a miserable night and a pleasant sleep. Nothing is more upsetting than to awaken at midnight and find youself in a little lake, or to be aroused by the sound of your tent collapsing on your face. With a little care all these mishaps can be avoided.

Introduction gives reasons for following directions

[2] When five or six o'clock draws near, begin to look about you for a good level dry place, raised some few feet above the surroundings. Drop your pack or beach your canoe. Examine the location carefully. You will want two trees about ten feet apart from which to suspend your tent, and a bit of flat ground underneath them. Of course the flat ground need not be particularly clear of brush or saplings, so the combination ought not to be hard to discover. Now return to your canoe. Do not unpack the tent.

First step—finding a suitable place

[3] With your little axe clear the ground thoroughly. By bending a sapling over strongly with the left hand, clipping sharply at the strained fibres, and then bending it as strongly the other way to repeat the axe stroke on the other side, you will find that treelets of even two or three inches' diameter can be felled by two blows. In a very few moments you will have accomplished a hole in the forest, and your two supporting trees will stand at either end of a most respectable-looking clearing. Do not unpack the tent.

Second step—clearing the area

[4] Now, although the ground seems free of all but unimportant growths, go over it thoroughly for little shrubs and leaves. They look soft and yielding, but are often unexpectedly tough under your bed. Besides, they mask the face of the ground. When you have finished pulling them up by the roots, you will find that your supposedly level plot is knobby with hummocks. Stand directly over each little mound; swing the back of your axe vigorously against it between your legs. Nine times out of ten it will crumble, and the tenth time means merely a root to cut or a stone to pry out of clean, fresh earth, level and soft, free from projections. But do not unpack your tent.

Third step—preparing the ground

[5] Lay a young birch or maple an inch or so in diameter across a log. Two clips will produce a

Fourth step—cutting the poles

tent-peg. If you are inexperienced, and have memories of striped lawn awnings put up on smooth grass, you will cut the pegs about six inches long. If you are wise and old and gray in woods experience, you will multiply that length by four. Then your loops will not slip off, and you will have a real grip on mother earth, than which nothing can be more desirable in the event of a heavy rain and wind squall about midnight. If your axe is as sharp as it ought to be, you can point the pegs more neatly by holding them suspended in front of you while you snip at their ends with the axe, rather than by resting them against a solid base. Pile them together at the edge of the clearing. Cut a crotched sapling eight or ten feet long. Now unpack your tent.

[6] In a wooded country you will not take the time to fool with tent poles. A stout line run through the eyelets and along the apex will string it successfully between your two trees. Draw the line as tight as possible, but do not be too unhappy if, after your best efforts, it still sags a little. That is what your long crotched stick is for. Stake out your four corners. If you get them in a good rectangle and in such relation to the apex as to form two isosceles triangles of the ends, your tent will stand smoothly. Therefore, be an artist and do it right.

Final step—putting up the tent

[7] Once the four corners are well placed, the rest follows naturally. Occasionally in the North Country it will be found that the soil is too thin, over the rocks, to grip the tent-pegs. In that case drive them at a sharp angle as deep as they will go, and then lay a large flat stone across the slant of them. Thus anchored, you will ride out a gale. Finally, wedge your long sapling crotch under the line—outside the tent, of course—to tighten it. Your shelter is up. If you are a woodsman, ten or fifteen minutes has been plenty to make sure that you will sleep cozily and well.

Conclusion—emphasizing time and safety from weather.

DISCUSSION

1. These directions for putting up a tent move step by step through the job; obviously the writer believes that the order is important. Has he convinced you that everything must be done in just the order he recom-

mends? If you are convinced, find the words and phrases the writer has used that helped to convince you.

2. Has everything the writer mentioned in the introductory paragraph been dealt with in the rest of the article? List the reasons given for pitching the tent properly and then find the comments that relate to those reasons.

3. Can you explain why the conclusion to this essay is so short? The writer has not even given it a separate paragraph but has instead made it the last two sentences of a paragraph. If you were writing the conclusion to this article, what else would you include?

4. Which paragraphs begin with echo transitions? What is the reader being reminded of that he has already been told? How does White tie the other paragraphs together?

5. What is the effect of repeating "Do not unpack the tent" at the end of paragraphs 2, 3, and 4? What would have been lost if White had ended the introduction by saying, "It is important not to unpack the tent until all the preparations have been made"? Why does the last sentence of paragraph 4 begin with "But" and the last sentence of paragraph 5 with "Now"?

6. Has White included anything not strictly necessary for the directions he has given, anything that seems to have been put in to make the article interesting? If you think he has, find the comments that are merely "interesting"; if you think everything said is important to pitching a tent properly, be prepared to defend your point of view.

7. Find the places where the writer seems to be encouraging the reader.

Canvassing for McCarthy

canvassing: finding out what people in a district think and urging them to vote in a certain way
technique: method of doing something
antagonize: annoy or make angry
roster: complete list of people

Adapted from literature distributed by the Oregon McCarthy-for-President Committee, 1968.

controversial: likely to cause an argument
abrupt: blunt or rude

[1] Door-to-door canvassing is undoubtedly one of the most effective campaign techniques. Properly handled, it can help undecided voters support your candidate; poorly handled, it can antagonize more voters than it influences. Thus it is particularly important that all the students who ring doorbells for Senator McCarthy make a good impression at every house.

[2] Before you start, you will be given a roster of registered voters for your area, listing each voter by name and address. Use the roster and follow these guidelines:

[3] Address the voter by name. You should know how to pronounce the name of the voter of the house you are canvassing. It is very important that you greet the person who answers the door with a smile, that you speak clearly and slowly. Do not let your approach become mechanical.

[4] Say you're a volunteer. When introducing yourself stress that you are a *volunteer* working for Senator McCarthy. A suggested introduction is "Good morning Mrs. Jones, I'm Jim Harrison. I'm a volunteer working for Senator McCarthy who is running for President in the primary on May 28."

[5] Be conversational. You might talk about the weather, pets, scenery. Mention that you are from out-of-town, that you have brought a sleeping bag, etc. Do your thing. You might lead into the issues by asking, "How do people in your neighborhood feel about Senator McCarthy . . . the war . . . inflation," etc. But be indirect in asking questions.

[6] Give out literature piece-by-piece. Literature is a useful point of reference. You can begin handing the literature to the person piece-by-piece, beginning with the least controversial, identifying each as you do. Most likely you will come to an issue which interests the voter.

[7] Never argue. Show every respect for the voter's opinions. Show interest in what the voter says, and try to agree with him. Say things like: "Yes, that's a very interesting point." Then try to move the voter some distance from what he has said to where Senator McCarthy stands. For example, if the voter says, "We must stop Communism," say "Senator McCarthy believes we must also, but that we have relied too heavily on military means." This is where you must be sensitive to each voter's attitudes.

[8] Be indirect. Never ask the voter for whom he is going to vote. In general you will gain a feeling for the voter's position.

[9] Ask the voter to consider. When leaving a house, you should say, "I hope you will *consider* voting for Senator McCarthy. I think he has proven himself worthy of everyone's consideration." This will usually produce a response.

[10] Even if you follow these guidelines step by step, you can't influence everybody. Whatever you say or do, some voters will be fearful or abrupt, but the canvasser who follows these suggestions carefully can cut down on

the number of times he must simply say "Thank you" and leave without any discussion.

DISCUSSION

1. Directions which give advice on how to behave in certain situations may follow a different kind of order from directions telling how to make something or accomplish a simple task. Can you justify the order that has been used in these guidelines? Could the order be changed without spoiling the canvassing interview? If you think so, explain where.

2. The very brief sentences which begin paragraphs 2 through 9 serve two purposes. First, they substitute for transitions by leading the reader to expect a *list* of do's and don'ts. And second, because they form a list, they serve as a short summary of what the article covers. Since these sentences do summarize all the main points, what is added by the paragraphs that follow? What would be lost by a canvasser operating from only the list?

3. Most of this article is written in fairly straightforward, standard English, but paragraph 5 contains the sentence, "Do your thing." What do you understand by "doing your thing"? Why has the writer used this phrase? Can you think of another way of saying it that would be just as effective?

Audience

Besides remembering to include all the necessary steps in the proper order, the writer has to keep in mind who his readers will be. The audience, as far as it can ever be known ahead of time, influences not only *what* the writer says, but also *how* he says it. If he expects most of his readers to be women, for instance, he may need to give a more complete explanation of mechanical matters and a less complete explanation of domestic items than if he were writing for men. And he will also need to use words and phrases he thinks his readers will feel comfortable with. His comparisons will move from the unfamiliar to what will probably be familiar to his audience. For women, he may compare a clutch mechanism to two pie plates; for men, he may compare an asbestos-lined hand heat protector to a catcher's mitt.

In writing from the point of view of his readers, it is also the writer's business to figure out what background information will seem obvious and include only what the readers actually need to be told. An article about shortcuts in radiator repair, written for mechanics, can take for granted a great deal of automobile knowledge that the general public would not have; a set of directions on how to patch a leaky radiator, intended for teen-age girls, may need to begin by explaining what a radiator is. If there is any question about how much his readers will understand, however, the careful writer plays it safe; he gives the information.

Wiring Homemade Lamps

accessory: something extra that makes things easier or pleasanter
baluster: a support for a railing
convert: change from one thing to another
basting: long temporary stitches holding two pieces of cloth together
earthy: direct; plain spoken
mooring: place to tie up a boat; here, anything securely fastened to
something solid
revealed: uncovered
terminal: mechanical device that forms an electrical connection
diffusing: scattering or spreading
invert: turn upside down
relic: something left over from an earlier time

[1] There is no accessory for the house that you can't make yourself—often from converting bits and pieces, as, for instance, lamps that can be made out of balusters, chair legs, old tin coffeepots painted, old vases, or bottles—in fact, many things that would be better left alone! For while I admit you can make a lamp out of practically anything, I've never been one of the convert-that-old-coffee-grinder school. As for lamp wiring, it's as simple as basting, and I learned how. Let me tell you, the field needs a woman's viewpoint.

The word "basting" makes it clear that the article is intended for women; furthermore, most men already know that attaching a plug is "simple"

[2] First, there's the cord. You buy it by the foot in a dime store, electrical supply place, or plain old hardware store. And it's important to a woman whether the cord is brown, white, or black, to harmonize with walls, rug, etc., and not stick out like a—cord. Then there are the two ends of the cord. On one end is the lamp, or will be, and on the other is the plug. They are very earthy in the electrical industry and call this, and anything with prongs that fit into anything else, a "male" connection. Your object is to somehow attach the lamp to one end of the cord and the plug to the other.

First things first: locating a supply of the cord. Again, this is information that would probably be left out if the writer expected his readers to be men

Adapted from pp. 99–103 *How to Live On Nothing*, by Joan Ranson Shortney, reprinted by permission of Pocket Books, a division of Simon & Schuster, Inc. Copyright © 1961 by Joan Ranson Shortney.

[3] Begin with the plug, which comes in a variety of shapes and several materials—usually rubber or plastic—and has two prongs. Let's say your plug is a round plastic one with a "grip" or projecting handle to aid pulling it out of the wall socket. Look inside the plug. You should see a round piece of cardboard. This is the insulation. Remove it and put it aside for the moment. Below this you will see four screws—two small ones and two larger ones. With a small screwdriver unscrew these as far as they'll go (that's turning to the left, remember). They won't come out of their moorings—they'll just be loosened. Now take your cord and push it into the plug from the direction of the closed part of the plug, not the part you've just been looking at. Push the cord in so that it comes through between the metal prongs for about three inches, and separate the two pieces of the cord.

The writer is not assuming that housewives will know *anything* about electric wiring

Concern about the direction to turn screws in order to loosen them is another indication of the audience expected

[4] Next you must remove the rubbery insulation from the ends of the wires back to about an inch. First you cut off the ends so that they are even and straight. Men do this with a pocketknife. I do it with a sharp scissors. The little strands of copper wire are quite soft—besides I'm more used to working with a scissors than with a pocketknife. Men also remove the insulation with a pocketknife. It has to be removed without cutting or nicking the wires. If you're good with knives, hold yours so that it faces the end of the cords that you'll be uncovering. I find it easy enough to start the insulation with a knife and after that I just peel the stuff off with my fingernails. After the black rubber is off, there will be a little bundle of beautiful copper wires revealed. Twist each little bundle (on the two cords, that is) so that you can work the bundles like single wires. Otherwise they'll be sticking out in every direction.

Scissors and fingernails used as tools

How many electricians would pause to mention the "beauty" of the copper wire? "Each little bundle" is almost nursery language

[5] Bring one of your cords around one of the prongs so that the curve of the cord (and this part still has insulation on it although no outer braid covering) is on the outer side of the prong toward the edge of the plug. Now curl the exposed copper strand around the terminal screw (one of the large screws that you loosened) that is near the prong. Bend your exposed copper strand neatly and tightly

around this screw and then tighten the screw with your little screwdriver. Your cord or wires should be covered with insulation up to the point where the cord bundle is attached to the terminal screw. There should be no little wires running off and wandering toward the other terminal screw. Each bundle has to remain on its own terminal screw or you'll have a short circuit. When you're satisfied that the terminal screw is as tight as you can make it, repeat this whole process with the remaining cord. Now your cord is properly attached to your plug. Put back the cardboard circle of insulation.

[6] Now you are ready to wire the lamp receptacle or socket to the other end of your cord . . . Look at the lamp receptacle carefully. It comes apart. Take it apart into four sections—the cap, which is shaped like a cap and has a screw on top to fasten it onto the body of your lamp. Around the bottom of this cap are little indentations which grip the next part of this socket fixture you're going to wire—the "body". To remove the cap from the body, press inward on the body. It may carry the word "press," to indicate where you push hard with your thumb while you pull on the cap to release the little grippers. Once you get body and cap apart you'll find an insulating shell inside the body. This looks like cardboard. Take it out of the body. The switch mechanism is inside the insulating shell. Push that out of the insulating shell.

"Shaped like a cap" may seem an obvious comparison, but it may help women who have never examined the parts of a socket

[7] Cut your cord end cleanly so that it is easy to thread it through the hole in the cap. If you have a hole for the cord to run through the side of the cap, you can work the cord through the cap and attach it to the switch mechanism. Otherwise, if there is no hole in the side of the cap, you have to run the cord through the lamp base and body first and then through the cap, which has been screwed to the lamp.

[8] Once you know this basic wiring technique you can make your own lamps. The electrical supply stores and mail-order houses and even ten-cent stores have many different connections and sockets. There are three-position sockets for three-way lights and diffusing bowls. Invert the sockets of dim bridge lamps and add diffusing bowls and larger shades for

Notice how this connecting sentence refers to all that has gone before

better lighting. You can buy pronged adapters or
adapters with cork on the bottom that can be whit-
tled to size to stick into vases or bottles that when
wired make the vases into lamps without cutting
the vases, so that if you change your mind or need
something to hold flowers you can once more have
a vase. Finally, screw adapters hold sockets in old
lamp bases so that you can convert that Victorian
relic in your attic, the relic that might cost you from
$35 to $100 if you bought it but that is now lying
idle and unused for want of wiring.

The comment about
"changing your mind"
refers to popular folk-
lore about the behavior
of women
It ends with another
piece of folklore, that
all good housewives
love a bargain

DISCUSSION

1. Although these directions are written in a very conversational style—
they sound like one woman talking to another—the article contains several difficult words. Why does the writer use them? Can you rewrite the
sentences, avoiding all the words that were unfamiliar to you before you
read this article? After you have rewritten the sentences, decide which
version you prefer—yours or the original.

2. What other details (beyond those mentioned in the marginal comments)
indicate that the article was written for women?

3. What is the main idea expressed in the introduction? Does the rest of
the article support the statement made in the first sentence of paragraph
1? Can you find any support for the last sentence in the same paragraph?

4. The directions given in paragraphs 6 and 7 are much less complete than
those in paragraphs 3, 4, and 5, although the job is at least as complicated. What steps seem to have been left out? How do you account for
these omissions?

5. If this article were used in a woman's magazine, some of the chatty comments might help the directions appeal to the audience. From the standpoint of simple directions, however, which of the comments seem off the
subject? Which ones are unnecessary for getting the job done?

Tandem on a Motorcycle

tandem: one behind the other
disenchanted: doesn't like it much after all
ingenuity: imagination; cleverness
surreptitiously: secretively; trying not to be noticed
novice: a beginner
inanimate: apparently lifeless; without motion
potential: possible, even probable

[1] If you are planning to carry female passengers on the back of your motorcycle—and what male rider isn't—there are certain practices to observe that will increase both the pleasure and safety of riding tandem.

[2] First of all, try to restrain yourself from taking a passenger until you have put at least 500 miles on your odometer. During these first 500 miles you will be learning to control your motorcycle, and it's a lot easier when you don't have the additional worry of a passenger.

[3] When you are ready to take on a passenger, here are some useful tips:

[4] If she's never been on a motorcycle before, don't just tell her casually to hop on. Certain preliminary instructions are in order *before* she gets on.

[5] The very first thing you should tell her, in a loud, attention-getting manner, is "NEVER TOUCH THE MUFFLERS." She will then look wildly about for the mufflers, so be sure to point them out. Warn her that if she touches a muffler with her leg, she will get a nasty burn. Many girls have become quickly disenchanted with motorcycling—and with their motorcycling partner—in this very way.

[6] Next, tell your passenger where she should put her feet. Almost every motorcycle comes equipped with foot pegs for passengers. Point them out, or your passenger is likely to plant her feet on something unsuitable or simply let them drag.

[7] Next, you must tell your passenger where to hang on. Years ago, there was only one thing for a motorcycle passenger to hang on to, and that was the rider. Then certain unromantic motorcycle manufacturers began to equip their saddles with center straps for the passenger to grasp. Soon, almost all motorcycles came with these straps. Male waists became less and less frequently clasped by female arms.

[8] However, ingenuity has come up with several ways to bring back the era of the clasped waist. One, of course, is to remove the strap entirely, but

you may want it for passengers whose embrace you can do without. Another is to surreptitiously pull the seat strap forward and sit on it, so that your passenger is unaware of its existence. If she does happen to spot it, warn her in urgent tones that it should never be touched, because pulling on it releases the whole rear-wheel assembly.

[9] Some even more heartless manufacturers have equipped their motor-cycles with rear rails or hand holds at the sides of the saddle. It's up to the rider to outwit these devices.

[10] Actually, all of these are perfectly sound safety devices, but so is the clasped waist, and it even has some safety advantages. An inexperienced pas-senger should lock her fingers together tightly after putting her arms around your waist. Besides giving her a feeling of security, this will save her from being jerked back suddenly if you should happen to take off sharply—most novice passengers are not prepared for the quick acceleration of a motor-cycle.

[11] When she is hugging you firmly, she is less likely to move indepen-dently of you and upset your balance. Moreover, with her arms already locked around you she won't suddenly—in a moment of panic—grab you by the shoulders or arms, causing you to lose control.

[12] Once a passenger has become more experienced in riding with you, she can place her hands lightly on either side of your waist. It is not, of course, necessary to volunteer this particular information.

[13] When your passenger is on the saddle behind you, her feet properly on the pegs, her knees in, her hands clasped about your waist, she's ready for further instructions. Tell her first to keep her feet up on the pegs at all times, even when you're stopped—this makes it easier for you to control the balance.

[14] Second, she should stay in one position, with no squirming, shifting, or any other movement that will change the balance of the motorcycle—and the slightest movement will.

[15] Third, tell her never to dismount until you give her the go-ahead. You don't have eyes in the back of your head, and if she gets off without warning she may upset the balance of the motorcycle.

[16] Fourth, she may know enough about motorcycling to understand that the rider leans into a corner—but that doesn't mean *she* should lean. You must control the turn with *your* leaning, and all she has to do is to stay put, neither leaning toward nor against the turn.

[17] Fifth, tell her firmly that conversation on a motorcycle is virtually im-possible. She may be given to yelling things into your ear like, "What did you think of Fellini's latest?" as if you were both sitting over steins in a cozy pub. The correct answer is, "Shut up," or something that will have the same effect. And don't turn your head even to say that, for obvious reasons. If you *must* converse while riding, the only solution is to equip yourself and your passenger with walkie-talkies.

[18] The ban on conversation includes back-seat driving. It is a wise pas-

senger who makes herself both inanimate and silent, although an occasional squeal of delight is permissible.

[19] Drive conservatively when you have an inexperienced passenger on the back. Being a motorcycle passenger for the first time is scarifying. She will think she's going much faster than she actually is. She will see all kinds of hazards, but she'll have no idea of whether you see them, too.

[20] So don't whip around corners or weave through traffic. Give her a chance to get the feel of riding on a motorcycle. Many potential converts to motorcycling have lost their enthusiasm because their first ride was terrifying instead of enjoyable.

DISCUSSION

1. Who is expected to read these directions? What is there in the article—information given or not given, the kind of wording used—that hints at who the audience is?

2. What is the writer's attitude toward his readers? Does he treat them as amateurs? As equals? As superiors? What effect does this attitude have on you as a reader?

3. What is the effect of the discussion of "holding" in paragraphs 7, 8, 9, and 12? What does the writer imply about the character of cyclists? How old does he assume they are?

4. Why does the writer use such phrases as "heartless manufacturers" and "outwit these devices" (paragraph 9)? What other words and phrases can you find that create a similar effect?

5. In talking about the passenger, the writer uses phrases such as "look wildly about" (paragraph 5), "occasional squeal of delight" (paragraph 18). Find other comments that deal with the passenger's reaction, and then describe the kind of girl the writer has in mind.

6. Make a brief plan of the order that has been used in these directions. Does it matter much whether the advice in paragraphs 4 through 7 comes in that order? How important is the order of the numbered advice given in paragraphs 13 through 17? Both these sets of advice are really directions for the passenger. Does it matter which set is given first?

7. Does the conclusion fit the introduction? How?

Shooting Underwater Pictures

yen: desire

strobe: a high-powered lamp connected to the camera

alternative: another way to do it

exposure: amount of light allowed on the film

diaphragm: device to control the amount of light let through the lens

compensate: make allowance for

tripod: three-legged camera stand

prefocus: focus in advance

image: picture that appears in the viewfinder

illuminated: lighted

[1] Have you ever had a yen to shoot underwater pictures? Here is the way to do it. You don't need a piece of underwater equipment, and you don't have to leave your living room. Shoot them in the fish tank.

[2] If you do not have a fish tank, you can buy a glass fish bowl for less than $1 or a small tank for around $3. Tropical fish cost as little as 25 cents each. All you need are the bowl, the fish, and some water.

[3] The setup is simple. Place a black cloth behind the tank. Set or hold the strobe or flash above the tank. An alternative would be to put the light at the side of the tank. Do not put the light in front of the tank because it will reflect off the glass and will cause a hot spot on the film. If you have two strobe or flash units, put one on each side of the tank. This will give a strong rim lighting. Calculate the exposure on the basis of the distance from the fish to the main light source. Then open the camera diaphragm one extra stop to compensate for the light which reflects from the glass wall of the tank.

[4] There are two ways to shoot the picture. The first is to put the camera on a tripod, prefocus, and then feed the fish at the spot on which you have focused. The second method is to hold the camera in your hand, focus it to its closest distance, and then follow the fish through the viewfinder. Keep the image sharp by moving the camera closer to or farther away from the fish. Do not constantly try to change the camera focus. Whichever focusing method you use, make the exposure when the flat surface of the fish will be fully illuminated by the light from the flash or strobe.

[5] When you make the print, show the fish in full detail and let the background go completely black.

Page 149 from *100 Camera Projects for Fun and Profit,* by John Durniak, Harvey Shaman, and Andrew V. Wahlberg is reprinted by permission of American Photographic Book Publishing Company, Inc.

DISCUSSION

1. Why do these directions tell the reader where to put the light, where to hold the camera, but almost nothing about taking the picture?

2. Paragraph 2 lists the equipment the writer says will be needed for taking underwater pictures, but the list is obviously incomplete. In paragraphs 3 and 4 what other equipment is mentioned? Why has the writer left these items out of the list in paragraph 2?

3. How satisfactory is the conclusion for these directions? What does the writer say to make the article sound finished?

4. Is the title of the article misleading? Why or why not?

5. Notice the number of technical terms: *strobe, exposure, diaphragm, tripod, prefocus, image.* "Tandem on a Motorcycle" also contained quite a few difficult words, yet the tone of the two sets of directions is quite different. What, in each writer's attitude toward his subject and reader, accounts for the difference?

Tips on Taping FM-Stereo Broadcasts

component: separate pieces for radio, amplifier, and speaker
outputs: sockets that can lead out of the radio
canine: dog
monaural: sound recorded and reproduced as though it came from a single source. Stereo separates the sound into two or more sources
input: a socket feeding into the recorder
fidelity: how accurately the original sound is reproduced

[1] Taping FM-stereo broadcasts has become more and more popular. If you have decided to tape a program, you may think the thing to do is to set up a microphone in front of the radio speaker and start recording. *This is exactly what you should not do.* Because the microphone does not "hear" the speaker the way you do, this method produces an only so-so recording with a harsh, rather tinny sound. Furthermore, the microphone not only hears the program, but everything else going on in the room and you may end up with a program sprinkled with telephone bells, a cough or two, and the yowl of a dog who doesn't like the music.

[2] The proper method is very simple. Just about 95 per cent of all current,

quality, component systems which include radios have extra outputs from the amplifier for recording. Marked "Tape" or "Auxiliary," they are at the back of the set and deliver the same program to the recorder that the speakers reproduce. But since the sound goes directly to the tape, nothing but the program is recorded—no extra noises, human or canine.

[3] Using the outputs for stereo recording requires two connecting cables—one for each channel—from the amplifier to the recorder. Most record and audio-supply stores have the cables already made up in various lengths from 3 to 6 feet long. Plug them into the back of your set and leave them there. All stereo tape recorders are equipped with extra inputs, but should you have a monaural recorder with only one input, you can still record a stereo broadcast using only one cable with perfectly pleasant, if not altogether brilliant, results.

[4] Making the actual recording with cables is a breeze. First connect the cables from your set to the recorder. The recorder inputs are marked "Microphone" and "Radio/Record Player." Sometimes the second set of inputs is marked "Auxiliary." Plug the cables into the "Radio" or "Auxiliary" inputs, then select a tape which has a playing time equal to the length of the program you plan to record. Most tape recorders today operate at two speeds: $7\frac{1}{2}$ inches per second and $3\frac{3}{4}$ inches per second. The first speed, $7\frac{1}{2}$, usually gives somewhat better fidelity; the second, slower speed makes the same amount of tape last twice as long. With the improved quality of today's tape heads and tapes, the difference between the two speeds is often hard to hear. A short test at each speed will help you to decide which speed is best for you.

[5] Before the program, turn on the radio to the station you intend to record, and set the tuning and the volume at the desired level to produce the amount of sound you most enjoy. Then turn on the tape machine and put it at the "Record" position. With the radio on and the recorder set, the volume indicators on the recorder will show the amount of sound being recorded. Get out your tape manual and follow the instructions for setting these indicators very, very carefully. Then, at the beginning of the selected program, start the recording. The only attention you need pay the machine now is to turn it off during the commercials if you want an uninterrupted program. Or, if your machine has a pause button (a very useful little gadget), you can skip the commercials without even turning off the machine.

[6] Taping broadcasts is an easy way to build a collection that would be hard to buy.

DISCUSSION

1. How much of this article is introduction? What does the introduction do? Would the directions be more effective if the introduction gave reasons for taping broadcasts and the warning about what *not* to do came later in the directions? Give reasons for your answer.

2. The vocabulary list suggests these directions are written for a fairly specialized audience. What is the audience and how can you tell?

3. Is it cheating for the writer to refer his readers to the tape manual instead of telling them how to set the indicators (paragraph 5)? Again, justify your answer.

4. If you didn't already know the meaning of *canine,* how could you guess it by pairing the last sentence of paragraph 1 with the last sentence of paragraph 2? What is the effect of this repetition?

5. Are these directions perfectly clear? In paragraph 3, does "your set" in "Plug them into the back of your set" refer to the recorder or the amplifier? Can you find any other places where the directions might seem confusing?

6. Does paragraph 4, beginning "Making the actual recording with cables is a breeze," deal with making the recordings? What does the paragraph cover?

Object Lesson

gratifying: pleasant; delightful
casual: effortless
workmanlike: adequate, though not brilliant
spiritedly: with enthusiasm
propels: moves rapidly
memorable: something worth remembering
immeasurably: more than can be measured
furtive: sneaky; secret

[1] A child psychologist, whose name we will not reveal because of a genuine concern for his safety, now comes forward with the suggestion that the child should be given what's known as an object lesson. This involves taking a child to a restaurant and doing all the things the child does. We can understand how this would be gratifying to the child, but we shudder to think of the effect on the other customers. For example:

[2] 1. Knock the milk over, yourself. To beat the child to it you will have to strike with the speed of a cobra. Try to hit the glass in such a way that the milk flows across the table and into the lap of an adult. You will probably

Reprinted by permission of Bernard Geis Associates from BACK TO ABNORMAL. Copyright © 1963 by Caskie Stinnett.

never achieve the casual, sure touch that the child displays, but you can do a good workmanlike job if you apply yourself spiritedly.

[3] 2. Kick the table so as to spill coffee into the saucers. A well-placed kick during the soup course can get the entire party moved to another table.

[4] 3. Twist around in your chair until, as nearly as possible, you have your back to the table. This permits you to see the coming and going of waiters, the seating of customers, and makes it possible to ignore the food completely.

[5] 4. Most of the food, of course, goes on the floor where it belongs, but a certain amount should be saved for the tablecloth. Spear the lamb chop violently and let the fork strike the plate a glancing blow. This *propels* the peas across the table, which is better theater than having them dribble over the sides of the plate.

[6] 5. As part of the squirming process, it is interesting to tip the chair over backwards. Though this contains some excellent possibilities for upsetting the entire restaurant, there is always the possibility of getting hurt, so it can be recommended only when other efforts to make the occasion memorable have failed.

[7] 6. It's good social custom to get down from the chair and wander around other tables, staring at strangers and even inquiring what they are eating. This adds immeasurably to the sociability of the meal.

[8] These are the main points to remember in teaching the child a lesson, but there's one other thing. Keep your eye on the manager and be ready to leave as soon as you see him make a furtive telephone call from the cashier's desk. If there's a side door, take it.

DISCUSSION

1. Although this essay does give directions, it is obvious that the writer is also having fun. The middle sentence in the introduction defines the main term, "object lesson." How does the author show his attitude toward such lessons in the first and third sentences of the introduction? Does he expect these directions to be followed?

2. Who is the audience for whom this article is written? How can you tell?

3. The separate pieces of advice use numbers rather than transitions, although No. 4 and No. 6 also use echo transitions. The advice could probably be followed in any order, but using your own experience with a small child's table habits, can you explain why the steps are arranged as they are? Can you explain why No. 3 and No. 5 are separated, even though they both deal with "the squirming process"?

4. Does paragraph 8 offer one more step or is it some final advice about the main thing the reader must keep in mind? Does what is said in the conclusion change your mind about the way you answered question 1? How?

A Student Theme

Most people need to write more than one draft of a paper before they are fully satisfied with how they have worded it. Here is the first version of a student paper giving directions for trimming a poodle.

Cutting Your Dog's Hair

[1] Taking a dog to a vet shop to have his hair cut costs a lot of money and so do clippers, but if you own a poodle, you have to face it, his hair grows <u>and</u> grows <u>and</u> grows until the poor dog gets too hot in the summer, or he drags through the house like a wet rug in the winter and walks flat footed because he has so much fur in his feet. Besides that, he can't see because he has so much fur hanging down in his eyes.

[2] As I've already said, electric clippers are expensive, but you can get them cheaper. You can check the want ads for used ones, or you can get clippers for green stamps like one of my friends did. It took a lot of books and she saved up for a long time, but she decided pretty soon that she had saved enough money clipping her dog herself to buy the clippers anyway. Whichever you do, you will be glad you got the clippers. Neither one of you will have to stand so long, which is tiring especially if the dog gets nervous. If the dog gets nervous, feed him a tranquillizer. This should be done before you clip him. Some people do it before they bathe them. If tranquillizers are too expensive, feed him a large meal.

[3] All you need is a comb and some round end scissors. After you have dried the dog, use the wire brush to get the snarls out. Actually, you should brush him well between washings. It makes him feel more comfortable and he looks better.

[4] First clip his throat, then his ears and the side of his face. Don't cut his eyelashes. Be careful around his eyes.

[5] The next step is to cut his whiskers and his pompadour.

[6] After that has been done, clip his tail, leaving a ball cut in a circle, and then cut the hair around his feet or else on his body. It doesn't matter which comes first.

[7] Clipping a poodle is very easy if you know how to do it.

(Used by permission.)

Here is the second version. Do all the changes in the second version seem to you to be improvements? Try to figure out the *reason* behind each change.

Consider changes in wording, order, information given, attitude toward audience.

How to Clip a Poodle

[1] Poodles have to be clipped and professional cuts are expensive. You may think you will not clip your dog because you do not intend to enter him in dog shows, but you will change your mind because a poodle's fur grows constantly. Unless he is clipped he is uncomfortable because he can't see; he gets too hot in the summer, or too messy in the winter; and his fur mats in his paws so that he loses his poodle prance. You can solve the problem by clipping your dog yourself.

[2] You will need a wire brush, a comb, and curved ended scissors. Electric clippers are convenient, but don't try to use the family clippers, because dog fur is denser than human hair and it ruins clippers not made for dogs. When you use electric clippers, you must be careful to keep them cool because a dog's skin can be burned. Keep the clippers cool by dipping them into kerosene and wiping them thoroughly. Test the heat of the clippers on your wrist. If they seem uncomfortable, they are too hot. You cannot be too cautious; your dog can be cruelly burned.

[3] Step One: Wash and thoroughly dry the dog. Use a hair dryer to save drying time.

[4] Step Two: Brush and comb the coat to remove snarls and matted fluff in the undercoat.

[5] Step Three: Rest the dog's chin in your hand; clip up the throat and into the muzzle. If he is to have whiskers, stop clipping at the point the whiskers begin. Clip up and under the ears, around the side of the face and under the eyes, avoiding the eyelashes. Be very careful around the eyes. Clip up the back of the neck to the base of the pompadour.

[6] Step Four: Trim his whiskers and pompadour with the scissors. If you are handy with electric clippers, you may use them on the pompadour. Don't trim the top of the head too short; a poodle looks stupid with a butch cut.

[7] Step Five: Clip the tail to the ball of fur on the end. Clip closely around the anus, then less closely down the back to the hips.

[8] Step Six: Scissor trim the tassel on the tail. Flatten it in one hand and trim circularly.

[9] Step Seven: Lay the dog on his side. Clip the hind paws first. Clip up the top of each toe, over the top of the foot to the wrist, using the clipper edge. Clip the back of the paw from pad to wrist. Use scissors to cut hair from between the toes and pads; use the round end of the scissors, pointing away from the skin.

[10] Step Eight: Stand the dog up. Comb his body so that the fur stands straight. Clip him according to the pattern you have chosen. Do not pull the

strands of fur out as you clip; they will spring back and leave an uneven line. Clip the abdomen and inside the haunches cleanly.

[11] With practice, do-it-yourself-poodle-clipping becomes an easy way to trim your budget and your dog. Nothing can be lost but time and fur.

(Used by permission.)

WRITING TOPICS
FOR DIRECTIONS

There are probably hundreds of things you know how to do. The list below is more to suggest topics than to limit the range of things you can write on. Whether you pick one of these topics or use one of your own, be sure you are writing from your own knowledge and that you remember the needs of your audience as you write. It's usually a good idea to avoid giving directions on something most people already know how to do. For instance, you wouldn't want to tell girls how to hem a skirt, or boys how to change a tire.

How to   entertain a three-year-old
win a student election
stand up on water skis
prevent frostbite
find an apartment
break a lease
form a car pool
raise Cain
placate a policeman

"Head down a bit more, weight forward, keep your back straight—and follow through!"

Drawing by Dana Fradon. Reprinted courtesy of *The Saturday Evening Post.*

raise bail
judge a beauty contest
win a beauty contest
prune rosebushes
pick a lock
cut toenails
replace a broken window
cure a cold
cover a chair seat
lose weight
cure snoring
choose a wig
give a haircut at home
dress out a deer
spot and avoid a speed trap
fill out an accident report
turn a somersault
get a date
refuse a date
perform a card trick
leave the house without being heard
remove candle wax from a tablecloth
impress your boyfriend's mother
skindive safely
sell tickets for a benefit
recruit a baseball team
fix a leaky faucet
keep a beard looking trim
decorate a Christmas tree
blow an egg
kill time

How to make   a mobile
invisible ink
ice sculpture
earrings from seashells
a silkscreen print
a decorated candle
a checkerboard
homemade soap
a bonfire without matches
a mess
an enemy

How to build   a board fence
a treehouse
a swing
an entrance for a cat
a tie rack
a bird feeder
a sauna bath
a better rat trap
a burglar alarm
a secret compartment
a soapbox racer
a kite
a photographic darkroom
a simple telescope
a reputation as a wit

More "how-to" writing topics

How to make masks, pottery, enameled copper jewelry, merry

How to use a soil test kit, a Geiger counter, a sewing machine, a tear gas mask

How to stop smoking, oversleeping, insulting your friends

How to tie a fly, a necktie, a record

How to play a game, a harmonica, dead

How to tune a guitar, a piano, a sitar, a hopped-up V-8

How to organize a tutoring service, a cake sale, a demonstration, your time

readings on definition 2

DEFINITION

Definitions are necessary to make clear what words or terms or ideas mean. New words, and old words with new meanings, need to be explained. Words used very precisely by scientists and scholars need to be defined carefully enough so that other scientists and other scholars can tell exactly where the words fit. And words with strong emotional associations, whose meanings are usually very broad and fuzzy, need to be brought back to reality, to be connected with experience.

One reason we need definition is so we can understand how people in one region use terms not much heard outside that region. That is the kind of definition Mark Twain is giving in "Lagniappe." We need definitions for slang terms such as "no sweat" or for familiar words used in new ways by certain in-groups, such as the way some black communities use "soul" or some street gangs use "heart." For words like this, synonyms won't work; we have no other word that means exactly the same as *lagniappe* or *no sweat* or *soul*. A single sentence of explanation will not do either. Mark Twain would not have said enough if he had stopped with saying that lagniappe means "something thrown in, gratis, for good measure." We can't understand just where the word fits until he lets us hear and see it in use, not once, but two or three times. He has to write several paragraphs before we understand all the situations the word can cover.

Sometimes seeing the word in use is not enough to make its meaning completely clear. We need also to be shown some situations where the word will not fit, some places where it is not used. In telling us what "no sweat" means, Myers begins with a negative definition; he tells us that the term does *not* refer to the amount of work or the temperature of the room.

Whatever method of definition the writer uses, however, his main concern is to set limits to the meaning of the word. He makes sure his readers understand just where the term fits and where it doesn't. He makes his definition complete enough that the reader can say to himself, "That's it. I see what it means."

Lagniappe

facility: ease; skill
equivalent: the same thing as
gratis: free
countenance: face
edifice: structure; large building
gill: about half a cup

[1] We picked up one excellent word—a word worth traveling to New Orleans to get; a nice, limber, expressive, handy word—"Lagniappe." They pronounce it *lanny-yap.* It is Spanish—so they said. We discovered it at the head of a column of odds and ends in the *Picayune* the first day; heard twenty people use it the second, inquired what it meant the third; adopted it and got facility in swinging it the fourth. It has a restricted meaning, but I think the people spread it out a little when they choose. It is the equivalent of the thirteenth roll in a "baker's dozen." It is something thrown in, gratis, for good measure. The custom originated in the Spanish quarter of the city. When a child or a servant buys something in a shop—or even the mayor or the governor, for aught I know—he finishes the operation by saying: "Give me something for lagniappe." [2] The shopman always responds; gives the child a bit of licorice root, gives the servant a cheap cigar or a spool of thread, gives the governor—I don't know what he gives the governor; support, likely. [3] When you are invited to drink—and this does occur now and then in New Orleans—and you say, "What, again?—no, I've had enough," the other party says, "But just this one time more—this is for lagniappe." When the beau perceives that he is stacking his compliments a trifle too high, and sees by the young lady's countenance that the edifice would have been better with the top compliment left off, he puts his "I beg pardon, no harm in-

Where the word is used: New Orleans

Who uses it: everybody

What it means, in general: something thrown in for good measure

Situations where it fits: buying something

taking an extra drink

flattering a girl

From *Life on the Mississippi* by Mark Twain.

50

tended," into the briefer form of "Oh, that's for
lagniappe." If the waiter in the restaurant stumbles
and spills a gill of coffee down the back of your   spilling something on a
neck, he says, "For lagniappe, sir," and gets you   customer
another cup without extra charge.

DISCUSSION

1. After Mark Twain has shown you *lagniappe* in operation, you should be
   able to think of three more occasions where the word would fit. Make up
   three situations where somebody might say "for lagniappe," and see
   whether your classmates think the word would be appropriate there.

2. Although in general Twain works from the unfamiliar *(lagniappe)* to
   the familiar (the kind of situation we might all find ourselves in), he
   does use some uncommon words. He could have said *ease, free, face,* and
   structure, for instance, instead of *facility, gratis, countenance,* and *edifice.*
   Does he use these words when he's quoting what somebody says? Why
   do you think he uses them?

3. The last situation Twain mentions is a little different from the other
   three. What do *thrown in* and *gratis* mean in this situation that they
   didn't mean in earlier situations? Why do you suppose Twain saved this
   situation for the last?

No Sweat

> **apprehension:** a mild worry or fear
> **reassurance:** encouragement or comfort
> **terminates:** ends
> **confirm:** promise

[1] "No sweat" is one of the most descriptive slang terms that I have ever
encountered. I first heard the term used in Korea, where it appeared in almost

"No Sweat," by John D. Myers from *Assignments In Exposition,* Third Edition, by Louise E.
Rorabacher. Copyright, 1946, 1950 by Harper & Brothers. Copyright © 1959 by Louise E.
Rorabacher.

every conversation among the American soldiers stationed there. It is admittedly a somewhat vulgar expression for formal use, but for saying much in a few words, it is hard to beat.

[2] Strangely enough, "no sweat" does not refer to the amount of work involved in doing something, nor yet to the temperature. It refers to the absence of worry and apprehension involved in a certain action. Used properly, it carries a note of reassurance; it is a short way of saying, "Don't work yourself up over this matter, as it is all taken care of."

[3] For example, let us suppose that a lovely young lady, in backing her car out of a parking lot, accidentally scrapes a young man's fender. The young man gallantly releases her from all responsibility by saying cheerfully, "No sweat," and the situation probably terminates in a date instead of a lawsuit.

[4] But the expression means more than a release from obligation, as can be seen from the following example: A production engineer calls in his foreman and explains that he will need four thousand brake units by the end of the week. The foreman replies, "No sweat," and the production engineer knows he is safe in telling the company's sales representative to confirm delivery.

[5] If "no sweat" had been current in New Orleans at the time Mark Twain wrote "Lagniappe," the restaurant scene in which the waiter spilled coffee down the customer's neck would have had a different outcome. Before the careless fellow had had time to make any kind of apology, the injured patron would have looked up with a smile and said, "No sweat," and the incident would have been closed.

DISCUSSION

1. This essay, too, begins by telling us where the expression is used and who uses it. Is "no sweat" an expression you use? Have you heard others use it? Does what Myers says agree with your experience?

2. How does Myers set limits on the use of the word? How does he make clear when *not* to use it? What is the effect of explaining what it doesn't mean before he tells us what it does mean?

3. Of the three examples given, two situations are much alike and one somewhat different. Can you explain this difference? For which of the three situations would these translations of "no sweat" be appropriate:
   "It wasn't my fault."
   "Don't worry; I can do it."
   "I won't have to try very hard."
   "OK, I won't make a fuss about it."

4. Are you convinced that Mark Twain's restaurant scene would have ended differently if the customer had said "no sweat"? Why? What was the outcome, as Twain told it?

5. Notice that in both "Lagniappe" and "No Sweat" the words being defined appear in the first and last sentences of each essay. How does this make the essays sound finished?

Soul

poly-:   many, thus **polyrhythms:**   many kinds of rhythm
essence: what's left when the unimportant things are taken away
transmits: communicates
infinite: unlimited
tambourine: small hand drum with jingling metal discs around it

[1] When I walk on Eighth Avenue, man, I see rhythms I don't see downtown. *Polyrhythms.* You look at one cat, he may be doin' bop, bop-bop bop, bop-bop, and another one goin' *bop*-de-bop, *de*-bop. Beautiful, man. Those are beautiful people. Yeah. But when I go downtown to Thirty-fourth Street, everybody's walkin' the same, you dig? They don't put themselves into it. Their walk tells you nothing about who they are. *Polyrhythms.* That's what it is. Like a flower garden in a breeze. The roses swing a little bit from side to side, kind of stiff, not too much. The lilacs swing wide, slow, lazy, not in a hurry. A blade of grass wiggles. It's 'cause they're all different and they're being themselves. Polyrhythms, like on Eighth Avenue. That's soul.
[2] Soul is motion and sound. It is stomping and clapping with the gospel music of the First Tabernacle of Deliverance (Spiritual) American Orthodox Catholic Church on Harlem's One Hundred Twenty-fifth Street, and boogalooing the Funky Broadway to the Memphis gospel soul blues of Otis Redding while walking down the street. Soul is "Doin' the Thing" with the church-oriented funky jazz of Horace Silver and just moving back down home with John Lee Hooker's gutbucket folk blues. Soul is being natural, telling it like it is . . . When Mahalia Jackson sings, the gospel and the blues of Bessie Smith become the *essence* of soul. Ray Charles throws his head back and shouts "Oh, yeah!" and transmits an inner feeling goodness. When you've heard it like that, you know you have been moved. Then he comes in with, "Don't it make you want to feel all right," and it's like everything has been unraveled and you just lay in there and groove. Ray Charles turns you on. So does Aretha Franklin and "Mister Soul" James Brown.

[3] On a warm day in Harlem one can see and feel an infinite variety of rhythms. People stand on tenement stoops and on the sidewalks and sway to jukebox music here, WLIB and WWRL radio there. Some get caught up in front of record shops and just soul dance like they want to. All around you, Watusi, Boston Monkey, Shing-a-ling, Karate, Boogaloo, The Pearl, The Funky Broadway. Store-front-church tambourines ring and two young men in red shirts walk down the street, one playing a sheepskin drum and the other a cowbell or fife. A saxophone riffs, a trumpet wails and then there's the shout. The black poet LeRoi Jones calls it "Ka'ba . . . Our world is full of sound/ our world is more lovely than anyone's . . ."

DISCUSSION

1. How many *synonym definitions* (offering another word that means about the same as the first one) are used in this article? What are they? Do you think any one of the synonyms is enough by itself? Why or why not?

2. How many *single sentence definitions* can you find? What are they?

3. Can you find any *negative definitions?* Where? If you find some, explain how they help us understand what the word *does* mean.

4. Does Calloway explain what "soul" means by showing how it is like or different from something else? What? How do these comparisons help to make the meaning clearer?

5. What do you think are the most effective *examples* Calloway uses?

Heart

Richard Coeur de Lion: a twelfth century British king called "The Lion-Hearted" because he was very brave in battle
Warwick: a reform school
rumble: gang fight
jap: attack
audacity: acting very boldly, very daringly
ambush: setting a trap to catch someone by surprise

sounding: testing
sham: pretend
simulate: look or act like

[1] Heart is what passes on the street for bravery. Heart, as defined by the bopping clubs, is not the exact equivalent of courage, as, say, Richard Coeur de Lion understood it.

[2] "Heart, well, that's when a bop isn't afraid of anything or anybody," Dice tells you. "He will do absolutely anything. When the chips are down— if he has to fight five he'll fight five. He'll say, 'I'm the butcher, man. I'm the hatchet. If you need anyone to pull the trigger I'll pull the trigger.'

[3] "You take Chico," Dice says. "He has more heart than anyone I ever saw. He's crazy, that boy. Been up to Warwick three times. He don't care what he do. Once we had a rumble with the Chaplains. You know what he did? He went out alone right into Chaplains' turf. In daylight. Just walked in, inviting them to jap him, hoping they would jap him. He'll fight anybody. No matter how many they are. That Chico—he stays drunk all the time. Isn't ever sober. But, man, he sure have heart."

[4] Heart, as the bop defines it, is audacity, devil-may-care disregard for self and consequences. Heart is fourteen-year-old Snake walking up to a patrol-man on the corner and making a grab for his pistol. Heart is sixteen-year-old Rocky waiting in ambush outside a school and firing a rifle into a group of teen-agers as they come out, joking and unaware of danger. Heart is Dice taking a dare to jump down three flights of stairs (and only prevented from carrying it out when someone grabs his legs as he leaps).

[5] A boy shows heart by laughing at his attackers when he is japped out-side his neighborhood. He shows heart by sounding a street boy bigger and tougher than himself.

[6] The opposite of heart is punking out. When a cool has been on for some time gang leaders may order a "shin fight" (sham battle) between the Little People and the Big People. The shin fight simulates gang combat except that knives and guns are not used and blows are not supposed to be struck below the belt or in the face. A shin battle tests heart and shows which boys will be the most vicious and daring street fighters.

DISCUSSION

1. Why does Salisbury begin by letting Dice explain what *heart* means instead of doing it himself? Dice uses several gang terms that ordinary readers might not know; what are they? Does using those words keep you from understanding what Dice means?

2. Both Dice and Salisbury start by giving a general definition. Are their general definitions alike? If you think they are different, show what the differences are.

3. What kind of defining process is being used in "Heart is not . . . courage as . . . Richard Coeur de Lion understood it"? In "Isn't ever sober. But . . ."? In "The opposite of heart is punking out"?

4. Do you need to know the kind of courage Richard Coeur de Lion showed for this reference to be useful? Why or why not?

5. Would it help if Salisbury showed us somebody "punking out"? Why or why not?

Finding the Class: How Is It Different?

Most of the definitions in this next section deal with the way words are used by specialists working in their own fields. Instructors in social science or physical science, for instance, are not being needlessly fussy when they insist on precise definitions. Only by using precision can scholars and scientists, social workers and lawyers, avoid sloppy thinking and sloppy work.

In ordinary conversation we do not need to be so careful. Nobody cares whether we use the word *instinct* in a fairly vague way when we are talking to our friends. It's perfectly all right to say, after a party, "Some instinct told me to stay away from Andy's home brew," but it's not all right to be that imprecise in a sociology paper or a biology class. There we must use the scientific definition.

Scientific definitions make a greater effort to place exact limits on meaning than is needed for words we use in ordinary conversation. One way that writers try to establish these limits is to use a three-part definition:
1. term being defined =
2. the general class it belongs to +
3. whatever makes it different from other things in the same general class.

When Landis defines what sociologists mean by *instinct* he sets his limits by using a three-part definition. He does not stop there, however. His three-part general definition is backed up by specific examples. He is careful to make clear what he is defining does *not* mean.

In the same way, lawyers in some states define a felony as a crime (the general class) involving bodily harm or property worth more than fifty dollars (difference between felonies and other less important crimes called misdemeanors). We can be grateful that the law does set these exact limits. Without such careful distinctions, we might all be labeled felons for forgetting to fill the parking meter or sticking our tongues out at the mayor.

Instinct

species: classification by kind or family
migratory: moving from one part of the world to another
climatic: weather conditions
vary: change
environmental: all the conditions and influences that surround us

[1] For the daily routine of living and meeting the need for food and shelter, nature has provided animal life with built-in patterns known as <u>instincts</u>.

> Introduction tells what instincts are for—an indirect way of saying what they are

[2] All birds of a given species build a similar nest. The orioles swing their cradle from the weeping-willow branch. Robins plaster their sturdy nest bowl in the shaded crotch of a maple, elm, or oak tree.

> Example: birds build nests of a certain kind—
> orioles
> robins

[3] Migratory birds have a built-in sense of direction which guides them to their destination on their annual migrations of thousands of miles from north to south in response to climatic changes. The geese form their **V** in the sky and start south in fall, led by the call of the lead gander. They do not argue about the reasonableness of it, or debate whether to set their compass to right or left. Day and night they fly on, through bright moonlight or stormy sky, reaching their destination close to schedule. It is traditional that the swallows of Capistrano, California, will arrive on March 19. They vary little from schedule year after year as they return to build their nests in the old Spanish mission.

> Example: birds know where and when to fly
>
> geese
>
> swallows

[4] On the West Coast the salmon return after four years at sea to the stream where they were hatched. There they lay their eggs and die, completing nature's life cycle for them.

> Example: salmon return to birthplace to spawn

[5] Nature provides some insects with the built-in equipment for a very complicated social life. Instinct accounts for the complex community organization of bees and the complicated homes and habits of ants. Among such social insects one sees cooperation,

> Example: social life of insects
>
> bees
> ants

specialization of work, and even division of labor. These patterns work perfectly, or nearly so, yet they are not learned.

[6] Instinct is never learned by an animal. It is by definition a behavior pattern provided by nature, which functions when environmental forces are brought to bear on the creature.

Three part definition:
(1)
instinct =
(2)
behavior pattern +
(3)
provided by nature and functioning when environmental forces are brought to bear on the creature

DISCUSSION

1. Although Landis begins with a simplified general statement, he does not give us his complete definition until after he has produced several examples. Does this order make his definition harder or easier to understand? Why?

2. Just before the complete three-part definition, we are given a brief negative definition. Does this statement of what *instinct* is not belong in the definition? Defend your answer. Does this negative definition help in seeing why the term is not precisely used in the comment, "Some instinct told me to stay away from Andy's home brew"?

3. Using the definition given in Landis' last paragraph, decide which of the following kinds of behavior could be called instinctive. Why do you think so?
   a. a newborn baby crying from hunger
   b. a two-year-old's fear of a hot stove
   c. a man swearing when he hits his thumb with a hammer
   d. a cat suckling her kittens
   e. a boy swallowing his gum when the teacher comes in
   f. a girl dodging when a car swerves toward her
   g. a child liking ice cream
   h. a child disliking spinach

Two Definitions of Poverty:

I. Who Are the Poor?*

minimum: least possible
adequate: enough to meet actual needs
composition: what it contains; in this case, who is in the family

[1] The Social Security Administration uses the best definition of "poor." A family of a husband and wife and two pre-school children must have an average of 70¢ per person per day for a minimum adequate diet plus $1.40 for all other needs. That's $58.80 per week, or over $3,100 per year. SSA adjusts this standard up or down to account for family size and composition and whether farm or non-farm residents.

[2] By these standards, they estimate for the end of 1963 that there were 34½ million Americans living in poverty. Fifteen million of these were children under 18 and 5 million were adults over 65. Twenty-three and a half million were white and about 11 million were non-white. About half of the poor lived in or near cities of over 50,000, while the other half are non-metropolitan, or rural. If you add up all the money earned by all these poor people, the sum is 40 per cent less than they would have if they all lived right on the poverty line.

II. Poverty: Public Enemy Number One†

options: choices
material conditions: amount of money; kind of house and food
strive: try; work hard
ascetic: person who deliberately goes without physical comforts, usually for religious reasons

Poverty is associated with low income, but it cannot be identified with it. To be in a state of poverty is to be entrapped: that is, to be in a situation without choices, an environment without options. Hence, adherents of the New Left who plunge themselves into the ghetto, or graduate students in the major universities whose material conditions are not significantly different from those of the poor, are not actually impoverished; for them there is always another place: the middle-class environment to which they can return, the future toward which they can strive. Poverty produces the sense of being shaped by forces beyond one's understanding and control, which renders the self insecure in all its aspects—physical well-being, personal relationships, moral and intellectual beliefs. Finally, and as a result of these conditions, poverty is a feeling of personal unimportance. The conviction that the *self* is worthless is what distinguishes modern poverty from the "honest poor" of old or the ascetics of religious tradition.

DISCUSSION

1. These two short definitions use quite different methods of making clear what *poverty* means. Neither writer lets us see poverty in operation and neither gives any examples, yet both set limits. How would you describe the method used in the first definition? In the second?

2. Do either of these definitions give a clear three-part general statement? If you think they do, be ready to say what it is. If you can't find one, work one out on the basis of the information given. How much of the difference in the two definitions depends on the second part, the general class of things in which poverty is placed?

3. If you were trying to decide which people in your own city lived in poverty, which definition would be easier to use? Why? Which definition seems fairer? Why?

4. Would the "impoverished students" in the apartment decorating article be considered impoverished by these definitions? Why or why not?

How To File A Complaint Against Unlawful Job Discrimination

prohibited: forbidden; illegal
charges: official complaint
apprenticeship: learning a skill while working on the job

[1] Discrimination in employment because of race, color, religion, sex or national origin is prohibited under Title VII of the Civil Rights Law. The Equal Employment Opportunity Commission will act on charges of discrimination in employment committed by employers, labor organizations, state and private employment agencies and labor-management apprenticeship programs.

[2] Charges may be filed by any person who believes he has been discriminated against in an employment situation. You have a right to complain if:

Employer refuses to hire you when you are qualified for a job opening.

Employer refuses to let you file application but accepts others'.

Union or employment agency refuses to refer you to job opening.

Union refuses to accept you into membership.

You are fired or laid off without cause.

You are passed over for promotion for which you are qualified.

You are paid less than others for comparable work.

You are placed in segregated seniority line.

You are left out of training or apprenticeship programs.

AND . . .

The reason for any of these acts is your race, color, religion, sex, or national origin.

Also, if employer provides racially segregated lunchrooms, locker rooms, rest rooms, recreation facilities.

DISCUSSION

1. At first glance, this article looks like a set of directions. Would you consider it directions or definition? If it is directions, what do the directions cover? What are the steps to be followed? If it is definition, what is being defined? What method is used in defining it?

Reprinted from the pamphlet "How To File A Complaint Against Unlawful Job Discrimination" by permission of The Equal Employment Opportunity Commission.

2. If you wanted to file a complaint against unlawful job discrimination, which would you need to know first, the steps to follow in filing the complaint or the legal definition of discrimination? Could you use the information in this article to decide whether or not you were being discriminated against?

3. Make up three different job situations and let your classmates decide whether a complaint should be filed. Make your situations as complete and specific as you can: give names and dates, as well as events.

Who Is Family?

presumed: taken for granted
The Man Who Came to Dinner: a long-running Broadway comedy of 1939 about a man who was invited to dinner and stayed for several weeks
bequests: gifts left in a will, usually money
probate: court that handles wills
reciprocal: working both ways
voluntary: done from choice

[1] What is a family in legal terms? This goes beyond parent and child, brothers and sisters, and any other line of blood relatives, because of the many issues that can arise when family legal rights get into court. For example, room and board and similar services within a family are presumed by the law to be a gift, unless there is a contract to pay. Whether or not someone is within the legal meaning of family may shed light on whether a contract exists.

[2] A lady in Indiana moved into the house of her second cousin. She was uninvited, unannounced, and unexpected. More than the man who came to dinner, she stayed for 23 years, until she died. She paid not a penny and there was never a discussion between her and householder about money for rent or services or anything else. The woman had a good income and accumulated enough money to leave several bequests in her will, including one to the second cousin. The will, as usual, directed that the estate pay all just debts.

[3] The second cousin filed a claim in probate for room, board, care and companionship. The claim was denied, a lawsuit was filed. A trial judge,

Reprinted from "IAM Family Lawyer" in the June 27, 1968 issue of *The Machinist* by permission.

after hearing all the evidence, rendered judgment for the second cousin for $11,368, which, although less than the claim, was a reasonably good recovery. This case may have bearing upon any family obligations to pay which you may have, if you live with relatives or·they live with you.

[4] One well-known definition of a family in the law reads as follows: "A family, within the meaning of the family relation doctrine, is generally defined as a collective body of persons, who form one household, under one head and one domestic government." Whether or not you may have conceived of your family as a domestic government, there it is. Another legal definition has added the important phrase, "and who have reciprocal, natural or moral duties to support and care for each other."

[5] Was the old lady who moved in subject to the head of the household within a domestic government? The court reviewed the evidence and found she was not. The uninvited woman was independent in the extreme. She came and went when and as she pleased. She took most of her meals alone, cooked in her room, and entertained her guests alone. She occasionally did chores around the house, but the judge said it was voluntary because she was never asked to do anything. This was not a family relationship. Accordingly, the law could presume that there was an intention to pay and an expectation of payment.

DISCUSSION

1. The first paragraph of this article makes no attempt to begin with a general statement of what family means, but it does narrow the topic to one special area. What is the area? How is the narrowing done? What else does the first paragraph do?

2. Why does the writer give such a complicated example? Do you think several simpler examples would make his meaning clearer? Why or why not?

3. Where is the generalization given? If it is a three-part definition, what are the parts? Which pieces of the definition helped the second cousin to collect his money? Why?

4. This selection was part of a longer article talking about legal protection. If the article had consisted only of the section included here, what would you have added to make the article sound finished?

5. In one of his poems, Robert Frost defined *home* as a place where, "when you have to go there, they have to let you in." How does this more ordinary definition fit with the legal definition of family?

Two Definitions from the Physical Sciences:

I. Diffusion*

altitude: height

[1] Meteorologists give a great deal of thought to a process called diffusion. In general, the term means a spreading out. Usually, we mean the spreading produced by the smaller-scale air motions rather than the large, steady wind currents.

[2] Have you ever seen a small rocket fired into the air at a Fourth of July fireworks display? When it reaches an altitude of a few hundred feet, the head of the rocket explodes. It throws out a shower of colored lights. It also produces a puff of smoke. If you watch the smoke, you will notice several features of its movement. First, under the influence of the wind, the entire puff moves as a single unit. In addition, the size of the smoke region increases. This spreading comes about as a result of variations of small-scale air motions. They move the smoke particles farther away from the center of the puff. We say that they cause the smoke to diffuse.

II. Angular Momentum†

phenomenon: an observable event in nature
execute: do
maneuver: action
axis: where a line would be if it were drawn down the center of a turning object
rotatable: capable of being turned around and around

*From THE UNCLEAN SKY, Louis J. Battan. Copyright © 1966 by Educational Services Incorporated. Reprinted by permission of Doubleday & Company, Inc.

†Excerpt from "Other Worlds Than Ours," by Donald H. Menzel in November, 1955 issue of *The Atlantic Monthly* is reprinted by permission of the author. Copyright © 1955 by The Atlantic Monthly Company, Boston, Mass. 02116.

[1] Angular momentum is a phenomenon well known to ballerinas or fancy skaters. For example, a skater or dancer wishing to execute a whirl starts spinning slowly upon one foot with both arms and one leg extended. An ice skater often goes into a crouching position at the beginning of the maneuver. Then the person draws the arms and leg closer to the body, trying to achieve pencil slimness as far as possible. The nearer the arms and legs reach the axis of rotation the faster the spin becomes.

[2] Anyone possessing a rotatable desk chair or piano stool can make an even more spectacular demonstration. Holding two fairly heavy books at arm's length, start yourself spinning. Pull the books in toward your body and the speed or rotation increases noticeably. In fact, you can pull the books in only with considerable effort. They tend to fly off unless you hold them tightly.

DISCUSSION

1. Terms such as *diffusion* and *momentum* are sometimes hard to understand because we think of them as being outside our normal experiences. Why are the examples given in these two short definitions especially useful?

2. Would what happens to smoke from a pipe or a chimney be just as good an example of *diffusion* as smoke from a rocket? Why or why not?

3. Would the origin of the planets from a whirling, contracting sun (sometimes thought to have happened as a result of *angular momentum*) be as useful a way to explain the term as the ballerina and the rotating piano stool? Explain.

4. The *diffusion* definition begins with a generalization followed by an example. The *angular momentum* definition contains only examples. Can you work out a generalization defining *angular momentum* from the two examples given?

Public Opinion

milquetoast: timid; wishy-washy
monogamous: having only one spouse
hypochondriac: person who always thinks he is sick

[1] For our purposes here, we shall define public opinion as the *expression of attitudes on a social issue.* Notice that this definition includes three parts. First, unless an attitude is *expressed,* it is neither public nor opinion, since attitudes are feelings or notions that cannot be directly observed, and opinions are the expressions of those feelings or notions. We say that a milquetoast employee has no opinions in the presence of his boss even though we assume that he does have attitudes of some kind. Attitudes must somehow be communicated to others—that is, they must be expressed—to become part of public opinion. Suppose that three-fifths of the people in a country have secret attitudes disapproving of their rulers, but that they fail for some reason to express their disapproval in talking with their friends, in behavior at political meetings, in voting, in answering interviewers, or in any other way. Such attitudes would not be part of public opinion, although they might make up part of a potential public opinion. Unexpressed attitudes have an influence in government but only because public officials must make guesses as to what opinions a given course of action would bring out.

[2] Second, public opinion requires an *issue* of some kind. To say that John Jones has an opinion tells us practically nothing, except that he is not a vegetable. For the statement to mean something, we need to know the object of his opinion (Democrats, dry martinis, federal aid to education, etc.), and whether he is for or against it. Because of their pro or con characteristics, opinions always deal with something that can call forth favorable or unfavorable responses. Some accepted practices, such as the monogamous family in the United States, seldom present a public issue, so that nobody talks much about it. But when such a practice is questioned, that is, when an issue is made of it, attitudes are quickly changed into public opinion.

[3] Third, public opinion deals with *social* rather than purely private questions. A hypochondriac's operation, however enthusiastically he expresses opinions about it, is not a social issue. It becomes a social issue, and an object of public opinion, only if others begin to have opinions about it. Public opinion refers, then, to the opinions of a group of people rather than to those

Based on a definition in *The Politics of American Democracy,* 2nd ed., by Marian D. Irish and James W. Prothro, reprinted by permission of the publisher. Copyright © 1962, by Prentice-Hall, Inc., Englewood Cliffs, N.J.

of a single person. In spite of our tendency to think that the only *real* social issues are those *we* know are important, public opinions exist on a tremendous range of questions—from whether Roger Maris really broke Babe Ruth's home run record to problems of world peace. Any question on which a group of people have favorable or unfavorable attitudes can, in other words, become an object of public opinion.

DISCUSSION

1. This definition of public opinion is given in a political science textbook. How does the author let you know that he is writing a scientific definition to be used for a special purpose?

2. The writer points out that his definition has three parts, all equally important, but he doesn't count *public opinion,* the term he is defining, as one of the three. What would you consider the general class if you were putting this definition into the three-part structure shown on page 56 (thing to be defined = class + ways it is different from other things in the class)? What are the two ways we can distinguish public opinion from other things in the same class?

3. How do the writers organize their definition around the three parts they mention? Would the definition have been easier to read and understand if they had given a separate paragraph to the introduction? Does the definition have a conclusion? That is, does it sound finished? Why or why not?

4. How might this kind of organization help you in answering an essay question in one of your courses? In answering an essay question, how might giving an example for each main point help to convince your teacher that you understood the points you were making?

What Is Space?

meteorite: a mass of stone or metal that has fallen to earth from outer space
cosmic ray: very strong radiation in space

From SATELLITES, ROCKETS AND OUTER SPACE by Willy Ley. Copyright © 1957, 1958 by Willy Ley. Adapted by arrangement with The New American Library, Inc., New York.

versatile: able to do many different things
unimpeded: not hindered or stopped
aeronautical: concerned with airplanes
acclimatizing: getting used to conditions
erupt: burst forth
inevitable: certain

[1] A few years ago the *New Yorker* ran a cartoon showing the interior of an airliner. A small boy inquired of the hostess, "Are we in outer space now?" while his mother looked exceedingly embarrassed. Actually the question was quite justified, for if that plane was flying at, say, 20,000 feet, its passengers were at least near the borders of space in some respects.

[2] It all depends on the viewpoint, for there is no simple answer to the simple question: "Where does space begin?" Or, since it does depend on the viewpoint, there is no single answer to that question. There are several.

[3] The earth, as everybody has learned in school at an early age, is a rocky ball moving around the sun in empty space. Its surface is protected by a thin film of atmosphere that has an amazing variety of jobs. It sees to it that not too much of the ultraviolet rays coming from the sun reaches the ground. It stops the majority of all meteorites from hitting the earth. It takes care of most cosmic rays. In addition to all that, it circulates water and acts as a blanket to keep the surface warm.

[4] Considering this large variety of functions one can easily get the feeling that mother earth must have provided an atmospheric blanket many hundreds of miles thick to protect the life on the ground and in the waters. Actually this amazing blanket is not only versatile, it is also quite thin. We are much closer to space than we think. At three miles up the comfortable air pressure of sea level has dropped to half of its sea-level value. At ten miles up the pressure is down to ten per cent of what it is at sea level. At twenty miles it is down to just one per cent.

[5] So if you generously neglect that last remaining one per cent you might simply say that you are in space if you reach 100,000 feet. Since rocket-propelled airplanes have flown higher than 100,000 feet, their pilots can claim to have been in space—and probably do. But unfortunately things are not that simple. It all depends on the effects you have in mind.

[6] Radio engineers, as is well known, use certain layers in the upper atmosphere from which to bounce short radio waves in order to make contact with spots on the ground they could not contact otherwise. The highest of these so-called ionized layers is called the F_2 layer, which has been found as high as 300 miles. A radio engineer is, therefore, justified in saying that from his point of view there are 300 miles of atmosphere above his head. The air may be extremely thin that high up, but he can still find a layer that does something.

[7] The rocket expert looks at the same question with something entirely different in mind. A rocket motor works best in a vacuum, where there is

no air to slow down the exhaust blast of the rocket. By the same token so does the rocket body itself when unimpeded by any air resistance. In short, the expert looks for a place where there is no resistance left. If he finds no resistance whatever, he feels he is in space. And is happy about it.

[8] Strangely enough, his figure comes out much lower than the figure of the radio engineer. The artificial satellites have raised his original figure of 120 miles to about 160 miles. Above that there seems to be no measurable resistance left. So, to the rocket engineer space begins 160 miles up.

[9] The aeronautical engineer again feels differently about the whole thing. He does want some air resistance because without air he cannot produce any "lift" with his wings. He will reason that he is in space if even a very fast-moving airplane cannot obtain any lift any longer. Just where that would take place depends on a number of things, like the assumed speed of the plane. But the figure will be somewhere near 35 miles; that is the height where space begins for the aeronautical engineer.

[10] But all these people, radio men, rocket men and aeronautical men, are thinking in terms of machines. When the medical man enters the discussion he thinks in terms of people. And when you do that, space is awfully near. The first mile above sea level presents no problems whatever, as the inhabitants of Denver will be eager to testify. Two miles up is not much of a problem either; you merely have to (and can) get used to it.

[11] At three miles you can still get along if you grew up at such a height or took enough time acclimatizing yourself, but flatlanders need extra oxygen. Of course, inside a building, or an airplane cabin, you can simply compress the external air until you get a pressure you like. That is still workable for another two miles. Even at five miles a man can expose himself to what is left of the atmosphere without fatal results. He does need oxygen and had better be warmly dressed since the temperature is around *minus* 40 degrees Fahrenheit. But it can be done.

[12] Above five miles another factor comes in.

[13] The boiling point of water, and of all other substances that are normally liquids, depends on air pressure. If the air pressure is lowered, the boiling point is lowered too; even on a not very high mountain it takes hours to boil potatoes; the water simply does not get hot enough.

[14] To a physician the pilot is, among other things, a container holding liquids at a temperature near 100 degrees Fahrenheit. When the air pressure drops so low that 100 degrees Fahrenheit is the boiling point of water no oxygen mask will do any good any more. The body fluids will erupt, boiling, even though they haven't changed temperature, and death is inevitable. Moreover, it is the same kind of death that would strike a man far out in space, a million miles from earth.

[15] The height at which the body fluids would start boiling is twelve miles and space medical researchers have called this altitude the "space equivalent altitude." That is where space begins as far as the human body is concerned.

DISCUSSION

1. In paragraph 2 the writer says, "It all depends on the viewpoint . . . " From how many viewpoints does he define *space?* Name them.

2. Before the writer can talk about *space,* he must explain what he means by *atmosphere.* Why do you think he did not begin with defining *atmosphere* as "the gaseous envelope surrounding the earth," or *space* as "the region beyond the earth's atmosphere" as a dictionary does? How does discussing *atmosphere* in terms of what it does, rather than simply what it is, prepare us for the rest of the article?

3. How does the fact that some radio techniques will work only in atmosphere affect a radio engineer's definition of space? What is his definition?

4. How does the fact that rockets work best in a vacuum (that is, in the absence of atmosphere) affect a rocket engineer's definition of space? What is his definition?

5. How does the fact that airplanes must have atmosphere affect an aeronautical engineer's definition of space? What is his definition?

6. Why is a doctor's definition of space discussed after the other three? Why is it given more space than any of the others? What is the doctor's definition?

7. Do you think this definition would be more satisfactory if it gave a single point of view rather than four? Why or why not?

8. Since the article does consider four points of view, do you think it would be clearer if it had a summary conclusion, reminding the reader of all four points of view? If you think it needs more conclusion than it has, what would you say to make the article sound more finished?

Emotionally-Loaded Terms

Probably the hardest terms to define, and the most important, are words that have strong emotional associations. Whenever we use a word that makes a comment on how people behave or how they feel and react, our emotions are likely to get so tangled up with our observations that we cannot straighten them out without a good deal of care.

Usually these emotion-laden terms are abstract words—words that stand for ideas, for concepts that cannot be seen or heard or smelled or measured. Because such concepts cannot be measured, there's an excellent chance that other people's feelings about them are not just like ours. The phrase "law and order" is a good example of such an emotion-laden expression. For some people, "law and order" may mean, "I don't like being afraid on the streets at night; I hate and fear Negroes." For others it may mean, "I don't like being afraid on the streets at night; I hate and fear whites." *Law and order* may mean "Anyone who threatens my own position or my own property must be punished," or "Anyone who dresses or acts or thinks differently from me ought to be arrested." To some people, the phrase can even mean "Laws ought to be as fair to the poor as to the rich" and "Order exists when everybody is left alone to do his own thing, when nobody is being hit over the head."

Whatever definition people give to *law and order,* they are likely to be in favor of it. Can you imagine how many votes a politician would get if he campaigned on a platform of "lawlessness and disorder"? Unless we ask, every time we hear it, "What do you mean by 'law and order'?" we may be tricked by the speaker's words instead of enlightened by his plans. Even more important, unless we ask ourselves what we mean by such emotion-laden words, we may become the victims of our own emotions and keep ourselves from thinking clearly. By forcing ourselves to give precise definitions, we find out something about ourselves, and we begin to free ourselves from unexamined opinions and meaningless slogans.

No matter how careful a writer is to be precise, however, he can't expect to write a definition everybody will agree with. The best he can do is to make what he means definite and clear—to set limits almost as exact as those the scientist uses. By using carefully chosen examples and by making clear what he does not mean, he can produce a "working definition" that will explain what he means in the present circumstances, at the present time. His definition has succeeded if he can answer "yes" to these questions: "Whether they agree with me or not, can my readers tell what kind of situation or behavior I'm including when I use this word? Can they tell what I'm excluding?"

As readers, we have a right to ask these questions, too. If they can't be answered, the definition isn't good enough.

The Nature of Prejudice

conspicuously: so as to attract attention
associative: connects one thing with another
deplore: dislike and disapprove of
brothel: house of prostitution
iniquity: great wickedness

From "Reading the Nature of Prejudice" by Gordon W. Allport, *Claremont College Reading Conference 17th Yearbook,* Claremont College Curriculum Laboratory, 1952. Reprinted by permission of Alpha Iota Chapter of Pi Lambda Theta.

debauchery: overdoing bodily or sexual pleasures
rapacious: greed so great it can't be satisfied
perfidious: false; treacherous
sufficient warrant: enough cause
categorization: putting people into groups and assuming that all members of the group are alike
parenthetically: as an aside—actually, a comment enough off the subject to be put in parentheses

[1] Before I attempt to define prejudice, let us have in mind four instances that I think we all would agree *are* prejudice.

Introduction begins with term to be defined and announces writer will first give situations

[2] The first is the case of the Cambridge University student who said, "I despise all Americans. But," he added, a bit puzzled, "I've never met one that I didn't like."

First situation: English against Americans

[3] The second is the case of another Englishman, who said to an American, "I think you're awfully unfair in your treatment of Negroes. How *do* Americans feel about Negroes?" The American replied, "Well, I suppose some Americans feel about Negroes just the way you feel about the Irish." The Englishman said, "Oh, come now! The Negroes are human beings!"

Second situation: English against Irish

[4] Then there's the incident that occasionally takes place in various parts of the world (in the West Indies, for example, I'm told). When an American walks down the street the natives conspicuously hold their noses till the American gets by. The case of odor is always interesting. Odor gets mixed up with prejudice because odor has great associative power. We know that some Chinese deplore the odor of Americans. Some white people think Negroes have a distinctive smell and vice versa. A brave psychologist recently did an experiment; it went as follows. He brought to a gymnasium an equal number of white and colored students and had them take shower baths. When they were nice and clean he had them exercise vigorously for fifteen minutes. Then he put them in different rooms, and he put a clean white sheet over each one. Then he brought his judges in, and each went to the sheeted figures and sniffed, guessing at the subject. The experiment seemed to prove that when we are sweaty we all

Third situation: other people's dislike of American smell—and thus smell in general

smell bad in the same way. It's good to have experimental demonstration of the fact.

[5] The fourth example I'd like to bring before you is a piece of writing that I quote. Please ask yourselves, who, in your judgment, wrote it. It's a passage about the Jews.

Fourth situation: prejudice against Jews

[6] The synagogue is worse than a brothel. It's a den of scoundrels. It's a criminal assembly of Jews, a place of meeting for the assassins of Christ, a den of thieves, a house of ill fame, a dwelling of iniquity. Whatever name more horrible to be found, it could never be worse than the synagogue deserves.

[7] I would say the same things about their souls. Debauchery and drunkenness have brought them to the level of lusty goat and pig. They know only one thing: to satisfy their stomachs and get drunk, kill, and beat each other up. Why should we salute them? We should have not even the slightest converse with them. They are lustful, rapacious, greedy, perfidious robbers.

[8] Now who wrote that? Perhaps you say Hitler, or Goebbels, or one of the local anti-Semites? No, it was written by Saint John Crysostom, in the fourth century A.D. Saint John Crysostom, as you know, gave us the first liturgy in the Christian church still used in the Orthodox churches today. From it all services of the Holy Communion come. Episcopalians will recognize him also as the author of the prayer that closes the offices of both matin and evensong in the *Book of Common Prayer*. I include this incident to show how complex the problem is. Religious people are by no means necessarily free from prejudice. In this regard be patient even with our saints.

[9] What do these four instances have in common? You notice that all of them indicate that somebody is "down" on somebody else—a feeling of rejection or hostility. But also, in all these four instances, there is indication that the person is not "up" on his subject—not really informed about Americans, Irish, Jews, or bodily odors.

Analysis of what the four situations have in common

[10] So I would offer, first a slang definition of prejudice: *Prejudice is being down on somebody you're not up on.* If you dislike slang, let me offer

Common element leads to two definitions

the same thought in the style of St. Thomas Aquinas. Thomists have defined prejudice as *thinking ill of others without sufficient warrant.*

[11] You notice that both definitions as well as the examples I gave, specify two ingredients in prejudice. First there is some sort of faulty generalization in thinking about a group. I'll call this the process of *categorization.* Then there is the negative, rejective, or hostile ingredient, a *feeling* tone. "Being down on something" is the hostile ingredient; "that you're not up on" is the categorization ingredient. "Thinking ill of others" is the hostile ingredient; "without sufficient warrant" is the faulty categorization.

Analysis of what the two definitions have in common

[12] Parenthetically I should say that of course there is such a thing as *positive* prejudice. We can be just as prejudiced *in favor of* as we are *against.* We can be biased in favor of our children, our neighborhood, or our college. Spinoza makes the distinction neatly. He says that *love prejudice* is "thinking well of others, through love, more than is right." *Hate prejudice,* he says, is "thinking ill of others, through hate, more than is right."

Thus a final definition

DISCUSSION

1. Many of us are used to thinking about prejudice in terms of majority attitudes toward minorities. We think of white attitudes toward Blacks in America, of Nazi attitudes toward Jews in Germany. How do Allport's first three situations help us to see prejudice from a new angle?

2. Normally we think of religion as promoting tolerance rather than preaching bigotry. What does the fourth situation do to destroy this idea? What does it tell us about how widespread prejudice is?

3. How much space is given to each of the four situations? Can you find any relation between the amount of space and the seriousness of the prejudice? (Consider "seriousness" in two ways: how violently the prejudice is expressed and how great its effect is likely to be on the victim.) Can you justify both the amount of space and the order of the examples?

4. What means does Allport use to make his situations vivid? What means does he use to make it obvious that the prejudices are not justified?

5. Which of the three definitions do you like best? Be specific as to your reasons.

A Just Law

degrades: cheapens; lowers in quality or dignity
distorts: twists or deforms
relegating: placing in an inferior position
devious: shifty, underhanded

[1] How does one determine whether a law is just or unjust? A just law is a man-made code that squares with the moral law or the law of God. An unjust law is a code that is out of harmony with the moral law. To put it in the terms of St. Thomas Aquinas: An unjust law is a human law that is not rooted in eternal law and natural law. Any law that uplifts human personality is just. Any law that degrades human personality is unjust. All segregation statutes are unjust because segregation distorts the soul and damages the personality. It gives the segregator a false sense of superiority and the segregated a false sense of inferiority. Segregation, to use the terminology of the Jewish philosopher Martin Buber, substitutes an "I-it" relationship for an "I-thou" relationship and ends up relegating persons to the status of things. Hence segregation is not only politically, economically and sociologically unsound, it is morally wrong and sinful . . .

[2] Thus it is that I can urge men to obey the 1954 decision of the Supreme Court, for it is morally right; and I can urge them to disobey segregation ordinances, for they are morally wrong . . .

[3] Let me give another explanation. A law is unjust if it is inflicted on a minority that, as a result of being denied the right to vote, had no part in enacting or devising the law. Who can say that the legislature of Alabama which set up that state's segregation laws was democratically elected? Throughout Alabama all sorts of devious methods are used to prevent Negroes from becoming registered voters, and there are some counties, in which, even though Negroes constitute a majority of the population, not a single Negro is registered. Can any law enacted under such circumstances be considered democratically structured?

DISCUSSION

1. In defining one abstract term, *just law,* King uses another abstract term, *moral law.* From the example he gives and his discussion of it, can you decide what King's definition of *moral law* would be?

2. There are two parts to this definition, but the example used for both parts is the same. Why do you think King stays with this single example? Can you think of other examples that would fit the first part of the definition? The second part?

3. What connection does King's definition of a just law have with the phrase "law and order"?

4. This definition of a just law is part of a much longer article, King's "Letter from a Birmingham Jail." King gives the definition because he needs it for other points he is making in the letter, rather than as a definition intended to stand by itself, and so it has less introduction and conclusion than definitions written as separate articles. Try your hand at writing an introductory paragraph and a concluding paragraph that would fit with what King says, and then see whether your classmates think what you have written does fit.

The Politician

dickering: haggling over price
candor: openness; honesty
pretensions: pretended claim
caucus-bound: voting whichever way a group tells him to

[1] The politician is a business man with a specialty.

[2] The commercial spirit is the spirit of profit, not patriotism; of credit, not honor; of individual gain, not national prosperity; of trade and dickering, not principle. "My business is sacred," says the business man in his heart. "Whatever prospers my business, is good; it must be. Whatever hinders it, is wrong; it must be. A bribe is bad, that is, it is a bad thing to take; but it is not so bad to give one, not if it is necessary to my business." "Business is business" is not a political sentiment, but our politician has caught it. He takes essentially the same view of the bribe, only he saves his self-respect by piling all his contempt upon the bribe-giver, and he has the great advantage of candor. "It is wrong, maybe," he says, "but if a rich merchant can afford to do business with me for the sake of a convenience or to increase his already great wealth, I can afford, for the sake of a living, to meet him half way. I make no pretensions to virtue, not even on Sunday." And as for giving bad government or good, how about the merchant who gives bad goods or good goods, according to the demand?

From *Shame of the Cities,* by Lincoln Steffens.

[3] No, the condemned methods of our despised politics are the master methods of our braggart business, and the corruption that shocks us in public affairs we practice ourselves in our private concerns. There is no essential difference between the pull that gets your wife into society or a favorable review for your book, and that which gets a heeler into office, a thief out of jail, and a rich man's son on the board of directors of a corporation; none between the corruption of a labor union, a bank, and a political machine; none between a dummy director of a trust and the caucus-bound member of a legislature; none between a labor boss like Sam Parks, a boss of banks like John D. Rockefeller, a boss of railroads like J. P. Morgan, and a political boss like Matthew S. Quay. The boss is not a political, he is an American institution, the product of a freed people that have not the spirit to be free. [4] The spirit of graft and lawlessness is the American spirit.

DISCUSSION

1. In spite of the first sentence ("The politician is . . .") would you consider this article a definition of *politician?* Why or why not? Could you use what Steffens says to measure whether or not an office-holder you know is or is not a politician? If the article had begun with the statement, "A bad politician is . . . ," would you consider the article a definition?

2. In paragraph 2, Steffens uses a comparison between the attitudes of businessmen and politicians; in paragraph 3, he uses a number of brief examples of people's behavior. What do these attitudes and examples have in common? Working from the kinds of behavior Steffens discusses, can you suggest what Steffens might actually be defining? Does the last sentence give you any help? If you think the article could be considered a definition of something besides *politician,* decide what is being defined and then make a three-part definition that fits Steffen's examples.

3. Steffens wrote this article more than sixty years ago. Can you find any words or phrases or examples that make the article sound old-fashioned? What are they? Do any of the ideas seem old-fashioned? Which ones and why?

Honest Graft

Tammany: a tight political organization in New York in the 1800s
disorderly people: euphemism for prostitutes
foresight: planning ahead
watershed: hill land from which water drains
condemnation: seizing property for public use

[1] Everybody is talkin' these days about Tammany men growin' rich on graft, but nobody thinks of drawin' the distinction between honest graft and dishonest graft. There's all the difference in the world between the two. Yes, many of our men have grown rich in politics. I have myself. I've made a big fortune out of the game, and I'm gettin' richer every day, but I've not gone in for dishonest graft—blackmailin' gamblers, saloon-keepers, disorderly people, etc.—and neither has any of the men who have made big fortunes in politics.

[2] There's an honest graft, and I'm an example of how it works. I might sum up the whole thing by saying': "I seen my opportunities and I took 'em."

[3] Just let me explain by examples. My party's in power in the city, and it's going to undertake a lot of public improvements. Well, I'm tipped off, say, that they're going to lay out a new park at a certain place.

[4] I see my opportunity and I take it. I go to that place and I buy up all the land I can in the neighborhood. Then the board of this or that makes its plan public, and there is a rush to get my land, which nobody cared particular for before.

[5] Ain't it perfectly honest to charge a good price and make a profit on my investment and foresight? Of course it is. Well, that's honest graft.

[6] Or, supposin' it's a new bridge they're going to build. I get tipped off and I buy as much property as I can that has to be taken for approaches. I sell at my own price later on and drop some more money in the bank.

[7] Wouldn't you? It's just like lookin' ahead in Wall Street or in the coffee or cotton market. It's honest graft, and I'm lookin' for it every day in the year. I will tell you frankly that I've got a good lot of it, too.

[8] I'll tell you of one case. They were goin' to fix up a big park, no matter where. I got on to it, and went lookin' about for land in that neighborhood.

[9] I could get nothin' at a bargain but a big piece of swamp, but I took it fast enough and held on to it. What turned out was just what I counted on. They couldn't make the park complete without Plunkitt's swamp, and they had to pay a good price for it. Anything dishonest in that?

From *Honest Graft*, by G. W. Plunkitt.

[10] Up in the watershed I made some money, too. I bought up several bits of land there some years ago and made a pretty good guess that they would be bought up for water purposes later by the city.

[11] Somehow, I always guessed about right, and shouldn' I enjoy the profit of my foresight? It was rather amusin' when the condemnation commissioners came along and found piece after piece of the land in the name of George Plunkitt of the Fifteenth Assembly District, New York City. They wondered how I knew just what to buy. The answer is—I seen my opportunity and I took it. I haven't confined myself to land; anything that pays is in my line . . .

[12] I got rich by honest graft.

DISCUSSION

1. What does Plunkitt accomplish in his first paragraph, besides letting the reader know what term he is going to define?

2. Does the sentence, "I seen my opportunities and I took 'em" fit all the situations Plunkitt describes? Would you consider it a complete definition of what Plunkitt means by *honest graft?* That is, could you use it to decide whether or not office-holders you know were using honest or dishonest graft? If you can think of some kinds of behavior that might come under "seeing an opportunity and taking it" that you would not consider honest graft, what are they?

3. What effect does Plunkitt create by repeating the statement, "I seen my opportunity and I took it"? What is the effect of having this article written just as Plunkitt would have talked, rather than in more formal standard English?

4. Using Plunkitt's examples, work out a general three-part definition that would fit what he means by honest graft. Begin "Honest graft is . . ."

5. Does the fact that Plunkitt uses himself for all his examples make this article seem more like a defense than a definition? If you think it does, point out the places where Plunkitt seems to be justifying his own behavior. On the whole, would you say Plunkitt was apologizing or boasting? Why?

6. Both Steffens and Plunkitt make a comparison between politics and business. Are their reasons for making the comparison the same? What do you think the differences are?

7. What do you think Steffens would say about Plunkitt's definition? What evidence can you find in the Steffens' article to support your belief?

Love, Like—How Different!

asperity: sharpness of tone
chided: scolded gently
intensive: a stronger form
scribes: those who wrote down what important people said
perverted: twisted; misused
ultimately: finally
imperative: absolutely necessary

[1] I took part in a college seminar recently, at which one of the participants was a nun. She was attacking some public figure with a great deal of asperity.

[2] "Sister," the chairman gently chided her, "I thought you're supposed to love your enemies." The nun smiled thinly. "I love him, all right," she returned. "But I just don't like him one bit!"

[3] Her answer was neither flip nor hypocritical. She knew that the verb "to love" is not an intensive of the verb "to like." Most people think it is, and that is why they often confuse the two.

[4] We cannot help what we like, but we can help what we love. Liking is a matter of taste and inclination, background and temperament. The food we like, the music we like, the kinds of people we like, are not subject to commandment or moral law.

[5] But we are commanded to love our neighbors and our enemies—who are so often the same people. How could the Bible be so psychologically stupid as to command us to love, if love were merely a matter of personal preference, like choosing vanilla ice cream over chocolate?

[6] Anybody can learn to love what he already likes; there is no trick in that. But the love spoken of by the scribes and prophets is love of what we do not especially like, or even actively dislike. This is the only kind that has any particular merit.

[7] Like is a feeling, and love is an act of the will. The nun may have intensely disliked the public figure she attacked, but nevertheless at some deeper stratum of her being she had trained herself to love him—which means to regard him as a human being co-essential with herself, as worthy of the same treatment, as sharing the same mark of creation.

[8] And only this kind of love can save the world from chaos and self-destruction. Without this absolute commandment—which is also a command-

ment of self-preservation of the human race—we embrace what we like and destroy what we do not like, and there is no end to killing.

[9] Modern man looks with suspicion on "moral laws" and absolute commandments of any kind, because in the past they have so often been perverted for evil ends. We must learn, however, to look upon them as psychological laws, which are true for the character and destiny of man. For if a moral law does not express a deep psychological truth, it is useless and ultimately false.

[10] "Love thine enemy" is not a piece of "spiritual" sentiment; it is a rule as imperative for our human survival as our need for air and water.

DISCUSSION

1. Although a good deal of this definition deals with the difference between *love* and *like,* the writer's main purpose seems to be to define *love.* What evidence can you find to support this belief?

2. In the first two paragraphs, Harris shows us a situation in which the word *love* is being used; in the third paragraph he tells us that the nun understands the definition. Why does he wait until paragraph 7 to tell us what her definition (and his) is? What does he accomplish in paragraphs 4, 5, and 6?

3. Is the distinction Harris makes between *love* and *like* the same one you would make? If it is different, what would your distinction be?

4. Would you consider Harris' definition a "special purpose definition"? If so, what would the purpose be?

5. It is often said that a "pure definition" should not come out in favor of the thing being defined or against it, but simply make clear what it is. At what point in the essay does Harris stop saying what *love* is and begin to argue for it? Does the argument weaken the definition or strengthen it? Why?

6. Harris implies that "to love" is never an intensive of "to like." Would you agree?

WRITING TOPICS
FOR DEFINITION

Write a paper of definition for one of the following terms or one of your own suggested by the list:

Chinook	chicken	split screen
tonic	shoo-in	anchor man
potlatch	WASP	animation
Skid Road	glamor	instant playback
moxie	charisma	special
dogie	mass media	rerun

"Sometimes I think—perhaps because they are more important *than grades—we here at State look for qualities of honesty, integrity, fortitude, aggressiveness, pertinacity, foresight, insight, leadership, loyalty, industry, maturity, sagacity, initiative, creativity, stamina, verve, mettle, vision . . ."*

Drawing by Whitney Darrow, Jr. Copyright 1967 The New Yorker Magazine, Inc.

skid
hang-up
sit-in
drop-out
cop-out
tune-out
Uncle Tom
brownie
cookie-cutter
square
straight
hip
rank
rumble
slander
libel
peer
bigot
racist
condominium
conglomerate
money
bug
buff
flop
transplant
bankruptcy
hurricane
tornado
cyclone
pornography
reliable
thrilling
co-op
boycott
adventure
caricature
neighbor
catalyst
parasite
conditioning
gossip
celebrity
pollination

conversation
demonstration
protest
dissent
egg beater
mirror
laundromat
compass
hydraulic brakes
magnet
light shows
mutual funds
passive resistance
free university
offset press
credit union
parachute brakes
clam gun
medicaid
negative income tax
osmosis
gills
prime time
channel
Nielson rating
talk show
sponsor
video tape
ghost
snow
closed-circuit TV
forest
jungle
wilderness
planet
star
symbiosis
photosynthesis
psychedelic
addiction
activist
criminal
urban renewal

flash-back
stop-light
monorail
piggyback
transmission
poverty
luxury
disappointment
caution
guilt
innocence
hope
incentive
antique
weed
nuisance
danger
safety
predator
parasite
laser
satellite
orbit
rehearsal
cook-out
conservation
uptight
militant
failure
compromise
negotiation
ghetto
core city
fair housing
discrimination
snob
stereotype
demagogue
freeway
erosion
status
racket
charity

readings on comparison 3

COMPARISON

Making comparisons—examining two things to see how they are alike and how they are different—is a human habit so natural that it seems almost automatic. In identifying people or things, we recognize what they are by distinguishing them from what they are not. We say, "That animal that ran across the road looked like a skunk, but it couldn't have been because it had no white stripe; it must have been a cat." When we move beyond such simple, automatic comparisons, however, we usually want to do more than identify; we want to explain or understand.

One of the commonest ways of using comparison to promote understanding is to contrast something familiar with something unfamiliar. A writer begins with what most of his readers know a little about and shows how that familiar thing resembles, or doesn't resemble, a thing that is strange to them. A custom or an attitude may be strange because it exists in another country, or it may be strange because it existed in another time, in places or periods we know little about. Because we are so much a part of our own time and our own place, we often forget that the way we do things or the way we look at things is not the only possible way. Comparing how we do something with another way of doing it can help us see both ways more clearly. It is this hope of better understanding, rather than a "Hurrah for us! Look how much better we are" approach that makes such comparisons really useful.

Ordinarily this kind of comparison, which moves from the familiar to the unfamiliar, puts most of the emphasis on differences. Starting from the things that are the same—in whatever country they are practicing, nurses must perform certain chores; in whatever period they live, people must get rid of their junk—the writer goes on to show that the attitudes, or the system, or the effects, are different. How a comparison deals with these differences will depend on the material being compared. Occasionally a writer will explain all about one thing and then go on to the other, as Johnston does in comparing old time tools with modern automated equipment, or the *Boston Herald Traveler* does in discussing ways of avoiding the draft. In more detailed comparisons, however, likenesses and differences are often intermingled, as they are in the nursing article and the garbage dump comparison.

But whatever the order is, or whatever the emphasis, comparisons between what others do and what we do ourselves provide both information and understanding. We learn about other places and other times and, while we are doing that, we see ourselves and our own customs with fresh eyes.

Nursing Practice from Dublin to London to Boston

entrusted: allowed to have or do
sutures: surgical stitches to hold a wound closed
unobtrusively: without calling attention to itself
utilization: use
orientation: becoming familiar with requirements of a new situation
theoretically: in theory, is supposed to; usually means practice doesn't conform to theory

[1] I left my native Ireland after I had completed a high school education. I studied to become a nurse and midwife in England, and I eventually came to the United States of America. Because I have worked five years in hospitals in England and the U.S.A., my friends frequently ask about differences, as I see them, in the practice of nursing on both sides of the Atlantic.

The writer introduces the subject, nursing, gives her qualifications for her comparison of nursing in Great Britain and the United States, and refers to the differences she has found between the two countries' nursing practices

[2] Until I realized how different the licensing laws of Great Britain are from those in the United States, I was surprised at the number of restrictions placed on a nurse's actions in this country. A nurse licensed in Britain may practice anywhere in the British Isles and in some countries abroad; in the United States, the nurse must apply in every state in which she hopes to work.

Licensing laws: (Difference #1)
a. In Great Britain, a nurse is allowed to practice anywhere in the British Isles and in some countries abroad
b. In the U.S., a nurse must apply in each state where she works

[3] In Britain, a nurse is a deeply respected, devoted woman, entrusted with a vast amount of responsibility. The patients place unquestioned confidence in her judgment and advice. The doctor relies on her report of her observations, and he seldom interferes in what is considered a nursing duty.

Responsibilities: (Difference #2)
a. In Great Britain, patients and doctors have more confidence in a nurse's judgment

"Nursing Practice from Dublin to London to Boston" by Mary T. Madden is reprinted, with permission, from the AMERICAN JOURNAL OF NURSING, April 1968.

[4] The nurse decides when the patient is allowed out of bed or what type of bath he may have. I do not recall ever seeing an order on a physician's chart such as "OOB in 24 hours" or "may take a shower". The nurse judges when a wound is healed and when sutures may be removed. She is always consulted about the patient's requirements and his progress. And because of the structure of most hospitals in England, the nurse is in view of the patient constantly. Whenever he needs attention, the nurse is there in the ward, and she may observe him, too, unobtrusively.

b. In Great Britain the nurse decides questions about a patient's requirements because she sees more of the patient than the doctor does

[5] Furthermore, the nurse is a member of the health team who sees the patient most frequently. To the patient she is the most familiar person in the strange hospital world.

c. In Great Britain, the nurse is the most familiar person to the patient because doctors practice as teams

[6] In the United States, the patient is likely to be under the care of the same doctor in and out of the hospital, so the doctor is the person the patient knows best and the one in whom he confides most easily. But though the patient's treatment and care are discussed with the nursing staff, a nurse is not allowed much freedom to advise a patient. Also, I have seen doctors visit patients without a word of communication to the nurse. Personally I think it difficult to be ignored when a patient's care is concerned and I think it prevents full utilization of the nurse's knowledge and skills.

d. In the U.S., the patient sees the same doctor in and out of the hospital and therefore knows him better

e. In the U.S., doctors do not consult nurses as they do in Great Britain

[7] I myself found nursing practice easier, in a way, under the so-called "socialized medicine" of Great Britain than the more individual type of medical care found in the United States. It involved much less writing and left me at the patient's bedside, where I am happiest. There was no need to write several charges and requests for the needs of the patient. Stocks of drugs and other medicines were kept on each ward, so that when medication was ordered, it was at hand. All charges were met by "National Health"—including all supplies and equipment used on the ward. The nurse tends a person who is free from much anxiety and hence more easily cared for while he is an inpatient.

Socialized Medicine: (Difference #3)
Nursing is easier under socialized medicine in Great Britain because:
1. all drugs and supplies are kept in the ward

2. Nurse tends a patient who is free from worry about costs

[8] On the other hand, I found that my introduction to an American hospital was a happy experience. As

Orientation: (Difference #4)

a new nurse, I was guided by an orientation program given by another nurse and quickly found my place on the patient care team. I had never experienced such an orientation in England.

[9] Policy, drug reference, and procedure books at the nurses' station provide a ready reference where a nurse may check facts when she is in doubt, and she can instruct a new nurse on the staff without confusion. The active U.S. nurse, while working, can keep informed about new trends, discoveries, and inventions in a rapidly changing world of medicine.

[10] Here in the United States the nurse is regarded as an individual person and her personal life outside the hospital is given consideration. She develops interests in arts, sport or a creative hobby; she is encouraged to further her education. Time and means are available to her to expand her horizons and to enrich her personality. Many nurses combine marriage and a career very ably in this country, but not in England or Ireland. All this tends to involve her more with people other than the sick. She is an interesting, informed, and happy person and at the bedside she can show understanding and perception.

[11] In Britain, like most nurses, I lived in a nurses' home on the hospital grounds and was thus isolated in a special hospital community. Theoretically I worked eight hours each day that I was on duty. But these hours were so arranged that one went to work twice in one day. One might work four hours in the morning, have a few hours free, and then go back to the ward for the evening. This schedule demands most of one's waking hours, and so mingling in the larger community outside the hospital was quite limited. The nurse was expected to find full satisfaction in her vocation, and thoughts of increases in salary were considered unworthy. Now, such attitudes are beginning to change and the winds of unrest are blowing through nursing in England, ruffling many a well placed cap.

Side notes (right column):

In the U.S. hospitals have helpful orientation programs

Reference books and information: (Difference #5)
U.S. practice keeps a nurse better informed than in Great Britain

Personal Life: (Difference #6)

In the U.S. a nurse has more time for outside activities

In Great Britain a nurse lives a more isolated life with a more demanding schedule

In Great Britain, nurses are now beginning to want changes in their profession

DISCUSSION

1. The nurse who wrote this comparison is measuring the advantages of nursing in England against the advantages of nursing in America. Does she

reach a clearcut decision as to which is better? Back up what you say by reference to the essay.

2. Based on what you are told in this essay, decide whether American or British nurses would be more likely to be able to do these things:
    a. decide that a patient with a sprained ankle would be better off walking on it
    b. offer an aspirin to a patient with a headache
    c. attend a night school class in sculpture
    d. deliver a baby
    e. move from the north of the country to the far south without taking another examination
    f. suggest to a patient that he is ready to go home
    g. notice a restless patient about to fall out of bed
    h. get a baby-sitter for her four-year-old so she can take a job in a hospital
    i. advise expensive medicine for a patient without worrying about whether he can afford it
    j. discover where things are kept in an unfamiliar ward without wasting time looking for them
    k. offer advice to a doctor about a patient

3. In which country does the writer think there are likely to be changes in nursing practice? How do you know? What are the changes likely to concern?

Then and Now: Three Comparisons:

I. Of Zaag-Bocs and Snitzel-Banks

precipitously: suddenly; without much thought
barter: trade of goods, rather than money

[1] In olden times a Dutch do-it-yourselfer invented a novel tripod on which to rest logs to be sawed. He called it the *zaag-boc* or saw goat. It eventually acquired a fourth leg and identity as the sawbuck, which is when children found another use for it. Many a good time did Esau and Buck have see-sawing on the sawbuck. In more recent times, the sawbuck came to be identified as the sawhorse.

From B. Johnston in the March, 1969 issue of *Mechanix Illustrated*, p. 4. Reprinted by permission of *Mechanix Illustrated*.

[2] There also was the *snitzel-bank*. This was a shaving horse which held a piece of wood while it was reduced with a draw knife. There were big shavers (chamfer knives) and little shavers (spokeshaves).

[3] But back to the log. After it was cut into shorter lengths, a man might want to construct a rail fence. To split rails he drove a glut into the wood with a maul. A good woodsman never used his axe as a sledge to drive the glut. This would widen the eyes, split the cheeks or ruin the head. On the other hand, if he wanted to split shingles, he hit a droe with a beetle.

[4] A few tools, including the adze, the axe and the knife, came down from the Stone Age. The adze was a shaping tool and has long since split from the scene. The axe also has precipitously gone out of fashion with the advent of the chain saw. Its most persistent survivor is the Boy Scout hatchet. But it survived for 10,000 years and, as late as 1868, catalogs pictured as many as 47 different axe patterns.

[5] The tools of early craftsmen became more than tools. They were extensions of a man's hands. He might have to buy or barter for the head or blade, but the rest he made himself. Early planes, especially, were much decorated, with ornately carved wooden parts reflecting the personality of the owner.

[6] With progress, foundries required pattern makers who made wooden patterns for every form cast. And after the Civil War, hand tools went into decline.

[7] Today most of the romance has gone from tools. Saws whine, lathes whirr and sanders drone. A man pushes a button, guides the wood and turns out perfect work. His tools are like every other man's—steely cold, efficient, but sadly impersonal.

II. Hartford, Connecticut

[1] Compare the position of the millions of men who are today unemployed to the position of our pioneer forefathers of a hundred years ago. At the beginning of the last century, Brillat-Savarin, the famous Frenchman who wrote *The Physiology of Taste,* made a long visit to the United States. In the fourth chapter of his book he tells the story of a visit of several weeks which he made to a farm which is now within the densely populated region of Hartford, Connecticut. As he was leaving, his host took him aside and said:

[2] "You behold in me, my dear sir, a happy man, if there is one on earth; everything you see around you, and what you have seen at my house, is

From *Flight From the City: The Story of a New Way to Family Security,* by Ralph Borsodi, Harper & Bros., 1933. Reprinted by permission of the author.

produced on my farm. These stockings have been knitted by my daughters; my shoes and clothes came from my herds; they, with my garden and my farmyard, supply me with plain and substantial food. The greatest praise of our government is that in Connecticut there are thousands of farmers quite as content as myself, and whose doors, like mine, are never locked."

[3] Today the farm on which that happy man once lived is cut up into city streets and covered with city buildings. The men and women of Hartford no longer produce their own food, clothing, and shelter. They work for them in stores and offices and factories. And in that same city, descendants of that pioneer farmer are probably walking the streets, not knowing what to do in order to be able to secure food, clothing and shelter.

III. Buying Out

[1] During the Civil War a Northerner with $300 could buy his way out of the draft and over 200,000 men chose to do so. The situation today is not much different from Civil War times. It's just that we have learned the art of subtlety.

[2] Now, instead of giving the money to the government, a rich young man gives it to a university. Once inside the university he is safe from the draft, assuming he has a reasonable amount of intelligence. When he graduates, all he has to do is enter graduate school, or get married and have a child, or find what is called a sensitive job (made possible, of course, by his college degree) and his deferment continues.

[3] It's a convenient system. Convenient, that is, for everyone except the poor youth who either can't qualify for a university or isn't smart enough to win a scholarship. Instead of spending his time in a university, he spends his time in Vietnam.

DISCUSSION

1. In the first article, the writer deliberately uses the names of many tools the modern reader will not know. How many such words can you find in the first three paragraphs? Why do you think the author uses these old words?

Editorial from the *Boston Herald Traveler*, May 12, 1966, p. 22, is reprinted by permission of the Boston Herald Traveler Corporation.

2. In the fourth paragraph of the tool article, why does the author emphasize how ancient some of these tools are? What does the information in paragraph 5 have to do with the conclusion in paragraph 7?

3. Why is so little space given to present-day tools? Do you think this weakens the comparison? Why or why not?

4. In the second article, what advantage does the author gain by quoting what the farmer said instead of depending on his own impression of what life was like a hundred years earlier?

5. How many kinds of things does Borsodi deal with in his comparison? What are they? In making your list, consider what is mentioned in both paragraphs 2 and 3.

6. All three of these articles are comparing American life a hundred or more years ago with American life in this century. How does each of them make it immediately clear which aspects of American life the comparison will deal with?

7. Which of these articles emphasizes differences? Which emphasizes likenesses? For each article, write a main idea sentence that will show clearly where the emphasis will lie.

8. Which of these articles ends with a judgment? How does the judgment rest on the comparison that has been made?

Playing The Game

> **adulation:** strong praise; worship
> **senile:** childishly old
> **allegedly:** said to be
> **recoil:** turn away in horror
> **repository:** container
> **bromide:** overworked remark

[1] The American athlete has become the spoiled brat of the New World, cuddled and coddled, pampered and petted. Too much money, either in salary or expenses, or both, and too much adulation are lavished on him. He has become a prince of privilege in the thriving Republic.

[2] By contrast, in Britain the athlete remains a working bloke like the rest of the British. He receives no great sums of money for playing, no special

From "American Athletes Are Sissies" by Iddon in *Coronet,* February 1952, pp. 34–36. Reprinted by permission of Esquire, Inc. Copyright © 1952 by Esquire, Inc.

privileges, no fancy fees for radio and television appearances. He is not allowed to accept gifts. And he has never been known to accept a bribe.

[3] British sports are tough, British sportsmen are tougher—probably because British sport is more adult. It is my belief that almost every major American sport derives from English children's games.

[4] In England we call baseball "rounders" and it is played only by toddlers and young girls. Basketball is "net ball" in our language, and strictly for girls and infants. Bowling is "skittles," a juvenile or senile diversion in our islands. And, as for ice hockey, allegedly the toughest of sports, this was adapted from English field hockey, the national sport of British schoolgirls.

[5] At the risk of offending, I have to tell you that whenever an American newsreel showing American football players in their outlandish padded costumes and helmets appears on an English screen, the audience hoots with laughter. Why the armor plate? The crash helmet? The shoulder and knee pads?

[6] We play a type of football similar to yours. In Britain it is called Rugby and it is a rugged game. No one ever wears any padding or a helmet, and it is even considered affected to put on a pair of shin guards or ear protectors. The current crop of Rugby players troop on the field and stay there (there are no substitutes), wearing a pair of studded shoes, stockings, pants, and a jersey. And that is all.

[7] The American practice of substitutions—the incredible platoon system in football is the worst example—has little relation to sport. To replace a man because he is playing badly, or even when he is injured, would be unthinkable in Britain. The basic appeal in sport should be the sense of contest and of hazard. A team fighting with its back to the wall, perhaps short two men and with another injured, is a gallant and inspiring spectacle.

[8] Such spectacles are common on the Rugby and soccer grounds of Britain. For a coach or manager to be able to remove a man at whim is a practice from which the British would recoil. The only time a football player, or a cricket player for that matter, is ever ordered from the field, is when he is offensive to the referee or umpire. Sometimes, of course, a player is compelled to leave the playing field because of an injury, but then he is carried out on a stretcher.

[9] British football players have been known to carry on in many games with broken collar bones, sprained ankles, and torn cartilages. What we do is to put the injured player "on the wing," where he is least likely to sustain further injury . . .

[10] It seems to me that the strangest phenomenon in American sports is the coach. Apparently he is regarded as a combination of elder statesman, father confessor, and mother superior. From what I hear and see, he is also the mastermind, a repository of all the talents. I have seen him as the inspired orator, haranguing the cowed team in the dressing room, admonishing, gesticulating, sweeping from stanza to stanza until the eloquent climax, with finger pointed to the field, the "go in to win for dear old _____."

[11] We have, of course, coaches in British sports, but the man's position is not one of great power. The key man is the captain of the team, who takes the field himself. Once on the field the team is on its own. There are no orders shouted from the touch line or bench. The captain is in charge and what he says goes. And if he has a bad day and his direction is incompetent, then it is just too bad for himself and for the team.

[12] Managers of teams give guidance and help during the days before the match, but their role is mainly administrative. The great emphasis in all British sports is on team spirit. There is an old British bromide—"the game's the thing"— and it is considered more important to play a good and fair game than to win it.

[13] We do not pamper our players. The stars of a football team or cricket team, if they are professionals, receive no more money than a mediocre member of the team. Even Alex James, the wonder player, whose appearance in a game added 15,000 to the gate, was paid the same salary as any raw newcomer. James earned a little on the side, writing newspaper articles and endorsing advertised products, but he never received fabulous sums on the Babe Ruth or DiMaggio scale.

[14] Temperament and temper are not tolerated in British sports. A couple of years ago, a major-league soccer team paid a fabulous sum for an international player. Soon afterwards, the man had an argument with the referee and was ordered off the field, and his team played the rest of the game one man short.

[15] The international player never played on that British team again. He was traded to a minor team for almost nothing, and although his genius as a soccer player was recognized everywhere, no major club has ever tried to buy him. If you don't have the guts to play according to the rules, you have no place in English sport.

DISCUSSION

1. What, according to the writer, is the main difference between American and British athletes? How—and where—does he back up what he says about this main difference?

2. Do you consider paragraph 4 part of the comparison? If so, what piece of the main point is it supporting? If not, what purpose does it serve? Why does the writer include it?

3. How many specific examples does Iddon use as he develops his comparison? In what paragraphs do these examples appear?

4. What is not stated about American players that would make the comparison complete in paragraphs 13 and 14?

5. What kind of order is the writer using? How does he arrange the similarities and differences?

6. Does it seem to you that Iddon is generalizing about American athletes—writing as though all teams and coaches and games were the same? Would you disagree with any of the generalizations he makes? Which ones?

7. Paragraph 1 discusses the American athlete; paragraph 15 discusses British athletes. Even so, would you consider the conclusion restates the main idea in different words? Defend your answer.

Down in the Dumps

nostalgia: longing for a time that is gone
imminent: just about to happen
diversified: varied; different
municipal: city-owned and controlled

[1] It was a hot summer day in the early forties. A teenager then, I was at one of my favorite pastimes, poking around in a dump I'd found in the woods near our New England farm. A towering birch tree arched high out over the big pile of cans, bottles, papers and trash. Against its white trunk leaned my little Stevens .22 rifle. In my pocket there were four shells, the last of fifty I'd talked a friend out of way back in the spring. I fingered them thoughtfully. Shells were harder to come by than butter in those wartime days and there was little prospect of getting any more when these were gone.

[2] That's when I saw the box, high up on the pile, half covered by a rusty can. Picking my way up over the rubble, I leaned over and flipped the can to one side. The yellow box, a big red X blazing on its face, was the same as the one my shells had come in. "Western Super-X". But there was something else about this box that stirred excitement in me.

[3] "Oh, it couldn't be," I thought, half aloud, "It couldn't be." I'd picked up every cartridge box I'd seen in the woods since shells had become scarce; none had contained a single bullet. Yet, this box looked different somehow, and when I reached out and picked it up my excitement flared, it was heavy.

[4] Straightening up, I quickly tore open one end of the box, hooked my thumbnail over the lip of the cartridge tray, and yanked it out. The squirrels for a mile around must have shot up their trees at the sound of my war whoop—the box contained fifty, shiny brass cartridge cases tipped with lead.

[5] When I recall that moment so long ago, I can feel the excitement and thrill it gave me. But I feel a twang of nostalgia, too; for it reminds me that

"Down in the Dumps," by Fred L. Thombs in the February 4, 1968 issue of *Northwest Magazine, The Oregonian,* is reprinted by permission.

progress has robbed me of one more thing in life that seemed worthwhile—rummaging in the dumps.

[6] Today I lug my castaways and rubbish to the barrel out behind the house. Once a week the sanitary outfit sends a truck around to cart it all off to the dump for me. I never see that stuff again once I drop it into the barrel. Which isn't the point, the point is: I never get to see the other guy's either. Even if I do haul a lot of junk off to the dump some weekend I still don't get to rummage. I'm watched with an eagle eye. Like a visitor to the U.S. mint, I must leave empty handed, despite all the goodies I may see lying around everywhere. The joyful feeling of quickening curiosity, the rising excitement of imminent discovery—they are lost to me forever.

[7] Yesterday things were different. By the time a lad was fourteen, though he still perhaps might not know if his sweater belonged on a hanger in his closet or went under the bed with his shoes, pajamas and white shirts, he did know the location and exact contents of every dump for miles around.

[8] How many dumps that was depended on how many houses there were; everybody had a dump. Usually the dump was out back somewhere, just into the woods a few yards, and always in a depression or gully if there was one. But sometimes if the occupants of the house were very old (or very lazy) the dump was practically against the back of the house. In that case the dump prowler had to go to a lot of trouble to learn when the owners would be gone away from home for a few hours before he could get in there and poke. Which caused a bit of resentment.

[9] That sort of resentment, plus keen interest, were the only feelings one had towards another and his dump. Nobody looked down his nose at another because of his unsightly pile of rubbish, for dumps weren't unsightly at all; dumps were dumps; they had their rightful place.

[10] Whether the dump was in the back yard or the front yard, it did, admittedly, create somewhat of a health hazard. Even so, it had a real value. It answered an age old problem: how to give to the needy without creating ill feelings. In those days neighborhoods were quite diversified, and the dumps of the more wealthy were an unending source of needed items for the less fortunate (or less ambitious).

[11] Besides being a neighborhood charity agency, the dump served a more common purpose, that of the neighborhood swap shop. People always want to throw away something they don't need, or to get something they do need—and for nothing. Today you can easily satisfy the first want, but that's it. The dump is a big, community affair with an "in" gate and an "out" gate somewhere along its prison-like wire enclosure. You pay to get in, and brother, you'd better come out "clean," or you'll pay a lot more.

[12] Yesterday people swapped these things by way of their own dumps, and sometimes the take was fabulous. I remember one occasion when my cousin (Mom was trying to raise him along with the six of us) came home nearly breathless, stammering excitedly to me, "Fred, you gotta see it . . . I found a new dump . . . c'mon!"

[13] All the way across the big lower field and for two miles up the railroad tracks I tried to pry it out of Warren. "Naw, ain't tellin'," he kept saying, plodding on ahead of me, "you gotta see it yourself . . . man, you just gotta see it!"

[14] Turning off the tracks beyond the swamp we tramped through the woods for a half mile or more, finally coming to a deep gully behind a deserted-looking, green and white house, and there it was. From the edge of the lawn at the opposite side of the gully, clear on down its 50-foot bank, draped a huge pile of radios and parts of radios. I could see dozens of radio chassis glistening with tubes, radio cabinets, speakers, ear phones, wire, and all kinds of stuff associated with radios. Down the steep slope we raced, half running, half stumbling, and up onto the pile on the other side.

[15] A month later, and after several tiring trips back from that dump, Warren and I sat on the edge of our chairs in our upstairs bedroom. We'd just flicked a switch and now Warren was slowly turning a small black knob. Suddenly, "Wahoo!" his slap to my back nearly sent me flying right out of my headset; our first homemade, battery-powered radio—somebody else's junk—was making music in our ears.

[16] Then the great war came along, and the beginning of the end for the dump prowler. All across the country the dumps—from the largest of the municipals, to the deep in the woods, tiny piles of junk that only young boys knew of—got churned through and through in a frantic quest for scrap metals to aid the war effort.

[17] After the war the professionals waged a war of their own—a battle for a monopoly over the municipal dumps. One by one those big dumps fell to the steel fences and the "in" and "out" gates. The atmosphere of them became appalling. I recall one victor, who after wrangling a contract with a nearby town to be its "Dumpmaster," got a permit and strapped a big revolver to his hip.

[18] Once the municipals all were secured, a great wave of progress swept across the land. Overnight, feelings changed. Dumps became unsightly, unsanitary blights upon the beautiful landscape. They had to go. And go they did. From the rear yards, the front yards, from along the country roads, the dumps were gathered up and packed off to the wire enclosed stockades. The days of the dump prowler had ended. The "Dumpmaster" now reigns supreme.

[19] Or does he? I wonder. My little guy does have some weird ideas about his sweaters, shoes and shirts. And now and then he comes home with an article which stirs something deep down inside of me: a slightly broken toy; a golf club that doesn't seem to have a thing wrong with it; a stool or chair that needs just a little mending.

[20] And when I ask him, "Ricky, where'd you get that?" he'll reply, "Oh . . . I found it."

[21] I wonder. By gosh, has that little rascal found a dump and isn't telling his Dad?

DISCUSSION

1. A big part of this comparison is made up of personal memories of what the writer did when he was a boy. Do you think he is regretting the disappearance of the dumps or the disappearance of his boyhood? Find parts of the article to support what you say.

2. Most of this article is written in an easy, conversational style. It uses words such as "stuff" and "guy," and an occasional sentence fragment found more often in talking than in writing. Does the informality fit the subject?

3. In paragraphs 10 and 11, the author suggests two social advantages of old-time family dumps. Do you think he suggests these advantages seriously? Why or why not?

4. Does the use of the term "Dumpmaster" tell you anything about the author's real attitude toward dumps? Do you know any city or town that has a "Dumpmaster"? What are such officials usually called? How does the title of the article tell you something about the author's attitude?

5. There are three transition paragraphs in this article, helping the reader to move from the past to the present, 5, from the present to the past, 7, and back to the present again, 11. But the other paragraphs, too, are carefully linked together. Point out the transitions used between paragraphs 5 through 12 and 16 through 20.

Language

> **innumerable:**   more than can be counted
> **assuring:**   making sure
> **miserly:**   stingy

[1] Do animals have language? We know that many forms of animal life do have elaborate systems of communication. Bees give information by dancing. Wild geese in flight have complicated signalling systems. There are innumerable stories about "counting" and "talking" dogs who "speak" by barking sounds. Parrots, of course, can be taught to imitate human speech. While all of these animals do communicate, none of them have language in the same sense that man has language.

[2] One language feature that man has, that animals do not have, is sometimes called "feedback." Unlike the barking dog, talking man can listen to

his own stream of words and respond to his own ideas while talking. This is what we mean by "thinking out loud."

[3] Another feature is the ability to say things that have never been said or heard before and yet be understood by other speakers of the language. If the chimpanzee uses a call, it is one of a limited number of familiar calls. His system is a closed system. Human language is an open system in the sense that men can arrange familiar words and pieces of words in new ways and be understood by the people who are listening.

[4] The most important feature of human language is the ability to talk about things that are not present, that are distant in time and space. Chimps and baboons have cries for food and cries for danger. But they are unable to discuss with their neighbors the ripeness of the bananas they had last week, or the problem of assuring a steady supply of bananas in the future. Man, on the other hand, can talk about the funny thing that happened at the office yesterday, or the strange animals that probably roamed the earth millions of years ago. He can explain the design of a space ship that doesn't yet exist and discuss the plans to use it on a trip to the moon. He can tell stories, make promises, tell lies, predict consequences.

[5] Unlike men, animals are unable to talk about abstract ideas like happiness, loneliness or love. They can't classify their friends as miserly or generous, courageous or cowardly, conformists or non-conformists. Not only can man talk about his own behavior, he can also make statements about the facts of nature and events that he has observed. He can talk about the speed of light, the atomic structure of matter, the principle of the internal combustion engine.

[6] Men can do all this through the use of symbols. Just as men agree that the color red will stand for "stop," that a ring on the finger will signify marriage, that pieces of silver and paper will represent buying power, so too men agree that certain sounds will stand for objects and ideas. Men agree that the sound "hat" will stand for a covering for the head; that the sound "hope" will stand for an idea or feeling that something will happen the way we want it to happen. The hat and the hope may belong to somebody out of the past, Napoleon Bonaparte or Abe Lincoln, or to an imaginary character in a novel like Holden Caulfield in *Catcher in the Rye*. But men can talk about the object *hat* and the idea *hope* even though they cannot be seen or experienced at the moment. Men do this through their ability to use sounds as symbols. This is the big difference between the language of men and the communication of animals.   (Used by permission of R. Wasserman.)

DISCUSSION

1. What is being compared in this article? Do you think it is a comparison between what we mean by *communication* and what we mean by *language?* Why or why not?

2. Find the sentence in paragraph 6 that comes closest to restating the same idea as one of the sentences in paragraph 1. How do these similar sentences help you in seeing what the main point of the article is?

3. Make a plan showing how the writer deals with the likenesses and differences he wants to discuss. You may find it easier if you mark everything he says about animal communication as *A* and everything he says about human communication as *B*.

4. Go back through the comparison marking all the specific examples the writer uses. How do these examples help you understand the comparison?

5. What is the familiar thing in this article? What is the unfamiliar thing? Which of the two—animal communication and human language—is the writer helping us to understand? Support what you say by referring to the article.

Analogies

All the articles in the first section compared two things that had some obvious likenesses—sports in America with sports in England, or the tools we use now with the tools we used to use. There is, however, another way of comparing the familiar with the unfamiliar. Beginning with something simple and easy to understand, something almost all readers will know about, the writer can go on to something that seems strange and complicated, something his readers do not understand. By showing how the two are alike, a good writer can often make what is complicated seem simpler.

For instance, Helen Keller, who was deaf and blind from babyhood, uses a comparison to make clear what her six years without language, without words, felt like:

> Have you ever been at sea in a dense fog, when it seemed as if a tangible white darkness shut you in, and the great ship, tense and anxious, groped her way toward the shore with plummet and sounding-line, and you waited with beating heart for something to happen? I was like that ship before my education began, only I was without compass or sounding-line, and had no way of knowing how near the harbor was. (From Helen Keller, *The Story of My Life*, Doubleday, Inc.)

Such comparisons as this, which bring together two things that seem quite different, are called *analogies*. Analogies usually concentrate on the likenesses that will help us understand (the dense fog that shut the ship in is similar to the lack of language that cut the child off from other people) and ignore the obvious differences (a ship and a six-year-old girl are quite different in size, shape, price, and purpose). As Miss Keller does, however, writers sometimes point out differences that have something to do with what they are concerned with: the ship did have some ways of finding out its location (the compass and the sounding-line), whereas the child had none.

Fisher uses an analogy to help us understand the climate, and Jeans uses another to explain light waves. And although it is not exactly an analogy, de Sales is using much the same method to make his readers understand American attitudes toward love by comparing them with attitudes toward cookery. Hoffer is telling us what pioneers were like by comparing them to homeless tramps. What all these articles have in common is that the things being compared are unexpected; all the writers show us resemblances we did not know were there.

Temperature: Mud Pies and Climate

unpalatable: bad-tasting
perceptibly: noticeably
infinitesimal: very tiny
sultry: hot and humid
incursions: sudden entrances
unhindered: without any obstruction
fluctuates: changes back and forth

[1] No one has ever earned a fortune selling home-made mud pies. They're unpalatable, indigestible, and hard to cook. If you put one under a broiler on a gas stove, the upper crust may burn to a crisp. But the filling will remain raw and muddy because heat is not easily transmitted through the pie.

Explains that mud pies will not broil evenly

[2] You'll be more successful if you set a dishpan of water under the broiler in place of the pie. Water cooks readily. As the surface warms under the gas flame, heat gradually circulates through the pan. Water at the bottom grows about as hot as water on top. Yet there is a drawback here, too. Although water can be cooked, it cannot be sold for pie.

Water does cook evenly
First comparison: difference in the way mud pies and water cook

[3] Broiling either mud pies or water seems impractical. But the experiment has important implications for the weather. Suppose the mud pie were the continent of the United States, the dishpan of water

Second comparison: an analogy—

Mud pies and land, dish-the oceans around it, and the gas flame the sun. When the sun rises, what happens?

[4] The surface of the earth, like the upper crust of the mud pie, warms rapidly. All the heat it receives from the sun is absorbed within the first foot or so of topsoil. But the dishpan of water—the ocean—warms little. The sun's rays are distributed through a large volume of water. All this water must be heated before the temperature at the top changes perceptibly. By midafternoon, the surface temperature of the land may have risen 10 degrees. That of the ocean may be less than 1 degree higher.

[5] After sunset, the process is reversed. The earth cools quickly. Much of its heat stays close to the surface and escapes. The ocean, on the other hand, keeps at about the same temperature. The heat it gives off during the night represents an infinitesimal part of what it has stored up in its depths. Over a twenty-four hour period, the surface temperature range may equal 20 degrees for land but only 1 degree for water.

[6] Because the mud-pie earth cannot be cooked to any great depth—and because the dishpan ocean can—a blizzard in San Francisco occurs as rarely as a winter without snow in St. Louis. Westerly winds travel over San Francisco from the Pacific Ocean, which evens out the seasons by being relatively cool in summer and warm in winter. Average monthly air temperatures in San Francisco vary over a narrow 12-degree range—from about 50 degrees in January to 62 degrees in September. At no time on record has the mercury risen above 101 degrees or dipped under 27 degrees.

[7] The mild climate of the west coast, however, extends only a few miles inland. For our western mountain ranges. which run almost north-south, keep the tempering influence of the Pacific Ocean close to shore. At the same time, they leave the rest of the continent open to invasions of frigid air from the north and sultry air from the south. These incursions of comparatively cold and hot air seldom reach the mountain-protected west coast. But they sweep unhindered over St. Louis.

[8] The people of Missouri thus live surrounded by a continent of land over which the air temperature

pan of water and ocean, gas flame and sun

Analogy makes clear why the land gets hotter than the ocean

Analogy makes clear why the land cools more quickly than the ocean

Third comparison: climate of San Francisco with climate in St. Louis

effect of ocean on San Francisco—very little temperature change

Analogy not used here because it won't work —there is nothing in mud pies and water that is like the Rocky Mountains

Effect of surrounding land on St. Louis—a

fluctuates widely. St. Louisans first shiver and then perspire as average monthly temperatures vary over a 48-degree range—from about 33 degrees in January to 80 degrees in July. Although St. Louis lies at nearly the same latitude as San Francisco, the mercury in St. Louis goes to much greater extremes.

wide temperature change

DISCUSSION

1. This paper of comparison does not begin with a main idea sentence, nor does it ever directly state one. There is a main idea in the essay, however. Which of these sentences comes closest to expressing it—the second sentence in paragraph 3? The first sentence in paragraph 6? The last sentence in paragraph 8? Why?

2. There are three comparisons in this essay, one beginning in paragraph 2, one in paragraph 3, and one in paragraph 6. Which of these comparisons is the most important to the main point of the paper? What makes you think so?

3. Why does Fisher mention in his opening paragraph that mud pies are bad tasting and hard to digest? Does this have anything to do with his comparison? Does the fact that they are hard to cook have anything to do with his comparison?

4. How do the last two sentences of paragraph 2 relate to the point Fisher is making? Why do you think he includes them?

5. Fisher explains the analogy he is using in paragraph 3 and the first part of paragraph 4, then doesn't mention mud pies and dishpans of water until paragraph 6. In paragraph 6, how does he remind us of the analogy? How does this reminder help the reader?

Sea Waves and Sunlight

formidable: powerful; superior
impinge: strike; collide
interposes: places between

From pp. 25–27 of *Stars In Their Courses* by Sir James Jeans. Reprinted by permission of Cambridge University Press.

prism: a transparent solid body used to separate light into the various
             colors
constituents: the parts that make up the whole

[1] Imagine that we stand on any ordinary seaside pier, and watch the
waves rolling in and striking against the iron columns of the pier. Large waves
pay very little attention to the columns—they divide left and right and re-unite
after passing each column, much as a regiment of soldiers would if a tree
stood in their road; it is almost as though the columns had not been there.
But the short waves and ripples find the columns of the pier a much more
formidable obstacle. When the short waves impinge on the columns, they
are reflected back and spread as new ripples in all directions. To use the
technical term, they are "scattered." The obstacle provided by the iron
columns hardly affects the long waves at all, but scatters the short ripples.

[2] We have been watching a sort of working model of the way in which
sunlight struggles through the earth's atmosphere. Between us on earth and
outerspace the atmosphere interposes innumerable obstacles in the form of
molecules of air, tiny droplets of water, and small particles of dust. These are
represented by the columns of the pier.

[3] The waves of the sea represent the sunlight. We know that sunlight is a
blend of lights of many colours—as we can prove for ourselves by passing it
through a prism, or even through a jug of water, or as Nature demonstrates
to us when she passes it through the raindrops of a summer shower and
produces a rainbow. We also know that light consists of waves, and that the
different colours of light are produced by waves of different lengths, red light
by long waves and blue light by short waves. The mixture of waves which
constitutes sunlight has to struggle through the obstacles it meets in the
atmosphere, just as the mixture of waves at the seaside has to struggle past
the columns of the pier. And these obstacles treat the light-waves much as
the columns of the pier treat the sea-waves. The long waves which constitute
red light are hardly affected, but the short waves which constitute blue light
are scattered in all directions.

[4] Thus, the different constituents of sunlight are treated in different ways
as they struggle through the earth's atmosphere. A wave of blue light may be
scattered by a dust particle, and turned out of its course. After a time a second
dust particle again turns it out of its course, and so on, until finally it enters
our eyes by a path as zigzag as that of a flash of lightning. Consequently the
blue waves of the sunlight enter our eyes from all directions. And that is
why the sky looks blue.

DISCUSSION

1. Where does Sir James Jeans first mention sunlight, the thing he is explaining? What does the first paragraph cover? What is gained by postponing
   the discussion of sunlight?

2. In which paragraph does Jeans lead the reader from the first thing he is explaining (sea waves) to the second thing (sunlight)? How does the transition work? That is, how do you find out that sea waves are being compared to sunlight?

3. Does the analogy Jeans uses serve as an effective explanation of why the sky is blue? Why or why not?

4. The conclusion is the last sentence: "And that is why the sky looks blue." Have you ever been warned not to begin a sentence with "and"? Do you like this sentence as it stands, or would it be better added to the sentence before it? Why? Would you like this conclusion better if it summarized the points that have been made in the rest of the essay? Why or why not?

Love and Cooking

esoteric: understood only by specialists
innate: inborn
flourishing: doing well; increasing
amorous: wanting to make love
panorama: broad view
imponderables: things that can't be measured

[1] The difference between an American cookbook and a French one is that the former is very accurate and the second exceedingly vague. A French recipe seldom tells you how many ounces of butter to use to make *crêpes suzette,* or how many spoonfuls of oil should go into a salad dressing. French cookbooks are full of esoteric measurements such as a *pinch* of pepper, a *suspicion* of garlic, or a *generous sprinkling* of brandy. There are constant references to seasoning *to taste,* as if the recipe were merely intended to give a general direction, relying on the experience and innate art of the cook to make the dish turn out right.

[2] American recipes look like doctors' prescriptions. Perfect cooking seems to depend on perfect dosage. Some of these books give you a table of calories and vitamins—as if that had anything to do with the problem of eating well!

[3] In the same way, there is now flourishing in America a great crop of

From "Love and Cookery" by Raoul de Roussy de Sales in the May 1938 issue of *The Atlantic Monthly.* Reprinted with permission. Copyright © 1938, 1966 by the Atlantic Monthly Company, Boston, Mass.

books which offer precise recipes for the things you should do, or avoid doing, in order to achieve happiness and keep the fires of love at a constant temperature. In an issue of *Time* magazine, four such books were reviewed together. Their titles are descriptive enough of the purpose of the authors as well as the state of mind of the readers: *Love and Happiness, So You're Going to Get Married, Marriages Are Made at Home, Getting Along Together.*

[4] I have not read all these books, but, according to the reviewer, they all tend to give practical answers to the same mysterious problem of living with someone of the opposite sex. They try to establish sets of little rules and little tricks which will guarantee marital bliss if carefully followed, in the same way that cookbooks guarantee that you will obtain pumpkin pie if you use the proper ingredients properly measured.

[5] As the publisher of one of these books says on the jacket: "There is nothing in this book about the complicated psychological problems that send men and women to psychoanalysts, but there is a lot in it about the little incidents of daily married life—the things that happen in the parlor, bedroom, and bath—that handled one way enable people to live together happily forever after, and handled another way lead to Reno."

[6] *Time's* review of these books is very gloomy in its conclusion: "Despite their optimistic tone," it says, "the four volumes give a troubled picture of United States domestic life—a world in which husbands are amorous when wives are not, and vice versa; where conflicts spring up over reading in bed or rumpling the evening paper—the whole grim panorama giving the impression that Americans are irritable, aggravated, dissatisfied people for whom marriage is an ordeal that only heroes and heroines can bear."

[7] But I believe that the editors of *Time* would be just as dejected if they were reviewing four volumes about American cooking, and for the same reasons. You cannot possibly feel cheerful when you see the art of love or the art of eating thus reduced to such automatic formulas, even if the experts in these matters are themselves cheerful and optimistic. Good food, the pleasures of love, and those of marriage depend on imponderables, individual taste, and no small amount of luck.

DISCUSSION

1. This essay makes a double comparison. What two things are being compared in paragraphs 1 and 2? Is the writer emphasizing likenesses or differences in this comparison? What does he say the likenesses or differences are?

2. What is the comparison being made in paragraphs 3–7? Is the writer emphasizing likenesses or differences here? What does he say the likenesses or differences are?

3. How does the last sentence of paragraph 4 refer to the first comparison?

When is the next time that de Sales reminds the reader of the first comparison? How does he tie the two comparisons together?

4. Can you tell at the end of paragraph 2 which of the two things being compared the writer thinks is better? How? Can you tell at the end of the essay? How?

5. Which of the comparisons do you think is the most important? That is, if you were asked what the main point of this essay was, what would you answer? What is the author's judgment about this main point? How do you know?

Pioneers

transient: person who moves from place to place, never staying long anywhere
indomitable: can't be defeated; full of courage
habitat: place one lives
migratory: moving from place to place
visualize: make a mental picture

[1] In April, when the hot winds began blowing, I shouldered my bedroll and took the highway to San Bernardino. It was the next morning, after I had got a lift to Indio by truck, that a new idea began to take hold of me. The highway out of Indio leads through waving date groves, fragrant grapefruit orchards, and lush alfalfa fields; then, abruptly, passes into a desert of white sand. The sharp line between garden and desert is very striking. The turning of white sand into garden seemed to me an act of magic. This, I thought, was a job one would jump at—even the men in the transient camps. They had the skill and ability of the average American. But their energies, I felt, could be quickened only by a task that was spectacular, that had in it something of the miraculous. The pioneer task of making the desert flower would certainly fill the bill.

[2] Tramps as pioneers? It seemed absurd. Every man and child in California knows that the pioneers had been giants, men of boundless courage and indomitable spirit. However, as I strode on across the white sand, I kept mulling the idea over.

[3] Who were the pioneers? Who were the men who left their homes and went into the wilderness? A man rarely leaves a soft spot and goes deliberately

From "The Role of the Undesirables" by Eric Hoffer in the December 1952 issue of *Harper's Magazine*. Reprinted by permission of the author.

in search of hardship and privation. People become attached to the places they live in; they drive roots. A change of habitat is a painful act of uprooting. A man who has made good and has a standing in his community stays put. The successful business men, farmers, and workers usually stayed where they were. Who then left for the wilderness and the unknown? Obviously those who had not made good: men who went broke or never amounted to much: men who though possessed of abilities were too impulsive to stand the daily grind: men who were slaves of their appetites—drunkards, gamblers, and woman-chasers; outcasts—fugitives from justice and ex-jailbirds. There were no doubt some who went in search of health—men suffering from TB, asthma, heart trouble. Finally there was a sprinkling of young and middle-aged in search of adventure.

[4] All these people craved change, some probably actuated by the naïve belief that a change in place brings with it a change in luck. Many wanted to go to a place where they were not known and there make a new beginning. Certainly they did not go out deliberately in search of hard work and suffering. If in the end they shouldered enormous tasks, endured unspeakable hardships, and accomplished the impossible, it was because they had to. They became men of action on the run. They acquired strength and skill in the inescapable struggle for existence. It was a question of do or die. And once they tasted the joy of achievement, they craved for more.

[5] Clearly the same types of people which now swelled the ranks of migratory workers and tramps had probably in former times made up the bulk of the pioneers. As a group the pioneers were probably as unlike the present-day "native sons"—their descendants—as one could well imagine. Indeed, were there to be today a new influx of typical pioneers, twin brothers of the forty-niners only in a modern garb, the citizens of California would consider it a menace to health, wealth, and morals . . .

[6] I talked with several old-timers—one of them over eighty and a native son—in Sacramento, Placerville, Auburn, and Fresno. It was not easy, at first, to obtain the information I was after. I could not make my questions specific enough. "What kind of people were the early settlers and miners?" I asked. They were a hard-working, tough lot, I was told. They drank, fought, gambled, and wenched. They were big-hearted, grasping, profane, and God-fearing. They wallowed in luxury, or lived on next to nothing with equal ease. They were the salt of the earth.

[7] Still it was not clear what manner of people they were.

[8] If I asked what they looked like, I was told of whiskers, broad-brimmed hats, high boots, shirts of many colors, sun-tanned faces, horny hands. Finally I asked: "What group of people in present-day California most closely resembles the pioneers?" The answer, usually after some hesitation, was invariably the same: "The Okies and the fruit tramps."

[9] I tried also to evaluate the tramps as potential pioneers by watching them in action. I saw them fell timber, clear firebreaks, build rock walls, put up

barracks, build dams and roads, handle steam shovels, bulldozers, tractors, and concrete mixers. I saw them put in a hard day's work after a night of steady drinking. They sweated and growled, but they did the work. I saw tramps elevated to positions of authority as foremen and superintendents. Then I could notice a remarkable physical transformation: a seamed face gradually smoothed out and the skin showed a healthy hue; an indifferent mouth became firm and expressive; dull eyes cleared and brightened; voices actually changed; there was even an apparent increase in stature. In almost no time these promoted tramps looked as if they had been on top all their lives. Yet sooner or later I would meet up with them again in a railroad yard, on some skid row, or in the fields—tramps again. It was usually the same story: they got drunk or lost their temper and were fired, or they got fed up with the steady job and quit. Usually, when a tramp becomes a foreman, he is careful in his treatment of the tramps under him; he knows the day of reckoning is never far off.

[10] In short, it was not difficult to visualize the tramps as pioneers. I reflected that if they were to find themselves in a singlehanded life-and-death struggle with nature, they would undoubtedly display persistence. For the pressure of responsibility and the heat of battle steel a character. The inadaptable would perish, and those who survived would be the equal of the successful pioneers.

DISCUSSION

1. In writing this comparison between tramps and pioneers, Hoffer begins with the transient workers he knows and then tries to figure out what kind of men the pioneers must have been. What does he think their characteristics were? How does he reach that conclusion? Once he has decided what the pioneers must have been like, what does he do to test his impression?

2. This comparison really has two parts: the kind of men the pioneers were, and what they had to do in conquering a new land. How does Hoffer show that the transients might have been like pioneers in their ability to survive in the wilderness?

3. Look again at paragraph 2 and paragraph 5. What is the point in saying "Every man and child in California knows . . ." and then in later saying ". . . the citizens of California would consider it a menace to health, wealth, and morals"?

4. Obviously, this article emphasizes some unexpected likenesses. Work out a main idea sentence for the article, beginning, "Even though tramps and pioneers . . ." and then compare your sentence with the ones your classmates have written.

Being Objective

Not all comparisons contrast the known with the unknown or the familiar with the unfamiliar. Some compare two things we may know a little about but have not thought about very carefully. Such comparisons help us see both things more clearly by relating them to each other. We may discover differences which, though important, usually go unnoticed; we may see similarities that will help us understand. Often we use this deepened understanding to decide which of the two things we think is better, or the writer uses it to try to convince us that we should prefer one to the other.

In comparing education and income in one part of Chicago with education and income in another part, Martin Luther King makes no attempt to force his judgment on us. He simply presents the information, and if his readers want to find the differences unfair, they can reach their own conclusions:

> The Chicago Urban League recently conducted a research project in the Kenwood community on the South Side. They discovered that the average educational grade level of Negroes in that community was 10.6 years and the median income was about $4,200 a year. In nearby Gage Park, the median educational grade level of the whites was 8.6 years, but the median income was $9,600 per year. In fact, the average white high school dropout makes as much as, if not more than, the average Negro college graduate. (From A TESTAMENT OF HOPE, Copyright © 1968 by the estate of Martin Luther King, Jr. by permission of Joan Daves.)

Averages and incomes can be measured fairly easily; attitudes and beliefs are harder to deal with. Nevertheless, in this paragraph also the writer is careful not to say which attitude is better or even which one he thinks is right:

> In the end, the difference between Conservatism and Liberalism seems to be this: both are devoted to liberty as we have known in the West, but the Conservative thinks of liberty as something to be preserved, the Liberal thinks of it as something to be enlarged. The Conservative suspects that a country like the United States or Britain has got just about as much liberty as it will ever have, that the liberty we enjoy cannot be increased but only redistributed among ourselves, and that persistent efforts either to increase or redistribute it may bring the whole structure of freedom down in ruins. The Liberal, on the other hand, is confident that no country has yet approached the upper limits of liberty, that giving new freedoms to some men does not necessitate taking away old liberties from others, and that the structure of freedom will fall slowly into decay if it is not enlarged by the men of each generation. (From p. 57 of *Conservatism in America* by Clinton Rossiter. Reprinted by permission of Alfred A. Knopf, Inc. Copyright © 1955, 1962 by Clinton Rossiter.)

Showing Where You Stand

Not all writers manage to remain that impartial. Some writers use their comparisons to make judgments of their own, and tell their readers clearly which side they are on, as this author does:

> It is significant that both the American Friends Service Committee and the Selective Service System have the word "service" in their titles. The meaning of the word, however, in the two cases is drastically different. For the American Friends Service Committee, service is the gift of the self to man's need; it is a service that rises out of love and an identification with those who are served. It cannot be coerced, it cannot evolve from fear. It is a service that is universal in its concern, it excludes no one, not even enemies, from its all embracing circle of good will.
>
> For the Selective Service, by contrast, service is coercive in its intent and structure, it drives men by fear and not by love. Where it invokes love, it is only for a portion of mankind; it has an ethic of selective disservice, that we should seek to do good to some and do harm to others. It is part and parcel of what has been called the threat system, that is, that part of the social structure which seeks to alter behavior and change organization by threatening harm. It is concerned with the production of "bads," not the production of "goods." (From THE DRAFT? A Report Prepared for the Peace Education Division of the American Friends Service Committee. Copyright © 1968 by Hill and Wang, Inc. Reprinted by permission of Hill and Wang, Inc.)

Comparisons such as this come very close to persuasion. Whenever a comparison deals with very controversial ideas, such as the use of force and the maintenance of order in Cleaver's and Shearer's articles, the comparison is likely to end in a judgment. Or, if the judgment is not stated, the points of the comparison are likely to invite us to share the writer's opinion.

Boxed In by Lack of Choice

perverse: stubbornly determined to do the opposite
durables: equipment that should last for several years, such as stoves and refrigerators
unethical: unfair; not right
fictitious: made up; untrue
verbal: spoken rather than written down

capitalize: take advantage of
sophistication: experience or knowledge

[1] One day three women went into a slum neighborhood store at different times and asked the price of the same TV set. Each was quoted a different price—$125 to the white college student, $139 to the Puerto Rican housewife, and $200 to the Negro mother. With friendly neighborhood merchants like that, you could say, who needs enemies?

Limits topic: comparison will cover differences in prices

[2] The incident was not an exercise in race prejudice, though that may have played some part. It was prejudice in the sense that the merchant prejudged just how poor each of these customers was and set his prices accordingly.

Gives main idea sentence

The Un-Sanforized Income

[3] The buying problems of the poor are many and varied, and are not very different in kind from those faced by all consumers. But the poor are often boxed in by their lack of choice.

Mentions likeness (buying problems are the same kind for all) and the main difference (the poor have little choice)

[4] Particularly in the area of housing, low-income people have relatively little choice. The combination of little money and often large families limits the possibility of selecting from a variety of at least partially desirable places. A U.S. Bureau of Labor Statistics survey found that the poor get substantially less per dollar in terms of space, facilities, and upkeep than the higher income people. In other words, $80 per month rent buys more in moderate income neighborhoods than in poor ones. In this situation racial discrimination operates most clearly.

In housing

[5] In utilities there are rarely any bargains. In fact there are times when a poor person has to pay a deposit for electric, gas, or telephone service, even though his references are good, because his address is in a low-income neighborhood, while persons in wealthier areas pay none. Similar practices, in the auto and life insurance industries, are now under Senate investigation.

In utilities

[6] It is in the areas of food, clothing, and durables (furniture, household equipment and cars) that low income people have the most buying difficulty.

Transition paragraph— promises to compare prices of food and durables

Food Prices

[7] Recently, the papers have been filled with stories of price differences for food in different sections of the same city. Logic seems to say: sure, higher prices in richer neighborhoods. But several studies have found that, in general, supermarket prices in poor neighborhoods run higher, from 5 to 10 per cent and more, than prices at the same chains in high-income areas and suburbs. For many small grocery stores the difference is often higher.

[8] Does this mean A & P and Kroger and Safeway and other industry giants are out to gouge poor people? Probably not. They are competitive within limits. The problem is, there are far fewer supermarkets in poor neighborhoods, where the competition tends to be with moderate size groceries or "ma and pa" stores. The supermarkets really only have to meet the competition in the area, not beat it . . .

Local or Downtown Prices?

[9] It is in the area of durables that the poor most clearly pay more. Some typical examples: a 19" Admiral TV selling for $139 in a downtown discount store in New York but priced $179 to $200 in Lower East Side stores; the same washing machine selling for $179 at Macy's, going for $369 in a Harlem store; a furniture store in a poverty area buys a mattress for $30 and sells it for $89.50 while a downtown department store sells it for $59.95.

[10] But these are only the most obvious methods of overcharging. The process is often more devious. First, comparable products often can't be found in both areas. The U.S. Bureau of Labor Statistics, studying price differences within a number of large cities, found it very hard to make comparisons. In many cases the merchants in poor neighborhoods carried brands no one has ever heard of, styles and models that were no longer current in other stores, or used and reconditioned merchandise (often not identified as such).

[11] Second, items sold in poor area stores are many times of the shoddiest sort. Yet their prices equal or exceed those for better and sturdier products in stores out of the area. This is particularly true of furniture. And to go along with shoddy merchandise,

shoddy selling practices—the clearly illegal and the
merely unethical.

[12] Bait and switch advertising, fictitious list prices
or no fixed prices at all, high-pressure selling, empty
verbal promises and guarantees—these are the stock
in trade of many slum merchants. They capitalize on
three disadvantages every person suffers at some time
in his life but which poor people face most of the
time—lack of buying income, lack of sophistication,
and lack of credit.

Conclusion: summary of ways in which the poor are forced to pay more

DISCUSSION

1. How do the three examples given in paragraph 1 tell the reader what the comparison will cover? How do they arouse his curiosity?

2. What is the main idea sentence of this article? How does it let the reader know that the article will emphasize differences?

3. Instead of telling all about prices in richer neighborhoods and then all about prices in poor neighborhoods, the writer does a step-by-step comparison. Do you think it would have been more effective if he had told us all about one and then all about the other? Why or why not?

4. For each section of the comparison the writer gives specific examples. How do these examples help us see the differences more clearly?

5. The purpose of this article is to compare, not to convince; the writer never says "The poor *ought not to have to pay more.*" Yet it is hard to read the article without realizing that the writer does think these differences are unfair. See how many words or comments you can find that hint at the writer's attitude.

Protest in the Early 1900s

disfranchisement: not being allowed to vote; not being treated as a citizen
accommodation: being obliging; doing what you're expected to do
conciliation: giving in for the sake of peace

From Report of the National Advisory Commission on Civil Disorders (also known as "the Kerner report"), March 1, 1968, p. 101.

acquisition: acquiring; getting
Jim Crow laws: laws discriminating against Negroes
advocated: spoke in favor of
caste: a system of higher and lower positions to which people are born and in which they are forced to stay

[1] Between his famous Atlanta Exposition Address in 1895 and his death in 1915, Booker T. Washington, principal of the Tuskegee Normal and Industrial Institute in Alabama and the most prominent Negro in America, privately spent thousands of dollars fighting disfranchisement and segregation laws; publicly he advocated a policy of accommodation, conciliation, and gradualism. Washington believed that by helping themselves, by creating and supporting their own businesses, by proving their usefulness to society through the acquisition of education, wealth, and morality, Negroes would earn the respect of the white man and thus eventually gain their constitutional rights.

[2] Self-help and self-respect appeared a practical and sure, if gradual, way of ultimately achieving racial equality. Washington's doctrines also gained support because they appealed to race pride: If Negroes believed in themselves, stood together, and supported each other, they would be able to shape their destinies.

[3] In the early years of the century, a small group of Negroes led by W. E. B. Du Bois formed the Niagara Movement to oppose Washington's program. Washington had put economic progress before politics, had accepted the separate-but-equal theory and opposed agitation and protest. Du Bois and his followers stressed political activity as the basis of the Negro's future, insisted on the inequity of Jim Crow laws and advocated agitation and protest.

[4] In sharp language, the Niagara group placed responsibility for the race problem squarely on the whites. The aims of the movement were voting rights and "the abolition of all caste distinctions based simply on race and color."

Although Booker T. Washington tried to crush his critics, Du Bois and the Negro "radicals" as they were called, enlisted the support of a small group of influential white liberals and socialists. Together, in 1909–1910, they formed the National Association for the Advancement of Colored People.

DISCUSSION

1. What method of organization does this article follow? That is, does it compare likenesses and differences step by step as "Boxed In by Lack of Choice" did, or does it tell all about one man, then all about another? Do you think the order would be more effective rearranged? Why or why not?

2. Partly because of the way it is organized, this article does not contain a clear main idea sentence. Can you work out in your own words what the

main idea sentence would be, beginning with "Although Washington and Du Bois both . . ."?

3. Can you tell which attitude the writer favors, the one represented by Washington or the one represented by Du Bois? Is your answer based on what the writer says or on your own knowledge of which side is favored by most people today?

4. More than fifty years ago, when Washington and Du Bois were leaders in the Negro movement, the National Association for the Advancement of Colored People represented the radical side of the movement. Can you work out a comparison between NAACP's position in 1910 and its position in 1970? If you don't know much about Black organizations, you may have to check the Reader's Guide for more information.

Politicians and Statesmen

> **compromise:**   give up part of one's beliefs to get part of what one wants
> **dividends:**   payment in return for money invested
> **tolerate:**   put up with
> **alleviation:**   relief

[1] There is a big difference between politicians and statesmen. Politics means the art of compromise. Most politicians are all-too-well schooled in this art. They compromise to get nominated; they compromise to get elected; and they compromise time and time again, after they are elected, to stay in office. In times of crisis, the politician flexes his muscle. During these next few months, you will see other Presidential candidates flexing their muscles, twisting arms politically to get delegate votes at the party conventions or offering the dividends of political appointment for delivering the vote in November.

[2] The statesman, on the other hand, flexes his mind in times of crisis. Like myself he is a dreamer, with a vision of the very best life has to offer and a determination to see all men have their rightful share of this offering; not as a reward, but because justice will tolerate nothing less. The statesman's devotion is to humanity, to the alleviation of suffering, to the creation of a decent and peaceful human environment throughout the world. The statesman cannot compromise with what he knows to be right, nor can he make any

political deals which will allow a form of evil or injustice to be even temporarily victorious. These are indeed times of crisis in America. Lest there be the slightest doubt in the mind of any voter, I am serving notice *now* that I will be a statesman and not a politician.

DISCUSSION

1. Although the organization of this brief comparison is very simple—all about politicians, then all about statesmen—the comments Gregory makes about each of them are very neatly matched. They do not come in exactly the same order, but you should be able to find a sentence in paragraph 2 that contrasts with each statement in paragraph 1. When you try matching them, do you have any left over? What are they?

2. Gregory uses comparisons within his comparison. For example, he compares the behavior of a politician with that of a wrestler. What is the point of his comparison between flexing muscles (paragraph 1) and flexing the mind (paragraph 2)?

3. Which does the author ask you to approve of, statesmen or politicians? What is there in the comparison that tells you that?

Domestic Law and International Order

cordon off: fence off; isolate
rejuvenated: made younger artificially
permeated: soaked
hybrid: mixed breed

[1] The police department and the armed forces are the two arms of the power structure, the muscles of control and enforcement. They have deadly weapons with which to inflict pain on the human body. They know how to bring about horrible deaths. They have clubs with which to beat the body and the head. They have bullets and guns with which to tear holes in the flesh, to smash bones, to disable and kill. They use force, to make you do what the deciders have decided you must do.

[2] The police do on the domestic level what the armed forces do on the international level: protect the way of life of those in power. The police patrol the city, cordon off communities, blockade neighborhoods, invade homes, search for that which is hidden. The armed forces patrol the world, invade countries and continents, cordon off nations, blockade islands and whole peoples; they will also overrun villages, neighborhoods, enter homes, huts, caves, searching for that which is hidden. The policeman and the soldier will violate your person, smoke you out with various gases. Each will shoot you, beat your head and body with sticks and clubs, with rifle butts, run you through with bayonets, shoot holes in your flesh, kill you. They each have unlimited firepower. They will use all that is necessary to bring you to your knees. They won't take no for an answer. If you resist their sticks, they draw their guns. If you resist their guns, they call for reinforcements with bigger guns. Eventually they will come in tanks, in jets, in ships. They will not rest until you surrender or are killed. The policeman and the soldier will have the last word.

[3] Both police and the armed forces follow orders. Orders. Orders flow from the top down. Up there, behind closed doors, in antechambers, in conference rooms, gavels bang on the tables, the tinkling of silver decanters can be heard as icewater is poured by well-fed, conservatively dressed men in horn-rimmed glasses, fashionably dressed American widows with rejuvenated faces and tinted hair, the air permeated with the square humor of Bob Hope jokes. Here all the talking is done, all the thinking, all the deciding. Gray rabbits of men scurry forth from the conference room to spread the decisions throughout the city, as News. Carrying out orders is a job, a way of meeting the payments on the house, a way of providing for one's kiddies. In the armed forces it is also a duty, patriotism. Not to do so is treason.

[4] A strange thing happened in Watts, in 1965, August. The blacks, who in this land of private property have all private and no property, got excited into an uproar because they noticed a cop before he had a chance to wash the blood off his hands. Usually the police department can handle such flare-ups. But this time it was different. Things got out of hand. The blacks were running amok, burning, shooting, breaking. The police department was powerless to control them; the chief called for reinforcements. Out came the National Guard, that ambiguous hybrid from the twilight zone where the domestic army merges with the international; that hypocritical force poised within America and capable of action on either level, capable of backing up either the police or the armed forces. Unleashing their formidable firepower, they crushed the blacks. But things will never be the same again. Too many people saw that those who turned the other cheek in Watts got their whole head blown off. At the same time, heads were being blown off in Vietnam. America was embarrassed, not by the quality of her deeds but by the surplus of publicity focused upon her negative selling points, and a little frightened because of what all those dead bodies, on two fronts, implied. Those corpses spoke eloquently of potential allies and alliances. A community of interest

began to merge, dripping with blood, out of the ashes of Watts. The blacks in Watts and all over America could now see the Viet Cong's point: both were on the receiving end of what the armed forces were dishing out.

[5] What is true on the international level is true also at home; except that the ace up the sleeve is easier to detect in the international arena. Who would maintain that American soldiers are in Vietnam on their own motion? They were conscripted into the armed forces and taught the wisdom of obeying orders. They were sent to Vietnam by orders of the generals in the Pentagon, who receive them from the Secretary of Defense, who receives them from the President, who is shrouded in mystery. The soldier in the field in Vietnam, the man who lies in the grass and squeezes the trigger when a little half-starved, trembling Vietnamese peasant crosses his sights, is only following orders, carrying out a policy and a plan. He hardly knows what it is all about. They have him wired-up tight with the slogans of TV and the World Series. All he knows is that he has been assigned to carry out a certain ritual of duties. He is well trained and does the best he can. He does a good job. He may want to please those above him with the quality of his performance. He may want to make sergeant, or better. This man is from some hicky farm in Shit Creek, Georgia. He only knew whom to kill after passing through boot camp. He could just as well come out ready to kill Swedes. He will kill a Swede dead, if he is ordered to do so.

[6] Same for the policeman in Watts. He is not there on his own. They have all been assigned. They have been told what to do and what not to do. They have also been told what they better not do. So when they continually do something, in every filthy ghetto in this shitty land, it means only that they are following orders.

[7] The police are the armed guardians of the social order. The blacks are the chief domestic victims of the American social order. A conflict of interest exists, therefore, between the blacks and the police. It is not solely a matter of trigger-happy cops, of brutal cops, who love to crack black heads. Mostly it's a job to them. It pays good. And there are numerous fringe benefits. The real problem is a trigger-happy social order.

[8] Meanwhile, blacks are looking on and asking tactical questions. They are asked to die for the System in Vietnam. In Watts they are killed by it. Now—NOW!—they are asking each other, in dead earnest: Why not die right here in Babylon fighting for a better life, like the Viet Cong? If those little cats can do it, what's wrong with big studs like us?

[9] A mood sets in, spreads across America, across the face of Babylon, jells in black hearts everywhere.

DISCUSSION

1. Discuss Cleaver's use of concrete, specific detail to help the reader *see* the conditions he is describing. Refer to specific sentences which use this detail.

2. Cleaver's first sentence states the main idea of this comparison. What details in the rest of the first paragraph make clear his attitude toward the "arms of the power structure"?

3. Would you say that Cleaver was more interested in police and armies or in the power structure? That is, is he using the comparison between police and armies to back up what he wants to say about the power structure, or are his comments about the power structure a part of the comparison? Why?

4. Does Cleaver hold either the police or the army responsible for what they do? How responsible? Find sentences that support your answer.

5. In what paragraph does Cleaver describe the people who give orders? Clearly his description is strongly slanted against those who give the orders. Does he merely resent their power, or does he find something else objectionable about them? In spite of the slanting, how sound do you think his description is?

6. Nearly every paragraph makes a statement about the police, then makes the same statement about the army. How does this prepare the reader for the comparison in paragraph 4 between Watts and Vietnam? How does paragraph 5 prepare the reader for the conclusion?

What Would You Think of a Bearded Cop?

truncheon: billy club
emulate: admire and copy
corruptible: dishonest; likely to take bribes
misanthropic: hating people
gratuities: tips, bribes

[1] British constable Malcolm Gair patrols his beat in London's Hyde Park wearing a full beard but no gun. Like all British policemen, Gair works unarmed except for a truncheon.

[2] To use a gun to apprehend someone, he would first have to explain to his commanding officers in the London metropolitan police district that the

From "What Would *You* Think of a Bearded Cop?" by Lloyd Shearer in the October 27, 1968 issue of *Parade*. Reprinted by permission of Parade Publications, Inc.

criminal in question was not only armed but in the possible course of resisting arrest was likely to shoot a civilian. Only then would Gair be granted permission to check out a weapon from the precinct arsenal. In Great Britain, unarmed police are expected to subdue armed bandits and murderers.

[3] Despite his lush and lovely beard, constable Gair is not regarded by the Londoners he serves as a kook, a hippie, a weirdy, a queer, an artist, or an eccentric. They consider him as they do most policemen, a warm decent, honest, brave, trustworthy friend whose job it is to help them. They do not regard him with fear, suspicion, or cynicism. They respect him and his position and the law he has sworn to enforce. Unlike many American policemen, he is not alienated from the community he serves. He is part of it.

[4] Over the years, most Englishmen have been reared to regard the cop on the beat as an ideal figure, someone to emulate, a man who stands for help, not punishment.

[5] In the U.S., on the other hand, the police have rarely been considered ideal models. As unfair as it may seem, many citizens regard them as authoritarian, corruptible, cynical, resentful, aggressive, Fascistic, racist, misanthropic, a subculture of males who basically dislike and do not trust others outside their own fold, and are yet constantly on the alert for "a handout." The status accorded the police is low on the U.S. occupational list. In a 1961 survey it ranked 54th out of 90 occupations, just about on par with railroad conductors.

Not "on the take"

[6] The average British policeman on the job does not smoke, loiter, drink, or accept free meals, samples, or other gratuities. He is not "on the take." He makes no distinction between "honest" and "dishonest graft." He accepts neither. Compared to the history of police department scandals in this country, the record of police honesty in Great Britain is a shining beacon of virtue.

[7] Because the British police do not carry guns, neither do most professional British thieves. The British Firearms Act of 1937 calls for the registration of all guns. If an Englishman wants to buy a revolver, he applies to the local police and is given the necessary firearms certificate allowing purchase from the gun dealer who registers the sale.

American "idiocy"

[8] In the U.S. more than 20 states require no license to own or sell guns and 31 have no laws against carrying concealed weapons. British police authorities regard this as the height of idiocy. Scotland Yard believes that police use of guns creates community resentment and leads to violence in kind. In 1967, in all of England and Wales, there were only 45 killings by shooting. In the U.S., a nation with four times the English and Welsh population, there were 7617 such killings in 1967—170 times the British total.

[9] It may well be, as many anthropologists suggest, that there is a fundamental flaw in the American character, or at least a fundamental contradic-

tion. The people want law and order, yet they are by nature and tradition, individualists who resent the authority necessary for the law enforcement they demand.

[10] There are no basic standards for policemen throughout the U.S. They vary from town to town. The need for better police training, higher requirements, more pay, better working conditions—all of this has been advocated countless times. What we seem to forget, however, is that the police today are more representative of U.S. society than ever before.

[11] If we do not respect them, the sad truth may well be that deep down many of us may not respect ourselves or our body of law.

DISCUSSION

1. This comparison deals with differences between British and American policemen and with differences between British and American attitudes toward policemen. How does the writer connect the two parts of the comparison? In which part is he most interested?

2. Why do you suppose Shearer starts with beards instead of guns? Which do you think is the more important part of the comparison? Why?

3. Both Cleaver, in "Domestic Law and International Order," and Shearer, in this essay, are discussing policemen. Cleaver is a Black militant writing for other Blacks and sympathetic whites; Shearer is a white reporter, writing for middle-class readers of the Sunday paper. In spite of their different backgrounds and audiences, what similar judgments do Cleaver and Shearer make? What differences can you find in their judgments?

4. What have the audiences for which they are writing to do with the kind of details Shearer and Cleaver use? Which do you think would be more appealing to Sunday morning readers? Why?

A Student Theme

This student started with the topic "TV and Newspapers." He limited his topic when he decided that he preferred to get his news from a paper, not from a telecast. Answering the question, "Why do I like to read the news?" helped him shape a plan on which he could build his theme.

   1. A picture may be worth 1,000 words.

      a. But a picture on TV does not last very long.

      b. Pictures in newspapers are more permanent.

  2. TV brings immediate news; but it's gone immediately, too.

      a. The TV viewer can't turn back.

      b. The newspaper reader can return to the first paragraph.

  3. TV doesn't have enough time allotted to cover news properly; a newspaper is limited only by space.

      a. To cover big stories TV must have special shows.

      b. Newspapers do in-depth coverage every day, not only once a month.

  4. TV is the lazy man's way.

He used this plan to write a first draft:

Newspaper vs. TV

Someone said a picture is worth a thousand words, but he didn't watch a TV newscast. If he had wanted the whole story, he should have read the evening paper.

It is true that pictures televised from on the spot are effective, but you see the same pictures in newsprint and they are there for you to look at carefully.

TV is great for learning the news immediately, but did you ever try to get the announcer to slow down and repeat the story when you've missed the first part of his flash bulletin? If it's a newspaper you have, you can go back to the lead paragraph and be sure of what you have been told.

It's equally hard to find out all of the details of a story when a TV newsbreak has to cover national, local, and sports news in 15 minutes between a cartoon and a soap opera.

Even when TV does a story in depth, it's such a production and such a rarity that the show gets special time and special advertising. The same story gets daily coverage in the papers. If it's important enough for TV to do a special on, the story will have been reported from a variety of points of view and levels of writing in the papers.

Television is the lazy man's way; it's no trouble to watch the Indianapolis 500, but I want to know more about those engines.

The man who said a picture is worth a thousand words was too lazy to read a thousand words.

This first draft followed the planned outline, but it was shorter than the assignment called for and it was not more specific. By adding more examples to illustrate the points he made, the writer was able to meet the assigned length without being aimlessly wordy, and at the same time wrote a more effective paper.

Confucius Would Have Read the Paper

When Confucius said a picture is worth a thousand words, he had not watched a TV newscast. If he had wanted the whole story, he would have read it in the newspaper.

It is true that events televised on the spot make you think you are there, but you can see the same pictures in newsprint and there you can look at them carefully and for as long as you need to.

Television depends a lot on interviews with eye-witnesses, yet the eye-witness is notably unreliable. How many people who are where something happens really know what is going on? At best, the eye-witness can see from only his point of view; at worst, his experience is so limited that he has no way to judge, or he is so emotional that he is not able to judge rationally what he has seen or what has happened. The testimony of eye-witnesses can be so contradictory that it has been inadmissible as court evidence; even Perry Mason has used the contradictory testimony of eye-witnesses to free the blonde accused of murder. But in spite of the well-known unreliability of emotional onlookers, TV announcers appeal to the man on the street as if he were an expert.

TV serves a purpose for learning the news immediately, but did you ever try to get an announcer to slow down, or repeat a story when you missed the first part of a flash bulletin? If you are reading a newspaper, you can go back to the beginning paragraphs to be sure of the facts. The reader can also choose what he wants to read; if he's not interested in a story he can turn a page. With television he can turn the set off, but in doing so he may also miss something he wants to know about.

It's equally hard to find out all of the details of a story when a TV newsbreak has to cover national, local and sports news in 15 minutes between "Huckleberry Hound" and the fiftieth rerun of "I Love Lucy." True, there's a lot of space goes to advertising in newspapers, but you don't have to interrupt a story about the Green Bay Packers to read about mouthwash, or to walk out of the room to avoid a car salesman.

Even when TV reports a current news story in depth, it's such a production, and such a rarity, that it gets special promotion and special time. The same story is sure to have been covered daily in the papers. If the story is important enough for TV to do a special on, the same story will have been reported from a variety of points of view and levels of coverage in the papers before the network gets around to the special.

Television is the lazy man's way. It's no trouble to watch the Indianapolis 500 on the living room set, but I want to know the specifications of those engines and I can only find that out by reading about them.

Had Confucius had a choice between TV and newspapers, he would have read the paper.

WRITING TOPICS
FOR COMPARISON

Some of these comparisons can be handled in a short paragraph; some of them would take several pages. Some will emphasize likenesses, some differences. For almost all of them, the writer will need to decide on a point of view before he begins. In using these lists, make sure that you choose a topic that can be handled in a paper of about the length you want to write, and that you choose something you are already familiar with.

compare	with
the Nina, Pinta, and Santa Maria	Apollo 11
the Beatles	Duke Ellington
Charles de Gaulle	Moshe Dayan
Mayor Richard Daley	Mayor John Lindsay
Minuteman missiles	MIRV

"It's awful the way they're trying to influence Congress. Why don't they serve cocktails and make campaign contributions like we do?"

Drawing by Herb Block from *The Herblock Gallery,* Simon & Schuster, 1968. Reprinted with permission.

compare	*with*
income tax	sales tax
motels	hotels
rifles	shotguns
a Harley	a Honda
a stick shift	an automatic shift
hamburger	ground round
Martin Luther King, Jr.	Malcolm X
a 10-year-old Ford	a 10-year-old Rolls Royce
a $3 shirt	a $10 shirt
low cost housing	slums
driving a new Jaguar to a protest march	walking to a protest march
a 45-year-old conscientious objector	an 18-year-old conscientious objector
used cars	pre-owned cars
"being broke"	being poor
a low-calorie diet	malnutrition
Little Orphan Annie	Peanuts
mini-skirts	pants suits
women jockeys	men jockeys
sexual discrimination	racial discrimination
sports cars	family cars
prunes	plums
the statement in your college catalog	your own experience in the same college
a planet	a star
George Washington	Ho Chi Minh
dentists	orthodontists
a guitar	a sitar
flower children	Maenads of Bacchus
mistake	serendipity
Christmas	Chanukah
letter grades	a pass-fail system
toothbrush	Water-pick
the CIA	the MVD
United Nations	League of Nations
hippies	remittance men
apartments	condominiums
folk rock	raga rock
parolee	trustee-at-large
psychedelic light shows	Chinese water torture
spectacles	contact lenses
Ten Commandments	U.S. Articles of War
Peace Corps	missionaries

compare	*with*
$3,000 a year	$10,000 a year
a furnace	a heat pump
oil heat	gas heat (or electric heat)
a remedy	a panacea
Easter	Passover
records	tapes
the Pueblo	the Lusitania
the war in Vietnam	the American Civil War
S. I. Hayakawa	Socrates
the draft law	the impressment of sailors into the English navy in 1812
the present U.S. Army	George Washington's troops
Playboy	*The Police Gazette*
General Westmoreland	General Cornwallis
relocation centers	concentration camps
Picasso	Michelangelo
Miss America pageants	fertility rites
zapping	jousting
pancake make-up	war paint
Lyndon B. Johnson	Andrew Johnson
Stokely Carmichael	Nat Turner
James D. Watson	Gregor Johann Mendel
Chief Sitting Bull	Hiawatha
Union of South Africa	the Southern Confederacy
air travel	rail travel
Harvard student strike	Boston Tea Party
the current stock market	1929 stock market
U.S. treaties with the Indians	U.S. treaties with France or Great Britain
the veterans' march of the '30s	the poor people's march of the '60s
Candy	*Little Women*
bugaloo	waltz
surveillance	spying
Eldridge Cleaver	Booker T. Washington
Cesar Chavez	Samuel Gompers
Confucius	Christ
women running for public office	blacks running for public office
George Wallace	Huey Long
George Wallace	Jefferson Davis
Lenin	Trotsky
Hitler	Mussolini
astrology	astronomy
doctors	quacks
alchemy	atom-breaking

compare	*with*
Sirhan Sirhan	James Earl Ray
karate	judo
wearing a beard	being unshaven
Bureau of Indian Affairs school	Harlem school
parent participation	PTA
Little League games	professional baseball
handouts	subsidies
state penitentiaries	army stockades
court martial	civil trial
op art	pop art
war	football
dialect	"bad grammar"
leftovers	a casserole

readings on classification 4

CLASSIFICATION

A third method of making what we mean clear is classifying. We are classifying when we divide things or people or ideas into categories—into groups that seem to belong together. Classifying starts with one general group, a collection of things that share some important likeness. Whatever the first group is, it can be divided into smaller groups, according to the differences we are interested in.

The general group of *teachers,* for instance, can be divided into smaller groups according to differences in the age of their students (grade school, high school, college), differences in the subjects they teach (English, mathematics, history, electronics), or differences in any other area that interests us. The categories into which the general group is divided depend on what the writer wants to explain.

Just as comparison does, classification makes meaning clear by showing likenesses and differences. But whereas comparison begins with two things and shows several likenesses and differences between those things, classification begins with things that are *alike in one way* and divides them according to *one difference at a time.* Even though the writer who was dividing the general group of teachers into three smaller groups—grade school, high school, and college—might later want to further divide college teachers into still smaller groups—English teachers, math teachers, science teachers, etc.—he should be careful not to make both divisions at once.

Many classification systems avoid this difficulty because they never go beyond the first big division; they stop with a single step. The post office, for instance, divides mail into four classes. First-class mail includes all letters or communications specially written from one person to another. Second-class mail includes group communications, usually mimeographed or printed. Third-class mail is magazines and pamphlets. Fourth-class mail is packages, without any communication in them.

Although the following classification of electronic devices by generation may seem complicated to people who are not electronics technicians, it too takes only one step. It divides electronic equipment into three "generations," mentions how each generation works, and gives an example of each generation:

> It has become fashionable to talk of the electronics industry in terms of generations. First generation equipment employs vacuum tubes. Second generation uses transistorized circuitry. Third generation uses integrated circuitry. And recently we have begun to characterize a fourth generation of equipment built from tens or hundreds of interconnected integrated circuits. These classifications are useful in order to assess the present status of our

industry and to better understand future trends. For example, your TV is a
first generation device, your car radio is second generation, and the computer
in your office is, or probably soon will be, third generation equipment. (From
Wall Street Reports, April 1968, p. 51.)

Most classification systems that group things according to what they are or
how they operate seem fairly clearcut and obvious, especially when the
classification explains the answer to a fairly clearcut and obvious question.
The next two essays, for instance, answer these questions:

How can you tell the three kinds of whales apart?
   (By what they eat: plankton, fish and squid)
What are the varieties of large sandpipers?
   (There are three main groups, which can be further subdivided)

But even though a writer sometimes needs to take more than one step
to complete his explanation, his second and third steps, if he subdivides that
many times, will still answer the original question.

Whales

latitude: geographical distance from the Equator
untenanted: not lived in
formidably: frighteningly
abundant: plentiful
quarry: prey; thing being hunted
writhing: twisting violently and painfully

[1] Eventually the whales, as though to divide the sea's food resources
among them, became separated into three groups: the plankton-eaters, the
fish-eaters, and the squid-eaters. The plankton-eating whales can exist only
where there are dense masses of small shrimp or copepods to supply their
enormous food requirements. This limits them, except for scattered areas,
to arctic and antarctic waters and the high temperate latitudes.
[2] Fish-eating whales may find food over a somewhat wider range of ocean,
but they are restricted to places where there are enormous populations of

schooling fish. The blue water of the tropics and of the open ocean basins offers little to either of these groups.

[3] But that immense, square-headed, formidably toothed whale known as the cachalot or sperm whale discovered long ago what men have known for only a short time—that hundreds of fathoms below the almost untenanted surface waters of these regions there is an abundant animal life. The sperm whale has taken these deep waters for his hunting grounds; his quarry is the deep-water population of squids, including the giant squid Architeuthis, which lives at depths of 1500 feet or more. The head of the sperm whale is often marked with long stripes, which consist of a great number of circular scars made by the suckers of the squid. From this evidence we can imagine the battles that go on, in the darkness of the deep water, between these two huge creatures—the sperm whale with its 70-ton bulk, the squid with a body as long as 30 feet, and writhing, grasping arms extending the total length of the animal to perhaps 50 feet.

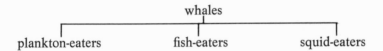

DISCUSSION

1. Although Miss Carson uses only a one-step classification system, she does more than just say, "Plankton-eaters eat plankton, fish-eaters eat fish," etc. For each group she gives some related information which could be the basis for a different classification. What is it? How would that classification work?

2. Miss Carson gives quite a lot of information about sperm whales, but all of it relates to her main point, that sperm whales eat squid. Show how everything she says about sperm whales is connected to that point.

Some Feathery Notes for Birdwatchers

prone to: likely to; in the habit of
provocation: cause; something that frightens or angers
solitary: alone
confined: limited to

From Irston R. Barnes in the August 18, 1968 issue of *The Washington Post*. Reprinted by permission of *The Washington Post*.

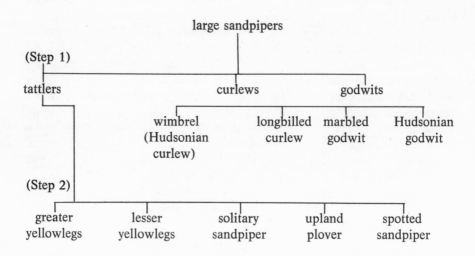

[1] The sandpiper family includes three groups of larger birds, the tattlers, the curlews, and the godwits.

[2] The tattlers are so called because they are loud voiced, easily excited, and prone to sound an alarm with little provocation. The best known of this group is the greater yellowlegs, a 14-inch sandpiper with bright yellow legs, and in flight showing a whitish rump and tail and dark wings. The lesser yellowlegs, 10 inches, is most readily distinguished by its shorter bill and its different call.

[3] Three other tattlers may be noted. The solitary sandpiper, 8 to 9 inches, is also a dark-winged bird with dark legs; otherwise it resembles the yellowlegs. The upland plover is a 12-inch sandpiper and not a plover. It is buffy brown with a notably small head and is confined largely to prairies and extensive fields, where it frequently perches on fence posts and other lookouts. The most familiar of all is the spotted sandpiper. It may be found on a beach or an inland shore.

[4] The most impressive of all shorebirds are the curlews, large birds with long, down curved bills. The wimbrel (or Hudsonian curlew) has a contrasting, striped crown and is about 17 inches in length. The longbilled curlew, 20 to 26 inches, is a more buffy bird and lacks the contrasting crown stripes. The latter is quite rare along the eastern coast.

[5] The godwits are large shorebirds also. They are distinguished by long, thin, slightly upturned bills. The marbled godwit, some 18 inches, with a buff and brown pattern, is more common in the West than along the eastern coast. The Hudsonian godwit, some 16 inches, is dark reddish on the breast in the spring, gray breasted in the fall, with a black tail having a broad, white ring.

DISCUSSION

1. What kind of difference does this classification emphasize? Does Barnes give the same kind of information about all three of the big groups? What kind of information does he give?

2. What audience is Barnes writing for? How can you tell? Do you think the audience influences the kind of information given? Explain.

3. Why do you suppose some people get more enjoyment from birds if they know what their names are? Do you know anybody who enjoys identifying cars? Flowers? Dress material? Can you see any connection between these pleasures and the pleasures of bird-watching? Any differences?

4. Does this article sound finished? Why or why not? If it sounds unfinished to you, what kind of conclusion would you give it? Does the purpose of the article have anything to do with how much conclusion it needs?

Do Chimpanzees Have Language?

predator: animal which eats other animals
characteristic: typical
audibly: loud enough to be heard
delicacy: especially choice or desirable food
grooming: hair-combing, lice-picking, etc.

[1] I am often asked, "Do Chimpanzees have a language?" They do not, of course, have a language that can be compared with our own, but they do have a tremendous variety of calls and gestures.

[2] The calls range from the rather low-pitched "hoo" of greeting, and the series of low grunts that is heard when a chimpanzee begins to feed on some desirable food, to the loud, excited calls and screams which occur when two groups meet.

[3] One call, given in defiance of a possible predator, or when a chimpanzee, for some reason, is angry at the approach of another, can be described as a loud "wraaaah." This is a single syllable, several times repeated, and is one of the most savage and spine-chilling sounds of the African forest.

Reprinted, with minor adaptations, from "My Life Among Wild Chimpanzees," by Jane Goodall, in the August 1963 National Geographic Magazine, copyright National Geographic Society, Washington, D.C.

[4] Another characteristic call is a series of hoots, the breath drawn in audibly after each hoot, and ending with three or four roars. This is the cry of a male chimpanzee as he crosses a ridge. It seems to be an announcement to any other chimpanzees that may be in the valley below: "Here I come."

[5] In addition, chimpanzees communicate by touch or gesture. A mother touches her young one when she is about to move away, or taps on the trunk when she wants it to come down from a tree. When a chimpanzee is anxious for a share of some delicacy, he begs, holding out his hand palm up, exactly as we do. He may pat the branch beside him if he wants a companion to join him there. When two animals are grooming each other and one feels that it is his turn to be groomed, he often reaches out and gives his companion a poke.

[6] Once, when three males were all grooming one another, I saw a female going round poking at each of them in turn. But she was completely ignored —and so sat down sadly and groomed herself!

[7] There are also many gestures of greeting and friendship. Sometimes when two friends meet after a separation, they fling their arms around each other in a delighted embrace.

[8] These calls and gestures, while they are not a language in our sense of the word, are understood by other chimpanzees and certainly form a means of communication.

DISCUSSION

1. The question the writer asks in the introductory paragraph is answered by "No, but . . ." The "but" leads to another question, actually answered by the article. What is the second, unstated question? How does the answer to this question lead into the first step of the classification?

2. How does the conclusion relate to the introduction? How does it make the article sound finished?

3. If, as the writer says, the chimpanzee's calls and gestures are not a language in our sense of the word, what is our sense of the word? Do you and the other members of your class all agree on what is meant by language?

4. If you wanted to classify the kinds of human communication, what sort of chart would you make?

THE CHIMPANZEE'S MEANS OF COMMUNICATION

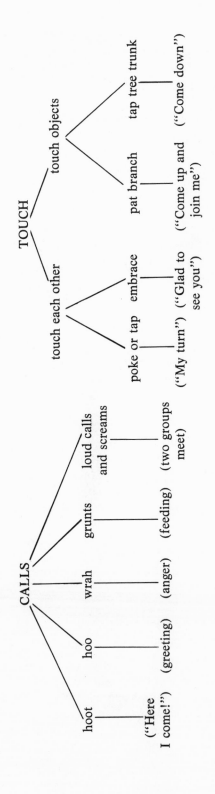

The Marine Rainbow

marine: of the sea
azure: sky-blue
diatom: tiny one-celled creatures that float in the sea
elude: escape
larvae: first stage after leaving the egg
hues: colors
raiment: clothing

[1] In a curious way, the colors of marine animals tend to be related to the zone in which they live. Fishes of the surface waters, like the mackerel and herring, often are blue or green; so are the floats of the Portuguese men-of-war and the azure tinted wings of the swimming snails. Down below the diatom meadows and the drifting sargassum weed, where the water becomes ever more deeply, brilliantly blue, many creatures are crystal clear. Their glassy, ghostly forms blend with their surroundings and make it easier for them to elude the ever-present, ever-hungry enemy. Such are the transparent hordes of the arrowworms or glassworms, the comb jellies, and the larvae of many fishes.

[2] At a thousand feet, and on down to the very end of the sun's rays, silvery fishes are common, and many others are red, drab brown, or black. Pteropods are a dark violet. Arrowworms, whose relatives in the upper layers are colorless, are here a deep red. Jellyfish medusae, which above would be transparent, at a depth of 1000 feet are a deep brown.

[3] At depths greater than 1500 feet, all the fish are black, deep violet or brown, but the prawns wear amazing hues of red, scarlet, and purple. Why, no one can say. Since all the red rays are strained out of the water far above this depth, the scarlet raiment of these creatures can only look black to their neighbors.

DISCUSSION

1. What is the question which this classification answers?

2. What point of view does the writer take? How many categories are included in the first step of the classification? What are they? See whether the categories you decide on agree with those of your classmates. If the class disagrees on the categories, can you explain the disagreement?

From p. 49 of *The Sea Around Us* by Rachel L. Carson. Copyright 1950, 1951 by Rachel L. Carson. Reprinted by permission of Oxford University Press, Inc.

3. What transitions does Miss Carson use to help the reader move from category to category?

4. Another way the article is tied together is by contrasting similar forms of marine animals. What marine animals mentioned in paragraph 2 correspond to animals mentioned in paragraph 1? How does the writer remind you of this relationship?

5. Why does Miss Carson mention prawns in the last paragraph? Does the color of the prawns spoil the point she is making? Why or why not?

Classifications that group people by behavior or attitudes may seem much more complicated, much less straightforward, than classifications that group things according to what they are or how they operate. For instance, food can easily be classified as meat, vegetables, fruit, grain products, and dairy products, but people's reactions to food are much harder to pin down. Part of the difficulty is that while the categories of food are well known, the categories of people's reactions to food have to be set up by the writer and can be done in any manner he likes.

In sorting out reactions, then, the writer's reason for making the classification is especially important, since it limits the topic and determines the kind of question he asks before he begins his classification. If his question is, "How do people react to artichokes?" his categories might be (1) people who think artichokes are a delicacy (2) people who hate them (3) people who are afraid of them and (4) people who never heard of them. By including the fourth category, people who never heard of artichokes, he has made allowances for all the possibilities.

In general, it is a good idea to make each new division include everything that was in the group being divided. If dairy products were divided into butter, cheese, and cream, for instance, readers would be justified in asking what happened to milk. Sometimes, the writer can take care of this danger by including a category labeled "other," to include the things he is not interested in discussing.

Notice, too, that the writer who classified people's reactions to food didn't attempt to cover everybody's reaction to every kind of food. Instead, he narrowed the subject to one kind of food, artichokes, and then asked his question.

The first essay of the following group classifies man's attitude toward animals, but before the writer begins he restricts the topic even more, to man's tendency to compare himself to animals. In the two articles on cars, the first writer limits himself to "used cars" and the second to "borrowed cars." But neither writer is interested in classifying cars according to what they are or how they work; instead, both writers are asking questions about people's attitudes toward cars or their behavior concerning them. That is, both writers have a special *point of view* about cars, and the point of view is reflected in the categories each writer uses.

Back to the Ark

idiom: an expression difficult to translate word for word
Example: "He takes after his father."
ruminant: a cud-chewing animal
embodiment: the concrete form of an idea or attitude; a perfect example
perfidy: treachery or betrayal
expletive: a strong word expressing insult or anger
minimal: as little as possible
ultimate: final; worst or best
repertoire: collection
unsavory: distasteful

[1] There is a strong tendency in Man to compare his qualities and actions with those of the animals. In some countries there is a common feeling of fondness and friendship for animals which shows up in phrases like "Don't whip a willing horse," "Cat may look at a king," and "Love me, love my dog." In others, particularly in France and Germany, the everyday idioms are loaded with insulting references to the realm of beasts. — *Introduction explains what will be classified—man's tendency to compare himself to animals—and indicates main categories— comparisons showing fondness / comparisons showing insult*

[2] The cow, for instance—that peaceful ruminant —is to the Frenchman the embodiment of perfidy and wickedness. *Ah, la vache!* (What a cow!) is the Frenchman's passionate expression of overwhelming indignation. If somebody plays a dirty trick on him there is no fouler expletive than *Vacherie!* — *Second suggested categories: in France / in Germany / in other places (implied)*

[3] And since his respect for the guardians of the law is minimal, he shouts *Mort aux vaches!* (Death on the cows!), meaning, of course, "Down with the cops!" But logic never loses out with a Frenchman, so it is only mildly surprising to learn that in France a policeman riding a bicycle is called *une vache a roulettes* (a cow on rollers). — *Example of insulting comparison: French use of cow*

[4] If the French are down on cows, the Germans apparently can't stand dogs. In fact the ultimate insult in their language is *Du Hund!* unless you prefer the *Schweinhund* (pig-dog). — *Example of insulting comparison: German use of dog*

Reprinted from p. 54 of "Back to the Ark" by Paul Brock in the January 1969 issue of *Quinto Lingo* by permission of Rodale Press, Inc.

[5] The Germans find stupidity characteristic of a large variety of animals. Not only the ass *(Esel)*, who has an international reputation for it, but the Ox (Ochs or Rindvieh), the sheep (Schaf), and even the camel (Kamel) are also regarded as blood-brothers to a blockhead or a boob.

More examples of German insults

[6] If a guy from another country falls for a gal, he might not "say it with flowers" but might express himself instead in zoological terms. If she is young and inexperienced she is a "goose," and in France a "turkey-hen" *(une dinde)*, in Germany a "fried fish" (Backfisch).

Examples of fond comparison

in France
in Germany

[7] As she yields to a man's advances he calls her by the sweetest names in his repertoire—but it's still the zoo! In several countries the girl becomes his "dove" or "ducky"; in Germany a *Mauschen* or *Katzchen* (little mouse or cat); in France, *ma poupoule* or *ma bichette* (my little hen or roe).

More examples of fond comparison in other places
in Germany
in France

[8] But it doesn't last. Later, when she's no longer a "chicken" she becomes a "vixen" or a plain "cat," or even a *Ziege* (she-goat). A *poupoule* is downgraded to the much less complimentary *poule,* or is substituted by a *piegrieche* (shrike or harpie).

Examples of insulting comparison
in Germany
in France

[9] The lady who remains a spinster is called a *rossignol* (nightingale—something on the shelf). And if she goes about chaperoning her younger sister, the *oie blanche.* And there is yet another animal's name for her—"the dragon."

Comparisons showing neither fondness nor insult

[10] Public life and finance ring with zoological names: social "lions," "bulls" and "bears" who gamble on the stock exchange, and "rats," thoroughly unsavory characters, and "chameleons," ever-changing politicians.

More miscellaneous comparisons

[11] So you see, we are ever inclined toward the kingdom of beasts. We see ourselves in the best and the worst of them. We are still sailing with Noah.

Conclusion repeats the two main categories—"the best" and "the worst"

Here is the classification chart apparently used by this writer:

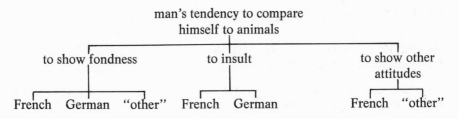

DISCUSSION

1. Actually the main idea sentence of this article is never directly stated, although it can be worked out from what is said in paragraph 1. Put into your own words what you think the main idea is, making sure your finished sentence includes both what is being classified and the main categories used in the first step.

2. Although the main purpose of this article is to classify, the first sentence might make you think the main purpose was comparison. Do you find the first sentence misleading? Why or why not?

3. The classification chart on which this article is based is fairly simple, and if the writer had merely changed the chart into sentences, he would have had a very short, and very dull, article. How has he added interest to the classification he began with?

4. Does the order of the article follow the order of the chart? What differences are there? What can you find in the article that justifies the order the writer uses? That is, what connection of ideas can you find between paragraphs 3 and 4, for instance? Between paragraphs 7 and 8? Between paragraphs 8 and 9?

5. What animal insults are used in America today? What animals are used to show fondness or to praise people?

6. Make a classification chart showing the animal comparisons you and your friends use.

Used Cars As Status Symbols

status symbol: a possession valued because it seems to show that its owner belongs to a desirable group
validly: accurately; logically
desirous: having a desire
ploy: device; tactic
vintage: age
explicit: exact; definite
bestow: give
concomitant: corresponding

Reprinted from "Used Cars As Status Symbols," by Diana Bartley in *Esquire* (March 1968), by permission of *Esquire* Magazine © 1968 by Esquire, Inc.

[1] The whole subject of cars as status symbols is very confused these days. Even back in the Thirties it wasn't simple. But then at least generalities could be made based on whose opinion of your status you were after, and genuine status-symbols cars, such as Stutzes, Duesenbergs and Pierce-Arrows, did exist. In those days a used Packard was superior to a new Willys-Knight for the country-club set. A used Buick (only doctors had new ones) was better than a new Ford. And any car was better than none. Today it can happen that none is better. Some New York City men, for example, walk ten midtown Manhattan blocks from an east side co-op penthouse to a Seagram Building office and hire a limousine with chauffeur for all other movement (to and from airports, mostly). Boats, country houses, trips to Ischia or Molokai have replaced cars in the status scale for a lot of people.

[2] But, cars are still in the running, so to speak. You'll have to decide just where they fit in your own system. Does your boss, neighbor, brother-in-law or colleague count higher points for, say, a new option-loaded Mustang or a 1966 Cadillac, which cost about the same. And indeed, which status-symbol league are you most interested in—your boss's, brother-in-law's, neighbor's, etc. The following generalities may not help much, but they're about the only ones that can still validly be made.

[3] 1. If you are very conservative and a bit snobbish (any age), a recent-model used Cadillac is better to own than a new anything else. (It is presumed you can't afford a new Caddy.)

[4] 2. If quite conservative (any age), you probably can count a used Lincoln Continental on a par with the Cad.

[5] 3. If rather conservative (any age) but would like to surprise people who think you are very, a year-old Dodge Charger is better than a new Dodge Coronet DeLuxe Six (both $2400 or so), and a year-old $3500 Riviera is better than a new Buick LeSabre at a similar price.

[6] 4. If young and eager (eighteen to thirty) or desirous of appearing same (thirty-to-not-more-than-forty-five), either a two-year-old Pontiac G.T.O. or a four-year-old Corvette at around $2100 gives a better image than most new cars at half-again-to-double the price.

[7] If just plain young (under eighteen), anything is acceptable, even your mother's car if it's reasonably available.

[8] For average men (any age) no generalities can be made, though a good ploy for certain of the up-and-coming ones (twenty-five to forty-five) is a third car, any kind or vintage, "for the kids" or "just to knock around in out at the lake."

[9] Beyond this, it's hard to be very explicit. Campers bestow status in some circles today, Land Rovers in some others, motorbikes not much anymore but motorcycles *lots* (more's the pity, in light of the concomitant increase in the number of badly broken heads), and there are even sections of the country where a snowmobile gets higher points than any other piece of transportation. So you see how difficult it has gotten.

DISCUSSION

1. Why does the writer begin each category with a description of the owner rather than a description of the car?

2. In this selection, the writer has used numbers instead of transitions. Her numbering scheme makes it appear that she has six distinct categories. Actually, however, she has four, one of which is subdivided. Which one is subdivided? What are the categories in the second step?

3. Notice that the last category, "average men," is a kind of catch-all group intended to include any people who weren't mentioned in groups one through five. What groups of used car owners has the writer left out?

4. How does the conclusion tie into the introduction and make the writing sound finished?

Liability on a Loaned Car

defective: has something wrong with it
negligence: carelessness; neglect
liability: legal responsibility
crucial: so important it decides things one way or another

[1] It is common courtesy, when you lend your car to a friend, to fill it up first with gas. But what about checking the brakes or inspecting the tires? If the car is defective and there is an accident, are you legally liable for the consequences?

[2] You may be indeed. Take this case:

[3] A man allowed the woman next door—an inexperienced driver—to borrow his car. Although he knew it had a "grabby" clutch, he didn't tell her so. She lost control of the car, crashed into a tree, and suffered painful injuries.

[4] She later sued him for damages, and the court decided he must pay for his negligence. The judge said that, under the circumstances, this was the kind of accident he could reasonably have foreseen and prevented.

Reprinted from "Liability on a Loaned Car," by Will Bernard, which appeared in the *St. Louis Post-Dispatch* (March 30, 1969), © 1969 American Bar Association, by permission of the American Bar Association and the author.

[5] What if there is an injury not to the borrower but to some third party whom you don't even know? Even then, you might incur liability.

[6] Thus, a man who loaned a car with faulty brakes, without giving fair warning to the borrower, was held responsible for the resulting death of a schoolboy. The fatal accident occurred when, at a crucial moment, the brakes gave way.

[7] That does not mean you have to make a thorough examination of your car before lending it, to discover defects you would not ordinarily know about. Accordingly, a car owner was held not to blame when the steering gear—seemingly all right until then—suddenly jammed while a friend was using the car.

[8] Nor must you warn a borrower about things he can and should see for himself. A man who loaned a car with a dirty windshield was held not responsible for a later collision. The court said he had a right to assume that the borrower would have enough sense to clean the windshield on his own.

[9] All the law demands is that you show, along with your generosity in lending the car, a decent concern for the safety of other people.

[10] As one court said:

> "When a person lends, he ought to confer a benefit and not do a mischief."

DISCUSSION

1. The introduction to this essay has one sentence about "common courtesy" and two questions, one about the condition of the car and one about the responsibility of the lender. Do the two questions seem related to the first sentence? Do they seem an effective introduction to the rest of the paper?

2. The obvious purpose of this writing is to explain about the responsibilities of the person who lends his car. What does it classify? What categories are included in the first step?

3. How do the last two paragraphs, beginning "All the law demands is . . ." relate to the introduction?

What News Story Do You Read?

Freud: Austrian doctor who analyzed motives of human behavior
corruption: crookedness in public affairs
vicarious: imagining you are feeling other people's experiences
ominous: threatening
stable: not moving; unchanging
predisposition: built-in habits or interests

[1] I think it is self-evident that a person selects news in expectation of a reward.

[2] This reward may be either of two kinds. One is related to what Freud calls the Pleasure Principle, the other to what he calls the Reality Principle. For want of better names, we shall call these two classes *immediate reward* and *delayed reward*.

[3] In general, the kind of news which may be expected to furnish immediate reward are news of crime and corruption, accidents and disasters, sports and recreation, social events, and human interest.

[4] Delayed reward may be expected from news of public affairs, economic matters, social problems, science, education, and health.

[5] News of the first kind pays its rewards at once. A reader can enjoy a vicarious experience without any of the dangers or stresses involved. He can shiver luxuriously at an axe-murder, shake his head sympathetically and safely at a tornado, identify himself with the winning team or (herself) with the society lady who wore a well-described gown at the reception for Lady Morganbilt, laugh understandingly (and from superior knowledge) at a warm little story of children or dogs.

[6] News of the second kind, however, pays its rewards later. It sometimes requires the reader to endure unpleasantness or annoyance—as, for example, when he reads of the ominous foreign situation, the mounting national debt, rising taxes, falling market, scarce housing, cancer, epidemics, farm blights. It has a kind of "threat value." It is read so that the reader may be informed and prepared. When a reader selects delayed reward news, he jerks himself into the world of surrounding reality to which he can adapt himself only by hard work. When he selects news of the other kind, he retreats usually from the world of threatening reality toward the dream world.

[7] For any individual, of course, the boundaries of these two classes are not stable. For example, a sociologist may read news of crime as a social

Reprinted from "The Nature of News," by Wilbur Schramm in *Journalism Quarterly* (September 1949), by permission of the publisher.

problem, rather than for its immediate reward. A coach may read a sports story for its threat value: he may have to play that team next week. A politician may read an account of his latest successful rally, not for its delayed reward, but very much as his wife reads an account of a party. In any given story of corruption or disaster, a thoughtful reader may receive not only the immediate reward of vicarious experience, but also the delayed reward of information and preparedness. Therefore, while the division of categories holds in general, the predispositions of the individual may transfer any story from one kind of reading to another, or divide the experience between the two kinds of reward.

DISCUSSION

1. In the first two paragraphs, the writer divides news stories into two categories: those that give immediate reward, and those that give delayed reward. What subdivisions does he make within each of the two main categories?

2. Schramm says he thinks "it is self-evident that a person selects news in expectation of a reward." Do you agree that it is self-evident? If his point is self-evident, why would anyone want to read his essay? If it is not self-evident, how does the first sentence work to get the reader engaged in the writing?

If we use classification properly, it can help us see relationships more distinctly and think more clearly. If we use it badly, however, it will confuse the relationships and muddy our thinking. One way of misusing classification is to let it lead us into pigeonholing or stereotyping. We begin to pigeonhole whenever we forget that a classification system works only for the question it begins with. Dividing draftees according to how they feel about the draft is a very handy way of examining reactions, as long as we remember that the boys who go to Canada belong together *only in terms of going to Canada.* If we were dividing them according to religious preference, some would be Catholics, some Protestants, some Jews, and some nonbelievers. If we were classifying them according to political preference, some would be Republicans, some Democrats, some Socialists, and some would never have voted at all. The category in which people are placed is not permanent or fixed; there are always other categories, just as there are other questions to be asked.

Another way of misusing classification is to let the categories overlap. Since the purpose of classification is to sort things into clear divisions, we must keep the divisions clear. In the essay, "What Kind of Language Are You Using?" the writer is very careful that his categories do not overlap. He points out that the purposes of language can be classified under one system, but that words are classified under another. Two questions are involved, and even though the questions are similar, he needs two separate classification systems. Unless we remember that there are two systems, and that the systems are different, we will miss the writer's point.

All the essays in this group use classification for different reasons, from special points of view, but whether the purpose is playful, as in "Inanimate Objects Cut Man's Lifespan," or serious, as in the long essay, "Hell, No, We Won't Go," the question the writer begins with determines the categories, and the writer keeps the categories straight.

What Kind of Language Are You Using?

function: purpose something is used for
rapport: sympathetic relationship
discourse: talking; speaking
convey: give or transfer
fraught: full of

[1] Language has more than one purpose. We might say that language operates on different levels, except that the word "levels" suggests higher and lower planes in a scale of value, and this is not intended here. We shall deal with three functions: the informative, the expressive, and the directive. To say that language has these three functions is to say that there are three different reasons for speaking. One reason, or purpose, is to communicate factual information. This is the informative function. We speak also in order to express our feelings, to "blow off steam," or to stir the feelings and attitudes of the person we are talking to. We shall call this the expressive or "emotive" function. And, finally, we speak in order to get people to act. This is the directive function.

Introduction gives point of view: looking at language according to purpose

The three main categories, listed and defined:
1. informative

2. expressive

3. directive

From the book *The Art of Making Sense* by Lionel Ruby. Copyright © 1968, 1954 by Lionel Ruby. Reprinted by permission of J. B. Lippincott Company.

[2] Some illustrations are in order. A book on astronomy describes the solar system and the stars. We learn that the diameter of the earth is about 8,000 miles; that of the sun, about 800,000 miles; a ratio of 100 to 1. We learn that the star Betelgeuse has a diameter three hundred times that of the sun. This means that if the earth is represented by a baseball, about three inches in diameter, then Betelgeuse would have a diameter of almost a mile and a half. We may learn that there are as many stars in the heavens as there are grains of sand on all the seashores of the world . . . I have just been using language to communicate information.

Examples of informative language

[3] Expressive language is a second type. When I talk about the United States Senator I like least, I may let off some steam, and relieve my pent-up feelings. I may even infect you with my feelings, making you feel as I feel. The poet, of course, is a specialist in expressive language, as in the lines:

Examples of expressive language

> Comes the blind Fury with the
> abhorred shears
> And slits the thin-spun life.

These lines give expression to John Milton's feelings and perhaps make us feel as he felt. When we tell our friends a funny story, to get a laugh, we express our feelings, too, and affect theirs.

[4] The third type, directive or action-provoking speech, is illustrated by examples like: "Do unto others as you would have others do unto you," or "Praise the Lord, and pass the ammunition!" We say these things to get action. Ceremonial language, such as "I am happy to meet you," "What a beautiful baby!" and conversation about the weather, also have a directive purpose: to establish social rapport, and to get a friendly response.

Examples of directive language

[5] There are, then, at least three different purposes of discourse. We may also make a somewhat similar classification for words, that is, for words taken by themselves. A basic distinction here is between what we shall call neutral words, and emotive words. Neutral words merely convey ideas to us, as when I say, "The sun rose at six this morning." The words in this sentence do not arouse our emotions. But words like "God," "love," "freedom," and "communism" are so closely connected with our total

Second classification system: words taken by themselves
Categories:
1. neutral
2. emotive

attitudes to life that they are likely to arouse emotional reactions. This division of words into neutral and emotive, however, is relative to our personal experiences, for there is nothing in the word itself which makes it neutral or emotive. If a word conveys nothing but an idea to you, then it is neutral to you; if it arouses your emotions, then it is emotive to you. The word "bread" is a neutral word to me, but to a "fat boy" or a starving man, it may be fraught with emotion. Nevertheless there are some words which can be counted on to make almost everyone "see red," so to speak, like the word "traitor."

Explanation and examples of neutral and emotive words

[6] This classification of words is independent of our classification of the functions of language, for those who wish to inform may use either type, as may those who want to express their feelings, or to get action. In general, however, neutral words will be used when we wish merely to inform, emotive words when we wish to be expressive.

Warning that the two classifications are separate

DISCUSSION

1. The writer makes it clear that he is classifying language according to the purpose for which it is used. What are some other ways by which language might be classified?

2. Is the author using informative, emotive, or directive language in this essay? Why do you say so?

3. In your daily newspaper, what section (or sections) would probably contain informative language? Emotive language? Directive language? (You may want to bring samples to class to see whether other students agree with you.)

4. Can you think of any common purposes of talking or writing that would make use of all three of Ruby's levels? What are they?

5. What sort of situations can you think of where *neutral words* would be more useful than *emotive words?* What sort of situations can you think of where the opposite would be true?

6. Pick five things for which you can give a neutral word, a favorable emotive word, and an unfavorable emotive word.

Inanimate Objects Cut Man's Lifespan

in league with: combined together to accomplish something
plausible: believable
locomotion: movement; traveling
inherent capacity: built-in ability
negotiated: agreed upon
conciliatory: trying to smooth things over
baffled: completely puzzled

[1] Inanimate objects are classified scientifically into three major categories —those that don't work, those that break down, and those that get lost.

[2] The goal of all inanimate objects is to resist man and finally to defeat him, and the three major classifications are based on the method each object uses to achieve its purpose. As a general rule, any object capable of breaking down at the moment when it is most needed will do so. The automobile is typical of the whole category.

[3] With the cunning typical of its breed, the automobile never breaks down while entering a filling station with a large staff of idle mechanics. It waits until it reaches a downtown intersection in the middle of the rush hour, or until it is fully loaded with family and luggage somewhere on the Ohio Turnpike.

[4] Thus, it creates maximum misery, inconvenience, frustration and irritability among its human cargo, thereby reducing its owner's life span. How much reduction in human life span occurs as a result of the average car breakdown has never been scientifically measured, but when we consider the vast number of inanimate objects that break down at life's critical moments, the total life span reduction in the average family is obviously considerable.

[5] Washing machines, garbage disposals, lawnmowers, light bulbs, automatic laundry dryers, water pipes, furnaces, electrical fuses, television tubes, hose nozzles, tape recorders, slide projectors—all are in league with the automobile to take their turn at breaking down whenever life threatens to flow smoothly for their human enemies.

[6] Many inanimate objects, of course, find it extremely difficult to break down. Pliers, for example, and gloves and keys are almost totally incapable

of breaking down. Therefore, they have had to develop a different technique for resisting man.

[7] They are lost. Science has still not solved the mystery of how they do it, and no man has ever caught one of them in the act of getting lost. The most plausible theory is that they have developed a secret method of locomotion which they are able to conceal the instant a human eye falls upon them.

[8] It is not uncommon for a pair of pliers to climb all the way from the cellar to the attic in its singleminded determination to raise its owner's blood pressure. Keys have been known to burrow three feet under mattresses. Women's purses, despite their great weight, frequently travel through six or seven rooms to find hiding space under a couch.

[9] Scientists have been struck by the fact that things that break down almost never get lost, while things that get lost hardly ever break down.

[10] A furnace, for example, will invariably break down at the depth of the first winter cold wave, but it will never get lost. A woman's purse, which after all does have some inherent capacity for breaking down, hardly ever does; it almost always chooses to get lost.

[11] Some persons believe this is evidence that inanimate objects are not entirely hostile to man, and that a negotiated peace is possible. After all, they point out, a furnace could infuriate a man even more thoroughly by getting lost than by breaking down, just as a glove could upset him far more by breaking down than by getting lost.

[12] Not everyone agrees, however, that this indicates a conciliatory attitude among inanimate objects. Many say it merely proves that furnaces, gloves and pliers are incredibly stupid.

[13] The third class of objects—those that don't work—is the most curious of all. These include such objects as barometers, car clocks, cigarette lighters, flashlights and toy-train locomotives. It is inaccurate, of course, to say that they never work. They work once, usually for the first few hours after being brought home, and then quit. Thereafter, they never work again.

[14] In fact, it is widely assumed that they are built for the purpose of not working. Some people have reached advanced ages without ever seeing some of these objects—barometers, for example—in working order.

[15] Science is utterly baffled by the entire category. There are many theories. The most interesting holds that the things that don't work have reached the highest state possible for an inanimate object, the state that things that break down and things that get lost can still only work toward.

[16] They have truly defeated man by conditioning him never to expect anything of them, and in return they have given man the only peace he receives from inanimate society. He does not expect his barometer to work, his electric locomotive to run, his cigarette lighter to light, or his flashlight to illuminate, and when they don't, it does not raise his blood pressure.

[17] He cannot attain that peace with furnaces and keys and cars and women's purses as long as he demands that they work for their keep.

DISCUSSION

1. Make a classification chart showing the divisions that are being used in this essay.

2. How does the writer take care of the possibility of overlapping categories (see paragraphs 9 through 12)?

3. What distinction is the writer making between his first and third categories? Does it seem to you a real distinction? Why or why not? In this essay, does it matter?

4. In the first paragraph, Baker says that inanimate objects are classified *scientifically* into three categories. Do his categories strike you as "scientific"? What does the essay gain from Baker's frequent reference to the "scientific" study of inanimate objects? (See paragraphs 1, 7, 9, 15.)

5. How does Baker's difficult vocabulary contribute to the tone of this essay? Would the writing be more effective, or less, if Baker used more common words?

Why Technicians Get Fired

stupefying: putting into a state of dullness; grogginess
ostensibly: apparently
intolerance: unwillingness to listen to the other side
pilferage: petty thievery
recurrent: happening over and over
tenure: length of time on the job
laudable: praiseworthy
diligence: hard work

[1] In any newly hired group of electronics technicians, some, or many, work out satisfactorily, remain on the job, and in the course of time get raises and promotions. In any group, there are a number of technicians who don't stay hired because they are technically incompetent in one way or another. One of the most common failings is the inability to use technical knowledge. The sufferer from this fault can pass every written test, fill blackboards with correct formulas and wiring diagrams, discuss theory impres-

From "The Electronics Technician Shortage" in the September 1967 issue of *Popular Electronics,* pp. 60–61. Reprinted by permission.

sively, and generally act like a genius (junior grade)—but he cannot make anything work.

[2] Some relatively new employees are called to the security office after a few weeks of work and are seen no more. The trouble could be false statements on the employment application, concealment of a criminal record, or denial of security clearance for various reasons.

[3] The technician who shows up for work under the influence of anything intoxicating or stupefying usually goes on permanent vacation rather suddenly. Absences every Monday morning, the day after each payday, usually make the section chief suspicious. So do shaky hands on return to work after each reported bout with "the virus." Filling your thermos full of "Old Bust Head" instead of coffee sounds like an excellent idea, but the foreman's grandfather knew about that one, too.

[4] One sure way of getting plenty of leisure (without pay) is to try to force your religious or political beliefs on your fellow employees. If while ostensibly employed by an electronics company, you spend a lot of time recruiting for the Charles Ash Society, organizing compulsory prayer sessions during coffee breaks, or bawling people out for not attending the Whoop and Holler Pentecostal Tabernacle, you are greasing the skids under your feet.

[5] A related, but less serious evil, is taking off too many religious holidays. Most employers allow time off for religious observances, but if you take off on Good Friday, don't also take off for Yom Kippur and the first day of Ramadan.

[6] Unreasonable friction on the job is a cause of many firings, as is intolerance of the reasonably normal traits of your fellow employees. A department where a number of the employees are "not speaking" is an unhealthy one and usually undergoes changes in personnel pretty regularly. Meddling in the personal affairs of your fellow workers just won't do, and loud personal criticism of the man at the next bench is completely out of line.

[7] A very common employee trait, carried on the books as "stock shrinkage" or "pilferage," but more commonly known as stealing, causes a lot of technicians to change jobs involuntarily. This ranges from the occasional "borrowing" of a resistor to fix the home radio to wholesale thefts of expensive or scarce components for sale. Many employers are pretty liberal about a few small parts but get downright "unreasonable" about recurrent disappearances of special integrated circuits, machine tool parts, or even oscilloscope plug-ins. Great care in keeping "company property" separate from "personal property" will not hurt your job tenure or chances for promotion.

[8] There is also the recurrent and disturbing condition of a sterling character, of unquestioned competence and laudable diligence, who just doesn't fit in a given department. Very often the reason for this cannot be determined and nobody seems to be at fault. Happily, most of these individuals recognize the situation, get jobs elsewhere before a crisis occurs, and frequently do well at the new job.

DISCUSSION

1. How many categories—how many reasons for getting fired—does the writer give? What are they?

2. Are any of his categories subdivided? If so, which ones? Do any of the categories overlap? If so, which ones?

3. Does the writer give enough examples so that you can understand clearly what he means by each category? If you think he does not, suggest other examples that might fit.

4. If you were making a classification chart showing reasons that people "don't stay hired" in some job you have had experience with, what categories would you include? In making your chart, be sure to avoid overlapping categories.

5. Make a similar classification system showing the reasons that people are *hired* for some job you are familiar with.

The Bandanna

tawdry: showy and cheap
prevailing: general; usual
nattily: neatly; sharply
respirator: device for helping one breathe
apparel: clothing
wont: in the habit of
guidon: an identifying flag

[1] Modern cowboys seem to be giving up the bandanna handkerchief. Perhaps the moving pictures have made it tawdry. Yet there was a time when this article was almost as necessary to a cowboy's equipment as a rope, and it served for purposes almost as varied. The prevailing color of the bandanna was red, but blues and blacks were common, and of course silk bandannas were prized above those made of cotton.

[2] When the cowboy got up in the morning and went down to the water hole to wash his face he used his bandanna for a towel. Then he tied it

around his neck, letting the fold hang down in front, thus appearing rather nattily dressed for breakfast. After he had roped out his bronc and tried to bridle him he probably found that the horse had to be blindfolded before he could do anything with him. The bandanna was what he used to blindfold the horse with. Mounted, the cowboy removed the blind from the horse and put it again around his own neck. Perhaps he rode only a short distance before he spied a big calf that should be branded. He roped the calf; then if he did not have a "piggin string"—a short rope used for tying down animals—he tied the calf's legs together with the bandanna and thus kept the calf fast while he branded it.

[3] In the summertime the cowboy adjusted the bandanna to protect his neck from the sun. He often wore gloves too, for he liked to present neat hands and neck. If the hot sun was in his face, he adjusted the bandanna in front of him, tying it so that the fold would hang over his cheeks, nose and mouth like a mask. If his business was with a dust-raising herd of cattle, the bandanna adjusted in the same way made a respirator; in blizzardly weather it likewise protected his face and ears. In the swift, unhalting work required in the pen the cowboy could, without losing time, grab a fold of the bandanna loosely hung about his neck and wipe away the blinding sweat. In the pen, too, the bandanna served as a rag for holding the hot handles of branding irons.

[4] Many a cowboy has spread his bandanna, perhaps none too clean itself, over dirty, muddy water and used it as a strainer to drink through; sometimes he used it as a cup towel, which he called a "drying rag." If the bandanna was dirty, it was probably not so dirty as the other apparel of the cowboy, for when he came to a hole of water, he was wont to dismount and wash out his handkerchief, letting it dry while he rode along, holding it in his hand or spread over his hat. Often he wore it under his hat in order to help keep his head cool. At other times, in the face of a fierce gale, he used it to tie down his hat.

[5] The bandanna made a good sling for a broken arm; it made a good bandage for a blood wound. Early Irish settlers on the Nueces River used to believe that a bandanna handkerchief that had been worn by a drowned man would, if cast into a stream above the sunken body, float until it came over the body and then sink, thus locating it. Many a cowboy out on the lonely plains has been buried with a clean bandanna spread over his face to keep the dirt, or the coarse blanket on which the dirt was poured, from touching it. The bandanna has been used to hang men with. Rustlers used to "wave" strangers around with it, as a warning against nearer approach, though the hat was more commonly used for signaling. Like the Mexican sombrero or the four-gallon Stetson, the bandanna could not be made too large.

[6] When the cowboys of the West make their final parade on the grassy shores of Paradise, the guidon that leads them should be a bandanna handkerchief. It deserves to be called the flag of the range country.

DISCUSSION

1. For what audience is this essay written? How does the audience affect the kind of information the writer gives? Show some examples of what you mean.

2. Can you find a main idea sentence in this essay? What is it? Does the main idea sentence indicate what the point of view will be? Does it indicate what the categories will be?

3. This essay is organized according to time rather than by categories. Beginning with "When the cowboy got up in the morning . . . ," how many other references to time can you find? What is the last time reference and where does it appear?

4. Because the essay is organized according to time rather than categories, the purposes for which cowboys used bandannas may seem to be given in a haphazard list. Make a classification chart of the uses Dobie mentions, taking as your main categories such things as "for clothing," "for equipment in his work," etc. (Probably you will need more than three main categories.) After you have decided on the main categories for the first step, subdivide them to include all the specific uses Dobie mentions.

5. How does the conclusion relate to the main point Dobie has been making?

"Hell, No, We Won't Go!"

      compulsion: force
      elite: the best of the group
      elusive: hard to find
      nonideological: not resulting from conviction or belief
      extradite: to give up a prisoner to another state or nation
      pending: waiting to be taken care of
      demoted: reduced in rank
      noncombatant: somebody not fighting
      bona fide: genuine
      revile: speak abusively about
      impotent: powerless

Abridged from Bill Davidson, "Hell, No, We Won't Go!" Reprinted with permission from The Saturday Evening Post © 1968.

[1] A big interstate bus noses into the checkpoint on the Canadian border near Rouses Point, New York. Canadian customs officials come aboard, accompanied by two FBI men. The agents have warrants in their pockets, and they are looking for young Americans of draft age trying to flee the country. They tap one boy on the shoulder . . .

[2] It's 10 A.M. in the offices of a big utility company in Chicago. Two FBI men and two federal marshals enter and ask to speak with a young clerk. The youth is called out into the corridor, and the agents put him under arrest for violation of the Selective Service Act. They snap handcuffs on the young man's wrists . . .

[3] A Pfc. is standing at attention in the orderly room of a quartermaster company at Ft. Knox in Kentucky. A reservist, he is wearing civilian clothes. His company commander says, "I'm giving you a direct order to put on your uniform and report for duty." The young soldier says, "I cannot, for reasons of conscience." The company commander orders the soldier taken to the post stockade, where he is stripped and put in a steel isolation cell . . .

[4] Two FBI men are working their way up Avenue A in New York's East Village hippie colony. They are asking about a boy named Johnson who failed to register for the draft in his hometown and then disappeared. They walk right past Johnson without knowing it. Johnson hasn't been Johnson for a long time. Hiding out with the hippies in San Francisco, Los Angeles, Chicago and New York, he has used half a dozen names. In the East Village he is known simply as Scuby . . .

[5] Across the country such scenes are taking place nearly every day. "Open resistance to the draft," says columnist Clayton Fritchey, "is greater than at any time since the Civil War." Altogether the Selective Service System lists 15,310 "delinquents," men who have not responded to calls or correspondence from their draft boards. More than 22,000 men (not counting veterans) have won classification as conscientious objectors.

[6] The Selective Service System, like most operations of our government, relies to a large degree on voluntary cooperation; compulsion can go just so far. Now, for the first time in living memory, a sizable number of Americans are refusing to cooperate. The draft evaders, or "noncooperators," as some call themselves, vary tremendously in background. There are simple Mennonite farm boys as well as scholars with Ph.D.'s. There are Negroes from the ghetto and boys from America's richest families. Politically, they range from Maoists to Kennedy Democrats to Goldwater Republicans. It is possible, however, to group these young men in six major categories.

[7] The first is composed of those men who have gone to prison for their antidraft activity. These are the élite of draft-dodger society, the folk heroes of the resistance movement. Typical of them is Fred Moore, Jr., who was back on the antiwar picket lines just two days after completing his two-year sentence at the Allenwood Federal Prison Camp. Moore is a Quaker and a follower of Mahatma Gandhi. He regards himself as an out-and-out pacifist and says he would not even defend himself if attacked.

[8] In 1962 Moore's draft board classified him 1-A. That prompted him to apply for conscientious objector status so that instead of soldiering he could work in a civilian hospital or a social-service agency. In April, 1964, he received the 1-O classification he had asked for. "I had a strange reaction to the notice," Moore says. "I had no feeling of relief or gladness. Instead, I had the feeling that I was a moral coward, and that I had ended up cooperating with the Selective Service System in order to get special status for myself." He sent his classification card back to his draft board, and went on trial for draft evasion on October 21, 1965. The trial lasted three hours. Moore was found guilty and sentenced to two years in the federal penitentiary. In April, 1967, he was released seven months early on automatic "good time." He could have been released earlier, but he refused to cooperate with the parole system.

[9] Moore already has burned his new 1-O draft card, which was sent to him after he got out of jail, and he fully expects to be prosecuted a second and maybe even a third time. He says, almost casually, "I'm perfectly willing to go to jail for my beliefs." A Justice Department official says, "This boy is either nuts or so goddam sincere you have to respect him—but what can we do but throw the book at him again?"

[10] Less sincere and more elusive is the second category of draft evaders, "the Underground." These are the young men, registered and unregistered, who hide out in the ghettos and hippie colonies of the major American cities. No one in the Government will even guess at how many of them there are, but the Central Committee for Conscientious Objectors in Philadelphia estimates that they probably number in the thousands.

[11] In New York's East Village, the Underground member named Scuby was sitting in a delicatessen eating a pastrami sandwich. "Man," he said, "there are fifty of us within two blocks of here." A few minutes before, the two FBI men had passed him without recognizing him; they were showing his picture to shopkeepers and asking for Johnson. But the picture was not recent, and Scuby now has a full, reddish beard and wears dark glasses.

[12] Scuby doesn't participate in hippie demonstrations or antiwar protests. "The idea is to play it cool," he said, "and never do anything to call attention to yourself. You never know who's a fink for the feds." Scuby expressed no convictions about pacifism or the Vietnam War. He simply said, "I got better things to do than get shot at by a bunch of Viet Congs."

[13] Many of the young men in the third major category of draft resisters— those who leave the country—share Scuby's nonideological live-and-let-live attitude. Canada is a natural haven for these young men. Some flee to France or South America, but most find it simplest to cross the Canadian border, knowing that Canadians on the whole are not enthusiastic about the Vietnam War, and that Canada will extradite criminals only for offenses also illegal in Canada—since Canada has no draft, draft evasion is not a crime there.

[14] One of the more impressive of the refugees is John Phillips, a tall, blond, 22-year-old Quaker from Iowa. Phillips' pacifism is founded in his

religion, and ordinarily he would have had little trouble obtaining the conscientious-objector classification he applied for. But he bewildered the five farmers on his rural draft board; he was the first objector they had encountered, and they didn't know what to make of him. "They called me a coward and a communist," Phillips says, "and when they learned I had covered the Selma, Alabama, civil-rights march as a photographer, they said, 'Oh, so you went down there to help those niggers.' I told them I'd go to Vietnam as a combat photographer, anything so I wouldn't have to kill, but they didn't believe me. For the first time in my life I broke down and cried."

[15] Phillips filed an appeal and went so far as to report for his preinduction physical examination. He spent the night in a barracks where the other draftees—until they were stopped by an officer—tried forcibly to shave him from head to toe. That decided Phillips. He is a photographer for an agency of the Canadian government.

[16] But this attitude is not a common one in Toronto, where a large number of the refugees go. Most of them have turned against their country completely. They make statements like "They ought to tear down the Statue of Liberty because it doesn't mean anything any more." The left-wing draft dodgers say they don't want to live in the United States any more because it has become a "fascist dictatorship no better than Hitler's Germany." The right-wingers say they have fled from "a collective tyranny no better than Soviet Russia."

[17] The war resisters in the fourth category do not generally enjoy the luxury of escape. These are the young men who have already entered the armed forces and then decided they couldn't fight in Vietnam. The Department of Defense says it has about 400 applications pending. The Central Committee for Conscientious Objectors insists, on the basis of its correspondence from servicemen seeking legal help, that the figure is much higher.

[18] One of the most interesting cases in this category involved Michael Wittels, who joined the Army Reserves in 1962. His six months of active duty at Fort Knox were uneventful. "But suddenly," Wittels told me, "the whole thing jumped up and hit me in the face. An instructor was demonstrating a new rifle, and he said. 'This weapon can tear a hole the size of a fist in a man.' At that moment I knew I could never kill—that I was a conscientious objector at heart."

[19] Wittels finished his active duty, but in June, 1965, he sought legal advice from the Friends Peace Committee and learned that he could apply for a conscientious-objector discharge. On August 25, 1965, he turned it in to his company commander. The next March the application was turned down. Then he was demoted from Pfc. to Private and, as a punishment, was ordered to report to Fort Knox for 45 days of active duty. He did so, arriving in civilian clothes. He explained his position to his new company commander. "He was very kind and polite," said Wittels, "but he didn't know what to do about me."

[20] After three days, according to Wittels, the captain gave him a direct order to put on his uniform and report for duty. When Wittels respectfully refused, he was taken to the stockade, where a sergeant told him, "We've had your kind in here before, and we're going to break you." He was stripped of his shirt, shoes, and socks and locked in "The Box," a 6-by-8-foot isolation cell with nothing in it but a Bible and a steel slab for a bunk. The guards kept him standing until 2 A.M., when he was sent to take a shower. When he got back to the cell, his blanket was gone. "You don't want that blanket. It says U.S. Army on it." Wittels says he was in "The Box" for three days and then was put in a 24-man cell with the general prison population. There were eight other C.O.'s in the stockade. Two weeks later he went on trial, was found guilty and sentenced to six months at hard labor.

[21] On February 6, 1967, Wittels was released from the stockade. He went back to his Fort Knox company where an officer again ordered him to put on his uniform and report to a duty station. Again Wittels refused, and he was returned to the stockade. This time Wittels faced a general court-martial and a sentence of five years at Fort Leavenworth. He was made a maximum-custody prisoner, often with handcuffs and an armed guard.

[22] But Wittels' mother had appealed to a congressman who demanded that the Army investigate. In July, 1967, he received a general discharge "under honorable conditions . . . by reason of conscientious objection." Later one of the Fort Knox stockade guards wrote to him: "What you went through here took more guts than going to Vietnam."

[23] Wittels could have avoided his ordeal if he had obtained conscientious-objector status *before* going into the Army. This type of war resistance is perfectly legal. The more than 220,000 men who have been classified as C.O.'s by their draft boards make up the fifth and sixth categories of war resisters—the two kinds of legitimate C.O.'s recognized by the Selective Service System.

[24] One kind is the men who are classified 1-A-O. The 1-A-O's—there are 4,500 of them—go into the Army as draftees along with the 1-A's, but they are not required to handle weapons, and they perform only noncombatant duties, usually in the Medical Corps. Members of churches such as the Seventh-Day Adventist almost automatically get 1-A-O status from their draft boards when they apply for it; others have to prove their case.

[25] Getting to be a 1-O, the other type of legitimate conscientious objector, is a bit more complicated. The 1-O does not serve in the Army but puts in two years of so-called "alternative service" as a civilian. The type of work he does is severely restricted and must be approved by the draft board. Usually it's duty of some sort in a civilian hospital or social-service agency. Although 1-O's outnumber 1-A-O's by about four to one, some draft boards refuse to give the classification at all, even to bona fide members of pacifist religions; the feeling is that anyone taking such a stand is either a coward or a traitor. All the conscientious objector can do then is appeal. Appeals can be expensive

and those who do not have the money often become draft dodgers even though they are anxious and willing to fulfill their obligation by doing legitimate "alternative service."

[26] Robert Whitford, a young Quaker from Wisconsin who is doing his service at Casa Central, a social-service agency for the Spanish-speaking poor in Chicago, said, "I'm lucky. Most draft boards will approve nothing but bedpan handling in hospitals." He also said, "Many of my friends in the resistance think I'm copping out. They say I should have gone to jail. Why is going to jail better than doing something constructive for society?"

[27] As Whitford's comment suggests, the war resisters often disagree with each other. The 1-O's consider the 1-A-O's to be "cop outs," and the resistance people, those who are awaiting jail sentences, feel similarly about the 1-O's. All three groups revile the Underground and the refugees in Canada as lacking courage and "thinking only of themselves instead of the issues." The resisters who follow Gandhi's teachings believe that the only workable program is to fill the jails with sincere, educated, nonviolent war resisters who peacefully turn in their draft cards—until troubled public opinion forces the Government to change its policies.

[28] There is no question that resistance is spreading—especially among the more highly educated. Jeremy Mott, a Harvard student from New Jersey, was safely at work in a Church of the Brethren hospital as a 1-O, when he burned his draft card publicly in New York and helped found the group called Chicago Area Draft Resisters. He is now awaiting his arrest and jail sentence.

[29] David McCarroll, who has degrees from Princeton and the University of Virginia, is in medical training as a 1-A-O at Fort Sam Houston. In the presence of his commanding officer he told me, "I'm totally against the war in Vietnam, and if I'm sent there I'll have to make up my mind about going to prison instead."

[30] Even some of the runaways to Canada are returning to the United States in order to make a less comfortable, more forceful protest. When I interviewed 25-year-old Tom Zimmerman from Kansas, he was teaching in a Toronto high school and seemed happy. But on December 5 he appeared in the U.S. Attorney's office in Kansas City. He could get up to five years in prison for draft evasion. "I felt impotent in Canada," Zimmerman says. "Being up there just created tension for me, because all of us in Toronto were out of the mainstream of protest. I want to preserve my conscience, so I am ready to go to prison."

[31] As a Justice Department official told me, "I know most Americans wouldn't agree, and certainly the fighting men in Vietnam don't think so, but these boys, some of our brightest young men, represent the agony of our age."

DISCUSSION

1. Why does this essay begin with four different scenes—short specific accounts of something happening? What similarities are there between the events in paragraphs 1, 2, 3, and 4? What differences?

2. How many main categories does this classification system use? Are there any subdivisions? Why does the introduction include only four scenes?

3. Find the transitions the writer uses to move from one category to another. Are all the transitions alike? Do you think they are all equally effective? Why or why not?

4. How does the conclusion tie back to the introduction? To the main point of the paper?

5. This article would be considerably shorter if the writer had summarized what some of the people he interviewed said, instead of quoting them directly. Would you have enjoyed a short article more? Why? What is the effect of quoting exactly what they said? What have these quotations to do with the title?

6. Do you think the writer is sympathetic or unsympathetic to draft resisters? Justify what you say by referring to the essay.

Would the Real John Q. Customer Please Stand Up?

ESP: extrasensory perception
sanctuary: a safe place
idiosyncracy: odd personality trait

[1] Whoever said that the "customer is always right" must have always been a customer. But anyone who has experienced punching the keys of a cash register of any grocery store can sympathize with the poor grocery clerks. [2] They are exposed to the showers of sneezes which the customer excuses as his latest allergy. They are in constant danger of attack by the nation's latest popular virus. And they are firm believers that cigarette and cigar smoking is injurious to their health, especially when they receive the smoke second hand.

[3] A clerk could identify his customers and win a blue ribbon by smell alone. The picric acid odor of some customers is so great that you wonder what they do with all the soap they buy. Other customers are so heavily perfumed they smell like walking gardenias. Then there is the fanatic animal lover. This customer has so many dogs or cats that he not only walks and talks like his pets but also smells of them.

(Used by permission of Marie M. Schaper.)

[4] The grocery clerk not only has a good smell receptor but he also possesses ESP (according to some customers, anyway). While he is bagging the order he is told explicitly, "Don't squeeze the bockwurst." Or, maybe, "Don't put the hamburger on the bottom because if there is one thing I hate is to eat hamburger that is pressed too tight." (This is said all in one breath, of course.) Exactly how is the clerk going to pick out the bockwurst or hamburger from a bunch of five or six neatly wrapped, pink-paper bundles?

[5] Although the cash register does the adding, subtracting, and figures the tax for the grocery clerk, he also has to be an expert accountant. One lady is married to such a miser that she has two charges for the same bill. The original bill is hers and she gives a padded one to her husband.

[6] Prices also make the clerk's head spin. If oranges sell for 59¢ a dozen, how much are three? How much are four? Think quickly! Do you divide by three or is it four? Quickly now! The customer is waiting!

[7] The under-six group of customers are most fascinating. They will spend five minutes or longer debating what to buy with the nickel grandma gave to them. Or the little one comes with a note hurriedly scribbled by mother (probably when she was in the midst of changing little brother's diaper) that you cannot read. He, of course, doesn't know what mommy wants. Or, maybe a little one comes into the store without a note. He says he wants "something paper." Does he want paper towels, bathroom paper, wax paper or paper plates? No, he wants "the one that has words on it and Daddy reads every night."

[8] Some customers constantly have to know how much they pay for an item. Out-of-season vegetables are highly priced. But why do they say they don't want them *after* you have already rung them?

[9] The list of different types of customers is endless. But finally after close-up time in the private sanctuary of the employees, the clerks have their well-earned laugh about the idiosyncracies of their customers. Upon leaving the store the clerks tuck the peculiarities of the customers tightly under their hats and go home to enjoy a pleasant evening with their families.

DISCUSSION

1. In how many different ways does the writer classify grocery store customers? What are they?

2. Why do you think she chose the categories she did? What other point of view might she have chosen? How might you as a customer have classified other customers? How might you have classified grocery clerks?

3. How does the writer select the details to make her experience as a grocery clerk more vivid?

4. How does the conclusion remind us of the method of classification that is used? How does the conclusion tie in with the introduction?

5. Is the title effective? If you think so, why?

6. This essay classifies people according to behavior. Could you classify students in the lunchroom line in a similar way? Students waiting to register? Students studying (sitting) in the library?

A Comparative Teenology of Seattle

The species known as *Seattle contemporary teenager* can be broken down into four subspecies: *Hip, Quasi-hip, Hood* and *Straight.* It should be emphasized that the listings under each category are not comprehensive, but limited to those items which best typify each subspecies. (Under "Favorite National Recording Groups," the Beatles, the Rolling Stones, Cream and Bob Dylan have been omitted because their popularity cuts across the board.) Parents seeking enlightenment from the chart should not try to arrive at hard and fast classifications for their own offspring. For one thing, pure examples of each subspecies are extremely rare (most teenagers combine characteristics of several); for another, given the unreliability of teenagers in general, pigeonholing your progeny can be a risky business. Tell your teenage son he's a *straight,* and it's a good bet that the next time you see him, he'll have metamorphosed into a *hip.*

	Hips	Quasi-hips	Hoods	Straights
Political leaning	Radical or revolutionary	Vague unhappiness with "the system"	None	Liberal to radical conservative
Socio-economic class	Middle	Middle and upper-middle	Lower and lower-middle	Middle and upper-middle
Hairstyle (boys)	Shoulder-length	Over ears, thick in back	Greased and combed back or longish in front, short in back and on sides	Neat, "Princeton"-style; if long, only in front— never in back or on sides
Hairstyle (girls)	Long and straight	Ditto	Teased, beehivey or long and straight	Straight—either short or long
Places visited on Saturday night	The Last Exit, Eagles Auditorium, the mountains	Trolly Club, Eagles, "The Ave"	Dick's, Herfy's, Tiffany's, Alki Beach	A movie, Dick's, Herfy's, a private party
Radio stations listened to	KOL-FM, KYAC, KING-FM, KRAB	KOL, KJR, KOL-FM	KOL, KJR	KOL, KJR
Local publications read	Helix, Karma, parts of Seattle	Ditto	None	School paper
National publications read	Berkeley Barb, Rolling Stone, L.A. Free Press	Time, Life, Newsweek, Look, Rolling Stone	None	Time, Life, Newsweek, Look

	Hips	Quasi-hips	Hoods	Straights
Favorite national recording groups	Jethro Tull, The Byrds, Flying Burrito Bros., Youngbloods, Butterfield Blues Band	The Doors, Canned Heat, Jimi Hendrix, Steppenwolf, Big Brother & Holding Co., Vanilla Fudge	Johnny Rivers, Paul Revere & the Raiders, Tommy James & the Shondells	Ditto, plus Simon & Garfunkel and Glen Campbell
Favorite record shops	Discount Records, Campus Music, U.W. Bookstore	Ditto	White Front, House of Values, Bon Marche	Tape Town, Warehouse of Music, Bon Marche
Clothing shops frequented (boys)	Salvation Army, Goodwill, Bluebeard's, Gypsy, T.J.'s	Bernie's, Bluebeard's, Don's	Third Avenue Men's Shop, Bernie's, Penney's	Arnstein's, Yankee Peddler, Bon Marche
Clothing shops frequented (girls)	Arabesque, La Tienda, Goodwill, Salvation Army, Gypsy*	Jay Jacobs, Bon Marche	Penney's, Sears, Jay Jacobs	Nordstrom-Best, Frederick & Nelson, Bon Marche, Jay Jacobs
Recreational activities	Getting stoned, going to rock concerts and avant-garde art galleries	Getting stoned, going to rock concerts, skiing	Drinking, cruising in cars, going to dance halls	Drinking, partying, skiing, playing tennis
The High Schools Sorted Out**	**Straight** Forest Ridge, Holy Angels, Holy Names, Holy Rosary, Immaculate — **Hood-Hip** Ballard, Franklin	**Straight-Hip** Helen Bush, Lakeside — **Straight-Quasi-hip** Bellevue, Mercer Island, St. Nicholas — **Hood-Hip-Straight** Lincoln, Queen Anne	**Straight-Hood** East Side schools (except Bellevue), Highline schools, Ingraham, Nathan Hale, Seattle Prep, Shoreline schools — **Hip-Hood** Garfield	**Hood-Straight** Blanchet, Cleveland, J.F.K. Memorial, O'Dea, Rainier Beach, Sealth, West Seattle — **Quasi-hip** Roosevelt

* Among hip girls, it is more hip to make your own clothes or get them out of grandmother's chest than to shop for clothes.

** These Seattle-area high schools are classified according to their *general* character, which in most cases is highly mixed.

From *Seattle Magazine,* August 1969, p. 25.

WRITING TOPICS
FOR CLASSIFICATION

Classify according to kind:

cheeses	trees
beverages	native plants
meat	schools
vegetables	musical instruments
dwellings	holidays
recreation	vacations
books	planes
movies	boats
games	traffic violations
game animals	killings
game birds	TV programs
fish	magazines

"Where do you stash the porno, Cookie?"

Drawing by W. Miller. Reprinted with permission of *The New Yorker* Magazine.

Classify according to backgrounds:

place of birth	employment experience
racial origin	religious training
education	travel
length of residence	musical experience

Classify according to attitude toward:

the draft	race relations
the younger generation	education
personal appearance	law and order
labor	religion
political parties	United Nations

Classify according to how we use them:

animals	clothes
plants	cars
holidays	books
policemen	furniture
libraries	words

Classify according to behavior:

waitresses	guests
service station attendants	hostesses
used car salesmen	neighbors
dentists	automobile drivers
doctors	women at a bargain counter
sales clerks	men at a prize fight
shoppers in a grocery store	students taking a test
first sergeants	parents

readings on analysis 5

ANALYSIS

Sometimes, in order to explain something, we have to analyze it. Analysis means breaking something down or taking something apart to find out how it works. A biologist uses analysis when he explains how the blood, the heart, the arteries, the veins, and the capillaries all function together to make up the circulatory system. The chairman of a committee to plan the club picnic considers such separate items as food, cost, place to hold the picnic, the entertainment and cleanup, and special arrangements in case of rain.

Analysis can be of two kinds, *operational* and *causal*. An automobile designer is using operational analysis when he writes an article explaining *how* a steam engine can make an automobile move, but the automobile mechanic who writes an explanation of what made Art Peters' steam car stop in the middle of the freeway is using causal analysis—he's explaining *why* it happened.

It's easier to see the difference between classification and analysis, both of which work with groups of things, if we remember that classification sorts out a collection of similar things, whereas analysis begins with one thing or process or event and then examines the parts that make it up, whether these parts are the separate elements that make it work, or the separate reasons that something happened. We could, for instance, *classify* weather instruments by sorting them into mercury thermometers, barometers, barographs, and hygrometers. But if we wanted to explain the operation of one of these instruments, the mercury thermometer, we would *analyze* it:

> The mercury thermometer consists of mercury confined in a capillary tube from which all air has been removed. The volume of the mercury changes with changes in temperature. Fixed points on the thermometer are the melting point of pure ice and the boiling point of pure water under a pressure of 760 mm. of mercury. The freezing point is 0° on the centigrade thermometer and 32° on the Fahrenheit.

The necessary parts in a mercury thermometer, then, are four: an airless capillary tube, mercury, a freezing point, and a boiling point.

In much the same way, a biologist explains how birds can sing; he looks at the combination of physical structure and air vibration:

> A special charm of the birds is their songs. These are produced by means of a structure called a *syrinx* (Gr. "pipe") which is located not at the upper end of the windpipe *(trachea)* as is the *larynx* of mammals, but at the lower end, at the point where the bronchi branch off. The syrinx contains a fold on each side which, when stretched, vibrates with the flow of exhaled air as do the vocal cords of a mammal. It is most highly developed in the perching birds,

which are therefore often spoken of as "songbirds." (Excerpt from GEN-
ERAL BIOLOGY, 3rd Ed. by Leslie A. Kenoyer, *et al.* [Harper & Row].
Reprinted by permission of Harper & Row, Publishers.)

In fact, when we need to understand *how* anything works, from breaking
the sound barrier to using steam to run a car, we use *operational analysis.*

Filtering

scheme: method; plan
particles: small bits; pieces
percolator: kind of coffee pot

[1] One of the oldest schemes for separating large
things from smaller ones involves the use of filters or
sieves. Sand is separated from gravel this way. Coffee
grounds can be separated from the liquid with a
filter. The most essential feature of any filter is that
the hole sizes be such that all the substance below
the desired size can pass through the filter while the
other particles of greater size are held back. But that
is not enough.

*Introduction: shows
that the paper will ex-
plain how filters work
and
tells the first important
thing*

[2] In a coffee pot, the water passes through the
holes but the coffee grounds with diameters greater
than the holes are held back. At first glance, it would
appear that as long as the holes are smaller than the
coffee grains, the percolater will do its job. But this
is not really true. If the holes are too small, the flow
of water will be so slow that it might take an hour or
two for enough water to pass over the grounds to
make the coffee. Eventually, you would have a pot
of brown liquid resembling coffee in appearance at
least, but it probably would not taste very good, and
you would be late for work. You might say that the
difficulty of the slow flow through the small holes
could be overcome by making more holes. This is
true enough, but it represents only a short-term solu-

*Explains operation by a
familiar example
and
tells the second impor-
tant thing*

From THE UNCLEAN SKY, by Louis J. Battan. Copyright © 1966 by Educational Services Incorporated. Reprinted by permission of Doubleday & Company, Inc.

tion. Small holes become clogged more quickly than the larger ones and, after a time, the filter would be completely useless.

[3] In general, the characteristics of the coffee pot sieve are not very different from almost any other filter. You always have to consider the hole or *pore* size, as it is called, in relation to the size and quantity of the particles you wish to capture.

Main point re-emphasized: holes in the filter must be exactly the right size

DISCUSSION

1. Is this essay an operational or a causal analysis? Why?

2. The main idea sentence is the last sentence in the essay. What is gained by putting it there rather than in the first paragraph?

3. Why does the author spend so much time discussing how a coffee pot works?

4. How does Battan use transitions to take the reader from the first point about filters to the second, and from a mistaken idea about the second point to showing why that idea is a mistake? Look especially at the last sentence of paragraph 1, and the third sentence of paragraph 2. What other kind of transition does Battan use?

5. Battan's use of transitions helps make this essay very clear. What else does he do to make his writing easy to understand?

The Sound Barrier

supersonic: anything moving faster than the speed of sound
subsonic: anything moving slower than the speed of sound
cope: deal with; handle a problem

[1] Ask any youngster who is interested in flying and he'll tell you that the "sound barrier" has been successfully broken. This statement, which has appeared in print repeatedly, is oversimplified. The sound barrier does not need to be "broken" by brute force like a brick wall in the sky.

From SATELLITES, ROCKETS AND OUTER SPACE by Willy Ley. Copyright © 1957, 1958 by Willy Ley. Adapted by arrangement with The New American Library, Inc., New York.

[2] "But," I have often been told, "I live not far from a jet fighter base and I can hear them break through the sound barrier."

[3] Let's have a quick look at what the sound barrier really is like. Sound, at sea level, travels at about 765 miles per hour. Anything that moves faster than that is called supersonic; anything that moves slower is called subsonic. Now, if an airplane flies at half the speed of sound, the air moves over and under its wings in patterns that are now well understood. If an airplane flies at one and a half times the speed of sound the air moves around its wings and tail in a different pattern. Experts know pretty well now what this pattern is and how to cope with it. But if an airplane flies *near* the speed of sound you get both patterns at once, and that is the real difficulty. You cannot expect a plane to cope with a supersonic pattern on top of the wing and a subsonic pattern below the tail. Hence the speed of sound must be avoided; either you fly a good deal faster or a good deal slower. And if you have to make the transition from one to the other, the faster you can do it the better off you are.

[4] There is an additional complication and that is that the speed of sound is not the same everywhere. Eight miles up it may be only 660 miles per hour. The speed of sound depends on the temperature of the air. It is slower in cold air. Higher up the air is colder; it also happens to be thinner. The density of the air does not matter, however, only its temperature.

[5] Now what about that "boom" you can hear? Very simple. If a subsonic plane approaches you, you hear the noise it makes increase gradually and it is loudest when the plane is overhead. But if the plane travels as fast as its own sound, all the noise it produces (no matter which way) hits your eardrums at once. You can get that effect even if the plane is still a little bit slower than sound; it has nothing to do with the moment of passing that precise speed.

DISCUSSION

1. How does the introduction arouse the reader's interest?

2. Why is it necessary to define "subsonic" and "supersonic"?

3. What things are involved when the sound barrier is "broken"?

4. What additional information is offered in paragraph 4?

5. How does the conclusion tie back into the first two paragraphs?

6. How is it made clear that the essay is an operational analysis about breaking the sound barrier, not directions on how to do it?

The Little Engine That Could—
And Did

puny: small; weak
devoid: without
malfunction: failure to work right
embarked: started out

[1] Compared with the mighty Saturn 5, which generated 7,500,000 lbs. of thrust in its first stage alone, the little engine seemed puny indeed. But the importance of the Apollo spacecraft's 20,500-lb.-thrust Service Propulsion System (SPC) engine was far out of proportion to its 3½-ft. length. The engine's faultless operation made the difference not only between a relatively simple moon shot and last week's sophisticated mission, but also between life and death for the astronauts.

[2] Had the SPS engine failed to ignite, or burned too briefly during the attempt to place Apollo into lunar orbit, the spacecraft would have looped around the back of the moon and headed directly back toward earth. If the engine had cut off during one crucial 30-second interval of the scheduled burn, Apollo would have been left in an unstable orbit and crashed into the surface of the moon. And, if the astronauts had not succeeded in restarting the engine after orbiting the moon, they would have been left stranded in space without hope of rescue. This point was not lost on Astronaut Borman. Shortly before launch, he said of the SPS engine: "It simply has to work at that point. . . ."

[3] To ensure reliability, engineers tried to make the engine as simple as possible. Devoid of any frills, the SPS engine consists basically of a combustion chamber and propellant (fuel and oxidizer) tanks. When valves to these tanks are opened, fuel flows from one tank and oxidizer to the other to meet in the combustion chamber, pushed by pressurized helium that takes the place of potentially troublesome pumps. Because the propellants are hypergolic—they react chemically and ignite on contact—no ignition system is needed. And to avoid including a complicated throttle, the engine burns only at its fully rated thrust of 20,500 lbs. or not at all.

[4] In reliability tests that extended over a period of five years, Aerojet and NASA technicians fired SPS engines some 3,200 times without a malfunction before qualifying them for manned flight. Although the total firing time on the

Apollo 8 mission was scheduled to take no more than seven or eight minutes, the combustion chamber was designed to operate for 12½ minutes. During tests, it actually held up for more than 30 minutes without burning out.

[5] During the flight of Apollo 6, the SPS engine took over from an S-4B stage that failed to restart, and by itself propelled the unmanned spacecraft to an altitude of more than 13,000 miles. On Apollo 7, its first manned flight, it was started eight times. Thus, when Borman, Lovell and Anders embarked on their mission, they had a pretty good idea that their little engine could perform its tasks flawlessly.

DISCUSSION

1. This essay begins with a double comparison between two engines. What things are being compared in the first part of the paragraph? What things are compared in the last part?

2. What is the purpose of paragraph 2? How does this paragraph lead into the actual operational analysis which comes in paragraph 3? Could paragraph 2 have been left out without spoiling the point of the article?

3. Paragraph 2 begins "Had the . . . ," a fairly formal way to say "If the engine had . . ." Do you think the paragraph would have been better balanced if this first sentence had begun with "if" as the next two sentences do?

4. The first sentence of paragraph 3 is the main idea sentence. Since we already know that "the engine" means the Apollo SPS, all the main idea sentence needs to say about it is that it is "as simple as possible." What necessary parts does the engine have? What operations are necessary to make these parts work?

5. Paragraph 3 also mentions some parts that the Apollo SPS does *not* have. Why does the writer tell his readers about these parts?

6. What is the purpose of paragraphs 4 and 5? How do they relate to the introduction?

7. Although this article appeared in a news magazine intended for ordinary readers, some of the language is very technical. Can you think of any way it could be simplified and still be accurate? What does the writer do to help readers who are not engineers?

Is There a Ford Steamer in Your Future?

torque: the power that can be exerted by a turning part
inaudible: can't be heard
actuated: started; made to work
rupture: a tear or a break
compatible: can work with

[1] On the outside it looks like any other brand-new Ford. But twist the key and you hear a whomp as the burner ignites. The flame hisses contentedly while you wait 15 seconds for full steam to build up in the boiler. You shift into forward and step a little too heavily on the accelerator and the rear wheels spin wildly. The engine puts out maximum torque from stall, so you must tread lightly. You have to change a few driving habits this year (1975) as the proud owner of one of the first steam cars off the Ford production lines.

[2] Whether or not there is a Ford steamer in the future, no one really knows at the present time, but the company isn't taking any chances. Ford recently invested an initial $1 million in the experimental steam project of Thermo Electron Corp., Waltham, Mass. Thermo Electron, a small but growing company, has several experimental steam engines chugging quietly away in its cramped, temporary quarters. One is a 25-lb., 100 watt, ½-hp portable generator. The Army is interested in it because of its quietness; stand 30 ft. away and you can't hear it running. There's also a larger, 1.5-kilowatt, 3-hp unit powerful enough to run a golf cart. It weighs 150 lbs. complete with military accessories and is inaudible at 300 ft. The basic principles of this engine could be scaled up to power an Army tank. This is the power plant that could be developed for the Ford of the future. Here is how this engine works:

[3] A pump driven by a belt from the crankshaft forces water into the boiler. There, a burner (which burns kerosene, white gas, JP-4 jet fuel or Diesel fuel) heats the water past the boiling point. As the water turns to steam, it expands; the pressurized steam then is piped to the intake valves at the tops of the three cylinders and provides the force to push the pistons down for the power strokes.

[4] The spent steam is exhausted through the bottoms of the cylinders. In many earlier engines the steam was turned around and exhausted through

the tops of the cylinders; this was less efficient because, with the intake and exhaust close together, the cooler exhaust robs heat from the intake.

[5] Also, unlike most earlier steam engines, this one uses precise-acting poppet valves (like the ones in your car engine) rather than slide or reed valves. These poppet valves are actuated internally by the movement of the pistons. No camshaft. No rocker arms.

[6] Once exhausted from the cylinders, the steam is piped to the condenser, a component that looks and works much like a car radiator. It even has a geared down, crank-shaft-powered fan for added cooling. Here the steam cools and condenses back into water, and then starts a new cycle through the water pump.

[7] Because the water system is sealed, only about 2½ cups of water is required. If the system were open to the atmosphere, as in earlier engines, four or five times as much water would be needed. With so little water under pressure, a rupture in the boiler (highly unlikely) would cause only a harmless hiss rather than a dangerous explosion. Even if the engine were scaled up to automotive size, it would need far less water than did the old, explosive steam cars.

[8] The engine uses a positive-pressure lube system, with the oil pump powered by the crankshaft. An airtight seal keeps the oil and steam separated, allowing neither to become contaminated.

[9] In future engines the water may be replaced by a fluorocarbon (such as freon, the liquid used in refrigerators), and the conventional oil may be replaced with one of the new fluorinated oils that are compatible with the fluorocarbon. With mixing of the two no great problem, a simpler seal could be used between crankcase and cylinders.

[10] Fluorocarbons have another advantage: Their boiling and freezing points can be controlled. Water, on the other hand, freezes at an inconveniently high 32°F.; of course, it could be collected somewhere in the engine where its freezing would do no damage, but time-consuming thawing would be necessary to start the engine.

[11] Now that we're past the basics, let's get back to our Ford steam car of the future. What will it be like?

[12] It will be startlingly simple. Except for a glow-plug and a small battery to ignite the boiler, no ignition system will be needed. That's because, unlike the internal combustion engine, which requires a timed spark, the steam engine has a continuously burning external flame, like the gas jet on your stove. Such a flame is easier to control for clean burning because it isn't dependent on compression and other variables.

[13] Since torque remains constant from stall all the way through the normal operating range, the simplest transmission will suffice. It will have one reverse gear, and a neutral position for idling while the car is stopped.

[14] Actually, because of its torque characteristics, the engine could be stopped dead each time the car stops, thus eliminating the need for a clutch. The only drawback would be that in long traffic jams the car accessories

might drain the battery. The engine probably will have to idle to run the generator.

[15] One problem with steam engines is that the boiler builds up pressure relatively slowly. For the kind of accelerator response required in an automobile, the boiler will have to maintain constant pressure at all times; engine speed can then be varied sensitively with a throttle valve between the boiler and cylinders by controlling the flow of steam. Fuel consumption will still vary with load. As more power is required, steam flow will increase and the burner will have to work harder to maintain boiler pressure . . .

[16] Maintenance should be less expensive. After running their larger engine for 3,000 hours, Thermo Electron technicians needed an air gauge to detect any wear in the bore. The steam actually acts as a lubricant. Valves should also last longer, since they run much cooler and they aren't exposed to dusty outside air as they are in an internal combustion engine.

[17] The burner probably will have to be overhauled periodically (much like the oil burner in your home needs cleaning each fall). You'll need to do this about every 1,500 hours—which adds up to over two months of continuous, day-and-night running. And it's not a major job. Oil changes probably will be made as often as with internal combustion engines.

[18] Controls and instruments in the steamer will be similar to those in today's cars, except for added gauges or warning lights for boiler pressure, boiler temperature and condenser pressure . . .

[19] Whether or not there is a steam engine in your future, only time and technology will tell.

DISCUSSION

1. How far into the introduction do you have to read before you discover that this writer is discussing what might be rather than what is? How does he let you know? Why does the writer use this method of introducing his topic rather than a more straightforward statement?

2. What engine is being analyzed in paragraphs 3 and 8? Where does the writer stop telling what the working parts of the engine are? Where does he begin telling what ingredients are needed to make the parts work?

3. Paragraphs 3 through 8 also contain some comparisons. What are these comparisons? Why does the author include them?

4. What is the purpose of paragraphs 9 and 10? Of paragraph 11?

5. What is being explained in paragraphs 12 through 18? Is the main purpose of this section operational analysis or comparison? If you think it is analysis, what is being analyzed? If you think it is comparison, what is being compared?

6. Why does the writer talk about the Thermo Electron engine first?

7. Do you need to be an automotive engineer to understand paragraphs 2 through 8? Paragraphs 12 through 18? Which is easier to understand? Why?

We use operational analysis not only to show how machines work and natural events occur, but also to explain what steps men take in performing certain actions. Even though the operational analysis of a mercury thermometer lists the physical *parts* that must be present, and the following paragraph explains what *steps* a citizen must follow to obtain a driver's license, both of them are actually doing the same thing; explaining *how* something works:

> To operate a motor vehicle legally in this state, the applicant must do four things. First, he must obtain a score of 80 or better on a written examination covering the vehicle code. Second, he must demonstrate on a vision test that his depth perception and reading ability are adequate for safe driving. Third, he must take an actual driving test, in an inspected vehicle, to show that he can park, give the proper signals, and control the car in traffic. Finally, he must buy a license that contains his operator's number, so that the State Department of Motor Vehicles can keep a record of whatever violations he may incur.

Probably you will notice that this analysis of the process involved in getting a driver's license comes very close to giving directions. The main difference is that in giving directions the writer speaks directly to his readers, telling them how to do it successfully. He gives advice, and presumably what he writes will be useful only to people who are expecting to get drivers' licenses. In operational analysis, the writer outlines the process, but he does not necessarily expect his readers to get licenses themselves. He is merely explaining *how* it works, not telling people *what to do.*

For instance, most people who read the following article on dubbing films will never dub a film themselves. They read this operational analysis because they are curious about how the process works.

The Borrowed Voice

synchronization: making two or more things happen at exactly the same time
gesticulations: motions that convey, or help convey, meaning
mimics: motions without language

Reprinted from "The Borrowed Voice" by George A. von Ihering in the January 1969 issue of *Quinto Lingo,* pp. 60–61, by permission of Rodale Press, Inc.

[1] Of the two to four hundred foreign movies which every year are shown in France, Germany and Italy, practically all have been dubbed into the respective native language. The vast majority of European audiences do not care for subtitles, which distract the viewer from the action on the screen.

Introduction: what the topic is

[2] The early attempts at transforming foreign film dialogue into the native language were rather crude and clumsy. By and large, it was just a matter of having the native speaker begin and finish the translated text at the same time as the original actor, without regard to lip synchronization or speech rhythm.

Background of dubbing: early method

[3] Gradually, as recording techniques improved, dubbing procedures became more subtle and refined. First of all, lip movements were imitated as closely as possible. However, this goal was often attained at the expense of normal speech. The native language was tortured to the point of ridicule. No one in his right mind spoke the stilted language that came from the screen.

Disadvantages of this method

[4] Soon it became obvious that other factors are just as important, if not even more important, than sheer lip synchronization. Each language has its own tempo to be taken into account. Gesticulation and facial expressions which emphasize certain parts of the speech demand an equivalent in the transformed dialogue.

Needs not met by this method

[5] Nowadays, a variety of dubbing methods are used, but here is the customary procedure: First, the original film is shown to the principal dubbing team —the dialogue adapter or translator, the film editor or cutter, the director who eventually supervises and directs the recording, and his assistant who hires the speakers and technical personnel, and who is responsible for many administrative items.

Main idea sentence
and
First step in process

[6] After the picture has been seen by everyone concerned, its dialogue parts are cut up by the film editor in small pieces of about ten to twenty feet, depending on the difficulty of the dialogue. These pieces, called takes, are numbered, marked as such in the original script, and pasted into a loop with a few feet of blank film between the end and the beginning of the take.

Second step in process

[7] These individual loops are then projected on a screen where the dialogue adapter can watch that

Third step in process

particular fragment of the original from his desk
while he endeavors to find an adequate translation.
After listening a few times he switches off the sound
and tries to adapt a suitable text to the silent lip
motions and mimics on the screen.

[8] Once the text has been finished and mimeo-   Fourth step in process
graphed for the speakers to read and memorize it,
there follows the casting of the speakers of the different parts. These are usually professional actors.
Some are so much in demand that they have given
up stage work to make a career of dubbing.

[9] After the whole film has been shown to the cast,   Fifth step in process
recording starts in a large studio which has a normal
size screen on which the individual takes are projected, again as loops. To emulate the dispersed
sound effects of the original, the recording is mostly
done by several strategically placed microphones.
The director listens to several rehearsal runs of the
take before he gives his OK for the final recording.

[10] Depending on the length and difficulty of the   Sixth and last step in
dialogue and on the skill or thoroughness of the   process
director, with an average of 200 to 250 takes per
day, the recording of the entire film will be finished
in about three to five days time. Meanwhile the film
editor has begun the painstaking work of synchroniz-
ing dialogue tapes, film and the so-called I.T.'s
(International Tracks). The latter are the sound
tracks containing background music, noises and
other not-spoken sounds which have been recorded
separately during the actual shooting of the film.
When this work is completed the so-called "Mix" is
made in the studio, i.e., the exact combination of picture, dialogue and I.T.'s. At this final stage, the
director, sound engineer, and film editor make the
last corrections before the finished product is sent
to the printing laboratory to make the copies which
are later distributed to the theaters . . .

[11] And in the end, someone in the audience always   Conclusion
complains about the inaccurate translation.

DISCUSSION

1. What does the writer accomplish in his introduction? Can you tell what
   the topic of the paper will be? Can you tell what the purpose is? Can you
   tell the main idea? How?

2. What is the writer doing in paragraphs 2, 3, and 4—analyzing a process or explaining what the results of a process were? If you think he is analyzing, what are the parts in the process?

3. Each part of this operation is given a separate paragraph. What are the transitions that connect the paragraphs? Are they link or echo transitions?

4. Does paragraph 11 make this article sound finished? How? What is there in paragraphs 1 through 4 that justifies this concluding comment?

5. The author of this article has dubbed more than 200 English movies into German. Does an awareness of his background help you to understand the conclusion? How?

6. In the foreign movies you have seen, have you noticed that the lip movements sometimes did not fit the English words? Have you ever noticed that what the actors were saying didn't seem to fit their expressions? Or that what they said sounded stilted? If you have noticed these problems, which bothered you the most? Why?

The Language of Space

distribute: to arrange objects or people within a space
rigidized: tightly organized
proximity: relative closeness
verticality: distance measured in height
territoriality: a sense of personal area or territory

[1] We use space to communicate with one another. The distance between you and someone else may determine the nature of the communication. If you are a few inches away from someone's ear, chances are that you will whisper and the nature of the communication will be "secret." At a distance of several feet, the communication may still be private, but its tone and nature will have changed. The change is even greater if you are speaking to a large audience. Here the nature of the message may be determined in part by the distance between you and the most distant member of the audience.

[2] Space "speaks" also in the way that we distribute ourselves in a classroom, bus or lecture hall. As long as there is optional space, most people will tend to sit as far from strangers as possible. The distance they select to

Reprinted with permission of The Macmillan Company from *Communications: The Transfer of Meaning* by Don Fabun. Copyright © 1965, 1968 by Kaiser Aluminum and Chemical Corporation.

separate themselves from others in the audience—and from the speaker—is in itself a form of communication. In rigidized institutions, such as the military service, the distance to be maintained between persons of different ranks may even be a matter of regulation.

[3] There is a cultural difference in the way we distribute ourselves in formal space—as in an office building. Thus Europeans are most likely to put their desks in the center of the room, and authority flows outward from the center. Proximity to the center is one way of saying, "That person is important." Americans, on the other hand, tend to distribute their working space around the edges of a room, leaving the center open for traffic and casual communication. Another way that Americans communicate through their use of space is in size and verticality. Most often, the size of an office will "say" something about the importance of the man who occupies it; the larger the space, the more important the man. Similarly, for many business and government departments and bureaus, the vertical distance between ground level and a person's office may act as an indication of his importance. Usually executive offices are located at or near the top of the building they occupy. Occupying a large room at the top of a building not only "says" a great deal about the person occupying it, but in part determines the kind of communication that can be carried on with him.

[4] In addition to the cultural and social communications through the use of space, each of us has spaces we feel are our "own"—a favorite chair, a seat on the bus, a place at table, or even a favorite table in a restaurant. When someone (usually unknowingly) occupies one of these "private" spaces, we may become annoyed or upset. One is reminded of Goldilocks and the Three Bears: each successive violation of the bears' private space made communication more difficult.

[5] The private space that each of us has is sometimes called "territoriality." It is as if we walked around with a plastic bubble hovering over us. When this space is violated—when someone gets "too close"—we may become tense or even hostile, and this will affect the nature of the communication that is possible. Most Americans and Englishmen prefer a certain distance for normal discourse. They feel more comfortable if a certain space between themselves and the other person is maintained. People of Latin descent apparently like a smaller distance. You can imagine a situation where a Latin talks to an American, and the American keeps retreating, trying to maintain his "proper" distance, all the way down a long hall.

[6] In some situations—say riding on a crowded subway or bus—we are willing to sacrifice our personal territoriality and allow strangers to crowd up against us. We feel uncomfortable about it, but in the interests of getting someplace we temporarily allow our plastic "bubble" to shrink up about us. Such proximity in other situations would be intolerable. How close we allow others to get to us is one measure of our relationship to them, and helps establish the kind of communication that can take place. When we are face to face with another person, it is well to remember that he has his own

plastic bubble surrounding him and that violating his territory by crowding too close may affect our ability to communicate with him.

[7] As we travel more or are engaged in business with people from other cultures, it is well to remind ourselves that others see and attach importance to things that we might not see or attach significance to.

DISCUSSION

1. What aspect of "space communication" is taken up in the first paragraph? In the second? The third? The fourth? From your answers, can you discover what order Fabun has followed in this essay? It is neither chronological nor order of importance.

2. This essay deals with a fairly abstract topic: how space "communicates." What does Fabun do to keep it from being neither general nor dull? In your answer, refer to specific parts of the essay.

3. Two methods of explanation are used in this essay. First, the author is analyzing *how* space communicates; second, he is classifying several different ways by which it can communicate. Make a chart showing what these different ways are.

4. Can you classify your fellow students according to the way they use space in the classroom? Can you classify the teachers you have had by the same system?

5. Although the last paragraph concludes the essay with a recommendation ("... it is well to ..."), would you say that Fabun is trying to persuade us or to give us a possible way to use the information in the essay? Explain.

6. You might want to try some experiments based on what you now know about how space "talks":
   a. What happens when you rearrange the chairs in your classroom? When you move from your regular chair at the dinner table at home? When you talk close to someone? When you move back from someone during a conversation?
   b. What kind of office does the president of your college have? How big? How high? Does it follow the European style, located at the center of things, or the American style, removed and isolated? How about the office of the Dean? The Assistant Dean? The faculty? Custodial help?
   c. How does space show importance or intimacy at your home? Where you work? In business or government offices that you have visited?

Violence: The Inner Circle

tractable: peaceable; easily managed
premise: unproved belief
potential: possibility
escalate: increase continuously
intolerance: inability to bear something

[1] "I'm going to approach you now," said Psychiatrist Augustus F. Kinzel to his subject, who stood eight feet away at the center of a bare room. "Tell me to stop when you think I'm too close." He moved forward a pace. "Here?" Another step. "Here?" The subject, an inmate of the U.S. Medical Center for Federal Prisoners in Springfield, Mo., and a man with a long history of violence, shook his head. But as Kinzel continued his advance, the prisoner's hands clenched into fists and he backed off, like someone gearing for attack. It was almost as if he felt himself inside an invisible circle into which no one, not even an unthreatening psychiatrist, could safely intrude.

[2] Kinzel believes that such a circle exists, and that merely to invade it can induce, in violent men, a panic that swiftly expands into irrational assault. In the room at Springfield, he has tested his theory on a group of prisoners, some known to be violent, others tractable. On the average, the violent subjects stopped him at a distance of three feet, and showed markedly increasing tension and hostility as the circle shrank. The nonviolent subjects let him approach to half that distance. Moreover, the two areas of insulating space differed radically in shape. That of the violent prisoners bulged to the rear— an avenue of approach that they regarded as unusually menacing. The nonviolent subjects' personal zones were nearly cylindrical.

[3] Kinzel's study is further proof of a contemporary psychological premise —advanced by such theorists as Northwestern University's Edward T. Hall and Medical Center of Mount Zion's Mardi J. Horowitz—that man unconsciously projects a sphere of personal space that admits no trespass by strangers. Whenever this zone is penetrated without permission, the occupant responds by defending it, often with violence. Kinzel believes that the dimensions of the circle may provide a clue to the violence potential of its inhabitant: the larger the circle, the more intolerant its inhabitant to invasion of his personal space. A rapidly expanding circle may signal that dangerous moment when the panic invoked by intrusion is about to escalate into destructive action.

Reprinted from "Violence: The Inner Circle," *Time*, The Weekly Newsmagazine; Copyright Time Inc., 1969.

[4] To Kinzel, there are certain obvious implications of this thesis. He estimates that some 85% of the country's prison population are not violence-prone. If this can be proved, these nonaggressive convicts could safely be paroled from custody—and from an environment bristling with guns and guards that provides a spur to violence. Now a psychiatrist at New York's Columbia-Presbyterian Medical Center, Kinzel has applied to the New York State Department of Correction to retest his theory on prison inmates whose susceptibility to violence will not be known to him beforehand. By measuring their intolerance to physical intrusion, Kinzel is confident that he can pick them out of the crowd.

DISCUSSION

1. What is the main idea sentence of this article? How does it help you to decide whether this essay is operational or causal analysis? What is being analyzed?

2. Do you see any relation between Fabun's theory of territoriality and the premise Kinzel advances? What is it?

3. How does Kinzel's theory work?

4. The conclusion to this essay does not summarize the parts, nor does it repeat the main idea. What does it do? Do you think such a conclusion is out of place in an article of analysis? Why or why not?

5. Can you think of specific situations in which you invaded someone's "space"? When your own space was invaded? What happened?

Use an Employment Agency?

vice versa: the other way around
aggressive: bold and pushing

[1] Nearly every job hunter at one time or another has thought about going to an employment agency. But many shy away because they don't really know how agencies work, how trustworthy they are, and how fees are charged. So,

Reprinted by permission from "Use an Employment Agency?" by Roger Rattan in the summer 1968 issue of *Everybody's Money,* pp. 4–6. Copyright © 1968 by *Everybody's Money,* a magazine for credit union members.

what's the story? Is an employment agency a good place to find a good job? Or will you just get an expensive bum steer?

[2] In the simplest terms an employment agent is a person who keeps two files: one of job openings; and one of people looking for jobs. In a perfect world the agent could match the lists perfectly. In fact he seldom finds the perfect person for the perfect job, or vice versa. And there's his next and perhaps biggest problem.

[3] An employment agent is most importantly a salesman. He has a product on the shelf—a job opening. And you come into his shop looking for one. His object is to convince you he has what you want. If you are hired, he earns his fee.

[4] Somebody, of course, has to pay for this service. In most cases the applicant, that is, the job hunter, pays the placement fee. Fees are charged as a percentage of the first month's, or occasionally a year's, salary. A typical fee would be 50 percent for a job in the $400 per month range—that's $200 for a $400 a month job. In general, placement fees get lower as the pay gets lower, and higher as it gets higher. For straight salary jobs, minimum placement fees tend to run around 10 percent of annual salary. Clearly, job placement is an expensive service.

[5] Only seldom does the *employer* pay the placement fee. And this is usually for jobs in highly skilled trades or professions or where the labor market is very tight. Don't be misled; nearly all employment agencies work on an applicant-pays-fee basis.

[6] Usually agencies give you three months to pay the fee. It doesn't come out of your check in some magical and painless way, either. You have to make that payment out of your take home pay each month for the next three months. Say you landed that $400 per month job; your take-home is $310. From that you pay about $70 ($\frac{1}{3}$ of the $200 fee). So for the first three months your $400 job is worth only about $240. But if an agency finds a good job when you are able to turn up nothing on your own, it may be worth it.

[7] In general, employment agents have no special inside track to job openings. They build up their files of jobs by carefully going through the help-wanted sections of local newspapers and magazines. Large or specialized agencies read national and trade publications. Where they find jobs listed by individual firms they call and ask if they may list the job in their own files. They also keep abreast of local business, watching for new contracts or expansion programs, anything that might affect the local labor market.

[8] Employment agencies build up their files of job seekers mostly by placing newspaper ads. They may list in an ad a variety of good looking jobs with good looking salaries. Other times they just say something like "Jobs! Jobs! Many Fee Paid." Just as in retail advertising, these ads are designed to get people into the store. A job they list may well be open but, by the time you get there, it's best not to count on it. Especially, don't count on the "fee paid" jobs being open.

[9] When a job hunter comes into an employment agency the usual procedure is to have him fill out a registration card listing the usual personal information as well as education, job skills, and experience. Either on this card or another given at the same time the applicant will sign his name and in doing so will have agreed to pay the agency's fee if he takes a job they refer him to. It's a contract and it's legal.

[10] Even if you should get a job different from the one they sent you to interview for, if it's with a firm they sent you to, chances are you'll have to pay their fee.

[11] The employment agency field is a highly competitive, aggressive and profitable business, plagued with sharp practices. Although most states regulate employment agencies, many of the laws are loose, vague or not strictly enforced. Short of learning your own state's laws by heart, your best bet when you go job hunting is to be on the lookout for some of the sharp or unethical practices that may, or should be, against the law . . .

[12] Sometimes a job doesn't work out after the applicant has been hired. Maybe he gets laid off or fired, or perhaps he's asked to do things that weren't part of the job as he understood it. He had better ask the agency beforehand what happens in such a case. A good practice followed by some agencies is to refund the placement fee if the job doesn't work out in three months. But that has to be in writing or the money won't reappear . . .

[13] It's rough to be out of work. And rougher still to have a big new debt as soon as you start. So be resourceful. Do as much digging as you can on your own. Comb the newspapers, talk to friends, check with local trade and professional organizations, your trade union local and the state employment service. A commercial employment agency may be one alternative. But it may be an expensive one, too.

DISCUSSION

1. What is the purpose of this article—giving directions or operational analysis? Back up what you say by referring to specific things in the article.

2. Is the main idea sentence actually stated? If so, what is it? If you think it is not stated, put into your own words what you think it is.

3. Are all the questions asked in the introduction answered in the article? Where can you find the answers and what are they?

4. How does the conclusion of this essay relate to the contract the writer has made in the introduction?

5. If you have had any experience with employment agencies, how does your experience compare with what this writer says? Do you think his evaluation is fair?

How Does It Work?   Why Did It Happen?

Operational analysis answers the question, "How does it work?" Causal analysis tries to answer the question, "Why did it turn out that way?" The historian who tries to trace the causes of United States involvement in Korea and the newscaster who tries to account for the escalation of the Vietnamese conflict are both using causal analysis. So is the instructor who tries to discover why his students go to sleep during his lecture; so is the repairman who tries to figure out why the air conditioner stopped working.

One major difference between these two kinds of analysis, however, is that we can be very sure about the answer to *"How* does it work?" We can seldom be absolutely certain about *why* it happened. If the repairman finds a fuse blown and if, when he replaces the fuse, the air conditioner starts to cool the house again, he can be quite certain that the fuse caused the failure—but he still may not know what blew the fuse. The instructor will find it harder to discover why his students doze in the back row; he may come up with several reasons before his analysis is complete. As for why we got into Korea or Vietnam, or why a riot occurred in a certain city at a certain time, we can never be absolutely sure. The most we can ask of such causal analyses is that they take into account all the factors that were present in the event, and that they not overemphasize some and neglect others.

The following brief analysis explains why the Negro bus strike began where and when it did. Notice that this writer takes account of other possible causes before he goes on to what he believes "the truth is."

> "Lord, Child," a Mississippi woman once said to me, "we colored people ain't nothing but a bundle of resentments and sufferings going somewhere to explode."
>
> The explosion—and no one would have then taken it for that—came on December 1, 1955, the day Mrs. Rosa Parks boarded the Cleveland Avenue bus in Montgomery, Alabama. And the Negro revolt is properly dated from the moment Mrs. Parks said, "No" to the bus driver's demand that she get up and let a white man have her seat.
>
> There have been scores of attempts to discover why Mrs. Parks refused to move. The local white power structure insisted that the NAACP had put her up to it, but this charge was quickly disproved. The extremists spread the word that Mrs. Parks was a Communist agent, that the whole thing had been hatched in the Kremlin; that rumor collapsed under the weight of its own preposterousness. The truth is that Mrs. Parks was a part of the deepening mood of despair and disillusionment that gripped the American Negro after World War II. She had been an official in the Montgomery NAACP; Mrs. Parks was an alert woman, a dedicated Negro and fully aware of the continuing injustices Negroes all over the nation were enduring. The only way to account for Mrs. Parks is to say she was a part of the times; that, at long last, her cup ran over. (Excerpt from p. 81 in THE NEGRO REVOLT by Louis E. Lomax [Harper & Row, 1962].)

Rioting in Watts

decade: ten years

oppressors: people who treat others unfairly; people who use excessive authority

erosion: wearing away

Utopia: the mythical place where everything is perfect; heaven on earth

referendum: submitting a law or other decision to the voters for their approval or disapproval

dominant: most important; most influential

harangue: long, passionate speech

intervened: stepped in; became involved

substantiate: back up what you have said by giving evidence

vapid: dull; lifeless; without spirit or interest

canard: false story or rumor, usually intended to discredit

indignity: humiliating treatment

[1] To the superficial white observer, Watts seems a most unlikely place for mass violence to erupt, for its inhabitants have benefited from most of the civil rights advances of the last decades. The neighborhood is composed of clean, spruce, if modest, dwellings enclosed by clipped lawns—far from the diseased alleys of Harlem. Children attend legally integrated schools (99 percent Negro). Parents have the vote. Public accommodations are open to all. For a man from Mississippi, Los Angeles would seem a haven of freedom. And this very promise attracts 1,000 Negroes a month, 65 per cent of them Southerners, to Los Angeles.

Introduction: identifies topic (riot in Watts) and describes the appearance of the area and what seem the good conditions

[2] But the reality of Watts hardly fits the dream of the Southern Negro. Over 30 percent of the men are unemployed wanderers. Some 40 percent of the families are broken by divorce or desertion. The area is three times as crowded with human beings as any other quarter of Los Angeles. This breakdown of the family has predictable results: Children see their

Transition leads to contrast: the reality and the dream

Reprinted from "Rioting in Watts," by William M. McCord in *The New Leader* (August 30, 1965), by permission. Copyright © 1965 by The American Labor Conference on International Affairs, Inc.

195

father, if at all, "sitting around the kitchen drinking beer with his buddies while the mother works." The average boy comes to despise authority.

[3] Not unreasonably, the Negro adults in Watts regard the white merchants and police as their most visible oppressors. The area is ruled by 272 policemen, 90 percent white, who act like troops occupying enemy territory. White landlords own 70 percent of the homes and apartments. White businessmen control all but a handful of the stores, bars and gas stations. "Here, you have to pay the white man, jump when the white cop calls you 'nigger,' " a Negro labor union official told me. "Here is where the Negroes' hopes were to be fulfilled. When they find life so empty, what can they do? Where can they go?"

[4] The Negroes in Watts have sought release in drugs, rackets, and crime: a fact which Police Chief William Parker claims Negro leaders have ignored. (Actually, the area has always been the crime center of Los Angeles. A gangland tradition, established by whites, surrounded the Negroes who were first forced to move into the district 30 years ago.)

[5] Thus the reasons behind the revolt are not hard to discover: a well-nourished criminal culture; a constant erosion of faith in authority; a rootlessness born when immigration from the South did not bring Utopia; hopelessness. And there is no way out for the Negro victims: a year ago, California passed a law legalizing housing discrimination and insuring that Negroes would forever be kept in their ghettoes. Proposition 14—that ironic product of democracy's hope, the referendum—repealed a fair housing law and made it clear that California whites hated the Negro. This demonstration of white contempt did more than anything else to cause the riots. "They told us last year that they didn't want no niggers living near them," a Negro explained to me. "Now, we are showing them that we don't want them sucking our blood."

Summary of reasons resulting from the contrast between dream and reality
One new reason

[6] To my shame (since I am that rare breed, a third generation Californian), the state's residents refuse to recognize their guilt. They ignore Proposition 14 and prefer to ask, as one white Los Angeles lawyer asked me several days ago, "What *do* those

Transition into false causes

Negroes want? We have given them everything."
Now, the state's whites will launch themselves on a
search for the "real causes" of the riots. Laying aside
the comments which one usually hears ("Those niggers are just different from us. We have to keep them
in their place"), the most widely discussed "explanation" is that extremist elements or civil rights leaders
encouraged the riots.

[7] The truth is that the riots started spontaneously,
but soon came under control of a variety of groups
(none of them "Leftist" or oriented to civil rights)
drawn from the normally dominant segments of the
community. The Black Muslims, I was told, wore
red arm-bands to identify their members, harangued
the crowds, directed them to appropriate targets,
and bailed out comrades who suffered arrest. Various
criminal gangs also intervened. These gangs, operating independently of each other, went on a looting
spree. Other groups within Watts—rallying around
the cry, "We'll get them for Bogalusa"—attacked the
most Scrooge-like of white merchants.

[8] The riots, therefore, were neither an expression
of pure lawlessness nor the product of civil rights
demonstrations. The actual civil rights leaders had
repeatedly warned the city government that a rebellious situation was building up in Watts. They
requested but did not receive police cooperation.
"We knew months ago what was coming," one
leader told me. "Gangs of young men cruised these
streets every night. There was ample warning, but
no action."

[9] Some in the "Freedom Movement" go even
further. They claim that police butality caused the
explosion. Certainly, the original arrest could have
been handled more tactfully and particular officers
could have acted with less "vigor" against the mobs.
Surely, too, Chief Parker could have consented to
see Negro leaders who have sought conferences.

[10] Yet these actions hardly amount to brutality.
In a number of interviews, I found nothing to substantiate the charge that police have acted viciously,
or, as a group, even unfairly. Compared to the Bull
Connors, Chief Raineys, and Jim Clarks, the Los
Angeles police force is a model of civic responsibility. "What we need here are *more* police, *more*

patrolmen cruising around," one middle-class Negro in Watts commented.

[11] The usual canards in the civil rights movement about police brutality will not explain the Los Angeles riot, nor will the vapid generalizations produced by white politicians. The cause is clear and so simple that it hurts: The Negro in California, that paradise of civil rights, is still treated with indignity. Proposition 14 certified by an overwhelming majority that whites want the Negro kept in his ghetto. Now, the whites are suffering from their own backlash.

Conclusion summarizes the analysis: the Watts riots were caused by Negroes reacting to the treatment the whites gave them

DISCUSSION

1. The writer begins by describing Watts, and then shows how "the reality of Watts hardly fits the dream of the Southern Negro." How do the appearance of Watts and the dreams of Southern Negroes fit into a causal analysis?

2. In paragraph 5, McCord writes, "Thus, the reasons behind the revolt are not hard to discover," and then summarizes the reasons he has mentioned so far. That paragraph might well conclude the essay, yet it appears about in the middle. What does the rest of the essay analyze? Why does McCord do it this way?

3. How does McCord use specific details to convince the reader that the reasons he gives are actually the real reasons? Which details did you find most convincing?

4. How does the conclusion tie the two parts of the essay together—what McCord believes are the genuine causes and the various "explanations" that other people give?

5. Is McCord serious when he calls California a "paradise of civil rights"? Would you call it that in the light of current events? Why or why not?

6. Since this article was written, the Supreme Court has declared Proposition 14 unconstitutional. Does this ruling destroy what McCord says about the effect Proposition 14 had on Negro attitudes? Why or why not?

Why Harlem Liked the Muslims

haberdashery: men's clothing store
Harlem: a Negro section in New York City; thus "a Harlem" is any
   Negro ghetto

[1] The Black Muslim movement was closer to most Harlemites than any of
the other organizations, much closer than the NAACP or the Urban League.
These were the people who were right out there in the street with you. They
had on suits, but their grammar wasn't something that would make the
average Negro on the street feel ill at ease. The words that they used were
the same words that the people on the street used. You could associate these
people with yourself; you knew some of them. Since the leaders of this group
had come from the community, the crowd could identify with these people
more readily than they could with anybody else.
[2] The Muslims were the home team. They were the people, talking for
everyone. This was the first time that many of these people had ever seen the
home boys get up and say anything in front of a crowd. This was the first
time that many of these people had ever seen home boys who had been
junkies, pimps, or thieves speak to crowds of people and sound so serious
about it. It became a community thing.
[3] I suppose the Muslims did the same thing in other places, other Harlems
throughout the nation. They must have gotten members and speakers right
out of the community. This was a way in which they couldn't lose, because
when a guy got up on 125th Street and started talking about how Goldberg
who's got the haberdashery right there on the corner paid him something like
forty dollars a week for two years, when he was a grown man, and how he
started working for Brother So-and-So, down at his rib joint on 116th Street,
and is now making seventy-five dollars a week, everybody's got to get up
and say, "Yeah, yeah. That no-good Goldberg ought to go."
[4] The people would holler. "Yeah! Yeah! Them goddam Jews killed my
Jesus too!" It's easy to build up this sort of feeling among the home folks
when one of the people in the neighborhood, the boy who used to work in
the butcher store and became a Muslim, says, "Mr. Greenberg didn't sell you
any good meat. Some of that meat was years old. Some of that meat had been
in there for days, and it was almost blue, because it had spoiled so long. But
he'd shellac it or something to make it look like it was unspoiled, to make it
look like it was almost fresh."

From pp. 348–349 of *Manchild in the Promised Land*, by Claude Brown. Reprinted by permission
of The Macmillan Company. Copyright © 1965 by Claude Brown.

[5] The people could believe these speakers. They knew them. They knew that they had worked at these places, and that they should know what they were talking about. The Muslims became a very influential force in Harlem. They would never have been able to take over, because they couldn't acquire any political power. For one thing, many of their recruits had been in jail. Once a person goes to jail for a felony, he loses his voting rights. But if the Muslims were to run a candidate for Congress in Harlem, there might be a good chance that they could get enough support. I know if they had done this in 1960, they could have gotten quite a bit of support from sympathizers. Today they might stand an even better chance.

DISCUSSION

1. The first sentence sounds as though this selection might be argument. How can you tell that it is analysis?

2. In paragraph 1, how many reasons can you find for the popularity of the Black Muslim movement? Are any of these reasons picked up and developed in the other paragraphs? Which ideas in which paragraph?

3. In paragraphs 3 and 4, Brown gives two examples of what street speakers might say and how the audience might respond. How many things do the examples have in common? What are the differences?

4. It's impossible to tell from this selection whether or not Brown is sympathetic toward anti-Semitism; he merely gives it as one of the causes of Muslim popularity. If he disapproves, should he express his disapproval in a causal analysis? Why or why not?

5. Brown's analysis of Muslim anti-Semitism illustrates that people who are discriminated against can be prejudiced against others. What does this tell us about how humans learn to behave?

6. In an essay you read earlier, Altick defines prejudice as "being down on something you're not up on." Does "being up" on the fact that in many Negro districts the merchants who overcharge and underpay Negroes are Catholics, Protestants, and nonbelievers affect your attitude toward what the Muslims say? How?

The Swing Right

constellation: a group of bright stars that form a design
dissent: disagreeing publicly with popular ideas and beliefs
apathy: lack of interest
Socrates: A Greek philosopher and teacher who was put to death for advocating unpopular ideas

[1] Everyone agrees that the country is swinging to the right: that the American people were more conservative in 1968 than they were in 1964 and that they will probably be more conservative still four years from now . . . To speak of a swing *toward* conservatism, however, is inexact. What we are witnessing is a swing *away* from the ideas, usually called liberal, which have dominated American thinking for a generation. And what makes this swing-away important—important is too weak a word—is the fact that the constellation of ideas we seem to be rejecting is a constellation which has played a crucial part in American life not only since 1932 but since 1789.

[2] Take for example the chosen slogan of the Nixon campaign—chosen to blunt the Wallace campaign. Law and Order, translated out of its Aesopian sloganese, means that the power of the State should take precedence over the rights of the citizen when there is suspicion of crime or fear of public disorder. The rights of individual citizens to the equal protection of the laws are not to be allowed to interfere with the investigations of the police or the punishments of the courts, and the rights of citizens and groups of citizens to meet and protest are to be subordinated to the interest of the State in the preservation of order.

[3] This proposal not only challenges certain specific provisions of the Constitution, it has even more disturbing implications. It is a rejection of the fundamental principle on which the American system rests. What distinguishes the American system from its contemporary alternatives is precisely the fact that, in the American system, as opposed to the fascist system, Red or Black, the rights of individual citizens are put *above* the power of the State whenever the protection of individual rights is essential to the preservation of human dignity and freedom . . .

[4] Why has all this happened? Why has the American passion for individual liberty cooled? One reason may be that the American people, or at least a majority of white Americans, have enjoyed a high degree of personal liberty so long that they have ceased to value it. If this is so, time may set things

Condensed from "The Swing Right" by Archibald MacLeish in the February 1969 issue of *Civil Liberties*, pp. 6–8. Reprinted by permission of Houghton Mifflin Company.

right. Should the American people ever lose their right of dissent to a George Wallace they might rather quickly learn to love what they had lost as passionately as the people, say, of Czechoslovakia.

[5] Another reason may be the general political apathy. McGeorge Bundy, in his Godkin Lectures last year, asked his audience to agree that the purpose of government is freedom. This fundamental truth of self-government in a free society is not often spoken of in our generation. Government exists, for most of us, to keep things the way they are. We have quite forgotten that the key to the American system is the combination of majority rule and minority rights which prevents our government of ourselves from becoming that worst of tyrannies, a tyranny by numbers, and we are now beginning to forget that the key to that key is the constitutional guarantee of personal liberty.

[6] A third, and not unrelated, reason may have to do with our famous affluence. A nation which has become rich by turning itself into a single, vast, continental market for consumer goods has no need—no commercial need at least—for individual liberties. What it demands of its citizens is uniform, standard acceptance of standard, uniform products advertised by uniform, standard television received in standard, uniform living rooms. Dissent by a Socrates, however unwelcome to the Athenian majority, was essential to the greatness of Athens because the greatness of Athens was measured by the human mind and spirit. Dissent in Supermarket America is merely an economic embarrassment.

DISCUSSION

1. Although the questions at the beginning of paragraph 4 make it clear that this article is causal analysis, MacLeish makes no attempt to answer the question "Why has all this happened?" until half way through the article. Does the *all this* give any clue as to why he waits so late? Would the article be more effective if he had given the reasons first and the results afterwards? Why or why not?

2. MacLeish makes it clear in the first paragraph that he thinks "conservatism" is the wrong word to use. What would be his definition of "conservatism"? How do the date (1789, the date of the Bill of Rights) and the reference to the Constitution relate to the definition?

3. A constellation is a group of bright stars forming a design and used by mankind for centuries as a guide to navigation. What effect does Mac-Leish get by talking twice about a "constellation of ideas" rather than a "group of ideas"?

4. All school children are familiar with Aesop's Fables—short, simplified tales of animals acting like humans, each tale ending with a moral. Why does MacLeish call the campaign slogan, "Law and Order," Aesopean?

5. MacLeish gives three reasons in answer to his own question. What kind of transitions does he use to introduce each reason?

6. Are the reasons he gives more persuasive because he says, "One reason *may be* . . ." instead of saying, "The truth is . . ."? Why?

7. The second question MacLeish asks in paragraph 4 takes it for granted that his readers will agree that "the American passion for liberty [has] cooled." What are the reasons he gives for thinking so? Would you agree with him? Give examples that support what you say.

8. Between World War I and World War II, Czechoslovakia was a democracy; then it fell, first under German, and then under Russian, control. In the 1950s there was an attempt at rebellion, mostly led by students, which failed. How do you think American students would behave if a similar situation occurred in this country? Why do you think so?

9. Do you agree with McGeorge Bundy's idea of what the purpose of government is (paragraph 5)? Do you agree with what MacLeish says "most of us" think the purpose of government is? If you don't agree with either of these, what do *you* think the purpose of government is?

10. Has your experience led you to think of America as "a single, vast . . . market for consumer goods"? Give examples to back up what you say.

11. In the sentence in paragraph 6 beginning "What it demands . . ." MacLeish first says "uniform, standard" and then reverses the order to say, "standard, uniform." Would it have been better to keep the same order all four times he uses the phrase? What is the effect of changing it back and forth?

12. A great many historians consider that the Greek city of Athens was one of the world's great democracies. What does MacLeish mean by saying that Athens' greatness was measured "by the human mind and spirit"? Does the fact that Athens produced great philosophers, great dramatists, great sculptors have anything to do with your answer? How is America's "greatness" measured? Who—or what kind of people—are the most admired in America today?

Looking for Causes

Analysis can be a very useful way to understand why things happen, but it will be useful only if the writer is careful not to jump to hasty conclusions. He can't just settle for the first reason that presents itself; instead, he must look for all the possible causes and decide on only those that seem clearly related to what happened. In trying to find out why more than 5,000 sheep died suddenly in Utah, the writer of the next essay makes a much more convincing case because he carefully examines all the things that might have killed the sheep.

When we turn from physical events, with physical causes, to human behavior, where a wide and tangled set of motives affect the results of even quite simple actions, we have to be even more careful. The investigators who tried to find out why some students are considered dummies, even though they understand the material being taught, carefully tested their theories on some actual students before they decided they had found the cause.

In some situations, however, possible causes cannot be altogether discarded, nor can theories be tested. In explaining why presidential appointments were made so slowly, the writer has acknowledged that there are many causes, some of which he has probably not discussed. Another writer, explaining why lightweight crew members don't stay on the team, offers a group of reasons and he makes a convincing case because he is a crew member and these are reasons that affect him.

Sheep Die Near Nerve Gas Tests

autopsies: operations after death, to find out what caused the death
persistent: hard to get rid of
confounding: completely puzzling
culpable: at fault
flora: plants
noxious: poisonous
innocuous: harmless
inaccessible: impossible to reach

[1] On March 13 a plane flew by. On March 14 the deaths began. Within the first week some 5,000 corpses lay on the rugged slopes of Utah's Skull Valley. The victims were sheep, who simply began dying one day with no advance warning except a sudden loss of muscular coordination, followed by collapse. Autopsies at first revealed practically nothing, and Federal, state, and university investigators were at a loss.

Introduction identifies the event and makes clear that the cause was not easy to find

[2] There was one fact: Bordering the grazing area is Dugway Proving Ground, the U. S. Army's main testing facility for chemical and biological weapons.

First possible cause: nerve gas tests

The day before the sheep began to die, the Army had fired several 155-millimeter artillery shells containing Sarin, a U. S. variation of a nerve gas developed by Germany prior to World War II. That same afternoon, 160 gallons of an unnamed persistent nerve chemical were disposed of by burning in an open pit, and 320 gallons of a similar persistent agent were sprayed from a "high-performance" aircraft flashing along 150 feet above the ground. The spraying took place some 27 miles from the nearest sheep kill.

[3] At first the Army said it "definitely was not responsible" for the deaths, which by the beginning of last week had topped 6,400. Then it changed to the view that "no definite cause of death" had been established. As investigators chipped away at other possible causes, the official statements backed off even further. "We are still saying that as far as has been determined, we had nothing to do with it," an Army spokesman said a week after the first report. *Army unwilling to accept nerve gas as cause*

[4] Meanwhile, the dead and dying sheep were confounding doctors and scientists from the Federal and State Departments of Agriculture, the U. S. Public Health Service, the University of Utah and the Army itself; the bodies revealed hardly any symptoms of anything, let alone nerve gas. *Tests show no symptoms that point to cause*

[5] "We've pretty well ruled out contagious disease," reports Dr. Jordan Rasmussen, chief USDA veterinarian in Utah. Painstaking examination of a vast variety of tissues from the sheep showed no abnormalities. *Another possible cause: contagious disease ruled out*

[6] Nor did poisonous plants seem to be to blame. Investigators, looking for culpable flora, combed Skull Valley in vain. One noxious weed called halogeton has taken a heavy toll in the past, according to Utah State Agriculture Commissioner David Waldron, but it could never fit the killer's description. It is usually fatal only if the animal drinks water soon afterward, causing bloat, and the symptoms would be obvious. In addition, thousands of acres of the plant have been plowed under; there is not enough left in Skull Valley to do such terrible damage. *Third possible cause: poisonous weeds ruled out*

[7] Adding to the mystery was the fact that the affected sheep seemed to be limited to a fairly well- *More facts that might lead to causes*

defined area. "There are sheep to the north and sheep to the south," says Waldron, "and they're doing fine." Even more curious is the fact that sheep were the only animals affected. People—Skull Valley has a population of about 55—horses, cattle, rabbits, birds, rodents and other creatures showed no symptoms at all. Almost the only difference between the sheep and everybody else was that sheep are natural snow-eaters.

[8] This seemingly innocuous fact again suggested Dugway as the source of the killer. State officials theorized that wind carried the droplets of nerve gas spray over the low Cedar Mountains then allowed it to settle on the snow that had fallen on previous days.

"Snow-eating" suggests nerve gas again

[9] By this time the Army was just about ready to indict itself. "We fully recognize, with this occurring right on our doorstep . . . that we are highly suspect," admits Brig. Gen. William W. Stone, in charge of research and laboratories for the Army Materiel Command.

One army official agrees nerve gas might have done it

[10] Yet the Army couldn't even make its own rap stick. The reason, says Gen. Stone, was that it simply could not isolate its own nerve gas from the bodies of the sheep. By this time, after some 10 days of sleuthing, scientists had managed to determine from urine and tear samples that the deaths were apparently due to an organo-phosphate compound similar to those used in nerve agents, as well as in several insecticides. Such compounds kill by blocking the action of a blood chemical called cholinesterase, whose job is to suppress another chemical that causes muscular action. Without this suppression, the muscle operates continuously, causing convulsions. Unfortunately, this was not enough to pin down the Army compound. Traces from the spraying were easily found and identified by the Army on its own test range, and should, officials say, have been just as easily identifiable in the sheep.

Tests show strong possibility of nerve gas

[11] Another possibility raised last week was that the poison might have come from a chemical preservative used on seed grain that may have been fed to two herds of rams in the valley. A similar incident reportedly occurred in Turkey a few years ago. Even if such feed was used in the valley, however, it

Final possible cause: grain preservative ruled out

would have been virtually inaccessible to the sheep,
which were at least six miles from one of the buck-
herds and 20 miles from the other. Waldron writes
the idea off entirely. "I've heard quite a few ideas
that I thought were silly," he says, "but I'd have to
put that at the top of the list."
[12] So Dugway still looks like the culprit. If it
is, the Skull Valley incident is one of the biggest
chemical-warfare-agent disasters in U. S. history.

DISCUSSION

1. Why does the title of this article say "near" instead of "from"?

2. The article discusses four possible causes for the sheep's death. Do you
   think the reasons for discarding three of them are sound? Why or why
   not?

3. The three possible causes that the writer says were not responsible are
   discussed in paragraphs 5, 6, and 11. Why has the writer separated
   these three possible causes? Would the order be better if they were considered in paragraphs 5, 6, and 7? In paragraphs 9, 10, and 11? Give
   your reasons for preferring one order to another.

4. This article quotes exactly what four of the investigators said. Why?

5. Since this article was written, later investigations have shown that rabbits,
   too, were affected by the nerve gas, probably from eating grass in the
   area. Does knowing this additional fact damage the analysis that is
   presented here? Why or why not?

6. In March 1970, 43 scientists at Portland State University petitioned the
   President and Secretary of Defense to delay a shipment of 700 rail cars of
   nerve gas to Oregon. Look for articles dealing with public reaction to
   the nerve gas shipment to the Pacific Northwest. How did the Skull
   Valley incident possibly contribute to public reaction? List the essential
   differences in public involvement in the two situations.

Nixon Appointments Lag

confirmed: made official or valid
illustrious: famous; highly distinguished
stock option: an opportunity to buy stocks at less than their regular
price
affluent: wealthy
lucrative: profitable
prominent: important; well known
acquaintanceship: knowing someone without being a close friend

[1] The Nixon Administration has been remarkably slow in filling many key posts in the new American government. For example, its ambassador to Japan reported for duty only this week, and its ambassador to West Germany has not yet been confirmed—though these are clearly two of the most important diplomatic posts in the world.

[2] Even in Washington, many key appointments have not been made five months after President Nixon took over, and it is interesting to analyze why this is so.

[3] First, the Republicans have been out of power for 28 of the last 36 years. Most of their illustrious members have been in business and in the professions, where the financial rewards increasingly depend on stock options and retirement benefits, and usually confront them with serious financial losses when they come up against the Government's conflict-of-interest regulations.

[4] Second, the Republicans do not have as large a following as the Democrats among the talented intellectuals and technicians in the universities, and in these affluent days, when professors are increasingly following lucrative secondary careers with commercial firms, the intellectuals are hesitating to go to Washington unless they can serve under a particularly exciting Administration.

[5] This much, however, was expected by the President and his principal aides and recruiters. What has surprised them, however, is how many times they have considered prominent men with established reputations, only to discover after careful investigation some physical or psychological weakness that disqualified the man for the job.

[6] "I had never realized," one Cabinet member remarked the other day, "what a toll the fierce competition of American business and professional

life has taken on many of our most talented and successful men. Many of them have simply been worn out in the struggle. Many more have all kinds of family problems they cannot leave. In a great many cases, they have taken to drink to such an extent that the risk is too great. So we have had to go much slower than we expected."

[7] No doubt there are other reasons, less disturbing. For so political a President, Nixon came to office with very few job commitments, and he has wisely refused to hand over his appointive power to the Republican national and state political committees.

[8] Also, unlike President Kennedy, he neither had a wide personal acquaintanceship in the academic community, nor was he willing—outside of a couple of White House appointments—to take as many chances as Kennedy with men he didn't know personally or by reputation.

[9] There is also a feeling, in some quarters at least, that President Nixon has surrounded himself with a White House staff that is overly protective of his time and thus keeps him from meeting many talented men who might have been willing to join his Administration.

DISCUSSION

1. How does the first paragraph get the reader's attention?

2. The second paragraph is the main idea sentence of this causal analysis. Do you think it should be a separate paragraph, or the last sentence of the previous paragraph? Explain. Does it make any difference that the article was written for a newspaper?

3. Paragraphs 3 through 9 give the causes behind the lag in appointments. Is the order chronological? Order of importance? Some other order?

4. Do you suppose there is a relationship between your answer to Question 3 above and the fact that paragraph 9 gives one more reason rather than making the essay sound finished?

5. Would you say that Reston is blaming Nixon's administration? Defending it? Neither? Explain.

6. Is Reston's vocabulary unnecessarily difficult? What kinds of things do most of his difficult words refer to? How would the tone of the essay change if those words were replaced with more ordinary words?

7. When Reston wrote this article, he expected it to be read before the appointments had been made. Even though you are reading the article long after the vacancies have been filled, does the analysis still stand up?

8. How many of the reasons that Reston gives apply just to the Nixon situation? How many of them would explain why businessmen and intellectuals are not attracted to government positions?

9. Would any of the reasons Reston gives apply to government jobs in your city or your state? Which ones?

10. Why do you suppose Reston compares Nixon to Kennedy rather than to Johnson?

If I'm So Smart, How Come I Flunk All the Time?

standardized tests: tests which show how a student compares with other students all over the country
bias: inclination; established attitude
belligerent: aggressive; hostile
inadequate: not sufficient or suitable
image: appearance one creates for others

[1] Can twenty flunking students of varying intelligence raise their math and English a full year's level in only thirty working days?

[2] Dr. Lloyd Homme, chief of a special educational "fix-it" laboratory in Albuquerque, New Mexico, said "Yes" and put teams of behavioral scientists together with the flunking students to work on the problem. Any available technology could be used—teaching machines, programmed instruction, computer-assisted methods—to cram a year's knowledge into the boys.

[3] Were the experiments a success? The scientists said "Yes" but the students said "No." When grades were measured using standardized tests under strict laboratory conditions, marks went up more than one year on the average. Meanwhile, back at school, the students were still barely passing, at best. "The experiment was fine for the scientists. They proved their theory on paper and made a name for themselves, but most of us were still flunking in class," remarked one seventeen-year-old.

[4] The only clue to the mystery was this common remark: "The teachers ignore us—they've got it in for us."

[5] At first the scientists on the team thought the complaint was just sour grapes and told the boys to work harder. When grades still failed to rise, the scientists felt there might be some truth in what the young team members were saying. Not that teachers were to blame, necessarily, but there still might be some negative bias. "You should see what goes on in class!" said the boys.

[6] "The only thing to do was to take them up on it, go into the classroom with them and see what was holding back their grades," said Dr. Homme. [7] Hence, bearded behavioral scientists ended up in the back row of math and English classes and made observations about the behavior of students and teachers. Homme was surprised to discover that two simple actions made the difference.

[8] "With few exceptions, our students acted like dummies," said Dr. Homme, "even though we knew they were ahead of the rest in knowledge. They were so used to playing the class idiot that they didn't know how to show what they knew. Their eyes wandered, they appeared absent-minded or even belligerent. One or two read magazines hidden under their desks, thinking, most likely, that they already knew the classwork. They rarely volunteered and often had to have questions repeated because they weren't listening. Teachers, on the other hand, did not trust our laboratory results. Nobody was going to tell them that 'miracles' could work on Sammy and Jose."

[9] In the eyes of teachers, students seemed to fall into three groups. We'll call them: *bright-eyes, scaredy-cats* and *dummies.*

> *Bright-eyes* had perfected the trick of:
> 1. "eyeballing" the instructor at all times, even from the minute he entered the room.
> 2. never ducking their eyes away when the instructor glanced at *them.*
> 3. getting the instructor to call on them when they wanted *without* raising their hands.
> 4. even making the instructor go out of his way to call on someone else to "give others a chance" (especially useful when bright-eyes themselves are uncertain of the answer).
> 5. readily admitting ignorance so as not to bluff—but in such a way that it sounds as though ignorance is rare.
> 6. asking many questions.
> *Scaredy-cats* (the middle group)
> 1. looked toward the instructor but were afraid to let him "catch their eyes."
> 2. asked few questions and gave the impression of being "under achievers."
> 3. appeared uninvolved and had to be "drawn out," so they were likely to be criticized for "inadequate participation."
> *Dummies* (no matter how much they really knew)
> 1. never looked at the instructor.
> 2. never asked questions.
> 3. were stubborn about volunteering information in class.

[10] To make matters worse, the tests in school were *not* standardized and not given nearly as frequently as those given in the laboratory. School test-

scores were open to teacher bias. Classroom behavior of students counted a lot toward their class grades. There was no doubt that teachers were biased against the dummies. The scientists concluded that no matter how much knowledge a dummy gained on his own, his grades in school were unlikely to improve unless he could somehow change his image into a bright-eyes. This would mean . . .

1. Look the teacher in the eye.
2. Ask questions and volunteer answers (even if uncertain).

"Teachers get teacher-training in how to play their roles. Why shouldn't students get student-training in how to play bright-eyes?" asked Homme.

[11] Special training sessions were held at the laboratory. Dummies were drilled in eyeballing and hand-raising, which, simple as they sound, weren't easy to do. "I felt so square I could hardly stand it," complained one of the dummies. "That was at first. Later, when I saw others eyeballing and hand-raising and really learning more, I even moved my seat to the front. It flipped the teacher out of her skull. She couldn't get over it."

[12] Those who found eyeballing especially difficult were taught to look at the instructor's mouth or the bridge of his nose. "Less threatening to the student," explained Homme. "It seems less aggressive to them."

[13] Unfortunately, not all of the dummies were able to pick up new habits during the limited training period. Some learned in the laboratory but couldn't do it in the classroom. These became scaredy-cats—at least a step up. But for the majority, grades improved steadily once they got the hang of their new techniques. The students encouraged and helped each other to hand-raise and eyeball.

[14] Teachers' comments reflected the improvement. "There is no doubt that student involvement was increased by the program and as a result grades went up."

[15] By way of advice to others wishing to improve their own eyeballing and hand-raising, student Jose Martinez suggests: "Don't try to do it all at once. You'll shock the teacher and make it tough for yourself. Begin slowly. Work with a friend and help each other. Do it like a game. Like exercising with weights—it takes practice but it's worth it."

[16] Homme agrees. "In fact, results are guaranteed for life," he says.

DISCUSSION

1. No single main idea sentence is used in this causal analysis, although the main point is implied all the way through. Which of these statements comes closest to what you think is the main idea? Justify your answer by what the article says, and by the way it begins and the way it ends.

   (a) Students flunk because they know less than other students in their classes.

    (b) Students flunk because teachers have it in for them.

    (c) Students flunk because they want to.

    (d) Students flunk because they don't look the teacher in the eye and don't ask questions or volunteer answers.

2. How does the title of this article help you decide what the main idea is?

3. In analyzing why some fairly well-informed students get low grades, the writer uses two other writing purposes: *classification* and *giving directions*. Find what is being classified and make a chart showing the divisions the writer uses. Does this classification fit your own experience? Would you make a different classification of the behavior of the students in your own English class?

4. When do the directions appear? Why do you think the writer shifts from *telling why* to *telling how to do it?*

5. In several places in the article, the writer quotes exactly what people said, rather than telling us indirectly what the people thought. In paragraph 4, for instance, the writer might have said, "The students thought the teachers had it in for them." Look at the other direct quotes and decide what the change in effect would be if no direct quotes were used.

Merrily, Merrily, Merrily, Merrily

tycoon: businessman of great wealth and power
Mafia: secret criminal organization
Circle Line: a company that carries tourists around Manhatten on sight-seeing boats
steeplechase: a race over various high obstacles
simulate: have the appearance of something else
commitment: sense of obligation and devotion

[1] According to regulations, to be a member of the lightweight crew, one must be able to step on a scale the day of a race and not tip it above 155 pounds. According to tradition one should be reasonably intelligent, not naturally athletic, at a loss for an explanation for why one is out for crew and at the short end of the visible light spectrum politically. That is to say, lightweights are cruddy, weirdo slobs. During the strike of '68 they consid-

From "Merrily, Merrily, Merrily, Merrily," by James Kunen in the June 16, 1969 issue of *Sports Illustrated*, pp. 50–52. Reprinted by permission of the author.

ered themselves to be rowing for themselves, not for the university, and kicked around the idea of not rowing, or rowing without shirts or rowing with black armbands to protest the police bust. Things being the way they are, what keeps people like this out for the sport?

[2] Very little, apparently. The Class of '70 turned out 48 lightweights for the first freshman practice in 1966. In this spring of 1969, as juniors, three of them remain on the team.

[3] There are a lot of reasons not to stay out. For one thing, crew takes more time than anyone except a time tycoon is willing to spend. Practice begins the day before classes open in the fall and never ends. You row out- doors through mid-November, then indoors—except for an occasional super- masculine snow row—until March, then out until the season ends in mid- May. When all is said and done you've spent around 470 hours of your life serving the sport, which is more time than you spend in classrooms all year, or enough to earn one full semester's tuition at $2.25 an hour or read maybe 90 books. If rowing is going to be your prime endeavor in college, you don't want to be no good at it. But the Columbia lightweights didn't win a race this season . . .

[4] Of course, one might want to quit because, whereas the human body is 70% water, the Harlem River cannot make that claim. A staggering quantity and variety of raw sewage flows into the river, joining with dead dogs, arti- chokes, box springs and last year—under the crew dock—a Mafia casualty. One never knows what's going to come up on his oar. Too, the bridges one rows under have a very active bird population and kids along the shore throw rocks and shoot arrows and whatnot. Surviving that, one is always in danger of being run over and killed, or if lucky, merely swamped by the tugs, barges and "America's Favorite Boatride"—the Circle Line. The latter makes the average practice something between a steeplechase and group surfing. It takes a 30-minute subway ride to get to all this at the boathouse at Baker Field, which is one of the largest tracts of private property in Manhattan, another being the Columbia campus itself.

[5] This year, it must be confessed, the Columbia lightweight crew has been losing just about as badly as it could, let alone should, perhaps because the oarsmen are increasingly distracted by the intermittent turmoil on campus and are increasingly aware that crew is, after all, rowboating—a game.

[6] Games are fine for training children. Games simulate life situations. Games absorb energy that might otherwise cause trouble. But when the Columbia men row past the Consolidated Edison power plant on the river, they know that the same men run their school who run Con Ed and they see the air being polluted (clean fuel would cut profits) and they know *that* is not a game. When they walk past emptied buildings they know it was their school, their baby blue and white alma mater that threw the people out and they know that is not a game. And they don't feel like children, and they don't want to be trained and they think perhaps they could use some trouble-making energy.

[7] It begins to seem that crew may be a waste of time when there is so much to be done, so much trouble to be made. And it's a waste of more than time. An eight-oared shell with oars costs about $3,500. Columbia has 12 such shells. The captain of the lightweight crew agrees that it's absurd and probably obscene to be paddling around in something that's worth two years' rent to families down the hill from the campus. The names on Columbia's shells read like a list of people not to be with should the revolution come. If black-lunged coal miners in Appalachia have sweated to make a man rich and the man has given a shell to Columbia, who wants to row in it?

[8] The lightweight captain doesn't know what to do (any more than anybody else knows what to do). There's no way to convert crew shells into food or to redirect the funds of the people who give them. "It's like 'eat your potatoes, Johnny, there are people starving in China,' " the crew captain says. "You talk about waste—this whole country's that way." But he does feel continued commitment to crew entails "pretending that there is no real world," and he—concerned with helping a friend escape from the draft into Canada—finds such a commitment increasingly difficult.

[9] "If there were no past and no present," he says, "crew wouldn't be a bad way to live."

[10] He didn't mention the future.

DISCUSSION

1. Can you identify the song from which the title comes? If you know the other three lines, explain how they fit what the writer is saying in this article.

2. Put into your own words what you think the main idea sentence is. How is it related to the question at the end of paragraph 1? Does the article ever get around to answering the question? If so, where? If not, do you think the contract with the reader has been broken?

3. How does the description of the "traditional" lightweight in paragraph 1 contribute to our understanding of the reasons Kunen gives?

4. What is the reason suggested in paragraph 3? How do the specific details help to make the reason convincing?

5. Suggesting that no one except a "time tycoon" can afford the time to practice seems a deliberate overstatement. What other examples of overstatement can you find? Why do you think Kunen uses them?

6. What specific details help to make the second reason (paragraph 4) more valid to the reader?

7. How many reasons does Kunen give? What are they? Which do you think he considers the most important reason? Why? Which seems to you the most important reason? Why?

216

Read On, Write On

8. Although Kunen (a junior at Columbia University) was a member of the lightweight crew, he avoids saying "I thought," "I did." Instead he uses "you" (paragraph 3) and "they" (paragraphs 6 and 7). Would you like the essay better if he talked about himself? If he used "you" all through or "they" all through? Why?

9. Do you need to know anything about Appalachia to understand the point of the question at the end of paragraph 7? Why or why not?

10. Do you think the concluding line is off the subject? That it introduces a new idea? Why or why not?

11. Do the reasons Kunen gives for not turning out for crew apply to any other more common sports? If you think they do, explain how. If you think they don't defend your position.

12. Are any students on your campus involved in both sports and protest movements? If so, what parts of Kunen's analysis would you disagree with?

WRITING TOPICS
FOR ANALYSIS

OPERATIONAL:

a water saw
a weather vane
a subway turnstile
an electric light switch
water faucet
a door knob and lock
a thermostat
telescope
fireplace chimney
speedometer
compass
micrometer
transistor
transformer

poultry incubator
automobile suspension system
cash register
pool table
Ferris wheel
merry-go-round
swimming pool filter system
blow torch
election campaign
bobbin in a sewing machine
typewriter
guitar
piano
getting a withdrawal slip

"Well, Irene, I just figured it out. If I walked in front of a truck tomorrow, you'd be worth one hundred and four thousand dollars."

Drawing by Saxon, Copyright © 1957, The New Yorker Magazine, Inc.

home permanent
microfilm reader
overhead projector
steam table
reserving a library book
a zipper
telephone answering service
a churn

barbershop quartet
thermos bottle
pressure cooker
using a bus transfer
a dress pattern
a milking machine
a cream separator
getting public assistance

CAUSAL:

a quarrel
growth of junior colleges
success of a fund-raising event
student unrest
backlash
getting a good grade
speaking with an accent
attitudes toward dialect
pollution
failure to enforce pollution laws
some local rebellion
good reading
lowered property values
attitude toward minorities
your preference for a certain

     magazine
popularity of a certain TV show
popularity of a singer
a divorce
an attraction between two people
a fire
the success (or failure) of a party
getting fired
getting hired
an overdrawn bank account
a disappointment
scores on IQ tests
a traffic jam
resentment of school

readings on objective reports 6

OBJECTIVE
REPORTS

Writing a report poses quite a different problem from analyzing an event
or a series of events. A report does not explain why or how things happened
but simply tells that they did happen. Good reports are as clear, complete,
orderly, and objective as possible; they tell *who, what, when, where,*
and sometimes *how much.*

Most of us are familiar with minutes of meetings, automobile accident
forms, laboratory reports, and newspaper articles. A report of a meeting
gives date and time of day, place, business transacted, and decisions made.
Laboratory reports tell the purpose of the experiment, the apparatus used,
the quantities, the procedure, and the results. Accident reports give date,
time of day, names of drivers and passengers, place where the accident
occurred, road conditions, and amount of damage. Newspaper reports
almost always begin with dates, places, names, a brief statement of what the
event was, and then go on to give more details.

Whatever the report covers, whether it is a meeting, an accident, an
experiment, or some other event, the writer must limit himself to factual
information. He must resist the temptation to add his own opinions.
He must not interpret the events. Factual information means
details that can be checked.

A straight report may not be as interesting or as lively as an account
which includes opinion and interpretation, but often bare facts can
have an impact of their own, more dramatic than an interpretation of
those facts. In the following brief report the facts speak more
forcefully than any opinion the writer might have added:

Sportsmen Sack Litter

Some forty sportsmen from seven Portland area clubs took part in a clean-up
campaign on Sauvie Island recently. For five hours the group picked up beer
cans, pop bottles, paper plates and general refuse left by picknickers, fisher-
men and other recreationists.

Actually, the area covered was rather small, including Willow Bar beach,
two smaller beaches nearby and several footbridge areas. However, the
amount of litter cleaned up was far from small. The group collected *105
gunny sacks* of debris during the session!

Sportsmen's groups represented in the clean-up included members from the
Brotherhood of Boosters Rod and Gun Club, Oregon Bass & Panfish Club,
Western Rod & Reel, Multnomah Anglers & Hunters, Portland Spin Fishing

Club, Milwaukee Rod & Gun Club, and a member from the Mazamas. (From "Sportsmen Sack Litter" in the June 1969 Game Commission Bulletin. Reprinted by permission of the Game Commission, State of Oregon.)

Although the comments that the area covered was "rather small" and the amount of litter cleaned up was "far from small" might be considered subjective, in both cases the writer carefully follows through with factual statements. He designates the specific area covered and gives the amount of litter, "105 sacks of debris."

One criticism that might be made is that the opening fails to tell just when the clean-up campaign took place. The word "recently" is vague; it could mean last week, last month, or even last season. Aside from this one omission in the introduction, however, the report appears to be complete, precise and factual.

Flight to Cuba

diverted: changed from one course to another
en route: on the way

[1] MIAMI, June 28 (AP)—An Eastern Airlines jet with 104 persons aboard was hijacked and forced to fly to Cuba today, the third airliner diverted to the Caribbean island in a week.

Main idea sentence— tells *what, how many, when, where*

[2] The Boeing 727, en route from Baltimore to Miami, was flying along Florida's east coast just off Daytona Beach when the pilot announced he was being hijacked.

What happened

[3] The plane, Eastern Flight 173, with 97 passengers and a crew of 7, landed at Havana's Jose Marti Airport at 12:28 P.M., an hour after it changed course for Cuba.

Precise details: plane number, how many people, exact time

[4] The plane later flew to Miami. One of the passengers said the hijacker was a shabbily dressed drunk with a knife. The hijacker remained in Cuba.

More of what happened

[5] It was the thirty-second time this year that a commercial airliner had been forced to fly to Cuba. Six other attempts failed.

Related background information

Reprinted from the June 29, 1969 issue of the *St. Louis Post-Dispatch,* p. 26A, by permission of the Associated Press.

DISCUSSION

1. This straightforward news story, intended to tell the general public what happened, does contain opinion words in paragraph 4. What keeps the report completely factual, even though opinion words are used?

2. Eastern Airlines would probably ask its pilot to make a more detailed report than this newspaper article includes. What other details would the pilot need to give?

3. What would need to be included in the report made by the stewardesses on the plane? By the agent who took the tickets?

A Rainfall of Fish

mystifying: puzzling; bewildering
adjacent: next to
specimen: sample of a type
consumption: eating
velocity: speed
devaluate: belittle; doubt

[1] A rainfall of fish occurred on October 23, 1947, in Marksville, Louisiana, while I was conducting biological investigations for the Department of Wild Life and Fisheries. In the morning of that day, between seven and eight o'clock, fish ranging from two to nine inches in length fell on the streets and in yards, mystifying the citizens of that southern town. I was in the restaurant with my wife having breakfast when the waitress informed us that fish were falling from the sky. We went immediately to collect some of the fish. The people of the town were excited. The director of the Marksville Bank, J. M. Barham, said he had discovered upon arising from bed that fish had fallen by hundreds in his yard, and in the adjacent yard of Mrs. J. W. Joffrion. The cashier of the same bank, J. E. Gremillion, and two merchants, E. A. Blanchard and J. M. Brouillette, were struck by falling fish as they walked toward their places of business about 7:45 A.M. There were spots on Main Street, in the vicinity of the bank (a half block from the restaurant) averaging one fish per square yard. Automobiles and trucks were running over them. Fish also fell on the roofs of houses.

Reprinted from "Do Fish Fall from the Sky?" by A. D. Bajkov, in *Science* (vol. 109, April 22, 1949), p. 402, by permission of the publisher.

[2] They were freshwater fish native to local waters, and belonging to the following species: Large-mouth Black Bass *(Micropterus salmoides)*, Goggle-eyes *(Chaenobryttus coronarius)*, two species of sunfish *(Lepomis)*, several species of minnows, and Hickòry Shad *(Pomolobus medioris)*. The latter (last) species were the most common. I personally collected from Main Street and several yards on Monroe Street, a large jar of perfect specimens, and preserved them in formalin, in order to distribute them among various museums. A local citizen who was struck by a fish told me that the fish were frozen; however, the specimens I collected, although cold, were not frozen. There is at least one record, in 1896 at Essen, Germany, of frozen fish falling from the sky. The largest fish in my collection was a Large-mouth Black Bass, 9½ inches long. The largest falling fish on record was reported from India and weighed over six pounds.

[3] The fish that fell in Marksville were absolutely fresh, and were fit for human consumption. The area in which they fell was approximately 1,000 feet long and about 75 or 80 feet wide, extending in a north-southerly direction, and was covered unevenly by fish. The actual falling of the fish occurred in somewhat short intervals, during foggy and comparatively calm weather. The velocity of the wind on the ground did not exceed eight miles per hour. The New Orleans weather bureau had no report of any large tornado, or updraft in the vicinity of Marksville at that time. However, James Nelson Gowanloch, chief biologist for the Louisiana Department of Wild Life and Fisheries, and I had noticed the presence of numerous small tornadoes, or "devil dusters," the day before the "rain of fish" in Marksville. Fish rains have nearly always been described as being accompanied by violent thunderstorms and heavy rains. This, however, was not the case in Marksville.

[4] Certainly occurrences of this nature are rare, and are not always reported, but nevertheless they are well known. The first mention of the phenomenon was made by Athanaseus in his *De pluvia piscum* nearly two thousand years ago, and E. W. Gudger, in his four collective articles, reports 78 cases of falling fish from the sky. There is no reason for anyone to devaluate the scientific evidence. Many people have never seen tornadoes, but they do not doubt them, and they accept the fact that wind can lift and carry heavy objects. Why can't fish be lifted with water and carried by the whirlwind?

DISCUSSION

1. What is the main idea sentence of this report?

2. Although the order is mostly chronological, paragraph 3 does refer to events that happened the day before. Does this order seem unreasonable? Would it be better for the writer to tell about these "devil dusters" before he tells about the rain of fish? Why or why not?

3. Paragraph 2 uses unusual words, the Latin names for four species of fish.

Since the author also gives their more common names, what is the effect of his including the precise scientific terms?

4. Since this report concerns an event in Louisiana in 1947, is the writer getting off the subject by referring to events in Germany in 1896 and in some unnamed part of the world 2000 years ago? Why or why not?

5. What exact kinds of information about the event has the writer given? For each kind you mention, quote exact details from the article.

6. Even though it's very hard to tell what a writer may have left out of his report, how would you judge this article in terms of completeness? Can you think of any questions you would have asked that this article doesn't answer?

7. Accuracy is even harder for an outsider to judge than completeness is. Nevertheless, there are some things in this article that might make you think this writer is a reliable observer. What are they?

8. The writer makes two comments that contain opinion words in paragraph 1. What are they? Do these two comments spoil the objective tone of the report? Could they be left out without spoiling the report?

9. Where does the report end and the writer's comments on it begin? In these comments, what is the writer trying to do? Would the reports be more effective if the comments were omitted? Why or why not?

Tenants, Army Join in Housing Cleanup

renovated: repaired, made new again
conditional sales contract: an agreement to buy something, whereby the buyer gets a clear title when all the payments are made
equity: the amount the buyer has already paid on whatever he is buying

[1] About twelve young tenants from the Fairview Apartments in the 700 block of Brandywine Street S.W. and fifteen members of the Black Man's Volunteer Army of Liberation were out on the street Saturday morning clearing the block of glass and debris.

"Tenants, Army Join in Housing Cleanup," by Adrienne Manns in the August 18, 1968 issue of the *Washington Post City Life*. Reprinted by permission of *The Washington Post*.

[2] Col. Hassan Jeru-Ahmed, founder of the Army, said his organization volunteered to help Ulysses Robinson, the landlord of Fairview and president of the American Homeowners Plan, "do something realistic for our people."

[3] "After these buildings are renovated and cleaned, they will be offered for sale to the families," said Hassan.

[4] Robinson plans to build sandboxes and swings and set up a medical aid station in the 15-building complex staffed by volunteer doctors and nurses. Hassan said his Army is training local people in building trades and has branches in 50 cities.

[5] Robinson said the American Homeowners Plan will sell the buildings to the present tenants under conditional sales contracts that do not require a down payment.

[6] "We will give them the house and help them put the house in shape. That way they will earn their equity," he said. The tenants will work on painting and plastering or putting in new roofing. After the cost of the work is totaled, it will be credited as partial payment for the building. The Federal Housing Authority will "put a value on the place," Robinson said.

[7] The complex will be sold one building at a time with each tenant in each building owning his own apartment, Robinson said. Robinson's Phoenix Society, a self-help, job-training and housing enterprise at 2005 14th St. N.W. took control of the Homeowners Plan last spring when Matthew Mezzanotte, the landlord, turned over 51 per cent of the stock to the Society.

[8] The apartments were sold to American Homeowners Plan through Mezzanotte on May 20 when the former owner, Robert S. Farmer of Arlington, had accumulated five housing code violations and was being faced with a tenant rent strike.

[9] Robinson, a home improvement contractor, said he will have plasterers and plumbers working inside the buildings this month. Col. Hassan's group will be working mainly on landscaping.

DISCUSSION

1. What is the "event" being covered in this report? If you think there is more than one event, how are the separate events related to each other?

2. Beginning with paragraph 3, the writer uses "will" and "will be" throughout most of the rest of the article. Is he reporting on an event that has happened or making a prediction about what might happen in the future? Support your decision by referring to the article.

3. This report does not follow strict chronological order. Can you think of any reason for following the kind of order that is used?

4. Can you find any opinion words in this report? What specific details can you find?

The Fourteenth of April

starboard: right
port: left
inexorably: without any chance of being prevented or changed
disengaged: broken loose
doomed: headed for certain death or disaster

[1] Sunday evening, April 14th, was the *Titanic*'s fifth night out from Queenstown for New York. All day the sea had been like glass, which was unusual for that time of year. At 10 P.M. there was a change in officers' watches. First Officer Murdock came on the bridge to relieve Second Officer Lightoller. They were old shipmates, and Murdock stood chatting for a few minutes to adjust his eyesight after coming from the lighted desk into pitch darkness.

[2] Both officers remarked upon the flat calm. Never in their long experience in crossing the North Atlantic had they seen such an absolutely flat sea. It was like a lake of oil, slipping smoothly away from the sides of the hull without a trace of swell. They discussed the ice reports. There was always a possibility of meeting ice when crossing the Banks. Lightoller said, "It's a pity the wind hasn't kept up while we're going through the ice region."

[3] The stronger the breeze at night, the more visible the ice, or rather the breakers on the ice. As a rule, bergs have a side that has been crystallized through exposure which will reflect a certain amount of light termed "ice blink." It is this ice blink, often seen before the berg itself comes above the horizon, for which seamen are on the lookout.

[4] But on the other hand the side of an iceberg that has "calved" or broken away from its parent glacier will usually be black, due to the earthy matter and rock that are in all bergs. This dark side, until it turns white from considerable exposure, will not give off any ice blink. If ice of this dark character appears on a dead calm sea, there is no sign at all to give a seaman any indication that there is anything there. It is especially difficult to see from a height, since it blends with the ocean if a man is looking down at an angle. At sea level, it might loom up.

[5] At 11:30 P.M. First Officer Murdock stood against the forward rail, 60 feet above the sea. He had an unobstructed view right ahead and a couple of points on either bow. In an earlier watch he had asked the lamptrimmer, Hemmings, to close the forescuttle hatch as a faint glow was coming up from below. He wanted nothing to interfere with vision from bridge or

From "The Fourteenth of April," by Angela Stuart in the June 1968 issue of *Mankind*, Volume 1, No. 7. Reprinted by permission of the author and publisher.

crow's-nest. Seamen usually spot a berg first with the naked eye, and not through binoculars. Afterwards it can be examined through glasses.

[6] Suddenly, Frederick Fleet in the crow's-nest, 30 feet above Murdock, saw a dark shadow immediately ahead off the *Titanic's* bow. He grabbed the bell rope to his right and struck the hammer three times—object dead ahead. Then he picked up the receiver of the bridge telephone.

[7] "Iceberg right ahead."

[8] First Officer Murdock leapt for the telegraphs and rang them over to "Stop!" shouting, "Hard-a-starboard!" Then he rang "Full Astern!" almost in the same moment.

[9] At the wheel, Robert Hitchens put all his weight on the spokes. Glancing up at the wheelhouse clock he saw it was twenty minutes to twelve. The berg was about a quarter of a mile ahead when the bow, still cutting through the water at 22 knots, began to swing slowly to port.

[10] But the berg slid inexorably toward the ship, moving gradually over to starboard as the helm began to have effect. The men on the bridge saw it tower up 40 or 50 feet from the flat sea. Hitchens was still heaving the spokes of the wheel around with every ounce of his energy when he felt it jam.

[11] "Wheel hard over!" he called.

[12] "Hard-aport!" Murdock ordered.

[13] They felt a slight shock as the ship struck the berg well forward of the foremast. Evidently there had been a shelf protruding below the water, and this pierced the *Titanic's* bow as she threw her whole weight on the ice. The ice tore a gash in the forepeak, number 1 hold, number 2 hold, the baggage and mail hold, number 6 boiler room—a jagged wound stretching 300 feet in less than ten seconds before she disengaged.

[14] "Everything was against us," Second Officer Lightoller testified later at the Enquiry. Had there been either wind or swell, the outline of the berg would have been rendered visible through the water breaking at the base. As it turned out, the disaster "was due to a combination of circumstances that never happened before and can never occur again."

[15] The iceberg, wet and glistening, passed swiftly along the starboard side. It came so near the hull chunks of ice fell through an open porthole into a cabin. As it shot past the passenger decks it was picked out stark white in the blaze of the lights. Then it faded into the darkness astern, a mountain of ice standing black against the starlit sky.

[16] When the *Titanic* drew to a stop a half mile from the point of collision, she was a doomed ship. She had about two and a half hours to live. And while the engineers would give their lives to a man to save her, she was past saving.

DISCUSSION

1. The sinking of the *Titanic,* one of the great sea disasters, occurred April 14, 1912, with a loss of approximately 1,500 lives. This report, then, does not cover a recent event, but rather tells what happened in one part of a

well-known tragedy. What additional details are given in this reconstruction that you would not expect to find in a newspaper report published the day after the accident? What has been omitted that you would expect the newspaper report to have included?

2. This account also contains some causal analysis. What is being analyzed? Do you think the analysis should be left out of the report?

3. What factual details—who, what, when, where, how much—are given in the report? Does the report omit any factual details about which you are curious? What are they?

4. What description or interpretation does the report contain? Why has it been added? What does the audience for which the report was written have to do with these additional details?

5. What is the effect of adding such details as "to adjust his eyesight after coming from the lighted desk into pitch darkness" (paragraph 1) or "glancing up at the wheelhouse clock" (paragraph 9)? What is the effect of quoting exactly what the officers said to each other? How can the writer, half a century after the accident, know what the seamen said?

6. Does the last sentence of the report contain an opinion? If so, what is it? Or is it a statement of fact (all the engineers did die in the accident), reminding the reader of the seriousness of the collision?

Reports That Interpret

Although we often think of reports as telling what happened in one place on one day, some reports deal with conditions or problems rather than single events. They tell what happened, they try to be objective, but the writer is concerned with several related events rather than one single occurrence. For instance, a report may tell what happened on several occasions to people who listen to extremely loud music. It may tell what happened in several accidents in which a certain kind of safety equipment was used. Or, in an attempt to reconstruct what actually happened, it may report the same event from several different points of view. Such reports, like those that deal with a single event, will be useful only if they stick to the facts and leave the writer's opinion out.

Sometimes the word "report" is used more broadly to describe a piece of writing that contains not only an account of what happened but also an analysis of what caused it to happen. Occasionally such "reports" even include recommendations. For example, a commission appointed by the President of the United States studied the reasons for low voter turnout in America and recommended solutions. The results of the commission's investigation were written up and published as *A Report of the President's Commission on Registration and Voting Participation*. Since such reports combine what happened with causal analysis and recommendations, it might be more appropriate to call them "studies."

Similarly, the so-called "Walker Report," prepared by a commission in Chicago under the direction of Daniel Walker, and submitted to the National Commission on the Causes and Prevention of Violence, contains factual accounts of the disturbances in Chicago during the Democratic National Convention of 1968. But this nearly 400-page report also tries to analyze the underlying causes of the violence, points the finger of criticism where criticism is due, and then offers recommendations as to what should be done about it.

In this kind of report, however, the writer is careful to make clear where the "pure report" leaves off and where the analysis, criticism, and recommendations begin. Sometimes this separation is made clear by a paragraph or two of explanation, warning the reader that the reporting has been finished; sometimes the distinction is clear from the chapter headings. Whatever the method, a careful writer makes sure that his readers can tell when he is reporting what happened and when he is giving his opinion about it.

Wildlife Killed

toll: the count of damage or death resulting from some action
succumbed: died
immune: safe from something

[1] A great toll is taken on the nation's wildlife each year on the highways. In some areas, it surpasses that taken by hunters in the woods and fields. And the percentage climbs year by year, day by day.

Main idea sentence promises to cover many events related to single topic: wildlife killed on highways

[2] The highest tolls of deer are recorded in California, Michigan, Minnesota, Pennsylvania, and Wisconsin. Pennsylvania has the highest count: in 1966 alone, 20,126 deer were killed in collisions with cars. This total does not include those that were unreported and those that managed to drag themselves into the brush before they succumbed.

Exact numbers given

[3] Deer are by far the most prone to highway accidents of all large wild animals, but others are not immune. Alaska reported 75 moose killed in 1966,

Exact kinds of animals killed

Reprinted from "Protect America's Wildlife!" by Bill Thomas in the August 1968 issue of *Oldsmobile's Rocket Circle,* by permission of Oldsmobile, Division of General Motors Corporation.

Arizona and Colorado lost more than 50 elk, and Florida reported 10 bear, 500 wild hogs, and 250 wild turkeys killed along its highways. In the same year, Wyoming lost 200 antelope in vehicle accidents. [4] The greatest toll of wildlife, however, is among small game and birds. No count is kept of these, but Warren Wells, park naturalist of the Hamilton County Park District, Cincinnati, Ohio, kept a six months' tally recently that covered only roads within three county parks. His tally included: one gray fox, six squirrels, ten raccoons, nineteen opossums, seventy-five rabbits, three woodchucks, eleven skunks, one mink, three muskrats, two owls, one quail, four cardinals, and five box turtles. Wells estimates this was roughly one-tenth of total wildlife destruction on the highways for this one Ohio county alone.

More kinds and more numbers

[5] Last year, I was returning from a fishing trip in Eastern Kentucky. I counted 29 cottontail rabbits killed on a little-traveled state highway within a 15-mile stretch. It was only hours after a rain, a time which wildlife officials say is most critical.

One event: count for a single day

[6] Tom Lewis, a Kentucky Fish and Wildlife Division regional director said 90 percent of the deer kill reported on highways in his area were reported shortly after a rain. "Wildlife begins to move out along the roads after a rain," he said, "and motorists traveling through areas marked with deer crossing signs should take particular care at this time." . . .

Quotation from a man whose business is wildlife

[7] The National Wildlife Management Institute and conservation officials of every state are deeply concerned and are searching for ways to curb the annual toll of wildlife.

Conclusion: what's being done about it

DISCUSSION

1. The main idea sentence of this report contains an opinion word, "great." What factual information given in the report justifies the use of this opinion word? Would you like the report better if the word "great" were left out and just the facts given? If so, how would you word the main idea sentence?

2. The last sentence of paragraph 1 contains no opinion but it is a very general statement. Are there any facts given in the report to support this statement? If so, what are they? If not, does this omission make the report incomplete?

3. Although the writer has given exact figures, he makes it clear that the numbers are probably not accurate. How does he indicate this lack of accuracy in paragraph 2? In paragraph 3? In paragraph 4? Does the fact that the reader knows the figures are not accurate damage the report? Why or why not?

4. In paragraph 5, the writer shifts rather abruptly from giving figures from all over the country to telling what happened to him personally. Write a transition sentence that makes the shift less abrupt. You may also, if you like, re-word the rest of paragraph 5.

5. Paragraph 6 contains some advice and some opinion. How does the writer manage to include this advice and still keep his report objective? How does he manage to keep the conclusion objective?

6. Can you tell from reading this report whether the writer is blaming the motorists? Is he blaming anybody? Is he upset about the toll of wildlife? Justify your answers by referring to the report.

Going Deaf from Rock 'n' Roll

otologist: specialist in hearing
irreversible: can't be changed or corrected
susceptible: subject to; likely to be affected
decibel: a unit measuring the smallest sound a man can hear
acuity: sharpness
fortissimi: very loud sounds
dissipated: scattered; lessened
cacophony: harsh and unpleasant mixture of sounds, usually very loud
impairment: damage
resiliency: ability to spring back

[1] Otologists report that youngsters are going deaf as a result of blasting their eardrums with electronically amplified rock 'n' roll.
[2] The hearing specialists used to worry about loud noise as a cause of

deafness only in industrial and military situations. They knew that eight hours of daily exposure, year in and year out, to the din of the proverbial boiler factory would eventually result in permanent, irreversible hearing loss. Riveters were particularly susceptible. Then they learned that the same thing happened to aviators. And after the advent of jets, the hazard applied to ground crews at airports and flight-deck personnel aboard aircraft carriers—hence the introduction of insulated, noise-absorbing plastic earmuffs.

[3] From industrial and military experience, the experts set certain standards for safety. Any prolonged exposure to a noise level above 85 decibels will eventually result in a loss of hearing acuity for sounds in the frequency most important for understanding human speech. This range is roughly from 256 cycles per second, the pitch of middle C, to about 2,000 c.p.s., or the C three octaves higher. Acuity is impaired even earlier for higher pitches, such as violin overtones.

[4] In discotheques and rock-'n'-roll joints, the trouble is not so much in the instruments themselves, or even the sustained fortissimi or the close quarters. The blame goes to the electronic amplifiers. An old-fashioned oompah military band, playing a Sousa march in Central or Golden Gate Park, generated as much sound. But the sound was not amplified, and was dissipated in the open air. A trombonist sitting in front of a tuba player might be a bit deaf for an hour or so after a concert; then his hearing returned to normal. A microphone hooked up to a public-address system did not much increase the hearing hazard. What did was multiple mikes and speakers, and the installation of internal mikes in such instruments as guitars and bouzoukia.

[5] "With these," says Dr. Robert Feder, a Beverly Hills ear specialist, "everything is reamplified many times, and the noise becomes nearly intolerable." Dr. Victor Goodhill of Hollywood reports that sound levels in many rock-'n'-roll night clubs soar to 125 db. Dr. Charles P. Lebo of the University of California took measuring instruments into two San Francisco rock-'n'-roll joints, where the cacophony was produced mainly by amplified guitars and percussion instruments. Throughout the audible-speech range, Lebo found that the sound intensity averaged over 100 db at virtually all frequencies. It rose to 119 db at peaks in the center of the hall.

[6] Individuals vary in their sensitivity to loud noise. Lebo estimates that 10% of the people in such a hall would show no effects, 80% would have their hearing threshold raised by five to 30 db, and 10% would suffer a 40-db impairment, at least temporarily. As for permanent damage, some might suffer it after a week or two of steady listening, while others could take it for a year.

[7] The man who had the problem closest to home, and studied it there, was George T. Singleton, an ear, nose and throat man at the University of Florida. He noticed that when he picked up his teen-age daughter Marsha after a dance she couldn't hear what he said in the car on the way home. Singleton recruited a research team and tested the hearing of ten 14-year-old ninth-graders an hour before a dance. Then the investigators went to the dance hall, and found the average sound intensity to be 106 to 108 db in the middle of the dance floor. Directly in front of the band it peaked to 120 db. The test crew

had to move 40 feet outside the building before the level dropped to a safe but still uncomfortable 90 db.

[8] After the dance, the kids' hearing was tested again. Despite the youthful resiliency of their inner ears, all had suffered at least temporary hearing impairment, with the average loss at about 11 db. One boy showed a 35-db loss. The greatest damage was in the high-frequency speech range, involving consonantal sounds, similar to the loss felt by oldsters who complain that "everybody mumbles nowadays."

DISCUSSION

1. If the first sentence of this report is the main idea, how well is it supported by the rest of the article?

2. How many experiments are reported in the article? How complete is the information you are given?

3. Why does the account of the experiments come so late in the article? This article contains summaries of more complete reports made by the doctors; do you think the material given in paragraphs 2 and 3 would have been included in the reports that Dr. Lebo and Dr. Singleton wrote? Why or why not? Why have these two paragraphs been included here? What has the audience to do with whether this material belongs in the report and appears where it does?

4. If you consider that all the words listed at the top of this article are "big words," which ones are needed to make the report precise? For which ones could more ordinary words be substituted without spoiling the report?

5. Can you find any slanted language in this report? If so, what is it?

Roll Over Protective Structures Add to Safety

prime: principal
canopy: a covering suspended on a frame
materially: greatly, measurably

[1] An accident occurred recently on the Blue River Dam Project, being constructed by the Portland District, Corps of Engineers, in which a loaded 35-ton Haul Pak end-dump truck, operated by Lockheed Ship-building and

From "Roll Over Protective Structures Add to Safety," SAFER OREGON, June–July 1968, p. 4. Reprinted by permission of the Workmen's Compensation Board of the State of Oregon.

Construction Company, prime contractor for the main dam, went off the side of a haul road and rolled down a rocky slope to the bottom of the canyon, a distance of 240-feet on an 80% slope. The vehicle rolled through a minimum of 3½ full turns and came to rest in about 2-feet of water. The driver of the vehicle was thrown out of the cab through the windshield during the roll and severely injured. All the injuries to the driver apparently occurred after he had been thrown from the cab.

[2] Following recovery of the truck, which was equipped with a rollover protective structure, the vehicle was found to be in functional condition with all essential devices in working order, including the engine, the steering, and the battery powered emergency hydraulic pump. The cab, while battered and dented, still provided adequate protected space for the operator. The seat belt provided in the truck was apparently not being used by the operator at the time of the accident.

[3] A few days earlier, a 50-ton Haul Pak had a mechanical steering failure while traveling along the river side of the haul road. The operator was unable to stop the truck before it went over the bank and rolled over and into the river. The truck rolled through 270 degrees. The operator, while not wearing the seat belt provided, escaped with only a few bruises. Damage to the truck was minor although the radiator and engine could have easily been demolished. Each of these trucks had recently been equipped with a rollover canopy which functioned in accordance with its design by providing a safe protected space for the operator as well as materially reducing damage to the vehicle.

[4] Rollover accidents have been a major concern to contractors for many years. When this type of accident occurs it invariably results in severe injuries or death to the equipment operator and extensive damage to the machine. In 1960 the North Pacific Division of the U.S. Army, Corps of Engineers, began requiring steel canopies capable of resisting rollover on all crawler type tractors. Today, in the Willamette Valley, it is difficult to find any crawler tractors without such a canopy. Operators of this type of equipment have been fully convinced of the value of this protection.

[5] In 1964 the Corps required that seat belts be installed on all rubber tired vehicles. In 1967 this requirement was extended to include tracked tractors also. At this time steel canopies, or rollover structures, for all tractors, pneumatic tired earth movers, water trucks, and motor patrols became a requirement on all Corps of Engineer contracts throughout the United States. The two accidents described above show the wisdom and necessity for these devices.

DISCUSSION

1. What is the topic being covered in this report? Can you find a main idea sentence which includes the topic? If so, what is it? If not, put into your own words what you think it would be.

2. What kind of order is being used in the report? Why does the report begin with reports of two separate events?

3. In paragraphs 1 and 3, why are the names of the drivers left out? Why are the exact dates left out?

4. What exact details of the two accidents are given? What details are left out?

5. How does the use of "apparently" at the end of paragraphs 1 and 2 help to make the writer sound accurate and objective?

6. What statements in the report give the writer's interpretation of the facts rather than the facts themselves? Can you think of any way the report could be written without this interpretation? How?

Clearing Clark Street

batons: nightsticks
initiated: began
media: newspapers; radio; television
brandished: displayed threateningly
epithets: insulting names
distraught: very upset

[1] Chicago, August 26, 1968. One observer describes the clearing of Clark Street in these words:

> The demonstrators were forced out onto Clark Street and once again a traffic jam developed. Cars were stopped, the horns began to honk, people couldn't move, people got gassed inside their cars, police were the objects of stones, and taunts, mostly taunts. As you must understand, most of the taunting of the police was verbal. There were stones thrown of course, but for the most part it was verbal. But there were stones being thrown and of course the police were responding with tear gas and clubs and everytime they could get near enough to a demonstrator they hit him.
>
> But again you had this police problem within—this really turned into a police problem. They pushed everybody out of the park, but this night there were a lot more people in the park than there had been during the previous

From RIGHTS IN CONFLICT, a Report Submitted by Daniel Walker, Director of the Chicago Study Team, to the National Commission on the Causes and Prevention of Violence, Bantam, Dec., 1968, pp. 179–183.

night and Clark Street was just full of people and in addition now was full of gas because the police were using gas on a much larger scale this night. So the police were faced with the task, which took them about an hour or so, of hitting people over the head and gassing them enough to get them out of Clark, which they did.

[2] At this point, Task Force officers initiated a series of sallies into Clark Street to apprehend apparent rock and bottle throwers and highly vocal demonstrators. After each sally the officers returned to the police lines. [3] Later, a young couple was halted by police who used their batons on the man, leaving him sprawling against a mail box. The girl ran into the middle of the street and shouted: "Why do you do that?" Four officers moved off the east curb, grabbed the girl by her arms and legs, and dragged her toward a squadron behind the police line. A free-lance photographer, covering the clearance for a magazine, snapped pictures of the scene, but as he did, police pulled his strobe unit away from him, ripped off his battery pack and struck him in the arms and abdomen.

[4] By this time, a police line was pushing a crowd estimated at about 1,000 persons north from their position blocking the Eugenie Triangle. At the same time, further north, another line of police was pushing people south. [5] As the first line of police passed the southwestern tip of the park, they yelled to a Chicago attorney, his wife and five or six others standing behind a park bench, telling them they had better get moving. The attorney and his wife hesitated. Then a group of officers broke from the line toward them. As they did, the attorney and his wife started to walk south toward the Chicago Historical Society building in Lincoln Park. The officer who had warned them was joined by seven or eight others who started to run toward them. They shouted: "Run!"

[6] They ran about 20 or 30 yards, turned around and stopped. The attorney said to his wife: "Slow down, they're not following us." But then he heard his wife say, "Damn you." She had been struck on the back and head by an officer with a baton. The attorney was also hit.

[7] At approximately the same time, according to a resident of the area, seven police officers, carrying what looked like knives or other sharp weapons, slashed the tires of cars parked in a parking lot, just opposite Lincoln Avenue and Clark Street, between Clark and Stockton Drive. He says he also saw police break the windows of several cars.

[8] The editor of a Chicago community newspaper came to the same parking lot at 5 A.M. with a friend from California to retrieve a Volkswagen camper owned by the latter. They discovered the tires slashed and the windows bashed in. A guitar and luggage had also been damaged.

[9] An Assistant U.S. Attorney says that on Monday night he observed three police officers standing next to a vehicle on Stockton Drive, about one-half block north of North Avenue. "The three officers appeared to be joking as they moved away from the loudly hissing rear tires of the vehicle," said the attorney. "It appeared that the officers had either slashed or released the air

from the tires." He says he saw several other vehicles in the area with one or more deflated tires.

[10] The people were pushed, shoved, gassed and clubbed until they reached Wells Street and North Avenue. At this intersection Mayor Carl Stokes of Cleveland was walking through the crowds, talking to people, trying to calm them down. Some of the crowd argued with him. He left the area shortly thereafter.

[11] A Chicago Transit Authority bus stopped to unload passengers at Lincoln Avenue and Clark. One of them was struck by policemen swinging batons. The man asked two ministers: "Why did they hit me? I'm just returning from work."

[12] Another minister spotted a boy lying on the west sidewalk of Clark Street, at the foot of a line of police who were blocking foot traffic. The minister asked a sergeant for permission to aid the boy, who was bleeding. When he had finished treating the boy, the medic and the minister walked by the police line. As they did, an officer yelled: "You sons-of-bitches, you big fakes. Give us a target."

[13] As the crowd fled, chaos and confusion traveled with them. An NBC truck stationed on Wisconsin Street was stoned, a squad car attacked, properly identified media personnel were beaten and some with cameras were attacked, and their cameras smashed or film destroyed. There were reports of shots fired and windows broken. Police moved everywhere in pursuit of the demonstrators, charging up streets, walks and into hallways. Many were not wearing identification.

[14] The crowd called them "Pigs," and some of the police, brandishing their nightsticks, yelled back: "Give us targets. Come on, do something." Bottles were thrown, and the police charged the crowd up to Eugenie, pressing the demonstrators out from Eugenie onto Wells. Shouts of "Let's get the fuckers" were heard from the police.

[15] Police lines had also formed on Wells and on Schiller, and the crowd was forced back to Burton where they were pinched off by the line of officers moving south on Wells from the Old Town Triangle. They tried to move east down LaSalle where they encountered yet another line of advancing police. Discovering that lines of escape were blocked, many demonstrators panicked and began to run in all directions. Officers leaped from unmarked cars and struck demonstrators with their nightsticks.

[16] The scene was so chaotic that even residents attempting to assist the police were roughly handled. A doctor driving home that night saw "hippies" dumping trash cans onto the street and throwing objects at parked cars. When attempting to bring this to the attention of a policeman, he was met with, "Listen you god damn mother fucker, get this fucking car out of here." He tried again to explain his concern, but was interrupted with, "Listen, you son-of-a-bitch, didn't you hear me the first time?" The policeman then struck the man's car with his nightstick, causing a sizeable dent. The doctor gave up his attempt to assist and drove home immediately.

[17] Violence raged through the early morning hours and was not limited to police actions. Groups of all types, including "locals," stoned police cars, broke windows and street lights, and shouted epithets at the police. One police officer was driving his squad car on Clark Street when his car door was pierced by a weapon which may have been a pickaxe. The officer suffered abrasions to his left forearm.

[18] A young man got off a CTA bus near the Lincoln Hotel and walked north. A police officer walked up to him and hit him with his elbow in the chest and stomach. The young man, about 30 years old, folded over but did not fall. The officer walked away.

[19] As a crowd of demonstrators moved past one observer, he noticed a young man being moved along by a policeman holding him by the upper arm. The young man was wearing identification badges or credentials around his neck. "This isn't a police state!" he said. Two or three other policemen joined the first, pushed the young man into a doorway and began hitting him. Immediately two persons with cameras began to move into the area yelling: "Police brutality." The observer said that two or three other policemen turned after the men with the cameras and began beating one of them.

[20] By 1 A.M., police had cleared the Eugenie Triangle. At about that time a *Chicago Daily News* reporter became involved in an incident with the police.

[21] The tape of the Police Department radio log discloses the following conversation at 1:29 A.M. on Tuesday morning:

> Police Operator: "1814, get a wagon over at 1436. We've got an injured hippie."
>
> Voice: "1436 North Wells?"
>
> Operator: "North Wells."
>
> In quick sequence, there are the following remarks from five other police cars:
>
> "That's no emergency."
>
> "Let him take a bus."
>
> "Kick the fucker."
>
> "Knock his teeth out."
>
> "Throw him in a wastepaper basket."

[22] The Medical Committee For Human Rights and the Student Health Organization, an assisting group of medics, reported that they had treated 24 persons for injuries Monday night, almost all lacerations. They said three others had also been maced.

[23] Most police had been on duty over 15 hours. All told, 15 policemen were reportedly treated for injuries Monday.

[24] By 2 A.M., there was little activity left to observe on the streets. Several people had watched the action from the roof above an apartment building. Their presence, however, had inspired reports of snipers. Two policemen came to the door of the residence to investigate. "There's a sniper on your roof!" the officers exclaimed. They demanded to search the apartment. Other officers were searching the other apartments in the building. A dog began to

bark and one of the officers pointed a gun at it. "Get this dog back or the dog will die." Quite distraught, another officer asked simply: "Why do you call us pigs?"

DISCUSSION

1. This selection from the Walker report combines a number of separate incidents, each of which could have been reported separately. What do the events have in common that justifies their being included in a single section?

2. The investigating team which wrote this report was not present in Clark Street on Monday night, and the readers of the report understand this. What have the writers done to convince readers that they are being as accurate and exact as possible?

3. What has the investigating team done to convince readers that the report is as complete as possible? Does it seem complete to you? Why or why not?

4. With one exception (paragraph 10) names have been entirely omitted from this report. Do you think they should have been included? Why or why not? Why has a name been included in paragraph 10?

5. Does paragraph 17 give a different point of view from that in the earlier paragraphs? What is it? What transition does the writer use to prepare the reader for the change?

6. How many separate sources has the investigating team used in making this report? How many kinds of sources? Do all the kinds of sources seem to you equally objective? Discuss.

7. The report contains a number of direct quotations, all from people who were in Clark Street that night. Which quotations use the most objective language? Which the least?

8. The Walker report, from which this selection comes, is really a "study" rather than a pure report. If you separate what the writer says from the quoted reports of eyewitnesses, do you think the writer stays objective or does he interpret the events he is reporting? Support what you say by referring to the selection.

9. The introduction to the complete Walker report contains the following comment: "This edition . . . includes the extremely obscene language which was considered essential to the accuracy and effectiveness of the Report and was so significantly a part of the confrontation between demonstrators and police." Are some of the words included in this selection (words not usually printed in newspapers and magazines) "essential to the accuracy and effectiveness" of the report? Give reasons for your answer.

10. If you think the obscene words should not have been included, either in the complete report or in this selection, is it because you have not heard the words before? Is it because they might damage other people who have not heard them? If you have other reasons, what are they?

11. What does the writer do to make this section of the report sound ended? Consider both the first and the last sentences of paragraph 24.

12. If you were a member of the Walker Commission, what recommendations for change would you make on the basis of this report? If you think this brief selection, covering only a few hours out of a week, gives an incomplete picture of what happened in Chicago, read some other sections of *Rights in Conflict* before you make your recommendations.

Certainly good reports must stick to the subject; certainly they must be precise, orderly, complete, exact, and accurate; but perhaps the most important thing they must do is avoid making judgments about what has happened. On many topics or about many events, it is fairly easy to stay objective, particularly if we or our friends have not been personally involved. There are other topics and other events, however, which are hard to report objectively. One place where staying objective is difficult is in reporting events which are highly controversial. Although we may realize that not everybody agrees with us, our emotions are so deeply involved that we find it almost impossible to keep interpretation and judgment from mixing with our account of what happened. Topics such as the draft or the race question are likely to make objectivity hard to maintain.

Another place where objectivity is difficult is where what has happened includes behavior that almost all of us consider wrong—murder or betrayal of trust or bribery of public officials, for instance. We tend to assume that all "right-thinking" readers will agree with our judgment, or perhaps we forget that our condemnation is a judgment and think the "wrongness" is part of the fact.

Work Is Cut, Bid Bigger

specifications: exact list of work to be done, and details about materials needed

rehabilitation: putting back in good condition

Reprinted, with changes, from "Work is Cut, Bid Bigger," by Edward H. Thornton, in the *St. Louis Post-Dispatch* (June 25, 1969), by permission of the author and the publisher.

execution: putting into effect
comptroller: director of money and budgets
inequity: unfairness
pending: still unsettled; hasn't happened yet
grant: gift of foundation or government money

[1] Considerably less work was required in revised specifications for one rehabilitation project under the housing code enforcement program on which bids of three contractors were thrown out in favor of a much higher bid by the H. Kalicak Construction Co., Inc.

Main idea sentence—gives the point of the report, to be followed later in the article by more specific details

[2] This was shown today by an analysis of the original set of specifications prepared Feb. 21, 1968, by the housing section of Building Commissioner Kenneth O. Brown's office and the revised specifications, dated last March 17, on which the Kalicak company based its bid.

When (analysis made *today* June 23, 1969, although the specifications were written much earlier)
Who prepared the specifications—in general
What the specifications covered

[3] The work is proposed for the home of Mrs. Irma Bennett, 5190 Cabanne Avenue. The application for a grant and loan under the federally financed program is one of those awaiting approval by the Kansas City office of the Department of Housing and Urban Development, Brown said.

[4] Kalicak's bid of $4,302 was sent to the Kansas City office with the loan application. A rehabilitation contract between the Kalicak company and Mrs. Bennett has been prepared for execution when the loan is approved.

[5] The Kalicak bid is nearly $3,000 higher than the lowest of the three bids received last year on the project and discarded by Brown's office.

How much the difference in the bids was

[6] These were Ace Construction & Engineering Co., 4069 Laclede Avenue, $1,602; Jim Bennett, contractor, 4251 Wyoming Avenue, $1,700, and Sunny Baer Construction Co., 2515 North Grand Boulevard, $1,793.

[7] Meanwhile, a check of records in the office of Comptroller John H. Poelker showed that a former employee of the Kalicak company has been employed in the housing section of Brown's office since mid-February writing specifications for projects under the program.

Who works in the housing section of the Building Commissions office and *what* his present job is and *what* his background is

[8] He is William Schmitt, who admitted to the Post-Dispatch that he came direct from the Kalicak

company to Brown's office under a contract between the building commissioner's office and M-R Contractors, Inc., to furnish a "construction supervisor" for the housing section at $700 a month.

[9] Schmitt said he was authorized to sign bid proposals when employed by Kalicak and that he had signed bids for the company on rehabilitation projects under the code enforcement program.

What Schmitt said

[10] He said his duties in the housing section had dealt only with preparing specifications, but he could not recall whether he prepared the revised specifications on Mrs. Bennett's home.

[11] To obtain an unbiased analysis, the Post-Dispatch submitted copies of the original specifications prepared by Brown's office and of the revised specifications on which Kalicak bid to a contractor who is a recognized expert in home construction.

What the analysis showed

[12] After studying the two sets of specifications, he reported that the original specifications called for at least $200 more work than the revised specifications.

[13] The original specifications called for more plastering and for installation of fencing and concrete work, which were not included in the revised specifications, and removal costs not required in the revised set, he said.

[14] He pointed out that the revised specifications called for more tuckpointing, carpentry and painting work than the original set of specifications and some plumbing work not included originally.

[15] However, he estimated that the total amount of additional work provided in the revised specifications would cost about $375, whereas the extra work required under the original specifications and not covered in the revised set would cost about $575.

[16] When asked about the difference in the specifications, Brown said:

What the Building Commissioner said

[17] "To my knowledge, we have never rewritten specifications to require less work. This certainly should not be the case and I don't think it has happened. If it has happened, however, it would appear we've got an inequity.

[18] "When we rewrote specifications and took new bids, we scrapped the old bids and specifications because they were no longer applicable."

[19] Brown said it is possible that this project might

be reconsidered and that some of the other pending projects also might be reworked.

[20] As previously disclosed by the Post-Dispatch, most of the contracts for rehabilitation projects under the code enforcement program have been channeled to the Kalicak company since it became interested in the program last November.

Background material the reader might not have: information on winners of earlier bids

[21] Brown said last week that in the future he would seek bids from two contractors on each project.

What Brown said again

[22] The $2,658,542 program, to which the Federal Government is contributing $1,986,095, is being conducted in the Academy North and South and O'Fallon South areas of the city.

More background information:
a. *Where* the rehabilitation project takes place
b. *What* the terms of the grant are

[23] Under it, the property owners may obtain grants for amounts up to $3,000 to pay for necessary work to bring their properties up to minimum housing standards. Loans at 3 percent interest may be obtained for amounts required in excess of $3,000.

DISCUSSION

1. The main idea sentence of this report contains two opinion terms, "considerably less" and "much higher." How are these opinions justified by the details given later in the report?

2. What effect is created by the use of *thrown out* in paragraph 1, *admitted* in paragraph 8, *disclosed* and *channeled* in paragraph 20? What more neutral words could be substituted for them?

3. Evaluate this report for precision, order, exactness, and sticking to the subject.

4. Why do paragraphs 7 through 10 give background and statements from only one Housing section employee? Why doesn't the writer of the article explain why he interviewed Schmitt?

5. Paragraph 20 also contains an opinion word in the phrase "most of the contracts." Is this opinion justified by details given elsewhere in the report? What percentage would you consider "most"?

6. The writer has been careful to avoid making any comment about *why* the bid was awarded to Kalicak. Even the one opinion word that is used to describe the event (*inequity* in paragraph 17) is quoted from what Commissioner Brown said. Is *inequity* the word you would use to

describe what seems to have happened in the awarding of this bid? What opinion words would you use to describe it?

7. Who would have benefited had one of the earlier bids been accepted? Who loses on the Kalicak bid? Why doesn't the writer point this out?

A Color Discrimination Test

rural: in the country; not in or near a large city

frustration: being upset by a situation you can't change

[1] RICEVILLE, Iowa (AP)—A rural third grade teacher who gave her pupils their first lesson in discrimination said the results were "absolutely frightening."

[2] "I was sick. I was simply dumbfounded," said Mrs. Darald Elliott, 34. "We had all the problems you hear about being connected with intolerance and prejudice." But she said the children benefited from the experience, and she plans similar lessons in the future.

[3] To make the white youngsters in this northeast Iowa community aware of color discrimination, Mrs. Elliott divided the class into two groups—those with blue eyes and those with brown.

[4] She gave the brown-eyed children special privileges during a Friday "Discrimination Day." The following Monday the blue-eyed youngsters were given the superior role.

[5] Though they knew it was just a lesson, she said the "inferior" group reacted with real anger, frustration and despair while their "superior" class-mates lorded it over them.

[6] "The people with blue eyes could not do the things the people with brown eyes did," one youngster wrote of the first day. "I felt like giving them all black eyes."

[7] From another: "I felt like slapping a brown-eyed person. It made me mad. Then I felt like kicking a brown-eyed person. I felt like quitting school. The brown-eyed people got five extra minutes of recess."

[8] He added: "I would not like to be angry all my life."

[9] Pupils' grades suffered when they were in the less-favored position. "I didn't want to work. I didn't feel like I was very big," noted one boy.

[10] But he and the others perked up during their privileged day. "On Monday I was happy because we discriminated against the brown-eyed

Reprinted by permission of the Associated Press.

people and I felt smarter and gooder and cleaner than the brown-eyed people," noted a blue-eyed girl.

[11] Mrs. Elliott said three green-eyed youngsters who weren't specifically placed in either group leaned toward the underprivileged.

[12] What was the effect of the two-day experiment on the 28 children, aged 8 and 9? "Discrimination is not fun at all. I am glad I am not a Negro and being judged by my skin," wrote one.

[13] Mrs. Elliott said the children reacted that way "without exception."

[14] "I think these children walked in a colored child's moccasins for a day," noted the teacher, herself a white native of Riceville, which has no Negroes in its 1,000 population. "They wouldn't want to do it again. They wouldn't want to make it as difficult for him to walk in those moccasins again."

DISCUSSION

1. How many opinion words are used in this article? What difference does it make whether the writer himself uses these words or whether he quotes what others say? Can you tell what the writer thinks about the experiment?

2. What information usually included in a report *(who, what, when, where, how much)* has been omitted here? Why has it been left out? Does the omission matter?

3. Why does the writer use so many quotations?

4. Why does the writer use so many one-sentence paragraphs? What do the many quotations have to do with the paragraphing?

5. Does the article make clear why the teacher finds the experiment "absolutely frightening"? Can you explain it?

Pray-In at Ft. Jackson

    disperse: break up; go away
    interrogation: questioning
    dissenters: people who disagree with generally accepted beliefs
    unauthorized: without permission
    leniency: treating offenders easily, not harshly

[1] Columbia, S.C.—More than 20 antiwar GIs gathered at a chapel here the night of Feb. 13 for a "pray-in." Col. Chester W. Davis, the base's

Administrative Officer, told the men to disperse. Five men remained in front of the chapel and were charged with disorderly conduct. Pvt. Steve Kline and Pvt. Robert Tatar actually knelt to pray. "I give you a direct and lawful order to stop praying and leave the area," said one of the officers. Kline and Tatar stayed on their knees, were dragged to a nearby jeep and taken to base headquarters for interrogation. At first the Army told reporters that there would be no charges; later, the base Public Information Officer said that the two men would be court-martialed.

[2] The following week a second pray-in was scheduled. This time the Army was prepared. The most committed dissenters were put on special work details; it was made plain that anyone else who wanted to demonstrate would be given the same treatment as Kline and Tatar. From six o'clock that evening the main gates, which are always open on week nights, were closed to all unauthorized personnel.

[3] I managed to get onto the base, but as I was walking toward the chapel I was picked up by an MP: "I'm afraid I'll have to detain you at military headquarters until I get further instructions."

[4] It was like a precinct station in Detroit during last summer's riots. Squad cars kept reporting in. "Two unaccompanied females seen near movie theatre number one," I heard as I entered the station. "There are two reporters over at gate number 2," one MP phoned in. "Should I take their names?" "Should I write down the license plate number of the cars I turn away, sir?" another asked.

[5] As it turned out only two soldiers went to the chapel. They left when the MP's took their names.

[6] But that same night Fort Jackson officials began having second thoughts about punishment. Congressman William Fitts Ryan had called up the base commander and urged leniency. Reporters from *The New York Times* and *The Washington Post* had come to Fort Jackson to cover the story. Charles Morgan, the American Civil Liberties Union lawyer who had handled Howard Levy's case, was in Columbia preparing to defend Tatar and Kline. Court-martial proceedings against Tatar and Kline were dropped.

[7] Feeling against the war here is more widespread than the response to the pray-in suggests. "I'd say that about 40 percent of the guys in my company are against the War," said one private who is slated to go to Vietnam this week. "Yeah, I think you're right," said another. "But I don't know how many will act on what they believe."

DISCUSSION

1. What is the main idea sentence of this report? What order is used in giving the supporting details?

2. Does the writer add any information that doesn't stick to the subject? If you think there is any, what is it?

3. How complete do you find this report? That is, can you think of any questions you have about the incident that are not answered?

4. Cowan does not record all the short wave messages he overheard as he waited in MP headquarters. What basis do you think he used for choosing the ones he did quote?

5. How does the use of "managed" at the beginning of paragraph 3 tell you that the writer is "unauthorized personnel"? Is this transition enough to justify the use of "I" in paragraphs 3 and 4? Rewrite these two paragraphs so that Cowan does not discuss his own presence at all. Which version do you and your fellow students prefer, your own or the original?

6. Can you find any opinion words in the article? Can you find any sentences that seem to interpret events rather than give the factual material on which the interpretation is based?

7. Do you think this report is slanted? That is, can you tell what Cowan's attitude toward the Vietnam war is? If so, how can you tell? Can you tell whether he approves or disapproves of the Army's actions? If so, how?

High School Censorship

the Establishment: those in power
ironically: contrasting what might have been expected with what is
reinstate: to put back as he was before
ACLU: American Civil Liberties Union, an organization which defends the rights guaranteed under the first ten amendments to the United States Constitution
unassailable: not open to argument or challenge
disruptive: upsetting
precedent: an example that can be followed
skepticism: doubt or disbelief
seamier: uglier; more unpleasant

[1] Last year, John Freeburg, a senior at rural South Kitsap High School outside of Seattle, Washington, began to edit and publish a mimeographed newspaper for students. The paper reflected his own opposition to the

Reprinted from "Revolt in the High Schools: The Way It's Going To Be," by Diane Divoky, in the *Saturday Review* (February 15, 1969), by permission of the publisher. Copyright 1969 Saturday Review, Inc.

Vietnam war, as well as to the adult Establishment's reaction to long hair. John himself was clean-cut in every sense of the word. The son of a commercial airlines pilot, a boy who spent summers working with diabetic children, he was a principal's dream: a high honor student, one of three chosen by the faculty as "outstanding students," a student council representative, and ironically, regional winner of the Veterans' of Foreign Wars "What Democracy Means to Me" contest. Even in getting out his paper, he operated true to form, submitting articles to the school administration for approval before each issue.

[2] In spite of this, three months before graduation John was suspended, and his parents' efforts to have him reinstated by the school board were unsuccessful. The state Civil Liberties Union stepped in and obtained a court order for his reinstatement. An ACLU suit on his behalf for damages brought against the school district is still pending in the U. S. District Court. ACLU claims that John's civil rights were violated; the district's counterclaim uses the traditionally unassailable argument that his activities were disruptive to school operation.

[3] But even if his case should succeed—setting a precedent for the rights of high school students—John Freeburg has gone from idealism to skepticism about the "system" that found his exercise of freedom of the press an embarrassment to be eliminated in the face of pressures from right wing groups in the small community. His school said he was old enough to praise democracy publicly, but not to speak about its seamier aspects. Rather than practicing the ideals of freedom and tolerance it preached, the school used its power to suppress ideas. Something was terribly wrong, John decided, not just across the world in Vietnam, but in the institution that was supposed to educate him.

DISCUSSION

1. The main idea sentence of this article does not appear in the introduction. From the information given in the article, work out what the main idea sentence must be. Be as exact as you can, giving details of *who, what, when, where, how much.*

2. This article is a mixture of report and interpretation. What parts are objective report? Where does the interpretation begin?

3. What is the writer's attitude toward this incident? Explain your answer by referring to specific words or statements in the article.

4. In paragraph 3 would it be more objective to quote what John Freeburg actually said? Why or why not? Why do you think the writer did not quote directly?

5. What factual basis is given for "found [it] an embarrassment to be eliminated in the face of pressures from right wing groups"? Before you

can accept this interpretation of the school board's actions, what else would you need to know?

6. What is your own attitude toward the action the school board took? In considering whether students have a right to publish newspapers expressing their own beliefs, does it matter whether the paper opposes or supports a war? Whether it defends long hair or argues for close haircuts?

Hiroshima

deltaic: referring to the flat plain at the mouth of some big rivers
evacuated: moved out, usually because of danger
volition: personal wish or decision

[1] At exactly fifteen minutes past eight in the morning, on August 6, 1945, Japanese time, at the moment when the atomic bomb flashed above Hiroshima, Miss Toshiko Sasaki, a clerk in the personnel department of the East Asia Tin Works, had just sat down at her place in the plant office and was turning her head to speak to the girl at the next desk. At that same moment, Dr. Masakazu Fujii was settling down cross-legged to read the Osaka *Asahi* on the porch of his private hospital, overhanging one of the seven deltaic rivers which divide Hiroshima; Mrs. Hatsuyo Nakamura, a tailor's widow, stood by the window of her kitchen, watching a neighbor tearing down his house because it lay in the path of an air-raid-defense fire lane; Father Wilhelm Kleinsorge, a German priest of the Society of Jesus, reclined in his underwear on a cot on the top floor of his order's three-story mission house, reading Jesuit magazine *Stimmen der Zeit*; Dr. Terufumi Sasaki, a young member of the surgical staff of the city's large, modern Red Cross Hospital, walked along one of the hospital corridors with a blood specimen for a Wassermann test in his hand; and the Reverend Mr. Kiyoshi Tanimoto, pastor of the Hiroshima Methodist Church, paused at the door of a rich man's house in Koi, the city's western suburb, and prepared to unload a handcart full of things he had evacuated from town in fear of the massive B-29 raid which everyone expected Hiroshima to suffer.

[2] A hundred thousand people were killed by the atomic bomb, and these six were among the survivors. They still wonder why they lived when so many others died. Each of them counts many small items of chance or volition—a

From HIROSHIMA, by John Hersey. Copyright 1946 by John Hersey. Originally appeared in *The New Yorker*. Reprinted by permission of Alfred A. Knopf, Inc.

step taken in time, a decision to go indoors, catching one streetcar instead of the next—that spared them. And now each knows that in the act of survival he lived a dozen lives and saw more death than he ever thought he would see. At the time, none of them knew anything.

DISCUSSION

1. Like the sinking of the *Titanic,* the bombing of Hiroshima is a well known historical event. What are some of the differences between reporting an event that is genuinely "news" and reporting one that most readers already know occurred? What evidence of these differences can you find in this selection?

2. What is the purpose of including such normally insignificant details as "cross-legged" and "in his underwear"? Are such details given for each of the six people named in the report? What is the combined effect of all these details?

3. What more usual exact details are given about each person?

4. Do you consider the topic of this report controversial? In what way?

5. Is the information given in paragraph 2 fact or interpretation?

6. Does Hersey make any judgment about the dropping of the bomb? If he does, what is it?

7. This selection is only the opening paragraphs of a short book, *Hiroshima.* If you have read the whole book, can you say whether or not this brief selection is representative of Hersey's method throughout the book? Is what he does more effective than arguing against the bomb? Why?

8. Here are two more introductions to longer articles, both on another fairly controversial subject:

   [A] One bleak evening last winter a lonely highway in upper New York State became the scene of what is probably the most terrifying flying saucer encounter that any human being has yet reported. It was the peak point of an extended "flap" (a word used by saucer buffs to indicate an unusually large number of sightings in any specific area of the country or world) that began in October and was still going on when I visited Ithaca, N.Y. last February to interview personally the people involved. (From SCIENCE & MECHANICS, July 1968.)

   [B] The time was 1:15 P.M.; the date January 7, 1948; the place, the control tower at Godman Air Force Base outside Louisville, Kentucky. A call had just come in from the Kentucky highway patrol. It seemed that several people in Marysville, a small town some eighty miles from Louisville, were concerned about a strange object they had seen in the sky. (From *Rumor, Fear and the Madness of Crowds* by J. P. Chaplin. Copyright © 1959 by J. P. Chaplin, published by Ballantine Books, Inc.)

Which introduction is the more objective? What words or phrases in either paragraph show judgment or interpretation?

9. Compare the two introductions given in Question 8 with the introduction to "A Rainfall of Fish," p. 223.

The Secretary's Report

ward heeling: doing petty chores for a political machine or party boss
inducement: promise or reward
perpetuate: keep going for a long time
venerable: old; well established

[1] 19 April, 1967. A short and rather dreary meeting: no fights, no convictions. Mrs. Gallagher accused the secretary of smoking tea—a dated expression—but nothing came of it.

[2] Apparently we had planned for a treasurer's report, but the treasurer was not here nor had he been conferred with. Neither is his identity known, but it is believed that he is alive and well in Mexico. In his absence, the Association muddled through anyhow. Mr. Albertson is to be paid $12.50, to compensate for his political expenses in ward heeling; and some other startling and good financial news awaited us. Norm Randolph has paid up!

[3] Our president, Mr. Hobson, referred to a grossly inaccurate IBM list of Association members on which our number is shown to be 39. Your secretary was instructed to dun new faculty members to join the national chapter. Various obscene inducements are to be offered to prospects.

[4] Next on our exciting agenda a nominating committee to select officer candidates for the forthcoming year was appointed. Said committee consisted of Ellis Duncan encircled by three women: Mrs. Gallagher, Mrs. McPhergus, and Dr. Anna Mechanic.

[5] Elisabeth McPhergus once more told of the state Association convention to be held in Seattle, May 12–13, and once more nagged at all of us to go.

[6] Moving on to a new thrill, our booksale, an Association annual tradition, was discussed. As just indicated, this sort of thing has been going on for years. The first annual Association booksale was believed to have been held in ancient Athens to raise ransom for maidens held by the Minotaur. The

Minotaur was a freak creature, half man, half bull, who couldn't read any better than Paul Albertson.

[7] To perpetuate this venerable rite, a committee consisting of Paul Albertson, Ellis Duncan, Sheila Samuelson, Dick Steinbeck, and Stanley Stookly was appointed. Conservatively, our group decided not to sacrifice virgins this year, but the need for publicity in the local paper was discussed.

[8] Elisabeth McPhergus announced that Dr. Benson had mentioned with favor the actions of the Association investigating committee in Oregon. I was awed by the fact that Elisabeth was awed with the fact that Dr. Benson was awed.

[9] There followed an absurdist-type dialogue, a portion of which is captured herein:

A nameless voice: Do you mean Stevenson?
Elisabeth McPhergus: No, Kraft.
Georgia Gallagher: Died?
Stan Stookly: Marilyn Monroe died!

Following this there was no adjournment. People just drifted away.

> Respectfully submitted, your recording secretary,
> Edward Albee (alias Lew Sander)

DISCUSSION

1. Although the subject covered in this report can hardly be considered controversial, the minutes still show what happens when the secretary of the association indulges himself by commenting on everything. The comments here are undoubtedly deliberate; the secretary is being funny, and probably minutes were never listened to more attentively than during the year of his secretaryship. Fun aside, however, if these minutes were to follow the rules for a good report, what would have to be left out? What would have to be rewritten?

2. In spite of the goodnatured kidding, do these minutes seem relatively precise, orderly, accurate, and complete? That is, do they serve as an adequate record of business done at the meeting? If you think they do not, what should be added?

Fact and Opinion

Sometimes a writer appears to be writing a straight report, giving only facts, but actually slips in his opinion by *slanting*. Slanting is accomplished in two ways: first, by using words that contain built-in opinion; second, by including details that are favorable to the writer's point of view and leaving out those that are unfavorable.

In reports of the Poor People's Campaign of June, 1968, for example, we can see some illustrations of slanted language:

> (A) As a result, the impression conveyed to the public by the impoverished demonstrators was not that of the sympathy-deserving downtrodden, but rather that of a bunch of unruly, undeserving riffraff. (From *U.S. News & World Report,* July 8, 1968)

> (B) Whatever the reasons, Martin Luther King's final enterprise seems close to foundering. Resurrection City is an unhappy, unfriendly—and increasingly dangerous—collection of disparate groups of the poor. (From *Time,* June 28, 1968)

In example A, the words *unruly, undeserving riffraff* contrast unfavorably with *sympathy-deserving downtrodden,* favorably slanted words. In example B, the phrase *increasingly dangerous* is more unfavorably slanted than *unhappy* and *unfriendly. Foundering* suggests a sinking ship, and the word *disparate,* which means *unlike,* suggests that the groups had little in common.

Another report on Resurrection City written a month earlier gives a favorably slanted account of the Poor People's Encampment in Washington, D.C.:

> (C) Politically it remains to be seen what the Poor People's Encampment on Washington's Mall can bring about. Architecturally it is already a heartening accomplishment. With little more than a month of preparation, a team of young urban designers has created a functional, decent, safe and sanitary summer camp city of a pop art beauty all its own. Thirty-six years ago, on the mud flats of Anacostia, demonstrators lived in ramshackle huts made from old packing cases, odd bits of lumber, scraps of canvas and tin cans amidst half-buried garbage, flies and disease. Now their successors live in neat rows of ingeniously pre-fabricated plywood huts, clustered in "neighborhoods" around shower houses with hot water and community halls. There are chemical toilets, mess halls with steam tables for a daily hot meal, a health clinic and even a kindergarten where the kids can be parked while the parents demonstrate. (Reprinted by Permission of THE NEW REPUBLIC, © 1968, Harrison-Blaine of New Jersey, Inc., from the June 1, 1968 issue, p. 7.)

In speaking of the encampment as a *heartening accomplishment,* the writer is clearly giving his opinion. The next sentence, while not a direct statement of opinion, lets us know that the writer is favorably inclined toward the encampment by using words like *functional, decent, safe, sanitary,* and *pop art beauty,* all favorably slanted words. Other favorably slanted phrases are *neat rows, ingeniously prefabricated* and *clustered in "neighborhoods."*

Another method of slanting consists of mentioning only those details that support the writer's point of view and omitting those that don't. How this kind of slant works can be shown by examining three statements

that appeared in national magazines the same week. All of them are
reporting the police action at Columbia University on April 30, 1968:

> (A) But at 3:00 A.M. on Tuesday, April 30, after the Columbia name and all
> those connected to it had been thoroughly mutilated, one thousand police . . .
> moved onto the campus, and in little more than sixty minutes, against weak
> resistance . . . and without guns, without tear gas and with only minor force,
> cleared all the captive buildings. (From p. 500, May 21, 1968 issue of
> *National Review,* 150 E. 35th Street, New York, New York 10016.)

> (B) They [the police] arrived at 2:20 A.M., 1,000 of them, carrying clubs,
> rubber truncheons and handcuffs wrapped around their knuckles. (From
> *Life,* May 10, 1968.)

> (C) It was strictly a police affair—and the performance was uneven. In some
> areas the police behaved with restraint; in others they were vicious. One
> contingent tried to clear the entire campus, charging at a run into about 1,000
> bystanders on the College Walk, swinging clubs, herding them first into a
> corner at Ferris Booth Hall, then out the 116th street gate onto Broadway.
> One boy was left writhing in front of Ferris Booth, his nose smashed . . . At
> Avery, police threw dozens of students from inside the buildings to rows of
> police and plainclothesmen outside, where some were punched, kicked and
> hit with clubs and handcuffs. One blond girl was thrown to the brick sidewalk
> and beaten unconscious; students hysterically called for a doctor. (From "The
> End of a Siege—and an Era" in *Newsweek,* May 13, 1968, p. 60. Copyright
> Newsweek, Inc., May 1968.)

Notice that the first selection emphasizes what the police were *not*
armed with, and mentions only that they used "minor force," whereas
the second selection says specifically what arms the police were carrying, and
the third makes clear the kind of force that the first writer regards as
"minor." Unless we have witnessed events at firsthand, it is never
possible to tell what details have been omitted, what included. We can,
however, by comparing several accounts of the same event, often
tell what the writer's biases are.

Two of these selections include slanted words as well as different details,
but although the slant in Selection A is clearly in favor of the police, the
third selection slants both ways: favorably *(behaved with restraint)* and
unfavorably *(others were vicious)*. Such two-way slanting is often used
to balance the effect and makes the report seem more objective.

All the articles in the next group deal with this same event: student
protest and police action at Columbia.

What Magazine Do You Read?

I. The End of a Siege–and an Era

extensive: large
endowment: property or funds which an institution is given
sever: cut
consortium: combination or partnership of financial institutions
prohibition: rule against
amnesty: general pardon

[1] The seven-day siege of Columbia University ended last week, but the battle for control of the institution has really just begun.

[2] The reoccupation was brief and at times brutal. Acting on a request from university president Grayson Kirk, 1,000 New York City police cleared students from five "liberated" campus buildings, including Kirk's own office. In three pre-dawn hours, they arrested 720 demonstrators; the injured included 132 students, four faculty members and twelve policemen.

[3] The real meaning of the struggle, however, lay not in ugly statistics but in the fact that Columbia, with its extensive real estate and $390 million endowment, is no longer simply the property of the administration or of its trustees. President Kirk and his 26 trustees are being forced to share power with the faculty and the students. "Columbia," said Tom Hayden, 28, a founder of the militant Students for a Democratic Society, who (though not a student) was arrested in the Mathematics Building, "puts things at a new stage in this country. Universities will reform or be destroyed." (It is a hard lesson that other university officials around the U.S. are also taking to heart.)

[4] The original student demands that triggered the confrontation were, in SDS chairman Mark Rudd's eyes, "not very radical." The students demanded that Columbia halt construction of a gymnasium on public-park land separating the university from Harlem; that it sever its ties with the Institute for Defense Analysis, a consortium of twelve universities performing secret research for the Pentagon; that it lift its prohibition against indoor demonstrations—and finally that it grant amnesty to the students who sat in.

From "The End of a Siege—and an Era," in *Newsweek,* May 13, 1968. Copyright Newsweek, Inc., May 1968.

DISCUSSION

1. Often a statement contains both fact and opinion. Examine the following sentences from this article. Which parts are fact and which are opinion?
   a. The seven-day siege of Columbia University ended last week, but the battle for control of the institution has really just begun (paragraph 1).
   b. The reoccupation was brief and at times brutal (paragraph 2).
   c. In three pre-dawn hours, they arrested 720 demonstrators; the injured included 132 students, four faculty members and twelve policemen (paragraph 2).
   d. President Kirk and his 26 trustees are being forced to share power with the faculty and the students (paragraph 3).
   e. The students demanded that Columbia halt construction of a gymnasium on public-park land separating the university from Harlem (paragraph 4).

2. Which of the opinion statements in Question 1 are backed up by factual statements made elsewhere in the article?

3. What other statements that mix factual statements with opinion can you find?

4. Why has the word "liberated" been put in quotations?

5. Do you find any words that seem to you slanted? If so, what are they?

6. Can you tell from reading this report whether the writer is in sympathy with the students? With the police? With the university administration? If you think you can, how can you tell?

II. When Students Take Over Colleges

impinge on: to move beyond the proper limits
concession: agreement to do part of what the other side wants
intervention: interfering, usually with force or threat of force

[1] Columbia University, New York. A student upheaval—marked by

From the copyrighted article "When Students Take Over Colleges" in *U.S. News & World Report,* May 20, 1968.

clashes with police—virtually paralyzed for two weeks the core area of one of the nation's oldest and largest universities.

[2] Main issues were the proposed construction of a gymnasium, which rebellious students said was "racist" because it would impinge on a park used by Harlem Negroes, and objections to the university's part in a military-research program.

[3] The university agreed to halt construction of the gymnasium. But this concession was not enough, and it was only with massive police intervention that demonstrators were removed from buildings they had seized.

[4]· With unrest continuing, the faculty of Columbia College, the university's liberal-arts school, decided to terminate formal classes for the rest of the spring semester and to cancel final examinations.

[5] On May 7, university officials warned of possible "criminal and civil" legal action against demonstrators who took documents from administrative offices which were ransacked.

DISCUSSION

1. In the following sentences, how much is factual and how much is opinion?
    a. A student upheaval—marked by clashes with police—virtually paralyzed for two weeks the core area of one of the nation's oldest and largest universities (paragraph 1).
    b. But this concession was not enough, and it was only with massive police intervention that demonstrators were removed from buildings they had seized (paragraph 3).
    c. University officials warned of possible "criminal and civil" legal action against demonstrators who took documents from administrative offices which were ransacked (paragraph 5).

2. Which of the opinion words in Question 1 are backed up by factual statements made elsewhere in the article?

3. Do you find any words that seem to you slanted? If so, what are they?

4. Does the phrase "marked by clashes with police" imply whether the "clashes" were begun by the students or by the police? What is a "clash"? (See paragraph 2 of the first article) Is a "clash" different from "massive police intervention"?

5. Can you tell from reading this report whether the writer is in sympathy with the students? With the police? With the university administration? If you think you can, how?

III. Lifting a Siege—and Rethinking a Future

melee: confused, general fight
impasse: deadlock
vacillation: wavering; unable to decide
abdication: giving up power or position
hooligan: roughneck; rowdy
ad hoc: created for one occasion only
intransigent: unwilling to agree
insurgents: rebels
ossified: hardened into bone
immaculate: spotlessly clean
awry: out of order; crooked

[1] At 2:30 A.M., said one combat-wise cop, "Harlem is asleep." At that propitious hour, 1,000 New York City police, armed with warrants signed by Columbia University trustees, marched on the Morningside Heights campus and dispossessed the student rebels who had occupied five buildings for nearly six days. In the inevitable melee, more than 130 people—including twelve policemen—were injured; 698 people, mostly students, were arrested and charged with criminal trespass, resisting arrest or both. Although the action united hopelessly confused Columbia in anger over police brutality, it also moved the campus toward order—and touched off a much needed re-examination of the university's future.

[2] The decision to call in the police, said Columbia President Grayson Kirk, was "the most painful one I have ever made." Although the need for some drastic action to end the impasse was due partly to Kirk's own vacillation in handling the student protests, he had plenty of provocation to call in the police. For one thing, the strike had expanded well beyond its initial aims —getting the university to cancel plans for a gymnasium in nearby Morningside Park and drop its affiliation with the Institute for Defense Analyses, a Government-supported research center.

[3] After successfully capturing the campus buildings, the demonstrators— led by the far-left Students for a Democratic Society and the all-Negro Student Afro-American Society—seemed far more interested in a bloody confrontation

with the administration than in any meaningful negotiations. They demanded a complete surrender on all points at issue, including amnesty for all participants in the rebellion. Kirk refused, on the ground that this would mean a complete abdication of all disciplinary authority.

[4] A majority of the university's 17,000 students and 2,500 faculty members undoubtedly shared the initial goals of the strike. But many were also appalled by the hooligan tactics of the demonstrators, who had held university officials captive, broken into offices and overturned furniture. Kirk had reason to fear that some 300 members of the Majority Coalition of students, which included a large proportion of athletes, might touch off intramural violence by trying to dislodge the demonstrators. A fight did break out between some 40 of the burly "jocks," who had set up a blockade to starve out the occupants of Low Library, and 40 youths, mainly Negroes, trying to send in food. The attackers were thrown back, causing one of the school's disillusioned football fans to note that "it's probably the first time Columbia has ever held a line." Kirk was also aware of rumors that militant Harlem residents were vowing to "burn Columbia down."

[5] While classes remained canceled, an Ad Hoc Faculty Group, moving helpfully into the dispute, thought it had found a reasonable solution. It urged uniform punishment for all offenders, under rules to be drawn up by a panel of students, faculty and administrators, and called on the trustees to provide an alternative gymnasium plan. Kirk said he agreed with "the essential spirit" of the proposals, would appoint such a tripartite committee—but did not agree to be bound by its decisions. "He's taking the posture of a neutral party," protested one of the faculty leaders. After the demonstrators also rejected the plan, the Columbia Spectator observed that the battle had degenerated into one between "the intransigent insurgents and the ossified administration."

[6] With the agreement of university trustees, Columbia lawyers drew up complaints that students were trespassing on the private property of the trustees in occupying the buildings, filed the papers with police. Moving to the campus in vans and squad cars, the police sealed off all gates, and then, on the orders of Commissioner Howard Leary, marched toward the five occupied buildings.

[7] Inside Hamilton Hall, 85 Negro students, who had been advised by such cool heads as Negro Psychologist Kenneth Clark, decided that their most effective tactic would be to file quietly into the vans (unlike white demonstrators in other buildings, they had kept their occupied quarters immaculate). With the two highest Negro officers in the New York police force observing, it was a model arrest operation—except that no one had brought a key for the main door and it had to be forced open.

[8] Elsewhere, the police were less carefully supervised—and less considerate of the rebels. Professors and students who had linked arms to keep police and demonstrators apart were charged by wedges of plainclothesmen. Uniformed officers plunged into the breach to smash open the doors, while

others broke in through underground tunnels. At Fayerweather Hall, where protesters had preplanned every act by majority vote, students who intended to submit cleanly to arrest lined up at the door; those who preferred to be dragged out sat on an upper floor; those who decided to resist linked arms on another floor. The neat plans went awry as police kicked and clubbed their way through the building. For no clear reason, they even attacked newsmen, including a LIFE photographer and, of all people, Columnist Walter Winchell.

DISCUSSION

1. How much is fact and how much opinion?
   a. Although the action united hopelessly confused Columbia in anger over police brutality, it also moved the campus toward order—and touched off a much needed re-examination of the university's future (paragraph 1).
   b. Although the need for some drastic action to end the impasse was due partly to Kirk's own vacillation in handling the student protests, he had plenty of provocation to call in the police (paragraph 2).
   c. After successfully capturing the campus buildings, the demonstrators . . . seemed far more interested in a bloody confrontation with the administration than in any meaningful negotiations (paragraph 3).
   d. A majority of the university's 17,000 students and 2,500 faculty members undoubtedly shared the initial goals of the strike. But many were also appalled by the hooligan tactics of the demonstrators, who had held university officials captive, broken into offices and overturned furniture (paragraph 4).
   e. Kirk was also aware of rumors that militant Harlem residents were vowing to "burn Columbia down" (paragraph 4).
   f. With the two highest Negro officers in the New York police force observing, it was a model arrest operation . . . (paragraph 7).
   g. Elsewhere, the police were less carefully supervised—and less considerate of the rebels (paragraph 8).

2. Which of the opinion statements in Question 1 are backed up by factual statements made elsewhere in the article?

3. What other statements that mix factual statements with opinion can you find?

4. Do you find any words that seem to you slanted? If so, what are they?

5. Does the sentence in paragraph 4, "The attackers were thrown back, causing one of the school's disillusioned football fans to note that it's probably the first time Columbia has ever held a line" seem out of tone with the rest of the article? Why or why not?

6. Can you tell from reading this report whether the writer is in sympathy with the students? With the police? With the university administration? If you think you can, how?

IV. Eyewitness Report

truncheons: clubs
gauntlet: a punishment in which the offender runs between two rows of men who strike him as he passes
unchecked: not stopped or restrained
obstinacy: unwillingness to change

[1] As President Kirk was to explain later, the decision to call in the police was "the most painful one" he ever made. They arrived at 2:20 A.M., 1,000 of them, carrying clubs, rubber truncheons and handcuffs wrapped around their knuckles.

[2] I was standing 10 feet away as one column advanced upon Avery Hall—where 50 students sat on the steps—and waded in, flailing and shoving. Sixty seconds later, all 50 students had been hurled down the stairs and through a gauntlet of plainclothesmen who sent them along with punches and clubbing. At Fayerweather, a medical station on the lawn was overrun by fleeing students, some holding bloody heads.

[3] Just inside the main gate to the campus someone screamed, "They're charging!" A line of policemen came flying at the crowd, clubbing as they ran. We scrambled onto Broadway where six mounted policemen galloped at us unchecked. Two of them chased me for five blocks. I turned and saw one of them run down and trample a student. Finally I heard the horses turn back.

[4] Last fall, LIFE Reporter Bruce Paisner wrote (Oct. 20) that student activists would try to change the universities by threatening to shut them down. But he warned that obstinacy on both sides would cause trouble. Now, with this prediction fulfilled, President Kirk was able at last to regain his office. But many students and faculty members chanted "Strike! Strike!" and vowed there would be no return to normalcy. At the height of the action I had seen one plainclothesman lean over to snuff out three candles on a window

Reprinted from "Eyewitness Report," by Thomas Ehrich in *Life*, May 10, 1968 by permission of the author.

ledge of Mathematics Hall. He walked away, then came back, picked up the candles and threw them to the floor. The gesture said a lot.

DISCUSSION

1. How much is fact and how much opinion?
   a. They arrived at 2:20 A.M., 1,000 of them, carrying clubs, rubber truncheons, and handcuffs wrapped around their knuckles (paragraph 1).
   b. I was standing 10 feet away as one column advanced upon Avery Hall—where 50 students sat on the steps—and waded in, flailing and shoving (paragraph 2).
   c. Sixty seconds later, all 50 students had been hurled down the stairs and through a gauntlet of plainclothesmen who sent them along with punches and clubbing (paragraph 2).
   d. At Fayerweather, a medical station on the lawn was overrun by fleeing students, some holding bloody heads (paragraph 2).
   e. Two of them chased me for five blocks (paragraph 3).
   f. At the height of the action I had seen one plainclothesman lean over to snuff out three candles on a window ledge of Mathematics Hall (paragraph 4).
   g. The gesture said a lot (paragraph 4).

2. Which of the opinion statements in Question 1 are backed up by factual statements made elsewhere in the article?

3. What other statements that mix factual statements with opinion can you find?

4. Do you find any words that seem to you slanted? If so, what are they?

5. Can you tell from anything in the first three articles whether or not the writers actually saw the police raid? Does knowing that Ehrich actually was there affect your attitude toward what he says? How?

6. What details not mentioned in the earlier accounts are included in this one? Why (probably) have they been left out of the other accounts?

7. The last sentence of this article implies that Ehrich knows what the gesture said. What do you think it said? Could it be interpreted to say more than one thing?

8. Can you tell from reading this article whether Ehrich is in sympathy with the students? With the police? With the university administration? If you think you can tell, how?

V. Columbia's Real Estate Ventures

apartheid: racially segregated
self-perpetuating: able to keep itself in power
redoubt: military fortification
harassed: repeatedly interfered with; persecuted
cordon sanitaire: a barrier between two unfriendly areas
touted: advertised; praised

[1] The plans to build an apartheid gymnasium set off the siege at Columbia University, but this scheme is a minor facet of the enormous realty consortia the university is forming with private industry. The story involves a tangled set of relationships within the self-perpetuating board of trustees . . .

[2] Since World War II, Columbia and the others [15 New York educational and medical institutions along the upper west side of Manhattan on Morningside Heights] have slowly constructed a redoubt on the Heights, methodically pushing out 7,500 residents, most of them poorly off, who lived in the rent-controlled apartments or rooming houses which the universities bought. Many of them were black or Puerto Rican.

[3] Even now, after having promised the city that its expansion plans had reached their limits, Columbia and the others push on secretly with the land grab, driving north into Harlem, east into the rundown slums around Central Park, and south to 96th Street. The trustees are speculating in land across the Hudson River in Rockland County, New York, some 30 miles outside the city. Over the next decade the institutions of higher learning on Morningside Heights anticipate relocating 11,000 more people. All in all, Columbia is among the great real estate development corporations of the day. The details of these various operations are obscured because Columbia, like most other private universities, is governed by a board of trustees whose decisions are not open to public scrutiny or review. William Bloor, the treasurer, refuses to disclose the university's real estate or mortgage holdings, although it is known that they account for at least half the university's endowment fund . . .

[4] So as not to discomfit the people it wants out of the buildings it buys, Columbia maintains a relocation office run by Ronald Golden. Golden says he relocates perhaps 200 people a year, many of them poor, elderly and white who have been able to hang on in the Heights because they live in rent-controlled apartments. Golden relates with bitterness the tale of an Irish bus driver, who with his wife lived alone in a four-room apartment at $30 a

month. The man might have needed this large apartment with children grow-ing up, Golden says, but now he had no real use for it. Still, he was hanging on; meanwhile, saving enough money to go to Ireland every summer. Golden thinks he could find this man, and those like him, similar apartments at $10 to $20 a month more on the edges of Harlem or further uptown around Puerto Rican neighborhoods. But people don't care to go back near the ghettos, and so Golden has to track all over the city, out to Queens, up in the Bronx looking for substitute residences. Fortunately, Golden says, his job is made easier since Columbia will pay a building manager a finder's fee of several hundred dollars to skip over his list of waiting applicants, to sneak in Columbia's candidate . . .

[5] There have been complaints in the neighborhood that one way Columbia gets the residents out is to plug up their doors so they can't get back inside. Columbia says this is a lie; it has only been done once or twice. In describing how Columbia got three families out of a building which Columbia wanted to tear down to make way for a School of International Affairs, the *Spectator,* the student newspaper, said Golden "denied that Columbia had harassed the families in order to make them depart. Two weeks ago, however, the building's heating plant was demolished." As William Bloor, the university treasurer, described the policy, "when a tenant isn't behaving himself, we will move him out" . . .

[6] In one single-room occupancy dwelling on West 114th Street, inhabited by welfare clients and owned by the university, the rent was increased 25 percent in December 1967, with a promise of another increase for January. Charles F. Darlington, director of housing for Columbia, explained to the *Spectator* that the university raised rents "to encourage the few people who are still there to leave." Public pressure finally forced a postponement of the January increase. This rooming house was to be ripped down to make way for a new home for the School of Social Work.

[7] Meanwhile the university concluded its deal with the city for lease of the southern section of Morningside Park, which lies as a sort of *cordon Sanitaire* between itself and Harlem. Columbia leased this land on which it planned to construct a gymnasium, complete with duplicate facilities, one set with a door opening on the Heights for the university students, the other with a back door opening on the park into Harlem for the community. This deal is now up in the air because of the student-faculty rebellion . . .

[8] Twice now within a year Columbia has provided examples of how a private university's decisions affect the general public. In its promotion of the Strickman cigarette filter, Columbia advertised the invention as "revolu-tionary," when in fact . . . the university knew all along that it was not revolutionary, indeed little better than similar products on the market. Columbia touted the filter in hopes it would make money from the public's fear of getting cancer. Now the university is involved in a widening real estate venture which will affect the lives of people who have nothing to say about making the decision.

DISCUSSION

1. Unlike the first three articles, this one was signed with the author's name and appeared in a magazine which calls itself "A Journal of Opinion." Would you consider this article a report or an argument? If it is a report, what is being reported? If it is an argument, what is the writer's belief? Whichever you decide it is, work out (or find) a main idea sentence for it.

2. What slanted words can you find in the first three paragraphs? In paragraphs 7 and 8? What more neutral terms could be substituted for them?

3. What is the effect of the long quotations from *Golden* (paragraphs 4 and 5)? Of the quotations from the *Spectator* (paragraphs 5 and 6)? Of the quotations from Bloor (paragraph 5) and Darlington (paragraph 6)?

4. What do the references to articles that appeared in the student newspaper, the *Spectator,* tell you about the background of the student-faculty rebellion? How does this information put the earlier statements ("The students demanded that Columbia halt construction of a gymnasium on public-park land," [Article I] or "getting the university to cancel plans for a gymnasium in nearby Morningside Park," [Article II]) in a clearer light?

5. Compare the statement "Columbia . . . planned to construct a gymnasium, complete with duplicate facilities, one set with a door opening on the Heights for the university students, the other with a back door opening on the park into Harlem for the community" (paragraph 7) with the statement from Article II, "a gymnasium which rebellious students said was 'racist' because it would impinge on a park used by Harlem Negroes." Which set of facts comes closer to your own definition of "racist"?

6. Do you agree with Golden's belief (paragraph 4) that the Irish bus driver has "no real use" for this "large apartment"? Why or why not?

7. What is the irony in saying (paragraph 6) that the rooming house had to go to "make way for a new home for the School of Social Work"? Would it have been more effective if Ridgeway had pointed out this irony?

8. What proportion of the statements in this article are factual? What proportion contain judgment?

9. What is the effect of the contrast between "this is a lie" and "only been done once or twice"? Between "denied that Columbia had harassed" and "the building's heating plant was demolished"? Between these two sets of statements and Bloor's explanation of university policy (paragraph 5)?

10. Is the last sentence of the article supported by examples? Defend your answer by reference to the article.

11. Can you tell from reading this article whether Ridgeway is in sympathy with the students? With the police? With the university administration? If you think you can, how?

VI. Farewell Columbia

nomenclature: a set of names

supine: lying down on one's back

compliant: doing what is asked without protest

expropriation: seizure of other people's property

indictment: a formal list of accusations

ultimatum: a statement of conditions or demands, often accompanied by threats

impassivity: without speech or expression

syndrome: a group of symptoms

ethos: code of behavior or belief

reticence: tendency to be silent

metier: a field in which one has special training or ability

turbulence: disorder or commotion

[1] It's getting harder to tell the difference between students and thugs. Columbia University at Morningside Heights (once a place for eagles, but no one knows when any more), increasingly careless of its admissions, a place of liberal education; now, the last week of April, the harvest is early.

[2] On Tuesday, April 23, a group of professional grievance-seekers with the fanciful name "Students for a Democratic Society," tired of persuasion, tired (at nineteen) of democratic process, tried to cancel the construction of a new university gym in Morningside Park by illegally seizing the area. Because the park is actually the border between the university above and Harlem below, SAS (Student Afro-American Society—for Negroes only) permitted a discrimination long since cancelled in the rest of the university and joined in the waves of assault. After a melee of intolerant students and tolerant (up to a point) police, they were driven from the site—anarchy repelled by law. In their nomenclature, Police Brutality.

[3] Disappointed and sullen, regrouping on Tuesday afternoon they now seized Hamilton Hall (the main undergraduate building) where there are no police and no construction workers; only professors and deans, and other students, whose education was about to be sacrificed for ideology. Since there

From pp. 498–500 (in an article by Mark Edelson) of the May 21, 1968 issue of *National Review*, 150 East 35th Street, New York, New York 10016.

was no resistance, these generally affluent squatters took the building without fuss—and the university pattern of passive nonresistance had begun. The lobby of the building had the appearance of an intermission at some Broadway, or more nearly off-Broadway theater, except that the intermission never stopped and the debris of munch and snack began to rise from the floor.

[4] Since there was no performance, merely disruption, many went home in the pre- and after-midnight hours, and the group shook down to what are either the "totally committed" (their word) or the "totally disruptive" (the perceiver's word). Meanwhile the university had gone to sleep, dreaming and hoping who knows what, at a time when the action (already thoroughly illegal) could have been dissolved with a simple determination, which was apparently not there . . .

[5] The next morning the university awoke from bad dreams and found, like the hero in Kafka's stories, that the dream was real. President Kirk stayed out of his office. He was smart. Dean Coleman of Columbia College (and two other university officials) had been "detained" in his office all night—and finally left only by "permission" of the Negro students, in mid-afternoon. The building was now entirely theirs. They had expelled the university. The university, remonstrating and chiding all day, pulled itself to its ultimate strength about five o'clock and suspended all classes. The 20,000 students who used the university, many of them in the evening, working by day and sacrificing to get their education, now all found themselves part of a new sacrifice.

[6] In Hamilton Hall, the Negro students, under advisement from Harlem agitators (daintily described as "militants" in the largely supine press) who had been filtering in and out of the building all day (having found a new kindle-point), barricaded the building with its own furniture (chairs, tables, and filing cabinets) and began what amounted to a siege of the outside. Behind the table-obscured glass doors of the building were unfriendly black faces, keeping out "Whitey" (that is, strangers, not of the blood), and behind them, with the original students, were celebrities of the new campus—some identifiable, like Roy Innis and Charles Kenyatta, others anonymous and seeking a name. Coaching the students, preparing statements for them, staying over and becoming "In-Residence," a new faculty had been formed. It is not so hard to become a professor at Columbia as some have imagined.

[7] Outside the building an admiring (for the most part) crowd had formed, their color Compliant White. They hung strainingly on every entrance and exit full of mystery and disdain, and waited in the dark outside, observing the lighted building, hungering for crumbs of notice—the tag-a-longs for black dominion . . .

[8] But what about the white brother in expropriation, now distanced by a campus block—was he getting the attention he deserved? The president's office had been occupied by these democrats all day. It is on the second floor, spacious, possessed of huge windows and a fine perspective proper to a

president of one of the world's best-known institutions. Undergraduates do not usually spend much time there, but under the conditions of "Participatory Democracy," invitations are not necessary—anywhere. SDS, supplied with edibles and blankets from the outside, liquor and cigars from the inside (presidential stock), was in a buoyant mood. Having held a sort of kitchen town meeting, they had voted to stay until the gym was permanently stopped, till Columbia separated itself from the Institute for Defense Analyses, and until a guarantee of total amnesty was given to them. And, relating to their environment—a pity not to use it—they went through the desks and files of the president's office, copying material that interested them. They were now sophisticated looters. Or were they only children at play, as some sympathizers said? Or were they merely fully socially committed, as other sympathizers still say?

[9] Constantly posing at the windows with a homing instinct for the cameras, these young masters occupied miles of film. And, composing statements, remarks, indictments and ultimatums, shouted them to the press, which took them all down. Along the perimeter of the building was a corps of fifteen or twenty city police, also under indictment from the second-story group, who baited them openly and slyly (they're very good at that); who under the siege of their own emotions stood in silence and impassivity. The police were not permitting further entrance into the building, but they did permit packages of food to be tossed up into the open windows. Thus a stalemate had been reached, not bred by equal force or right, but by the syndrome of non-reaction.

[10] Inside, a pattern of faces emerged at the windows. Some diversity, but mainly, for the boys, an ethos of bristly side leaves and moustaches (that would bring back the moustache cup). And their valkyrie—girls long past all reticence. They were strange flowers. Already paranoid at nineteen, they saw a world all against them and were seeking out acts which could make their fantasy real . . .

[11] At 3:00 A.M. on Tuesday, April 30, after the Columbia name and all those connected to it had been thoroughly mutilated, one thousand police moved onto the campus, and in little more than sixty minutes, against weak resistance (for Fidelistas or Maoists) and without guns, without tear gas and with only minor force, cleared all the captive buildings. These young revolutionaries, so often filled with death rhetoric, have not yet found their *metier*. Several hundred were arrested and in a few hours released. Later on Tuesday, the young mutineers promised strikes and more turbulence, but they were now without their territorial imperative.

[12] A tragedy, a comedy, a history, a masque for dancers? We do not know yet. This is a play in many scenes and an unknown number of acts. But it seems certain that so far education is losing, and has been losing for several years. This week had a history, mainly defined by a university that turned the look of concession to the face of minority student intimidation. The tablets are broken—beyond repair? Nor had the break come suddenly, without warning.

DISCUSSION

1. In paragraph 11, Edelson calls the occupiers of the buildings, "Fidelistas or Maoists," followers of Fidel Castro or Mao Tse-tung. What evidence does he offer to show that all (or most) of the people in the buildings were sympathetic to those Communist leaders?

2. In the same sentence, Edelson mentions "weak resistance." Do you think he would have favored "strong resistance"? Discuss.

3. At the end of the paragraph, he says the "young mutineers . . . were now without their territorial imperative." The term "territorial imperative" has been used in two ways: to explain the way nations expand by colonization and to explain a tendency observed in animals to hold and defend a certain area. Which meaning do you think Edelson intends?

4. This article, more than the others, tends to use an unusually sophisticated vocabulary. Could any of the "big words" be replaced with ordinary words? Does the vocabulary tend to make the report seem more objective? More authoritative? Why?

5. Article III says that the Negroes "had kept their occupied quarters immaculate (see paragraph 7). Edelson doesn't mention that, but he does comment on "the debris of munch and snack" that "began to rise from the floor (paragraph 3). How do these included and omitted details contribute to the slant of Edelson's article?

6. Does this article give any specific details not included in any of the other articles? If so, what are they?

7. Does this article leave out any specific details included in any of the other articles (other than that mentioned in Question 5)? If so, what are they? Do the omitted details seem important or insignificant? That is, does leaving them out affect the reader's attitude toward what happened?

8. This article is also signed, and the *National Review* advertises itself as "about the quickest way you can find to turn a *potential* conservative into an *actual* conservative." Would you consider Edelson's article to be a report or a piece of persuasion? If it is a report, what is being reported? If it is persuasion, what is the writer's belief? What evidence can you find in the article that Edelson might be trying to turn his readers into "conservatives"?

9. What slanted words can you find in the first three paragraphs of this article? Can you find any paragraphs completely free of slant? Which ones?

10. Can you tell from reading this article whether Edelson is in sympathy with the students? With the police? With the university administration? If you think you can, how?

WRITING TOPICS
FOR REPORTS

1. Find some construction activity going on in your neighborhood; observe it for an hour and report on what you saw.
2. Report on the activities you observe during an hour spent at a bus depot or airport.
3. Station yourself at the fruit and vegetable section of the supermarket and report the actions of three or four customers choosing produce.
4. Report on an increase—or decrease—in prices of various food items.
5. Report on some unusual or mystifying incident that you have seen. Keep out all opinion and interpretation.

"About mid-February, the red squirrels' nut store ran out, and she left him. Then we had this terrible snow-storm and that dumb little spotted fawn got lost and— oh, yes, there was an awful row between owl and fox. It seems beaver told fox that owl said . . ."

Drawing by Edward Frascino. Reprinted with permission of *The New Yorker* Magazine.

6. Write a report on a windstorm, a flood, or any natural disaster that you have witnessed.
7. Write a report on weather conditions in your own area over a period of a week or a month.
8. Report on the accidents caused by a heavy snowstorm.
9. Report on a power failure.
10. Report on any recent disturbance in your neighborhood—a burglary, a dog fight, etc.
11. Report the behavior of teeny-boppers listening to a rock band.
12. Report on the response of the audience to a symphony concert.
13. Report on a visit to the barber shop or the beauty parlor.
14. Report on a day spent looking for a job.
15. Report on a job interview.
16. Report on the job situation in your area.
17. Report on the first day on a new job.
18. Report on your last conference with your draft board.
19. Report the attitudes of your fellow students toward the draft.
20. Report on the draft status of a group of your fellow students.
21. Report on the process you went through to register for classes this semester.
22. Report on the comparative size of the various departments in the college.
23. Report on your experience in renting an apartment or a house, or in buying or attempting to buy a house.
24. Report on a shift in property values in your own neighborhood.
25. Report on "moving day" in your family.
26. Report what happened at some rodeo you have attended.
27. Report on the background of one of the rodeo performers.
28. Report on a destruction derby you have seen.
29. Report on a stock car race.
30. Report on the accident statistics for race car drivers.
31. Report on a clean-up campaign.
32. Report on a money-raising project.
33. Report on a beauty contest.
34. Report on an election.
35. Shave your beard off for a week and report people's reactions. (Or grow a beard, etc.)
36. If you have ever dyed your hair or made a sudden, drastic change in your hair style, report on people's reactions.

readings on personal experience 7

PERSONAL
EXPERIENCE

To write successfully about his own experiences, a writer must do more than just tell what happened. If he merely says, "I did this, I did that, I saw something else, and then I went home," he will not interest his readers much. As readers, we are interested in what happened to other people only if we can see some reason for their telling us about it. If the reason is not there, we're likely to say, "Well, OK, but what was the *point*?"

In a paper of personal experience, the point can be a greater understanding of ourselves or others, a change in attitude, or a discovery of new relationships. But the greater understanding or the changed attitude or the sense of pattern must grow so naturally out of the event that the writer does not have to say openly what the point is. The successful writer knows before he begins what the event means to him; he knows what the significance is.

Sometimes the writer of personal experience is less interested in the event than in what the event shows about some person he knows well or how the event explains his relationship with that person.

Notice, however, that even though the writer is mainly interested in telling us about somebody he knows, he doesn't just talk *about* him; he lets us hear the person talking or see him in action or catch a glimpse of his appearance. When the writer does describe what the person looks like, he seldom gives a complete description of the kind the police ask for when they're hunting a missing person or the kind that appears on a post office WANTED poster. Instead, the writer picks out one or two vivid or characteristic details and lets his readers fill in the rest; he picks the significant details and omits those that are ordinary enough to fit anybody.

Joan Baez doesn't tell us how tall Archie is, or how much he weighs, but she does make us see him vividly. Richard Wright is able to give us a quick picture of his father by telling us that his stomach lapped over his belt; Clarence Day tells us all we need to know about his father's appearance by saying "His features were lumpy with gloom."

Notice, too, that all these writers have resisted the temptation to praise the people they are writing about. Clarence Day was undoubtedly fond of his parents, but he lets us see and hear what they said and did rather than telling us what splendid parents they were.

Little Archie, the Problem Child

[1] Little Archie, the problem child, eight operations on his eyes by the age of six, cleft palate, no taste buds or sense of smell, chewed his vitamins up in the morning, dropped his glass eye in the oatmeal and cried in noisy sorrow that he'd lost his eye—I felt sick trying to wash his face the first day, because both his eye sockets were infected and oozing, so at the breakfast table I couldn't eat, and when the head housemother said, "Is something wrong?" I said, "Archie's face, it's sort of icky," and began to cry.

Introduces Archie and describes writer's reaction

[2] "Oh, goodness, dear, we can't let a little thing like that get us down," she said brightly, and she took Archie off to wash his face and threw up her breakfast.

Emphasizes head housemother's reaction to Archie

[3] Archie's mother was always the first parent to drop him at the school on Sunday afternoons and the last to pick him up on Fridays, and the housemothers didn't give a damn about him in between because he was a bad boy and all the operations had made him hard to look at. I begged the women to quit calling him a bad boy, and said I would spend extra time with him.

Shows attitude of others to Archie

[4] It turned out that Archie didn't know how to hug. So every time he came around I'd grab all the children I could find and be hugging them when he got near. He had a tiny bit of vision in his one eye if he poked it with his fist, and he'd climb up over the kids to find out what was happening. I'd be saying, "Oh, Gail what a lovely hug, thank you!" and so Archie, with one fist jammed into his good eye, was beginning to see that he'd been missing something that looked like fun.

Writer's attempt to help Archie

[5] One night after I'd put him to bed, and we'd said the horrible little Perkins prayer, I gave Archie a kiss on the forehead and said goodnight. As I got up to go he said, "Hey, Miss Joan, don't I get a hug?"

Conclusion: what Archie did

Reprinted from *Daybreak*, by Joan Baez (New York: Dial Press, 1968), pp. 71–72, by permission of the author and the publisher.

After we'd had a big warm hug there was a fiendish
smile on his funny cock-eyed face on the pillow, and
he said, "You know what, Miss Joan? You're a
good kid."

DISCUSSION

1. Work out in your own words what the main idea sentence for this personal experience is.

2. In your opinion, would this article be more or less effective if the main
   idea sentence were stated rather than implied?

3. Can you see how the significance of this experience might apply to other
   experiences? Explain your answer.

4. Do the two people quoted in the first two paragraphs have different
   styles of talking? What words or expressions make the language sound
   natural for each speaker?

5. In this short article, Joan Baez uses plenty of specific details—Archie's
   appearance, when his mother came, what the housemothers called him,
   how she managed the hugging. Are all these details significant to the point
   of the article? Explain what the relationship is.

6. Paragraph 2 is one long sentence using two *and's*. How does using this
   stringy connector contribute to our surprise at what happens at the end
   of the sentence?

7. "Good kid" in the last line contrasts with "bad boy" used earlier. Can
   you tell from other words in the conclusion that the writer thinks Archie,
   too, is a "good kid"?

Father and the Ailing

colitis: a painful inflammation of the intestines

[1] From Father's point of view, Mother didn't know how to handle an ailment. He admired her most of the time and thought there was nobody like

her; he often said to us boys, "Your mother is a wonderful woman"; but he always seemed to disapprove of her when she was ill.

[2] Mother went to bed, for instance, at such times. Yet she didn't make noises. Father heard a little gasping moan sometimes, but she didn't want him to hear even that. Consequently he was sure she wasn't suffering. There was nothing to indicate it, he said.

[3] The worse she felt, the less she ever said about it, and the harder it was for him to believe that there was anything really wrong with her. "He says he can't see why I stay in bed so long," she once wrote to me, when I was away, "but this colitis is a mean affair which keeps one perfectly flat. The doctor told him yesterday the meaning of colitis, but he said he 'had never heard of the damned thing, thank God.' He feels very abused that he should be 'so upset by people with queer things the matter with them and doctors all over the place.' " (Mother underlined the word "people.")

[4] Even Mother's colds made him fretful. Whenever she had one, she kept going as long as she could, pottering about her room looking white and tired, with a shawl round her shoulders. But sometimes she had to give up and crawl into her bed.

[5] Father pished and poohed to himself about this, and muttered that it was silly. He said Mother was perfectly healthy. When people thought they were ill, he declared, it didn't mean that there was anything the matter with them, it was merely a sign of weak character. He often told Mother how weak it was to give in to an ailment, but every time he tried to strengthen her character in this respect, he said she seemed to resent it. He never remembered to try except when she could hardly hold her head up. From his point of view, though, that was the very time that she needed his help.

[6] He needed hers, too, or not exactly her help but her company, and he never hesitated to say so. When she was ill, he felt lost.

[7] He usually came up from his office at about five or six. The first thing he did was to look around the house to find Mother. It made his home feel queer and empty to him when she wasn't there.

[8] One night about six o'clock he opened the door of her bedroom. There was no light except for a struggling little fire which flickered and sank in the grate. A smell of witch-hazel was in the air, mixed with spirits of camphor. On the bed, huddled up under an afghan, Mother lay still, in the dark.

[9] "Are you there, Vinnie?" Father said, in a voice even louder than usual because of his not being sure.

[10] Mother moaned, "Go away."

[11] "What?" he asked, in astonishment.

[12] "Go away. Oh, go 'way."

[13] "Damnation!" he said, marching out.

[14] "Clare!"

[15] "What is it?"

[16] "Won't you *ple-e-ease* shut my door again."

[17] Father ground his teeth and shut it with such a bang that it made Mother jump.

[18] He told himself she had nothing the matter with her. She'd be all right in the morning. He ate a good dinner. Being lonely, he added an extra glass of claret and some toasted crackers and cheese. He had such a long and dull evening that he smoked two extra cigars.

[19] After breakfast the next morning, he went to her bedroom again. The fire was out. Two worn old slippers lay on a chair. The gray daylight was cheerless. Father stood at the foot of Mother's bed, looking disconsolately at her because she wasn't well yet. He had no one to laugh at or quarrel with; his features were lumpy with gloom.

[20] "What is it?" Mother asked in a whisper, opening her weary eyes.

[21] "Nothing," he said loudly. "Nothing."

[22] "Well, for mercy's sake, don't come in here looking like that, Clare," Mother begged.

[23] "What do you mean? Looking like what?"

[24] "Oh, go away!" Mother shrieked. "When people are sick, they like to see a smile or something. I never will get well if you stand there and stare at me that way! And shut my door quietly this time. And let me alone."

[25] Outside her door, when I asked him how Mother was, he said with a chuckle: "She's all right again. She isn't out of bed yet, but she sounds much better this morning."

DISCUSSION

1. In this essay, the writer, Clarence Day, appears only as an observer rather than a participant. Does this make the experience any less personal? Explain.

2. The main character in this essay is Day's father. What do we know about the father by the end of the essay? How do we know it?

3. What do we know about Day's mother? How do we know it?

4. What is Day's attitude toward his father? How can you tell?

5. Does Day's focus on what his father says and does in only one kind of situation make the writing more effective or less? Why?

6. What descriptive details are given in paragraph 8? In paragraph 18? In paragraph 19? How do they relate to the main idea of the essay?

7. The main event in this writing begins in paragraph 8. Why does Day open this writing with other incidents which presumably happened earlier? How do the earlier events relate to his main point?

8. How does Day make the account sound finished? What does the last sentence have to do with the introduction?

Father

orbit: circle within which one stays
alien: foreign; strange
literal: taking words for what they seem to mean, rather than as a
           figure of speech or an emotional outlet

[1] In Memphis we lived in a one-story brick tenement. The stone buildings and the concrete pavements looked bleak and hostile to me. The absence of green, growing things made the city seem dead. Living space for the four of us—my mother, my brother, my father, and me—was a kitchen and a bedroom. In the front and rear were paved areas in which my brother and I could play, but for days I was afraid to go into the strange city streets alone.
[2] It was in this tenement that the personality of my father first came fully into the orbit of my concern. He worked as a night porter in a Beale Street drugstore and he became important and forbidding to me only when I learned that I could not make noise when he was asleep in the daytime. He was the lawgiver in our family and I never laughed in his presence. I used to lurk timidly in the kitchen doorway and watch his huge body sitting slumped at the table. I stared at him with awe as he gulped his beer from a tin bucket, as he ate long and heavily, sighed, belched, closed his eyes to nod on a stuffed belly. He was quite fat and his bloated stomach always lapped over his belt. He was always a stranger to me, always somehow alien and remote.
[3] One morning my brother and I, while playing in the rear of our flat, found a stray kitten that set up a loud, persistent meowing. We fed it some scraps of food and gave it water, but it still meowed. My father, clad in his underwear, stumbled sleepily to the back door and demanded that we keep quiet. We told him that it was the kitten that was making the noise and he ordered us to drive it away. We tried to make the kitten leave, but it would not budge. My father took a hand.
[4] "Scat!" he shouted.
[5] The scrawny kitten lingered, brushing itself against our legs, and meowing plaintively.
[6] "Kill that damn thing!" my father exploded. "Do anything, but get it away from here!"
[7] He went inside, grumbling. I resented his shouting and it irked me that I could never make him feel my resentment. How could I hit back at him? Oh, yes . . . He had said to kill the kitten and I would kill it! I knew that he had

not really meant for me to kill the kitten, but my deep hate of him urged me toward a literal acceptance of his word.

[8] "He said for us to kill the kitten," I told my brother.

[9] "He didn't mean it," my brother said.

[10] "He did, and I'm going to kill 'im."

[11] "Then he *will* howl," my brother said.

[12] "He can't howl if he's dead," I said.

[13] "He didn't really say kill 'im," my brother protested.

[14] "He did!" I said. "And you heard him!"

[15] My brother ran away in fright. I found a piece of rope, made a noose, slipped it about the kitten's neck, pulled it over a nail, then jerked the animal clear of the ground. It gasped, slobbered, spun, doubled, clawed the air frantically; finally its mouth gaped and its pink-white tongue shot out stiffly. I tied the rope to a nail and went to find my brother. He was crouching behind a corner of the building.

[16] "I killed 'im," I whispered.

[17] "You did bad," my brother said.

[18] "Now Papa can sleep," I said, deeply satisfied.

[19] "He didn't mean for you to kill 'im," my brother said.

[20] "Then why did he *tell* me to do it?" I demanded.

[21] My brother could not answer; he stared fearfully at the dangling kitten.

[22] "That kitten's going to get you," he warned me.

[23] "That kitten can't even breathe now," I said.

[24] "I'm going to tell," my brother said, running into the house.

[25] I waited, resolving to defend myself with my father's rash words, anticipating my enjoyment in repeating them to him even though I knew that he had spoken them in anger. My mother hurried toward me, drying her hands upon her apron. She stopped and paled when she saw the kitten suspended from the rope.

[26] "What in God's name have you done?" she asked.

[27] "The kitten was making noise and Papa said to kill it," I explained.

[28] "You little fool!" she said. "Your father's going to beat you for this!"

[29] "But he told me to kill it," I said.

[30] "You shut your mouth!"

[31] She grabbed my hand and dragged me to my father's bedside and told him what I had done.

[32] "You know better than that!" my father stormed.

[33] "You told me to kill 'im," I said.

[34] "I told you to drive him away," he said.

[35] "You told me to kill 'im," I countered positively.

[36] "You get out of my eyes before I smack you down!" my father bellowed in disgust, then turned over in bed.

[37] I had had my first triumph over my father. I had made him believe that I had taken his words literally. He could not punish me now without risking his authority. I was happy because I had at last found a way to throw my

criticism of him into his face. I had made him feel that, if he whipped me for killing the kitten, I would never give serious weight to his words again. I had made him know that I felt he was cruel and I had done it without his punishing me.

DISCUSSION

1. Using a two-part main idea sentence for finding the significance in a personal experience (When ————, I discovered ————), work out a main idea sentence for this essay. Does what Wright says in the last paragraph help you to see why this incident was significant for him?

2. What was the child's attitude toward his father? How can you tell? Is there anything in the article to show whether the writer had the same attitude when he wrote this essay?

3. What specific details in paragraph 3 help you to get a picture of the father? Would it be more effective or less if Wright had told us what kind of clothes his father wore, or what his eyes looked like?

4. How old (about) is the child? How can you tell? Would it have made any difference to give an exact age?

5. Why does Wright include the long, somewhat repetitious, discussion between the two boys (paragraphs 8 through 14, and 16 through 24)?

6. Paragraph 15 contains more specific details. What do these details tell us about the boy's own attitude toward what he has done to the kitten? Why does Wright say "whispered" in paragraph 16?

7. What does Wright do to make the quoted conversations sound natural?

What's the Point?

Personal experience papers do not have to be built on colorful personalities or unusual events. In fact, no experience is too trivial, no incident too slight, to make an interesting essay of personal experience if the writer himself sees some point in the experience and can make his readers see that same point. Spending a sleepless night, hearing a casual comment made by a friend, watching a routine arrest on a busy street, shopping for a pillow and a suitcase, can all be made significant. The writer who can find significance in ordinary daily occurrences, in little events that might seem so trivial they are hardly worth writing about, has done two things: he has enriched his own understanding or enjoyment, and he has helped his readers share his enriched appreciation.

His readers will not share his appreciation, however, unless he chooses his details well. The significance of the experience helps him to decide what to include and what to leave out. He describes people and places, he quotes conversations, because he wants his readers to share his experience vividly; but he is careful about which details he includes and which conversations he quotes, because he also wants his readers to share the meaning that he found in the experience.

A Quiet Summer Night

discrete: separate and distinct
conspiratorial: like someone plotting
microcosm: a little world; any small world that includes all the important elements of a bigger one
reconnoiter: scout around

[1] There are jokes about city people who can't sleep in the country "because of the noise," and once on a quiet summer night the joke was on me. There is no steady roar of traffic here to shut out the discrete scratch of a mouse or a bird's insistent singing at dawn. But these "usual" sounds weave themselves into the silence; only the "unusual," like a clap of thunder, startles the country dweller.

Essay begins with the main idea sentence openly stated

[2] I had gone to bed, tired and content, when, only half asleep, I became aware of low insistent conspiratorial voices in the big meadow. "Well," I told myself, "you are imagining things, my girl." When I pulled up the shade and peered out, there was nothing to be seen but an empty field under a calm starry sky. Yet the mysterious voices murmured on, like a crowd of supers on a stage . . . and then, suddenly, I registered. It was bullfrogs, of course, having a conversation, and the wind was just right to carry their voices from the pond. Feeling like a great fool, I went shivering back to bed.

First unexpected sound —the croaking of bull-frogs

[3] But not to sleep. For, a half hour later, I sat up with a prickle of fear at the nape of my neck. I heard excited dangerous barking, the barking of a pack of dogs at large in my woods. Could their quarry be

Second sound: easily recognized this time but frightening because the dogs sound dangerous

the exquisite young buck that only the other day ventured within a few yards of the barn and stood there, gazing at me with great dark eyes, unafraid? [4] No village is perfect; it is a microcosm. Here we have had to absorb a new neighbor who chooses to keep a pack of mongrels and allows them to run loose. I listened to the barking as it grew louder and more murderous, and suddenly I was furious, too furious to think of risk, I got up, pulled on jeans, a sweater, and boots over my pajamas, grabbed a flashlight and my woodchuck-scaring rifle, and ran down the rough field toward my woods, and then over a tumble-down stone wall into the second—now overgrown—field. There I stood still, before crashing in through white pine and blackberry bushes, and listened. The barking sounded farther away than it had when I started out, but now I heard a woman's voice cry, "Help!"

Fright turns to anger—and then an unexpected cry for help

[5] "Stay where you are—I'm coming!" I'm no Davy Crockett, but there was nothing to do but plunge on over granite boulders, through old stumps and thickets of alder in the direction of the cry. Then, quite suddenly, I knew I was lost. I stood there, panting, scared to death, feeling like a wild animal myself, and called out again: "Where are you?" This time there was no answer, but I thought I heard mocking laughter. Well, the first thing was to get "found."

Chasing the cry, she gets lost

[6] After about 10 minutes of panic and thrashing about, I came out on the dirt road—a real stroke of luck—and from there could see lights at a neighbor's house, though it was past midnight. What a relief to tell someone my story! My neighbor suggested that it might be better another time to call the police, but we could still do that now.

After a frantic few minutes, she finds a road, and a neighbor

[7] Pretty soon our own more or less volunteer policeman turned up in the big car with a flashing red light on the roof, and went off to reconnoiter. No one but a fool about deer would go off into the woods alone at night, and I have an idea that he did not. When he came back he tried to convince me that I had been "had" by a crowd across the brook at another neighbor's who gives an occasional wild party. I wonder. Whatever the teasing human voices may have cried, the dog voices had been in earnest.

Policeman fails to find anything

[8] I went home, rather sheepish, determined to get some sleep at last, and was dozing off when a tremendous jangling of metal flung down on wood nearly made me leap out of my skin, this time to laugh with pleasure, for I guessed at once what the commotion must be.

Third noise: loud but not frightening because she recognizes it

[9] I crept through the big kitchen-livingroom in the dark and, at the door to the back porch, clicked on the outside light. Sure enough, there was a fat raccoon who had just managed to lift off the tight lid of the garbage can with her clever little hands. She looked up, bright eyes shining through her black mask, ring tail stretched out behind her, and we took each other in. Then I turned out the light and left her to her joys. "Tomorrow night," I said to myself, crawling happily back into bed, "remember to put out chocolate biscuits." (Raccoons are crazy about chocolate biscuits.)

Tracing down the identified noise

[10] All's well that ends with a merry wild face, unafraid, and I climbed back into bed, relaxed, and must have fallen into deep sleep almost at once. Not for long! A violent explosion, then shattering glass, rocked the house. I was too terrified to move at first. Had someone thrown a hand grenade through a window? Of course, I had to find out.

Fourth noise: sounds like an explosion

[11] I turned on all the lights, went through the house from attic to cellar . . . and there at the bottom of the cellar stairs on the cement floor I saw the shattered remains of an empty gallon cider bottle. From a secret hiding place in the stone foundation, Scrabble, one of my two speckled cats, stared at me with round, scared golden eyes. "So you thought it would be fun to knock that bottle down the stairs, you dunce!"

Tracing down the unidentified noise

[12] At 3 A.M., while Scrabble wound herself around my legs and purred, I sat in the big wing chair by the fireplace, drinking a cup of cocoa and thinking that country silence is wonderful—but I have to get home to it, sometimes, through some pretty strange noises.

Conclusion: comes back to the main idea, but in different words

DISCUSSION

1. What distinction between "country quiet" and "city quiet" does the writer make in the first paragraph? How does she define "noise"? What specific examples does she give?

2. What details in paragraph 2 help to establish the contrast between the expected and the unexpected?

3. How do the details of wearing apparel help us to visualize the situation? How are they related to the main idea? What about the description of the brush she crashes through (paragraphs 4 and 5)?

4. What is the connection between the "mocking laughter" mentioned in paragraph 5 and the constable's explanation in paragraph 6?

5. Paragraphs 6 and 7 give no details of sounds, but they do give visual detail. What does the writer mention that lets us see the scene with the writer?

6. In paragraph 7, Miss Sarton says "I wonder." Is it more satisfactory to leave the readers wondering too, or would it have been better to explain?

7. Although there are some people mentioned in this essay, they are not described at all. What animals are described? Are there specific details that help us see them? Which animal is described in the most detail? Why does it seem more appropriate in this essay to describe the animals rather than the people?

Chain-Link Fence

citation: honorable mention
interstices: spaces between lines

[1] Once I was with Richard in his hometown. It was his first visit in five years. We arrived in the middle of the night and had to leave before day-break because Richard was wanted by the local police. We were in his grand-mother's house. Besides Richard, there were his grandmother, his aunt, and two unrelated men, both long-time friends of Richard.
[2] The group was discussing the possibility of Richard's coming home to stay and weighing the probable consequences. In the middle of the discussion, Richard interrupted and nodded at me, "Now Ellix here is white, as you can see, but he's one of my best friends. Him and me are real tight. You can say anything you want, right to his face. He's real nice."

From *Tally's Corner* by Elliot Liebow, by permission of Little, Brown and Co. Copyright © 1967 by Little, Brown and Company.

[3] "Well," said his Aunt Pearl, "I always did say there are some nice white people."

[4] Whether or not there is more to these citations than "Some of my best friends are . . ." or "Yes, but you're different," the wall between us remained, or better, the chain-link fence, since despite the barriers we were able to look at each other, walk alongside each other, talk and occasionally touch fingers. When two people stand up close to the fence on either side, without touching it, they can look through the interstices and forget that they are looking through a fence.

DISCUSSION

1. In this essay, Liebow uses three paragraphs to set the scene for a scrap of conversation, and interprets the significance of that scrap in the last paragraph. Would the point of the first three paragraphs have been clear without paragraph 4? Explain.

2. Richard and Aunt Pearl are both praising Liebow. What is there in their praise that reminds him of a fence?

3. Do you think Liebow's comparison of color difference to a chain-link fence is effective? Why? Is it accurate? Explain. He also mentions "barrier" and "wall." What other words have been used to describe the differences?

On Becoming a Cop Hater

malignantly: in an evil and vicious manner
stratum: level
benign: calm; harmless (opposite of malignant)
bizarre: highly unusual; fantastic
apprehend: catch; arrest
bourgeoisie: the middle class
admonishment: warning; mild scolding
inquisition: harsh and prolonged questioning

[1] I had seen the two boys in the crosswalk, and I had seen the Thunderbird almost hit them. It was on Kalakaua Avenue in Honolulu, one early evening

in the late spring. "Watch it," one of the boys may or may not have said. I heard him say nothing, but whatever was said or not said affected the erring driver of the Thunderbird malignantly. "Stinking hippies," he screamed, jumping from the car. "Burning your draft cards, you should've burned Germany, you should've burned Japan, *stinking hippies*."

[2] "I don't know what you're talking about, Mister," one of the boys said. He was wearing a blue suit and a white shirt, and his blond hair was about as long as the average college freshman's. "I got my draft card."

[3] "Stinking cowards, stinking *hippies*."

[4] "Good for him," said an old man behind me. Quite a crowd had gathered by then, most of them the retired and the conventioneers who wander aimlessly up and down Kalakaua Avenue in the off seasons, and, when two police officers finally drove up, the crowd clapped. The man in the Thunderbird drove off then, and one of the police officers jumped out and grabbed the arm of the boy in the blue suit. "Listen, it wasn't my fault, I didn't do anything," the boy said.

[5] "Don't talk back," the officer said.

[6] "But I didn't *do* anything."

[7] The boy was finally arrested for resisting an officer. His friend was told to "move on." The friend looked bewildered. "But I'm with him," he said. "You aren't with him any more," said one of the officers. "No sir. I'm telling you you're not. You don't want to go where he's going."

[8] "But you can't take him in," I heard myself saying suddenly. "He didn't do anything." I had touched the arm of one of the police officers to attract his attention, and he recoiled as if touched by a snake. The other officer sprang forward and raised his arms in a defensive karate position. (I want you to bear in mind here that I am five-feet-two, and weigh 91 pounds.) Both of them fixed their eyes just over my head in that gaze peculiar to police officers and troops on review. "Move on, sister," one of them ordered. "I said move on." I last saw the boy in the back of the patrol car, on his way to the precinct house.

[9] I want to tell you a few things about myself. As it happens, I was raised in that stratum of society which teaches its children that the police are not merely their protectors but, in a world of hostile strangers, perhaps their only friends. When I thought of the police, certain images sprang obediently to mind: Look at the mounted policeman leaning to answer a small boy's question, then sweeping him onto his saddle for a trot around the park. Watch the patrolman leading the little children across the intersection. Policemen were there to rescue lost balls, and kittens, and, were a child to drop her ice-cream cone, a policeman would dry her tears and buy her another, with a nickel from his own pocket. A policeman was a true friend in blue.

[10] I had never actually come into contact with such a policeman, or in fact with any policeman, but I knew all that to be true because I had seen pictures of it happening, in school readers and coloring books. So benign was my view of the police that until quite recently, even when I knew myself to

be in technical violation of the law, I was confident that the police, should they by some bizarre error apprehend me, would recognize my essential "niceness"—*i.e.,* my status as a daughter of the lawful and propertied *bourgeoisie*—and deliver me to my doorstep with a friendly, and well, respectful admonishment. Some unexamined snobbery (as unattractive as any other snobbery, all right, but I am talking to you straight) led me to expect that to policemen I would ever be "Miss Joan."

[11] What I am telling you is that I was neither born a cop hater nor did I become one by way of some dramatic venture into the unlawful; I became one over the course of several years, by way of an accumulation of small encounters, insignificant confrontations. There was the time I called to report an accident in front of my house, and no one came for 40 minutes, and when I called a third time to say that the driver was pinned behind the wheel and intermittently unconscious and screaming, the desk man asked me if she was drunk. There were the extended inquisitions when people with whom I was driving were stopped for traffic violations. There was the point at which I began to notice that every time I saw a cop stop a car on the Sunset Strip, he was stopping either a juvenile or a Mexican. There were the belligerent crossed arms at police lines. On the whole the police make it a point to be nice to writers, once they see the press card, but now and then I would meet one who saw writers as just more of the enemy: The enemy, I began to perceive, was anyone not a cop, not on the force, not in the life . . . It has been a very long time since I thought of a cop as a friend in blue.

DISCUSSION

1. Would this essay have been more effective or less if the writer had stopped at the end of paragraph 8? Why?

2. Can you find any details in paragraphs 1 through 8 that could have been left out without losing some of the point? Has the writer left out any details that you are curious about?

3. Does it seem to you that the police are wholly at fault in the incident told in these first eight paragraphs? If anyone else is at fault, who is it? Why does the writer put the entire blame on the police?

4. Why does the writer tell us about her background in paragraph 9? Would what she says about her attitude be more convincing or less if she had grown up in a different "stratum" of society?

5. What indirect comment about school texts is being made in paragraph 10? Does this agree with your own experience of grade-school readers, or with your experience of the children's books sold in groceries and drug stores? If it differs, what is the difference?

6. This article might also have ended with paragraph 10. What is the purpose of adding paragraph 11? Does the additional material in paragraph 11 make Miss Didion's point more convincing or less?

7. What is the main idea of this essay? Is it stated in the essay? How far does this point correspond with your own experience? Where does it differ?

8. Does Miss Didion's present impression of a policeman come any closer to fitting all policemen than her childhood impression? What things do the two have in common?

Open Letter to Consumer Reports

hostile: actively unfriendly
hoosegow: jail
accosted: approached boldly
compressing: squeezing
knead: to punch, pound, and press, as in making bread
consistency: firmness; degree of density
disarray: disorder
hauteur: a mixture of pride and contempt
languish: become weak and feeble; droop and fade
ensue: follow

Gentlemen:

[1] Just reading *Consumer Reports* fills my window shopping needs, and makes me feel practical and economical, but this isn't my annual fan letter. Right now I want you to go bail for me.

[2] I set out for the January sales with your new Buying Guide Issue under my arm, love in my heart, and a wallet in my jeans that was nicely filled out with Christmas bonuses. I never thought of Boston as a hostile town, yet here I am in the hoosegow, and no one seems to care or understand. I am writing you because I feel perhaps you will understand, and in the hope that you will care.

[3] What happened is this: I headed for the department store area with two

Reprinted from the column "Ironic Board," by Betsy Cochran in *The Cape Codder* by permission of the author and the publisher.

particular items in mind—molded luggage, and bed pillows. First the luggage. I found stacks of it taking up half a room in the first store I tried. Whipping out the Guide, I followed its instructions:

[4] ". . . Check the frame's sturdiness by opening the case ninety degrees and seeing how hard it is to flex the edges; pull the lid sideways to see how readily it tends to deform . . . Try the handle for size and comfort. Pinch the lining in several places to see how firmly it is glued down . . ."

[5] It was while I was still pinching the lining of a $45 twenty-six-inch case that the salesman accosted me. "Can I help you?" he asked between clenched teeth.

[6] "Why no," I said, "as a matter of fact I find the linings of your cases are not well glued, and the lids don't stay open the way they should, so I shall have to look elsewhere."

[7] He accompanied me to the elevator and pushed the button. My next quest before I left the store was for bed pillows. I had read all you had to say about shredded foam and waterfowl down, so when I approached the generously stacked counters I knew just what to do. I compared them for resiliency by placing them on a flat surface (the only one handy was the floor) and compressing them to about half their original thickness. I made sure the openings used for inserting the filler were well-closed with both ends of the seam back-stitched (and not all of them were). I made it my job to "knead a synthetic fiber or feather-down pillow to determine whether its filling had uniform consistency," and at this point I was approached by the floor manager. He did not ask if he could help me.

[8] "Watcha doing to our pillows?" he asked, his face flushed. In truth, the display case was in some disarray, and a few tiny goose down feathers were gliding softly between us.

[9] "I was only giving them the necessary tests," I replied with hauteur. "They don't all measure up," I added. I balanced a couple of them on my arms, as you suggested, to see if the corners drooped, and then held them by the ends and shook them.

[10] "See here," said the manager, "quit it!"

[11] Indignantly I pointed to the section of page 96 of the Buying Guide that was giving me my instructions. "We must now fluff the pillows to see if they have good dome-shaped crowns," I pointed out, "and unzip the foam rubber ones to see if the filling is in one piece. We must make sure that zipper tapes are attached with two rows of stitching, tap and fold the ticking to see if it is heavily treated with sizing material, punch it and watch for signs of dust, and bury our face in it and sniff to see if the filler has been cleaned properly."

[12] "Must we indeed," he said, "we'll see about that." I turned away from him and began to fluff and punch. "I'll bury your face in them for you," he shouted, and we soon had a brisk pillow fight on our hands (another effective test), until stronger authorities intervened. It seems the law was on his side, though Virtue and Righteousness were on mine.

[13] This brings me to the spot where I now languish. I can only hope that the lawsuits which will ensue will turn out to be a Best Buy.
[14] Please get me out of here.

Faithfully yours,
B.C.

DISCUSSION

1. Why is this article written in the form of a letter to *Consumer Reports*? Do you think it was ever sent to *Consumer Reports*? Why?

2. Does the writer apparently keep on believing in the advice *Consumer Reports* gives? Look especially at the end of paragraph 12, paragraph 13, and the closing of the letter.

3. Why does the writer quote the exact directions the magazine gives for testing suitcases and pillows?

4. How is the price of the suitcase in paragraph 5 related to the point of this essay? The fact that not all the pillows had back-stitched seams?

5. Would this story be as funny if the writer had first tested the pillows and then been jailed after testing the suitcase? Why?

6. At first reading, you might think that the main idea sentence of this article is "When I tried to follow the directions in the Buying Guide, I discovered I was in trouble." But is the point of the essay that she got into trouble? What would a better main idea sentence be?

Sometimes a writer starts with a special problem he has been trying to solve or a situation that puzzles him. Instead of beginning with an ordinary incident and trying to isolate what it was that impressed him, he wants to share with his readers the solution to his problem or his puzzlement. In papers such as these, the significance is built into the experience, but the writer must still keep that significance in mind all the time he is writing.

Gregory begins with a particular problem—his worry about what he would do when some heckler called him "nigger"—and everything he includes is somehow related to that problem. Everything Robinson includes in his essay is related to the discovery he made when his son got an *F* in arithmetic. Gregory does not tell us what he was wearing or what he said to people who praised his performance, no matter how much he liked his clothes or how pleased he was with the compliments. Robinson does not tell us anything about his other children, or the size of his house, or what they had for dinner. Instead, although both writers help us to see the situation, they make sure that everything we see and hear does have something to do with the point.

nigger

heckler: person who deliberately baits a performer
honky-tonk: cheap night club
vicious: especially nasty or mean
comeback: quick answer

[1] In and out of Roberts in 1960, I had plenty of time to think. I realized that when I started working the white clubs, one of my big problems was going to be hecklers—especially in the beginning when I'd be in honky-tonk white clubs. Handling a heckler just right is very important to a comic. Unless you're well known as an insulting comedian, you can't chop hecklers down too hard or the crowd will turn against you. Most hecklers are half drunk anyway, and you will lose a crowd if you get mean with a drunk. On the other hand, you have to put a heckler down. If a heckler gets the best of you, that crowd will start to feel sorry for you. I had worked it out pretty well in Negro clubs. I'd put a drunken heckler down gently: "Man, I'd rather be your slave than your liver," and that would go even better in a white club. Whenever I got a vicious heckler, I could say something like: "Now, how would you like it if I came to *your* job and kicked the shovel out of *your* hand?" That would work fine, too. But some day, somewhere, I'd be in a white club and somebody would get up and call me a nigger.

Statement of the problem: what will he do when he is called "nigger"?

[2] I worried about that. When that white man calls me nigger, every other white man in that club is going to feel embarrassed. The customers are going to tie in that uncomfortable feeling with that club— even after I'm gone—and the club owner knows this. He would rather keep me out of his club than take a chance on losing customers. It was the same thing when I got kicked in the mouth as a shoeshine boy—

Why he worried about it

the bartender ran me out of the place, even though he felt sorry for me, because he couldn't afford to have the customers fight. But now I'm a man and I have to take care of myself. I need a fast comeback to that word. That split second is all the difference between going on with the show or letting the customers feel pity and a little resentment for the entertainer who got put down.

[3] I used to make Lillian call me a nigger over the dinner table, and I'd practice the fast comeback. Somehow, I couldn't get it right. I'd always come back with something a little bitter, a little evil.

First attempts to solve the problem

[4] "Nigger."

[5] "Maybe you'd feel more like a man if you lived down South and had a toilet with your name on it."

[6] "No, Greg, that's not right at all."

[7] I was lying around the house one night, watching television and feeling mad at the world. I'd been out of work for three weeks. The snow was so deep I hadn't even been outside the house for four days. Lil was sitting in a corner, so calm and peaceful, reading a book. There was no one else to pick on.

Another attempt to solve it; this one provides a clue

[8] "Hey, Lil."

[9] "Yes, Greg."

[10] "What would you do if from here on in I started referring to you as bitch?"

[11] She jumped out of the chair. "I would simply ignore you."

[12] I fell off the couch and started laughing so hard that old stomach of mine nearly burst. That was it. The quick sophisticated answer. Cool. No bitterness. The audience would never know I was mad and mean inside. And there would be no time to feel sorry for me. Now I'd get that comeback.

[13] I got my chance a few weeks later, in a rundown neighborhood club on the outskirts of town. The customers were working-class white men, laborers, factory hands, men whose only marks of dignity were the Negroes they bossed on the job and kept away from on weekends. It happened in the middle of the late show on the second night. Loud and clear.

A chance to try the solution

[14] "Nigger."

[15] The audience froze, and I wheeled around without batting an eye. "You hear what that guy just

Actual quotations let the reader share the experience

called me? Roy Rogers' horse. He called me Trigger."

[16] I had hit them so quick that they laughed, and they laughed hard because that was what they really wanted to believe the guy had called me. But I had only bought myself a little time. There was an element in the house that really knew what he had called me. I had the crowd locked up with that fast comeback, so I took a few seconds to look them over and blow out some smoke.   *The first part works*

[17] "You know, my contract reads that every time I hear that word, I get fifty dollars more a night. I'm only making ten dollars a night, and I'd like to put the owner out of business. Will everybody in the room please stand up and yell nigger?"   *What he said*

[18] They laughed and they clapped and I swung right back into my show. Afterwards, the owner came over and gave me twenty dollars and shook my hand and thanked me. I had made my test.   *How it worked*

DISCUSSION

1. Rather than dealing with a single event, this personal experience story deals with a single problem. What is it?

2. What discovery grows out of the next-to-last event, when Gregory is finally called "nigger"? How does this discovery relate to what his wife told him in paragraph 11?

3. Can you make a two-part main idea sentence for this article?

4. Gregory uses lots of "street words"—*honky-tonk, drunk, slave, nigger, kicked in the mouth, bitch.* Does the vocabulary seem appropriate to the story, or is Gregory merely using the words for their shocking effect? Explain.

5. Does Gregory use echo transitions? Where?

6. Do you think the last line is a successful conclusion to this paper? If you think it is, explain why. If you don't like it, write a concluding sentence you think would fit better.

One a Penny, Two a Penny

acclaimed: announced with loud applause; praised highly
forthcoming: about to appear
discomfited: made uncomfortable
decidedly: very much
namesake: a person named after someone else
Quixote: a fictional Spanish knight who has become a symbol for any idealist amusingly frustrated by reality
tilting: fighting on horseback with lances, trying to knock the other rider from his horse

[1] I had never paid much attention to my son's homework until the night I discovered that he was a moron! I had always assumed that he was a typical boy. He had never been acclaimed as a scholastic wizard, but then he was only in the third grade, and I doubt that even Shakespeare made his mark in the world at such an early stage.

[2] So I was unprepared for the shocking discovery that grew out of an innocent request for help with an arithmetic exercise.

[3] "I'm having trouble with the problem, Dad," he said. "The teacher said you might be able to help me."

[4] Mathematics, as you know, is my strong suit. You probably have read some of the articles I've published in this field. Moreover, I have the reputation of being an excellent teacher. So it was with a feeling of utmost confidence that I said, "I guess together we ought to be able to lick it, Son. What is the problem?"

[5] "It's about pencils, Dad. I'll read it. 'If you can buy three pencils for 5¢, how many pencils can you buy for 10¢?' "

[6] "Surely you can answer that, Son," I said. "What answer did you give?"

[7] "I thought 'five' might be the right answer, but the teacher said it was wrong. So then I thought it might be 'four.' The teacher said that was wrong, too. I can't seem to get the answer she wants."

[8] What was needed here, I told myself, was a simple, clear review of the proposition. Calmly ordering my best teaching tactics, I went to work. Still the correct answer was not forthcoming. Again we tried. And again. Horror was rising in me. My son *was* a moron. I could *not* get from him the correct answer although I did everything but whisper "six" in his ear. Finally, in

Reprinted from "One a Penny, Two a Penny," by Thomas E. Robinson, in *Today's Education* (January 1969), by permission of the author and the publisher.

desperation, I asked, "Why can't you solve this easy little problem? Are you really trying?"

[9] "I guess it looks easy to you, Dad. But I can do it in so many ways, and I always get different answers. Look, the problem says I buy 'three pencils for 5¢.' I could buy two 2¢ pencils and one 1¢ pencil. Or I could buy a 3¢ pencil and two penny pencils. For 10¢ I could buy three 3¢ pencils and one penny pencil, but the teacher says 'four' is wrong. Or I could buy five 2¢ pencils, but that's wrong too. Or I could buy three 2¢ pencils and four penny pencils. But 'seven' doesn't seem to be the answer. I just can't do it, Dad. I get a lot of answers, but the teacher marks them all wrong. I guess I'm just dumb!"

[10] Quick as a flash, my horror changed to pride. Deep, exciting pride. I had a genius in the family, whose only handicap was a moronic father who wrote arithmetic textbooks.

[11] In the full flush of that pride, I hugged him, and I said, "You tell your teacher the answers you have. Tell her again tomorrow. And just watch her eyes light up. And tomorrow night you tell me what she said."

[12] Wednesday I came home early and sat awaiting my genius son, anxious to hear the admission of a discomfited teacher with a decidedly altered conception of my namesake's ability.

[13] "What did she say, Son?" I asked, as he entered the door I opened for him. I should have guessed his answer, though, for his gloomy face was an unmistakable giveaway of her reaction.

[14] "It's no use, Dad. The teacher marked all of my answers wrong. She gave me a zero and said she didn't see how I could pass arithmetic this month."

[15] Instinctively, I dug into my pocket and gave him a dime. "Don't worry about it any more, Son. Go buy yourself a treat."

[16] He started out the door, already looking a bit happier, ticking off the endless combinations of flavors, the infinite range of colors, all sold at the corner shop where they advertise "Candy—3 for 5¢."

[17] I settled back in my chair, also feeling happier and strangely secure. Today's children were answering yesterday's questions with tomorrow's answers. I must have dozed, for I dreamed of a young Quixote tilting the exact sciences—with a licorice stick.

DISCUSSION

1. Could the first sentence be the main idea sentence of this article? What does beginning the article with this sentence lead the reader to expect?

2. What is the main idea sentence? Support your answer by referring to the essay.

3. How do the specific details and the many direct quotations make this

essay more effective, especially in telling how the boy solved the problem? Could the writer get the same effect by using generalizations?
Explain.

4. One reason this fairly short essay contains so many paragraphs is that
   there are so many direct quotations. In your own words, explain how
   the quotations affect the paragraphing, and notice how they are punc-
   tuated.

5. In paragraph 12, the author shifts from the conversational language he
   has been using and puts in several words like *discomfited, decidedly, conception, namesake.* Why does he change the tone here?

6. After the boy reports his second failure, the father might have sided with
   the teacher. If he had done so, how would this have changed the point
   of the paper?

7. As a reader, which interpretation of the boy's ability in arithmetic do
   you accept—the teacher's or the father's? Why?

8. In paragraph 16, why doesn't the writer tell us what else the corner
   shop sells? What difference does it make how many flavors and colors
   of candy there are? When there must be several signs in the shop, why
   is just one quoted exactly?

9. How effective is the conclusion of this essay? Why does the writer feel
   secure? What does the second sentence mean? Explain the reference
   to "a licorice stick."

10. What comment about the school system does this paper make? In decid-
    ing on your answer, look especially at paragraphs 11, 14, and 17.

11. Do you see any resemblance between the attitude of the teacher in this
    essay and the attitudes of the teachers in "If I'm So Smart, How Come
    I Flunk All the Time?" Explain.

The Way It Spozed To Be

delirious: hysterical with pleasure
regimen: carefully ordered, controlled program
tolerable: adequate

[1] When I went back to George Washington Junior High School after a month's absence, 7B and 8B seemed the same. They had few comments to make about the past month except for a few kids who said they were glad to see me back and a few others who said they wished they could still have Mrs. A., whose name I've forgotten.

[2] 9D, however, greeted me with an indignant and sincere-sounding outcry. Mrs. A. was a better teacher than I, she was a real teacher, I wasn't no real teacher, she really made them work, not just have them old discussions every day; no, man, they were learning spelling and sentences and all they was spozed to. Moreover she was strict and didn't allow fooling around—all in all they felt they'd been really getting somewhere. I looked in my grade book, up to now pretty empty of marks, and saw, sure enough, a whole string of grades after each name—mostly, however, F's and zeroes. Many of them had nothing but zeroes, which I took to mean they had been busy not-doing this important work. I pointed this out to the class, but it didn't matter. They had been back on familiar ground; strict teacher, no fooling around, no smart-off, no discussions about how bad school was, and plenty of work. That was, after all, what school was and they were in favor of it.

[3] 7H was in a similar temper. They too had tales of plenty of real work, strict discipline, no talking, no gum, reading aloud every day, everybody— and then they came out with a long list of all of them who had been sent to the office for talking or chewing gum or refusing to read or laughing or getting mad at the teacher. Mrs. A. gave them work on the board every day, they screamed, and she made them keep a notebook with all this work in it and they were spozed to bring it every day to work in and get graded on it. That was what real teachers did, they told me. I asked to see some of the notebooks; naturally no one had one. What about that? I asked. No use. She made us keep them notebooks, they all shouted. The fact that no one had kept or was keeping them notebooks didn't enter into it.

[4] A big change was that everyone had them spellers. May showed hers off triumphantly. Most of the spellers in 9D were empty of writing—all that copying of words and alphabetizing and putting in lines between syllables hadn't actually been done except by May, Josephine and Geraldine. Theirs were all filled out to date, but were also all wrong. 7H had spellers too, but after the first victorious outcry their tone changed and they issued a complaint about them. For while Mrs. A. was a great teacher, for evidence of which they had their non-existent notebooks and blank spellers, she had made a serious mistake; the spellers were second- and third-grade spellers. We in the seventh grade, Mr. Hern-don! She give us the wrong spellers!

[5] The state spellers tried to keep grade level a secret; they didn't say seventh grade or second grade anywhere on them, to keep the kids unaware of the fact they were working below (or above) grade level. What they did have was a number of dots, near the top, perhaps so the teacher could tell what grade level they were—seven dots for seventh-grade, two dots for second grade. It didn't take long for the slowest kid to figure out this system.

[6] 7H raised hell with me about the second- and third-grade spellers. They

needed seventh-grade spellers. They'd already had them second- and third-grade spellers for a number of years, they pointed out with some justification; they'd already not-done them a few times.

[7] Hell, I thought; it didn't seem very important to me all of a sudden, and I went over and grabbed a stack of seventh-grade spellers from the shelf and passed them out. Everyone was delirious. The holidays were only a couple of weeks off, and I told them it was a Christmas present.

[8] It was true the second- and third-grade spellers were of no use to them. What they needed was official spellers with seven big dots on them, to carry outside on the school grounds and home with them to prove they were too in seventh grade. I gave out a bunch of homework in spelling and ordered everyone to take the spellers home that very night to do the homework in; everyone carried those spellers home and back again every day from then on, until they were lost or swiped. I was, if not a real teacher like Mrs. A., at least a good guy again, and that was something. We were back to normal, ready to go.

[9] In my free period that first day back I conferred with Mrs. A., who was sticking around to let me know what she'd been doing. She was an extremely attractive woman, perhaps thirty, well-dressed, light colored, her hair nicely waved and under control; everything else was well under control, too, as I discovered. She told me, although not in so many words, that my classes had been a mess when she took over, that she considered them well on their way to straightening up after a month with her, and that it was now up to me to keep them that way. She got this across to me very nicely in the kind but firm manner some people have with training animals.

[10] She advised me to figure out a regular and consistent plan of work, or simply to accept the one she had devised, and see to it that the students did this, or if not that they at least did nothing else during the period. I should grade all papers immediately and hand them back so that students who did the work could see their rewards promptly.

[11] It was important, she said, to get them into the proper mood for schoolwork as soon as they entered the room. In particular, avoid beginning the period by talking to them, explaining, or lecturing, which they would not listen to and which only encouraged them to start talking themselves. She believed that I talked to the class too much anyway—there was no point in their expressing opinions about things they knew nothing about. Let them learn something first, she said, and then they might have something to say.

[12] The best method for getting them in order was to have a paragraph written out on the board when they entered, and get them in the habit of copying this paragraph in their notebooks immediately they sat down, giving a time limit for its completion, erasing the paragraph when the time was up, and grading the notebooks frequently. Copying was something they could all do without further explanation from me; it got them in the mood for schoolwork, quiet, their materials ready, all set for the day's lesson, whatever it was.

[13] I didn't have a lot to say to this advice. In the face of the nonexistent

notebooks and the unused or all-wrong spellers, the list of those trooping down to the office for misbehavior, I couldn't see that the regimen had been a great success. In any case, the advice wasn't new. I'd been getting the same advice since September, especially the part about the paragraph. Perhaps after a year or so of this it might work; I didn't think so, but it didn't matter either. I knew damn well they'd been getting this treatment for the past six years, that during this time they'd learned practically nothing about the "skills" this type of order was spozed to produce—no adverbs, not how to spell, no punctuation, not adding, subtracting, multiplying or dividing; many hadn't even learned how to read. I couldn't see my way had been a great success either—in fact, I didn't know what my way was—but the other was a failure and was going to be a failure. I couldn't see any reason to keep on doing it. I really couldn't.

[14] I didn't say any of this to her. After all, she began to tell me about her own life; how she'd taught for five years, then had kids, stayed at home until the kids were in school, and was now coming back into the profession. She had a job for next year, full-time, for the district. She thought that what these kids needed was to learn to conform to the ordinary standards of American society, morals, and language. She also thought that too many teachers, faced with these children—we ignored The Word—just gave up on them, considered them hopeless, wouldn't give them a chance.

[15] It wasn't surprising that we had so little to say to each other. She believed my classes were a mess because I was white and they were Negro kids and so I thought they weren't worth making an effort for. I thought she was working hard to help them in a way that hadn't ever helped them, wouldn't help them in the future, and was in fact cementing them into failure, rebellion, or apathy. She thought I couldn't imagine them ever being tolerable students or responsible citizens. I thought that she, a middle-class Negro woman in a lamb's-wool sweater, had less contact with these students than I, knew less about them, mistrusted them more, thought less of their capabilities, and disliked them, as they were now, utterly.

DISCUSSION

1. Put into your own words what you think the main idea sentence of this selection is. Begin with, "When Herndon went back to his junior high school classes after a month's absence, he discovered_____." Be ready to defend what you think the point is by showing how every paragraph in the article relates to it.

2. Some of this article is deliberately written in informal, non-standard English; some of it uses the kind of language you'd expect to find in an ordinary essay. Compare the language in paragraphs 2, 3 and 4, for instance, with the language in paragraphs 9, 10, and 11. What are the differences? Why does Herndon make this shift?

3. What is the effect of Herndon's using the hyphenated words, "not-doing"

(paragraph 2) and "not-done" (paragraph 6)? How do these words relate to what Herndon is saying in paragraph 2? To the comment Herndon makes at the end of paragraph 3? To Herndon's attitude toward Mrs. A.'s advice in paragraph 13? To the conclusion in paragraph 15?

4. The first sentence of paragraph 12 implies that one of Mrs. A.'s main aims was "getting them in order." How does this aim fit with what she thinks these students need (paragraph 14)? Do you agree that keeping a class in order is important? Why or why not?

5. Discuss Mrs. A.'s comment at the end of paragraph 11 in the light of your own school experience. Do you get more or less out of classes in which the teacher assumes that students "might have something to say"?

6. Is mentioning what Mrs. A. was wearing ("a lamb's-wool sweater") related to the main point of the essay or is it an unrelated detail? Explain your answer.

7. How much of your own attitude toward school—either high school or college—is affected by your expectations of what it "spozed to be"? What are these expectations based on: past experience, what other people have said, or logic?

8. "The Word" in paragraph 14 is *black* or *Negro*. What does the fact that they do not mention "the Word" tell you about Mrs. A.'s attitude? About Herndon's attitude?

9. What does Mrs. A. think the aims of education should be? What does Herndon think they should be? On what points would they agree? Where would they disagree? What is your own idea of what the main aims of junior high school or high school education should be?

10. Many of the strikes and protests that have taken place in schools and colleges have included the demand that more black teachers be hired. In the light of what Herndon says about Mrs. A., how well will this solve the problem?

Teaching

irrelevant: not related to what is going on
indignation: strong anger at something unfair
commensurate: on an equal scale
pronouncement: a final and authoritative statement

Reprinted from *Thirty-Six Children*, by Herbert Kohl (New York: New American Library, 1967), p. 45, by permission of the author and the publisher.

[1] I would arrive at the school at eight. Several of the children would be waiting and we would walk the five flights up to the room. One of the boys would take my briefcase, another the keys. Once in the room the children went their own ways. Maurice and Michael went to the phonograph, Alvin to his latest project with Robert Jackson. The girls would play jacks or wash the boards. Grace explored the books on my desk. Every once in a while one of the children would come up to my desk and ask a question or tell me something. The room warmed up to the children, got ready for the day. At first the questions were simple, irrelevant.

[2] "Mr. Kohl, what's today's date?"

[3] "Where is Charles this morning?"

[4] Then there was some testing.

[5] "Mr. Kohl, when are you going to be absent?"

[6] "Will you come back here next year?"

[7] By the end of October a few children were coming to my desk in the morning and saying things that nothing in my life prepared me to understand or respond to.

[8] "Mr. Kohl, the junkies had a fight last night. They cut this girl up bad."

[9] "Mr. Kohl, I couldn't sleep last night, they was shouting and screaming until four o'clock."

[10] "I don't go down to the streets to play, it's not safe."

[11] "Mr. Kohl, those cops are no good. They beat up on this kid for nothing last night."

[12] I listened, hurt, bruised by the harshness of the children's world. There was no response, no indignation or anger of mine, commensurate to what the children felt. Besides, it was relief they wanted, pronouncement of the truth, acceptance of it in a classroom which had become important to them. I could do nothing about the facts, therefore my words were useless. But through listening, the facts remained open and therefore placed school in the context of the children's real world.

DISCUSSION

1. Is Kohl's main idea sentence stated or implied? What is it?

2. Does he deal with a single event or several related events? Explain.

3. Kohl might have said, "At first the children's questions were simple, irrelevant. Later their statements shocked me," and then moved to his conclusion. How does quoting the children's own words add to the effectiveness of this account? How does the change between their earlier and their later comments relate to the point of the essay?

4. What makes the children's comments sound natural?

5. Are the big words in the last paragraph justified by what Kohl is saying? What happens when the paragraph is put into simpler language?

6. Would Kohl be inclined to agree with Herndon's notions of what children need in school, or with Mrs. A.'s? What is there in the essay that helped you to decide?

7. In what ways are the school attitudes in "One a Penny, Two a Penny" like those in Kohl's school? In what ways are they different?

Being a Negro Mother

decentralize: break up one big area into several smaller ones
vying: competing
alma mater: the school or college from which one has graduated
ejected: thrown out
rebuffs: refusals; making people feel unwanted
subterfuge: statement or plan that avoids the real issue

[1] Through the years the sounds change—the click, click of the ping-pong ball, the rock of the record player, and the thump, thump, thump of dancing feet. And the children change. I often wonder what happened to Eddie and that quiet, peaceful yard up in the east end of Xenia, Ohio—where the colored people lived. I know what happened to us. We moved to California.

[2] It was decided to decentralize the Air Force. The various branches and divisions were scattered to installations throughout the country. By this time my husband had proved himself to the point where the executives were vying for him.

[3] "Go with me to Ogden, Utah, Bill." ("For goodness sake, don't go out there; they are very prejudiced, Eva.")

[4] "Come up to Middletown, Pennsylvania." ("Well, not so bad, I lived in Harrisburg, not too far away, and . . .")

[5] "Out to California with me . . ."

[6] I didn't really care where, knowing that it wouldn't be Atlanta, which I had now begun to think of as heaven. When you read about the South with its diehard attitudes a fear stirs within you. But being there is different.

[7] Visiting in Atlanta, I would go from one spacious home to another—

Condensed and adapted from *The Trouble with Being a Mama* by Eva Rutland. Copyright © 1961 by Abingdon Press. Used by permission. Adaptation by permission of Science Research Associates from their *College Reading Program One*.

luncheon and bridge during the day, parties at night. Or we would visit the Lincoln Country Club—the Negroes' private club with its own little golf course. Or we would take the children to visit our alma maters and the other nearby Negro universities, stroll on the beautiful campuses, listen to a lecture, attend a University Players' production, walk through the library. How I wished my children could live there, go to school there. How beautiful it seemed—Atlanta, with its ermine-trimmed, diamond-studded, velvety cloak of segregation. How beautiful it seemed as I turned my back upon it and headed West.

[8] Bill went out first, to take care of some business and to find us a home. And here was the first indication that the cloak was gone forever. He tells a rollicking tale about his experiences in a white hotel, served by white bellboys and white waiters, and his searching desperately through the hotel for a black face to direct him to the colored section of town. He even wandered to the kitchen, where he was promptly ejected, but not until he had discovered that the cooks were white, too, or at least Mexican or Oriental. And when he finally cornered a Negro at the base who had been transferred out before him, he learned the astounding truth—there was no colored section. The cloak was gone.

[9] But the truth was that this left him rather naked. For he desperately needed a colored section. The housing official at the base had found houses for his white colleagues with little or no difficulty. Brand-new, better-than-average tract homes with an executive air, boasting of built-in modern appliances, and situated near the air base where they worked. And for about $250 down.

[10] But for Bill—nothing. Bill set out on his own. We had not planned to buy. Hospitals and doctors (for all their kindness) had left us rather broke. But renting, he soon found, was an impossibility. As if being colored weren't enough, he also had four children and a dog. He traveled with the real estate man to outlandish impossibilities, looked through the newspaper ads, lingered longingly over the three-bedroom, two-bath contemporaries—complete with modern electric kitchens, dishwashers, and garbage disposals—that could be handled with a very small down payment.

[11] After several rebuffs, he began to look for the "unrestricted" notation and to rely on the real estate man to direct him to where "they will sell to colored." And more often than not, it was in an old section that whites were gradually abandoning for the newer suburban tract houses. They would sell to a Negro because they could sell to no one else—no one to whom the newer suburban houses were also available. Usually the price they asked more than covered the brand-new house they would purchase. Eventually Bill found one. Not too bad, he assured me, glancing at me anxiously. They will sell it on contract for $1,000 down. We borrowed money on the car for the down payment and headed west.

[12] Sacramento, California—how green, how clean, how wonderful. I was so impressed by our own street—a neat, neighborly looking street lined with

tall elm trees (I had really expected palms like those on my husband's post-cards, but elm was good enough)—that I almost forgot my qualms. Integration qualms, that is. Integration in theory is a fine high-sounding utopia. In reality I shivered as I watched my children unknowingly shed the warm cloak of segregation, their happy isolation with Eddie, Carol Ann, and all their many Negro friends in the East End. That's another thing about Mamas. We are neither broadminded nor progressive. We just want the children to be happy.

[13] I didn't say anything. You don't, you know, until you have to. Just, "Oh, yes, you will like it here. Never mind, there will be other boys and girls to play with." And, "Of course the new teacher will be nice." And they didn't even notice. Of course, Bill and the twins were too young. But even Elsie didn't notice until that morning when I was brushing her hair. I don't know why Elsie introduces all of her serious conversations when I am brushing her hair, but she does. Almost as if the brush reaches down into the innermost recesses of her brain and releases a tremendous train of thought. I was brushing vigorously, one eye on the clock and the other on Billy, who was struggling half-heartedly with his shoelaces. Elsie was watching Billy, too. He could not go to school unaccompanied, so her movements were somewhat controlled by his.

[14] "Oh, hurry, hurry, Billy, hurry," she begged. "I want to walk to school with Bonnie." The next door slammed and I glanced apprehensively at Elsie, for this indicated Bonnie's departure. For the moment this escaped Elsie, reminding her only of Bonnie herself. "That's Bonnie," she beamed and immediately began to chant in a singsong voice, "Oh, Bonnie, I love you, Bonnie, I love you."

[15] Then—"Why, Mama," she said, "I love a little white girl. I never thought about it. I've been playing and playing. Why, I never even thought about it." And Elsie was as surprised by the fact that she had never thought about Bonnie's being white as I had been for the past two weeks.

[16] And the neighborhood went on its placid unassuming way, accepting —along with blue-eyed Bonnie, Alfred Shimizu, and Sheri Yee—the new Negro family in the neighborhood.

[17] But if the neighbors were nice the house was impossible. Well, not really impossible. At first, I was impressed—the large living and dining rooms with the solid redwood paneling almost to the beamed ceiling, the lovely stone fireplace and mantel, the big, big yard. All of these features made me praise Bill's choice. And I thought surely we could fix the crumbling walls upstairs, seal up the cracks, get new windows, finish the attic, install a bathroom upstairs, pull out the outmoded plumbing, remodel the present bathroom and kitchen, rewire, reshingle, repaint, add on a playroom. We even had an architect draw up the plans.

[18] Then an endless stream of contractors. My spirits went down. For as our prospects for a bright, shining remodeled house decreased, our need for it increased. Because for some reason, we became alarmingly popular. The

Negro community, scattered though it was, embraced us as one of its own. And, surprisingly, through Bill and his work, we accumulated a wide circle of white friends. Imperfect though it may be, there is something about an integrated community. It tends to release the hearts and minds of its people, leaves them free to choose their friends in the light of mutual interests.

[19] Hearts and minds notwithstanding, all this visiting back and forth made me self-conscious. Not only were my white friends better housekeepers than I. (This I do not attribute to the color of their skin. Take the Negro family who moved across the street from us who repapered, repainted, spit, polished, and shined their little house before I could say, "You think I should wash the windows?") But they had better houses to keep—those gorgeous three-bedroom, two-bath, family-room mansions with dishwashers and garbage disposals that they could buy. And we couldn't. My spirits hit rock bottom the day the Japanese contractor said to me, "Should I tell you the truth?"

[20] "Yes," said I.

[21] "You won't get mad?"

[22] "No."

[23] "You sure you won't get mad?"

[24] "No."

[25] "Well, why don't you tear this house down and . . ."

[26] So began the hunt for a new house—and our own private battle against subterfuge. For there are many subtle ways to circumvent the purchase of a house by a Negro. One price is quoted to you, another to a white buyer, your loan doesn't go through—many ways. Once we thought we had one. Really, I didn't like it. It was a multicolored brick monstrosity. My husband was enraged. "Why don't you like it?" he stormed.

[27] "Too small."

[28] "It has four bedrooms."

[29] "Like closets."

[30] "And a family room."

[31] "Just an extension of the kitchen. I could never get away from the children."

[32] "Two bathrooms."

[33] "I know."

[34] "And built-ins, and a big yard."

[35] "I know."

[36] "And they will sell it to us."

[37] This I couldn't beat. We signed the papers, gave the deposit. On the way home my husband sighed. "You know, I don't like that house either." We consoled each other. "We can extend the family room." "Paint the brick." "At least it's new."

[38] Next morning the phone rang. Our agent was most apologetic. The owner wanted $26,000 instead of the quoted $22,000, and he wanted cash (although it already had an $18,000 insurance loan on it). I recognized the subterfuge, but I could have kissed him. Hooray for discrimination! We

didn't have to buy the brick monstrosity. Happily clutching the returned deposit check, we resolved from then on to make no compromises. Nothing that we didn't want just because we could buy it.

[39] Failing in all efforts to buy, we decided to build. Not that a lot was easier to buy than a house. I searched, and found a lovely corner lot with a big oak tree. "I couldn't touch it," said my Negro agent. I got on the phone. (Bill was out of town and this was a good buy) and called one of our white friends. "I've found a lot. Will you buy it for me?"

[40] He didn't hesitate. "Of course."

[41] It still wasn't easy—finding a contractor who would build for us, getting a loan. Nor was it pleasant. Our white friend was called. How dared he sell to a "Nigger"?

[42] "Will you be happy," asked a casual white acquaintance, "knowing they don't want you?" But I was emancipated. I had picnicked in the public parks, played golf on the public fairways, taken the children to the public integrated dancing classes, lived on a lovely shaded, integrated street. I had tasted the fruit of full citizenship (well, nearly full) and found it delicious. Remembering the east end of Xenia, and the slums of Atlanta, I shed once and for all the stifling cloak of segregation.

[43] "It is where I want to be," I answered.

[44] "But the children . . . ," she persisted.

[45] I smiled. "They'll survive."

DISCUSSION

1. When Mrs. Rutland says, in paragraph 1, "And the children change," the reader thinks just of their growing up, moving from the age of ping-pong to the age of dates and dancing. By the end of the article, what other changes have taken place in the children?

2. What changes have taken place in Mrs. Rutland herself? (Compare "from one spacious home to another," paragraph 7, with "the slums of Atlanta," paragraph 42; have any of her definitions changed?)

3. How do these changes help you to decide what the main point of this article is? Is the main idea sentence stated or implied?

4. In paragraphs 3 and 4, why are some of the comments in parentheses?

5. All the way through the essay, Mrs. Rutland refers to "a cloak." Do you think this is a good comparison? Why or why not?

6. Why does the writer quote so many conversations directly? Would the article be just as interesting if she said, in paragraphs 19 through 25, for instance, "The contractor told us the house wasn't worth fixing"? What would be lost?

7. Much of this essay is written in what would normally be called incomplete sentences. Do you think the essay would be better if the style were more formal? Try fixing some of the sentences that might be marked "fragments" and see whether you think the effect is better or worse—and why.

8. From what Mrs. Rutland says, which seems to you more prejudiced, Sacramento or Atlanta? Why?

9. Would you describe the Rutlands as middle class? Why? Does Mrs. Rutland's comment in paragraph 12 help to explain her attitude? What would be Mrs. Rutland's attitude toward the students in George Washington Junior High School ("The Way It Spozed To Be")? What makes you think so?

Perhaps the hardest kind of personal experience to write is an account of some really unusual experience—unusual because it is a milestone in the writer's own life, or unusual because nothing like it has happened to most of the people he knows. The temptation here is to suppose that the event itself is so interesting that the only thing the writer needs to do is put it down on paper, sometimes as a bare announcement that it happened, without worrying about significance or vivid details.

And maybe if you are Deadwood Dick, captured by the Indians, adopted by them, and you finally escaped alive to tell the tale, that assumption may possibly be true. But Deadwood Dick didn't take a chance on it; he gave his readers vivid detail. It is much safer to remember the comment that Paul Roberts once made: "All subjects, except sex, are dull until some writer makes them interesting."

Whether the experience is driving a car across the country, riding in a bomber during the war, or spending a year in a far country with the Peace Corps, there still must be some point to what happened, other than just that it happened; there still must be details that relate to the significance of the event and help the reader share the writer's experience.

Coast to Coast to Coast in a Cadillac

grande dame: a great lady
trap: a light, two-headed carriage
Carlsbad Caverns: the largest caves in America

Reprinted from "Coast to Coast in a Cadillac" by Tom McCahill, from MECHANIX ILLUS-TRATED Magazine. Copyright 1968 by Fawcett Publications, Inc.

prone: likely
phenomenally: amazingly; unusually; extremely

[1] There is nothing unusual about going coast to coast. National Airlines does it all the time. And I've done it many times in the past—in cars. But my latest three-coaster was a dilly. Last winter it was decided that an up-to-date report on the *grande dame* of American automobiles, the Cadillac Fleetwood Brougham, was overdue. This test turned out to be a combination of Jack London's *Call of the Wild,* Doctor Frankenstein's *Fun & Games,* and *Tess of the Storm Country.*

> Introduction tells what the experience is—a trip from coast to coast in a Cadillac—why—and in general terms what it was like—"a dilly"

[2] I was given just 17 days to drive this de luxe trap from ocean to ocean to ocean. And in my spare time I only had to bat out three other test articles. This was to be my 75th and 76th cross-country runs and of the whole kit and caboodle, 75 and 76 turned out to be the wildest. Just about everything, aside from an earthquake and an Indian uprising, happened. One night I will swear I could hear Apache drums in the distance.

> Makes clear that the trip itself is not a novelty for the writer

[3] The day before my departure a brand-new 1968 Fleetwood Brougham was delivered to my house. This car had the new 472-cu.-in. engine, the biggest in the world. The rest of the rig was as loaded as a Kodiak bear after raiding a still. Everything about it was as lush and comfortable as a bathtub full of warm whipped cream. The stowage room shamed even the Carlsbad Caverns. In short, it is a large trunk.

> Praise for the appearance of the car

[4] Early the next morning, with a happy heart, I jumped aboard with my crew of two, plus dog, and headed for the wild, wild West. Before I'd gone more than a dozen miles I realized that this ocean-liner-type automobile was a special piece of transportation in many ways. It was fast in getting away from traffic lights (0 to 60 in 8.7) and the steering is so quick it could be dangerous for some retired oldster tooling down the highway at 75 or better—but for top drivers it's great. You can shift lanes with a wrist flick faster than with some of our hottest specialty screamers. This oversteer quality, however, might get Aunt Petunia and her bloomer girls into a bind if

> Praise for the performance of the car

she whips the smallish steering wheel too fast in an emergency maneuver . . .

[5] When darkness set in I discovered a real fault with our Fleetwood. I couldn't see more than 100 yds. down the road with the bright lights on and not more than 75 with the low beams. Now this car had been checked out by Cadillac before delivery but the headlights were so out of adjustment that I could have done as well with my Zippo held close to the windshield. These headlights, which had automatic shutoffs, included a real Mickey Mouse switching gizmo that simulated a Russian puzzle, even after several sessions with the owner's manual.

First difficulty: poor headlight adjustment

[6] From then on it was clear going to Phoenix, Ariz., where we ran into another nightmare. Brooks, my photographer, who fancies himself as the 20th Century's answer to Daniel Boone, wanted to see the off-the-road-desert country where I used to hunt with Clark Gable years ago. I've driven hundreds of miles over the hard-packed desert when tires were tires straight up from the tread. Today, with the blood-hound droopy-eyed low-profiles, things are different. Before you could count to three I had two flat front tires caused by cactus thorns that punctured the soft under-bellies of the sidewalls. There were eight thorns all the way through one tire and seven through the other. As they are prone to say on TV, "there we were," with one spare. Brooks is also pretty good at hiking and he eventually showed up with a service truck. The spare was put on and the other tire was temporarily blown up by a compressor on the truck.

Second difficulty: two flat tires and only one spare

[7] Incidentally, there was no good way to patch these thorn holes successfully so we installed two truck tubes. If any Fleetwood Brougham owner in the future discovers that he has two tubeless tires with truck tubes in them, the chances are he has our test car.

A side remark, acknowledged by the use of "incidentally"

[8] Bob Beason checked up on us in Palm Springs, Calif., to make sure we weren't wasting any of the company's time. After a run for another test on the coast, we finally headed for home.

The turn-around point

[9] As we recrossed the Calif. border back to Ariz., the snow started to fly. Before reaching Tucson that

More trouble: a blizzard

night the roads were not only iced but covered with snowdrifts. I made several hard brake stops to test handling on the ice and snow and it was phenomenally good. The traction was almost equal to my Jeep. It snowed and sleeted all night and when I left Tucson the next morning the roads were covered, but the Caddy kept pushing ahead without a wheel spin. I'm sorry to report that this wasn't typical for the rest of the cars on the road. Between two mountains hundreds of vehicles were stuck all over the road, facing every direction. There were trucks on their sides and buses in the ditches and fouled-up cars in between. The trouble was caused because the drivers in South Ariz., near the Mexican border, don't know how to handle snow and ice. For several hours we didn't move more than six ft. as there was no way to get through the maze of spun-out cars blocking the road. This was on Interstate 10.

[10] That night over 600 travelers spent the night in Benson, Ariz., in a high school gymnasium and various churches. We made our way back to Tucson and the same motel rooms we had vacated that morning. After two more days the roads were somewhat cleared and we wormed our way to El Paso, Tex., at an average speed of about 30. That night we learned via newscasts that another blizzard was about to hit. It was headed across our homeward path. When we left before dawn the next morning snow was falling hard but we managed to stay just ahead of the worst of this new blizzard that followed us all the way to the Gulf Coast.

A second blizzard

[11] By this time both my crew and I were running fevers as we had picked up the flu bug. When we finally reached our home state, instead of being thrilled by our jolly trip, we all hit the sack for days. It was one of the worst trips I have ever made in óne of the best big cars I have ever driven.

Conclusion: final difficulty—the flu
and
the experience summed up in a single sentence

DISCUSSION

1. McCahill begins this article by saying he was asked to make an "up-to-date report" on a Cadillac. Would you consider this article a *report*? What elements of a report does it have in it? How does it differ from a report?

2. The language used in this article is very informal. In the first paragraph McCahill says the trip was "a dilly." What other colloquial expressions can you find? Do you think they are appropriate to the tone of the article?

3. All through the article, McCahill uses abbreviations (*cu.in.,* paragraph 3, and *Ariz.,* paragraph 6, for instance). Would you prefer that these abbreviations be written out, as most handbooks would demand? Why or why not?

4. McCahill gets part of his effect by using colorful comparisons and exaggeration. What exaggeration (or comparison) can you find in paragraph 1? In paragraph 3? In paragraph 5?

5. Who are "Aunt Petunia and her bloomer girls"? Do you think this reference is more effective, or less, than simply saying "women drivers"? Why?

6. Is the comment in paragraph 7 a digression that should have been omitted? Why does McCahill include it?

7. What details given in the article back up the contrast in the last sentence?

8. Put into your own words what you think the main idea sentence is.

A Raid on a Fishing Village

napalm: jellied gasoline which sticks to whatever it hits and burns fiercely

antipersonnel: designed to kill and wound people (rather than set fires, destroy buildings, etc.)

monsoon: a tropical wind, bringing with it extremely heavy rain

sampan: a small Oriental boat, with a sail and an oar

composite: combined

[1] Our "Skyraider" was loaded with 750-pound napalm bombs and 500-pound napalm bombs, plus our four 20-millimeter cannon. Our wing plane carried 7,500 pounds of high explosive antipersonnel bombs, plus four cannon. We were the lead plane going in. My pilot was Major John C. Carson. [2] We were airborne for one and one half hours before we reached our

From "This Isn't Munich, It's Spain," by Bernard B. Fall in the December 1965 issue of *Ramparts* Magazine. Copyright *Ramparts* Magazine, Inc., 1965. By permission of the Editors.

primary target. But as we came over the target the monsoon came down with quite incredible force and completely obscured the ground. Then a decision was made, in accordance with established procedures, to switch over to the alternate target which was described as a "Communist rest center" in the Camau Peninsula. A rest center may, of course, be anything, any group of huts, or it may be just a normal village in which Viet Cong troops have put down stake for, perhaps, 48 hours.

[3] As we flew over the target it looked to me very much as any normal village would look: on the edge of a river, sampans and fish nets in the water. It was a peaceful scene. Major Carson put our plane into a steep dive. I could see the napalm bombs dropping from the wings. The big bombs, first. As we peeled back from our dive, I saw an incredibly bright flash of fire as napalm exploded at the tree level. The first pass had a one-two effect. The napalm was expected to force the people—fearing the heat and the burning— out into the open. Then the second plane was to move in with heavy fragmentation bombs to hit whatever—or whoever—had rushed out into the open. So our wingman followed us in and dropped his heavy explosives. Mushroom-like clouds drifted into the air. We made a second pass and dropped our remaining 500-pound napalm bombs. Our wingman followed. Then we went in a third time and raked over the village with our cannon. We came down low, flying very fast, and I could see some of the villagers trying to head away from the burning shore in their sampans. The village was burning fiercely. I will never forget the sight of the fishing nets in flame, covered with burning, jellied gasoline. Behind me I could hear—even through my padded flying helmet—the rear of our plane's 20-millimeter cannon as we flew away.

[4] Behind us flew a small, very dainty-looking aircraft, an OF-1, otherwise referred to as a "bird dog." It is a spotter plane—used to find targets for the bombers and to determine whether the targets have been hit and—as the word goes in Vietnam—award your "score." The "score" is usually worked out in numbers of structures hit and numbers of people seen dead on the ground. This information is reported to Air Intelligence, and eventually becomes part of the composite "score" for the week (the number of sorties flown plus what is called the "structure count" and the "body count"). These are the terms by which success is measured in the new Vietnam war.

[5] There were probably between 1,000 and 1,500 people living in the fishing village we attacked. It is difficult to estimate how many were killed. It is equally difficult to judge if there actually were any Viet Cong in the village, and if so, if any were killed. The observation planes are called the Forward Air controllers (FAC's). But it happens very often in Vietnam that, as a current joke goes, the FAC's have their facts wrong; that the raid information is stale; that there may have been Communists in the village—but the day before. You may very often get the proper number of structures awarded to your "score," but you may not have hit any Communist structures. So it is difficult to say whether you hit a Communist or whether you just hit the

village which, unwilling, may have been the host of a Communist unit for one night. Or maybe not at all. This has happened.

[6] During our attack probably ten to fifteen houses were hit. There is at least one family per house, and Vietnamese families average from six to eight persons. In each of those houses there must have been people maimed or killed—no one knows how many. I read an official report later which described the village as a Communist rest center, and said it had been successfully destroyed.

DISCUSSION

1. This article, too, has some elements of a report. What are they? How does the article differ from a straight report?

2. What details in paragraph 3 help the reader to visualize the scene?

3. What is the writer's attitude toward the bombing of the village? How can you tell?

4. On the face of it, the last sentence in paragraph 4 could be a simple statement of fact. How else could it be interpreted?

5. What is the point of the "joke" in paragraph 5? Does the writer find the joke very funny? Do you?

6. What is the effect of the two very short sentences with which paragraph 5 ends?

7. How does the writer use the final sentence of this article to contrast with what he has seen and described in paragraph 3?

8. How would you complete a main idea sentence beginning, "When I took part in a raid on a Vietnamese fishing village, I_____"?

9. Notice the copyright date on this article. It was published at a time when criticism of the Vietnam War was just starting to build up. What evidence can you find in the article which identifies it as an early one? When it was written, this article was considered a strong condemnation of the Vietnam War. Compared with later articles, it seems rather mild. Find a report of a later incident in the Vietnam War (for example, the My Lai incident) and compare it with Bernard Fall's article.

Fight with Yellow Dog

remonstrance: a protest
breastwork: hastily built fortress
subdued: defeated
captor: one who captures someone else
fancied: imagined
proclaimed: announced

[1] It was a bright, clear fall day, October 4, 1876, that quite a large number of us boys started out over the range hunting strays which had been lost for some time. We had scattered over the range and I was riding along alone when all at once I heard the well known Indian war whoop and noticed not far away a large party of Indians making straight for me. They were all well mounted and they were in full war paint, which showed me that they were on the war path, and as I was alone and had no wish to be scalped by them I decided to run for it. So I headed for Yellow Horse Canyon and gave my horse the rein, but as I had considerable objection to being chased by a lot of painted braves without some remonstrance, I turned in my saddle every once in a while and gave them a shot by way of greeting, and I had the satisfaction of seeing a painted brave tumble from his horse and go rolling in the dust every time my rifle spoke, and the Indians were by no means idle all this time, as their bullets were singing around me rather lively, one of them passing through my thigh, but it did not amount to much. Reaching Yellow Horse Canyon, I had about decided to stop and make a stand when one of their bullets caught me in the leg, passing clear through it and then through my horse, killing him. Quickly falling behind him I used his dead body for a breastwork and stood the Indians off for a long time, as my aim was so deadly and they had lost so many that they were careful to keep out of range.

[2] But finally my ammunition gave out, and the Indians were quick to find this out, and they at once closed in on me, but I was by no means subdued, wounded as I was and almost out of my head, and I fought with my empty gun until finally overpowered. When I came to my senses I was in the Indians' camp.

[3] My wounds had been dressed with some kind of herbs, the wound in my breast just over the heart was covered thickly with herbs and bound up.

From *Life and Adventures of Nat Love, Better Known in the Cattle Country as Deadwood Dick* by Nat Love, 1906.

316

My nose had been nearly cut off. These wounds I received when I was fighting my captors with my empty gun. What caused them to spare my life I cannot tell, but it was I think partly because I had proved myself a brave man, and all Indians admire a brave man and when they captured a man whose fighting powers were out of the ordinary they generally kept him if possible as he was needed in the tribe.

[4] Then again Yellow Dog's tribe was composed largely of half-breeds, and there was a large percentage of colored blood in the tribe, and as I was a colored man they wanted to keep me, as they thought I was too good a man to die. Be that as it may, they dressed my wounds and gave me plenty to eat, but the only grub they had was buffalo meat which they cooked over a fire of buffalo chips, but of this I had all I wanted to eat. For the first two days after my capture they kept me tied hand and foot. At the end of that time they untied my feet, but kept my hands tied for a couple of days longer, when I was given my freedom, but was always closely watched by members of the tribe. Three days after my capture my ears were pierced and I was adopted into the tribe. The operation of piercing my ears was quite painful, in the method used, as they had a small bone secured from a deer's leg, a small thin bone, rounded at the end and as sharp as a needle. This they used to make the holes, then strings made from the tendons of a deer were inserted in place of thread, of which the Indians had none. Then horn rings were placed in my ears and the same kind of salve made from herbs which they placed on my wounds was placed on my ears and they soon healed.

[5] The bullet holes in my leg and breast also healed in a surprisingly short time. That was good salve all right. As soon as I was well enough I took part in the Indian dances. One kind or another was in progress all the time. The war dance and the medicine dance seemed the most popular. When in the war dance the tribesmen danced around me in a circle, making gestures, chanting, with every now and then a blood curdling yell, always keeping time to a sort of music provided by stretching buffalo skins tightly over a hoop.

[6] When I was well enough I joined the dances, and I think I soon made a good dancer. The medicine dance varies from the war dance only that in the medicine dance the Indians danced around a boiling pot, the pot being filled with roots and water and they dance around it while it boils. The medicine dance occurs about daylight.

[7] My wounds were now nearly well, and gave me no trouble. It was a dark, cloudy night, and the Indians, grown careless in their fancied security, had relaxed their watchfulness. After they had all thrown themselves on the ground and the quiet of the camp proclaimed them all asleep, I got up and, crawling on my hands and knees, using the greatest caution for fear of making a noise, I crawled about 250 yards to where the horses were picketed, and going to the Indian pony I had already picked out I slipped the skin thong in his mouth which the Indians use for a bridle, one which I had secured and carried in my shirt for some time for this particular purpose. Then springing to his back I made for the open prairie in the direction of the home ranch

in Texas, one hundred miles away. All that night I rode as fast as my horse could carry me and the next morning, twelve hours after I left the Indians' camp, I was safe on the home ranch again. And my joy was without bounds, and such a reception as I received from the boys. They said they were just one day late, and if it hadn't been for a fight they had with some of the same tribe, they would have been to my relief. As it was they did not expect to ever see me again alive. But that they knew that if the Indians did not kill me, and gave me only half a chance, I would get away from them, but now that I was safe home again, nothing mattered much and nothing was too good for me.

[8] It was a mystery to them how I managed to escape death with such wounds as I had received, the marks of which I will carry to my grave. It is as much a mystery to me, as the bullet that struck me in the breast just over the heart passed clear through, coming out my back just below the shoulder. Likewise the bullet in my leg passed clear through, then through my horse, killing him.

[9] The fight with the Yellow Dog's tribe is probably the closest call I ever had, and as close a call as I ever want.

DISCUSSION

1. Part of the charm of this personal experience is that it sounds exactly as though the reader were listening to Nat Love talk, rather than reading a carefully planned essay. For example, notice how he repeats himself (see the first sentence in paragraph 6, the last sentence of paragraph 8). What other specific things in the essay help to give this conversational effect?

2. In spite of the conversational tone in most of the article, Love occasionally uses somewhat stilted wording: "as I was alone and had no desire to be scalped by them"; "considerable objection to being chased"; and "without some remonstrance," in paragraph 1. Is Love trying to sound scholarly or does he use these phrases for their humorous effect? If you think the latter, what makes them funny?

3. There are several possible main idea sentences for this personal experience. For example,
   (a) When I was captured by Yellow Dog, I learned that Indians are nice to their captives if the captives are brave.
   (b) When I was captured by Yellow Dog, I learned that Indians know how to use herb medicines.
   (c) When I was captured by Yellow Dog, I discovered that I could trick the Indians and escape.
   (d) When I escaped from the Indians, I learned that I was glad to get back to my outfit.

(e) When I was subdued by the Indians, I learned that I had had as close a call as I ever want.

Do you think that any one of these is *the* underlying main idea? Why or why not?

If you like none of the suggested main idea sentences, write one of your own.

4. Although it might appear at first glance that Love's fight with Yellow Dog and his escape are merely a list of pointless details, most readers agree that Love's experience makes good reading. What is there about Love and his experience that makes his account interesting even though he does not follow the "rules" about main idea sentences and about careful selection and omission of details?

Thrown onto the Edge of Asia

betel nut: an East Indian nut which the people are fond of chewing
toxic: poisonous
ultimate: the last word; the extreme of
incomprehensible: completely unable to understand
counter-insurgency: against the rebellion

[1] I was a Peace Corps Volunteer in the Far East. I lived for a short time on a government "self-help land settlement," and I tried to help self-help the settlers. Life is very slow there and plenty real. It is sporting at first—to be constantly adored as the strangest and most god-like individual ever to have turned his eye onto an isolated village otherwise unknown. Very soon, I think, the game goes out of it. Then you must know what you're there for, what you are going to do, and why.

[2] Here is a narrative of some of the events that I remember. They all happened to me, and they could have happened in any typical day in my life as a new Peace Corps Rural Community Action Volunteer.

[3] A chicken wakes me up; not even the chicken speaks English. Language is essential. The radio is rocking the house next door; it sounds like a government broadcast; I assume that it's a pack of lies. I wrap on a phakoma, sort of a bright cotton sarong, and walk down the front stairs. I begin sipping cold water from the rain barrel and pouring it on my head. Then I brush my

Adapted from "Thrown onto the Edge of Asia" by an anonymous Peace Corps Volunteer, in *The Peace Corps Reader,* Quadrangle Books, 1967.

teeth for awhile, not that they really need brushing, but this is a habit I've formed. The lady next door is watching from a screenless window. I feel a sense of pride that, having been awake for only ten minutes, I am already functioning as an Agent of Change. The Volunteer should brush his teeth publicly every chance he gets. Maybe it will become a fad. The lady next door has black teeth, however, and her lips are packed with that red, sour-smelling paste they use. She's as likely to begin brushing her teeth, after my modern example, as I am to begin chewing betel nut. But, I think, maybe her children will learn from me. There's hope in children.

[4] Later I am at the market, in the restaurant run by a woman who is either a reformed or retired prostitute, and she is swearing a blue streak at someone. I can't understand the words, but the blue streak is as clear as day. She puts a bottle of orange soda in front of me. I've been ordering this every morning partly because I don't trust the water in this particular restaurant and partly because it is the nearest equivalent to orange juice. She looks at me, in disgust, as if to say, "what the hell kind of man would drink orange soda pop for breakfast?"

[5] I order a few things to eat "with rice," as they say, and I get what I recognize to be the same hot curry, partly fried pork, and toxic intestinal stew I had for supper, all out of the same pot. A crowd begins to gather. Eating breakfast is my first big performance of the day. I sit as tall as I can and eat with vigor. I invite the nearest settlers to sit down with me—the ultimate of democratic gestures—but they refuse, as expected, because it's not their place to be seen eating with a superior. They're not sure whether I'm a superior or not, but they know I was placed there by some distant and very important machinery of government; they are, consequently, playing it safe. They gather, watching from nearby tables—men mostly, dressed in black. I notice some children, too, standing quietly in rows. All the faces express friendliness and infinite curiosity.

[6] One of the settlers speaks up, "Hungry, are you?"

[7] "Yes, sir," I say. "I am hungry a lot, sir."

[8] "Like our food, do you?"

[9] "I like it a little bit, sir." I make a mental note to stop using that polite word at the end of sentences too often.

[10] "Very hot, eh?"

[11] "Yes, sir, I think that your food is hot a lot." The crowd makes a general murmur of amusement.

[12] "Healthy, are you?"

[13] "Healthy."

[14] Encouraged by this communication, he produces a question so lengthy and incomprehensible that I stop eating and stare at him. I say, "Eh?" This is the word which I use most often during the day. He says it again, leaving me more confused. I hear one of the other settlers explaining to him that he must speak very slowly because the foreigner does not know "how to listen to our language." A couple of children giggle and repeat, "foreigner." In their

language the word also means the fruit, guava, and, with a short modifier, bird manure.

[15] My friend speaks slowly again, and I begin to understand. "Eat rice in the other place, do they?"

[16] I say, "Other place where?"

[17] He thinks for a moment. "The other country . . . the foreign country."

[18] "Oh, America."

[19] "Ah yes," he says, "America."

[20] "In America people do not generally eat much rice, sir," I say.

[21] He finds this very interesting, although I suspect he has already learned this from television. We sit there for about an hour at their table where I've moved. The conversation would be too much work to reproduce here, and it would be pretty dull. I struggle through a few communications about the weather, about getting drunk, about the brothels in town—the usual things —and, of course, they run through an inventory of all my personal belongings, getting the price for my watch, shirt, fountain pen, glasses. They're very persistent on prices.

[22] The crowd thins. This curious new thing in town, a full-grown man who does not know how to speak, can sustain interest for only so long. I walk around the market. I stop to thump a few pineapples. I don't know how a good pineapple should go when you thump it, but this seems to be the proper thing to do, like kicking tires in a car lot.

[23] Then I head on down the road. The weather is so warm that even the tall, dead trees on the cleared land seem to sweat. I notice a low, thatched construction beside the road, a kind of roof shading something. There is a government sign advertising what it is, but I can't read. Probably some experimental crop. A man is chopping weeds there. I approach him.

[24] "Greetings, sir."

[25] "Greetings. You have gone where?"

[26] "Just around. You go where?"

[27] "Just around."

[28] "The weather is hot."

[29] "Yes."

[30] We stare at each other. He says, "You speak our language strong."

[31] "Not strong. I speak a little, that's all." Then I go into my speech about how I studied his language in America and that I am a member of the volunteer friendship group (which is how Peace Corps translates) coming from America to help people. I give him my name. He's heard of me already.

[32] "This is what?" I say.

[33] "What where?"

[34] I point to the experimental crop. To my relief he answers with a word I can understand: coffee. I search my vocabulary for some appropriate comment. "Mmm," I say. "Very progressive." I don't know anything about coffee, except that it comes in cans. I look over the coffee with a seasoned old coffee-planter's eye. "Very interesting," I say. I examine a little plant

with all the bearing of Mr. Hills Brothers himself. The settler is watching me nervously. I am about to tell him he ought to pour fertilizer or something on it, when I decide to stop kidding myself. I turn to him. "I've never seen coffee before."

[35] The man begins to gesture and explain. I listen for several minutes, picking out a word here and there, trying to make him speak slowly, but I don't understand. Language is essential.

[36] I am walking down the road again. A jeep comes along. It carries the deputy assistant supervisor, who wears the government uniform but is unarmed, and his driver. "You get in," he says in English. We arrive at another market place. He walks to a thatched coffee shop, and I follow. We sit at a table with several settlers. The usual conversation follows: Is the weather hot? Do you like our food? How much did that cost? How much money do you make? How much did it cost to come from America?

[37] "Do you like our girls?"

[38] "Yes."

[39] "Do you have a wife in the other country?"

[40] "No."

[41] "Do you like that girl over there?"

[42] "Very pretty."

[43] "Would you like to marry with her? Will you take one of our girls to America?"

[44] "No."

[45] "Will you take my daughter to America?"

[46] "No."

[47] It happens every day. This is not a game.

[48] I sit in the coffee shop. They are talking about something, but I fail to catch the words. I decide I need a break from this noise of a foreign language. I stand up. The deputy assistant supervisor says, "Where you go?"

[49] I answer, "To the person who cuts hair."

[50] He follows me. There are a half-dozen men seated in the barber shop. He says a few brisk words in his language. The man in the barber's chair gets up and takes a place on a bench. I try to indicate that I want to wait my turn, but my language fails. The barber, smiling, waits with cloth in hand. All eyes watch me. The deputy says, "You to sit down there." I sit in the barber's chair. Everyone seems happy about it.

[51] After the barber is done and has refused payment, I walk out and down the road. The deputy assistant supervisor spots me and comes running after. The man is clearly harassed by this American restlessness of mine which makes it difficult for me to sit still for any more than two or three hours at a time. Obviously he has been assigned to watch over me for these first few weeks. He says, "Where you go?"

[52] There are four pints of rice whiskey on the table in a grass stall in another market. There are five glasses on the table: one for me, one for the deputy, three for the three soldiers. There are a dozen more persons around

the table, but they are only settlers. They are watching the soldiers drink. The sergeant at my right seems to be in charge here. He is a counter-insurgency soldier. He has explained that they have come to check over the settlement. He wears a pistol. He is drunk. He hates communists. By means of his G.I. English and my scanty knowledge of his language, we have reached a few understandings. He has assumed that we are in the same line of work. He is anxious to prove to me his knowledge of propaganda and other counter-insurgency methods. "Allies," he says in English.

[53] "Allies," I agree.

[54] "You and me." He gives the thumbs-up gesture, which to him means something like "number one." "The American country and our country— allies. You and me. We know how to kill the communist together."

[55] I hold up my hands. I announce, for the second time, as clearly and publicly as my vocabulary will allow, "I am not a soldier. I am a Volunteer come from America to help the settler because you and the American are a pair of friends together."

[56] The sergeant has another drink. "Allies," he says, and then, "Help the rotten settler. Look at this man." He orders one of them to stand up. "We do help this man. This man is always lazy. This man is always dirty. Look." He points to the old farmer's shirt, then to his own insignia, and he says something I don't understand.

[57] A young man who looks at me steadily asks a question. "You will help the settler how?"

[58] "I will help development, sir," I say, using the government term. There are no further questions. I decide to leave. I look over at the settlers who sit with their hands folded soberly. I had not even remembered to invite them to drink with us. The sergeant begins to abuse these farm people again; he tries to get me to agree that they are this or that. By way of a parting gesture, I order two bottles of whiskey. The soldiers protest, this is their party, they pay. Then I order six glasses, which I have passed out to the settlers. We drink. I shake hands with each person, including the soldiers and the deputy assistant supervisor. This is not the customary manner of taking leave, but they know that Americans always shake hands and say "okay," or "hello," or "goodbye." So I shake hands and say goodbye.

DISCUSSION

1. Which of the following seems to you the best main idea sentence for this personal experience?

   When I was a Peace Corps Volunteer in the Far East, I discovered

   (a) that I didn't know much about growing coffee.

   (b) that I couldn't prevent people from treating me as a superior.

   (c) that I couldn't prevent people from treating me as a curiosity.

(d) that language is essential.
(e) that the soldiers were more anti-communist than the people.
Support your answer by referring to comments and details used in the article.

2. How do the quoted conversations (paragraphs 6 through 14, for instance, or 37 through 48) give the impression that communication is difficult? How else does the writer make the same point?

3. How satisfactorily does the introductory paragraph serve to let the reader know what points the writer is going to make? Does the rest of the essay do anything with "Very soon . . . the game goes out of it"? What? Does he ever find out the answers to the implied questions in the last sentence of paragraph 1—what he is there for? What he is going to do? And why? Do we as readers find out?

4. Is the teeth brushing discussion in paragraph 3 part of the answer to what he is going to do? Does he think it is an important thing to do? How do you know? Do you think it is an important thing to do? Why?

5. What is the point of the parenthetical remark, "the ultimate in democratic gestures," in paragraph 5? How does it relate to the main idea of the essay—or do you think it does?

6. What is the effect of saying *"only* settlers" in paragraph 52? How does this relate to the main point of the article—or do you think it doesn't?

7. Do you think this article ends too abruptly? Why or why not? If you think it does end too abruptly, how would you end it?

8. When this article was first published, it carried the footnote, "This letter was written in 1964 by a restless Volunteer who resigned overseas." Does anything in the article support the idea that he was "restless"? What? If you were trying to put into your own words why he resigned, what would you say?

9. Does this article have some significance that might carry over into other experiences? What? Into your own experience, even though you may never have left your own area?

WRITING TOPICS
FOR PERSONAL EXPERIENCE

In considering this brief list of topics for personal experience papers, remember that the topic itself is not enough; the point of the paper will depend on the significance the event has for you. Only the person who had the experience can know why it was significant. All of these suggestions, therefore, are only a beginning. Unless the event they mention was important to you, and *you know why it was important,* none of them will make good papers.

When my father spanked me the first time, . . .
The first time I punished my child, . . .

". . . And then one day I suddenly asked myself why should neither snow nor hail nor dark, etcetera, stay me from my appointed round?"

Drawing by Ed Fisher. Copyright 1969 Saturday Review, Inc.

When my father spanked me the first time, . . .
The first time I punished my child, . . .
When I campaigned for a school office, . . .
When I helped a friend campaign, . . .
When I almost drowned, . . .
When I rescued a child from drowning, . . .
When we moved from a house to an apartment, . . .
The night I burned the dinner, . . .
The night my wife burned the dinner, . . .
When I spent two weeks in Paris, . . .
When I spent two weeks with my stepfather, . . .
When I took my first plane ride, . . .
The first time I spent a night away from home, . . .
When a friend spread gossip about my sister, . . .
When I broke up with my boy (girl) friend, . . .
When I took my first job, . . .
When I got fired, . . .
When a customer was rude to me, . . .
When I went Christmas shopping, . . .
After I flunked my first test, . . .
And almost any incident, no matter how small, if you discovered . . .

readings on persuasion 8

PERSUASION

All of us have convictions about a large number of things, ranging all the
way from what's the best hamburger in town to what's the best method of
preventing war, and most of us, if we're really convinced that one thing is
"better" than another, or that people "ought" or "ought not" to do something,
want to persuade other people to think so too. But just saying that
Bullyburgers are good because we like them, or wars are wrong because we
know they're wrong, will not convince many people. To forestall readers
who are bound to say, "Why do you think that? How do you know?"
the successful writer must give reasons for his belief, and his reasons,
in turn, must be backed up by something definite enough and specific enough
that readers will actually be convinced.

One of the easiest and most direct ways to support an argument is by
giving examples. Very few writers, except perhaps the man who does
the ads for Bullyburgers, Inc., will want to give examples of how crisp the
pickles are, how moist and thick the ground beef, how tender the buns.
On subjects of more general interest, however, an example that lets the reader
share the writer's experience or see the problem as the writer sees it will go
farther than pages of generalities toward convincing readers that a
problem does exist.

But examples will not convince unless they are fair. Readers must be
able to see that the incident they're told about is not unusual or uncommon;
they must believe that it really is typical. In his essay on civil rights, for
instance, Harris is able to convince us that the television program he
discusses is a fair example; if we watch detective shows or westerns very
often, we've seen something very like that situation.

Since one of the main reasons for using examples is to force readers
to share the writer's experience, good examples must be vivid. They must
give enough specific detail that the reader can see the event occurring and
can picture in his mind what it was like. O'Kane in trying to convince us
that the Land Rover may very well be the best car in the world, shows us
the car in action and lets us share the customer's delight at what it can do.

Very often the best examples come from the writer's own experience.
When he tells what happened to him, he can write with real conviction,
as Harris, O'Kane, and Stanton do. With some subjects, on the other hand,
many of us have had little personal experience. To believe that germ
warfare is wrong, we do not need to have experienced it; our belief may
be based on what we have read or heard, as the writer's is in the sheep article.

Rights Are for Rats

morality play: a simple, clearcut play in which the good are always rewarded and the bad are always punished
amorality: neither moral nor immoral
scabrous: evil; obscene

[1] When adults deplore the "bad examples" of violence and lawlessness on television programs for children—and don't most of the early evening programs seem designed for children's minds?—they are usually thinking of the crimes committed by the "bad guys" on the shows.

Giving the usual point of view

[2] But this alone would not necessarily have a harmful effect on children, who expect bad guys to do wrong, to be caught and overcome and punished by the good guys. This would be simply an old-time morality play in modern form: evil conquered by virtue.

Letting the reader know that this essay will take an unusual point of view

[3] What is sinister in some of these shows, however, is not the "immorality" of the villains, but the "amorality" of the so-called heroes. When the good guys themselves avoid the law in order to achieve their purpose, then our whole traditional structure of values is brought into question, and "good" and "bad" become meaningless sentimental tags.

The main idea sentence

[4] My older boy and I were watching an episode of a program called "Mission—Impossible," a few weeks ago, in which one of the heroes lured the master criminal into a hotel room and proceeded to beat a confession out of him.

Example that illustrates the main idea

[5] When the criminal protested that his constitutional rights were being violated—for the hero had posed as a Senate crime investigator—his attacker snarled: "Rights aren't for rats like you—they're just for decent citizens." (My boy, I'm happy to say, jeered at that remark.)

[6] But rights are for rats, even more than for

Examining what the ex-

"decent citizens." If the rats and the decent citizens aren't treated equally under the law, then any group that gets in power can decide that any other group consists of "rats." This is the whole point in carefully guarding the civil liberties of even the most scabrous member of society.

[7] And this is a lesson in American history and civics that we seem increasingly to have forgotten, if the present generation has ever known it. Equal treatment under law is precisely what distinguishes the good guys from the bad guys; and when the good guys begin to give up this difference, then the bad guys have already triumphed philosophically.

[8] In today's practical atmosphere, many people seem to feel that any means will do to get rid of the rats; an attitude that is more dangerous, to my mind, than the activities of the rats. Unless our children are shown exactly what makes the "good guys" good, they will judge essential morality only by such trivial trappings as white hats and blacks hats—on or off the TV screen.

(margin notes:)

ample shows

Example applied to the main idea

Conclusion returns to the idea of "good guys" and "bad guys" which introduced the article, and reinforces the main idea

DISCUSSION

1. Can you restate the main idea of this selection in your own words? How does the main idea relate to Harris's opening paragraph?

2. Do you think that Harris would make his point more effectively or less effectively if he began with the ideas in paragraphs 6 and 7 and then illustrated his point with his personal experience?

3. Could the comment in parentheses in paragraph 4 have been left out? Why does Harris mention his son at all?

4. What is the distinction that Harris makes in paragraph 7? Does this distinction make any difference in whether you consider the "hero" in paragraphs 4 and 5 as a "good guy"?

5. How is the title of this essay related to the main idea sentence? How is it related to the example?

6. From your own experience in watching television, especially programs that show violence, what other examples can you find that illustrate Harris's point? Can you think of examples that contradict it?

In Praise of the Land Rover

embodiment: an actual example of an abstract idea
indomitable: can't be defeated or subdued
Brunhilde: legendary queen of Germanic warriors
Atlantis: a mythical land that is said to have sunk into the sea
intrigued: very interested
archetype: genuine one, of which others are just copies
cataclysmic: like a violent upheaval
John Bull: the typical Englishman

[1] I got into the Land Rover thing about ten years ago when trying to sell business machines to Mom-and-Pop grocery stores in an economic disaster area finally got to my soul and my bank balance simultaneously. So I wound up in a very small, very informal Land Rover agency as a salesman, sometime mechanic, chief gopher and seat warmer.

[2] The first thing you learn about a Land Rover is that it has a personality which is uniquely its own. To me, a Land Rover is a safe, warm, comfortable place to be. When in a Land Rover you're safe from any assault by man or nature. The Bomb could land right on top of it, but somehow you're sure that it would only blister the paint a little. A Land Rover is the wheeled embodiment of the spirit of one of the sturdiest, most indomitable nations on earth. This is not just a heavy-duty vehicle; this is *John Bull's* heavy-duty vehicle. And there's a difference. There it is—Rule Britannia and Press On Regardless!

[3] Okay, yes, I'm sure your 4wd vehicle is just as good, if not better. But it can't have anywhere near the Land Rover's class. And when it comes to tradition, well . . . hang around Land Rovers long enough and you'll wind up convinced that if Rover ever stopped making them, the whole continent of Africa would sink like Atlantis into the sea. Anyway, two days after I started, I was a confirmed Land Rover nut. Those things are more fun to drive than anything this side of a Ferrari! They'll go over, under or through anything, the visibility's marvelous, and you have to be really creative to make one break. And for sheer startle value, a Land Rover just can't be beat.

[4] When you took a customer out for a demonstration ride, you'd get him (or often, her) firmly strapped in and take off down the street, which was separated from an expressway by a rather steep grassy embankment about 10 feet wide, and during the winter, this strip always had snow piled up on it about three feet deep. You'd get up to about 20, say very casually, "Hey, why

Reprinted, with changes, from "O'Kane on Land Rovers," by Dick O'Kane, in *Road and Track*, July 1969, by permission of the author and the publisher.

don't we take the expressway—it's quicker," and suddenly swerve right. As you swerved, you banged it into 4-wheel drive and "whumph!" Into the snow, churn up the embankment, pull out into the disbelieving traffic and go, hood and fenders festooned with hunks of snow, customer still softly going "gah . . . gah . . . gah . . ." to himself. Then down to the river where you'd demonstrate the thing's ability to climb sheer cliffs, charge through the woods, wade through hub-deep sand and generally do unreasonable things without a whimper. Then you'd let the customer play for awhile and it was *your* turn to hang grimly on while *he* tried to destroy the car, the object being to let him get so intrigued that he could be relieved of his sack of coin. And oddly, there was only one instance of customer-caused damage to our demonstrator. And not in the bush, either. This happened in downtown traffic. You remember Land Rover's claim that the thing's built to withstand the full charge of a bull rhinoceros? Yeah, well, they'll even do better than that.

[5] On this particular day, my prospect was one of those marvelous old ladies New England's so full of. There's a whole class of them; great, huge, jolly people with master's degrees and sometimes doctorates—always from Smith—and they're really into living. They do things like sail star boats single-handed, dig bushels of clams for dinner, march in demonstrations, lecture at the library and talk like a fascinating blue streak while they get genteelly swacked on sherry. This one was the archetype of the species, and she was having a ball with the Land Rover, giggling and cooing as she howled through a trafficky, one-way circle in a beautifully-controlled drift. Then, ohmigod, here comes a great Mother Buick the wrong way, and with a cataclysmic bang the two cars married fairly, front to front.

[6] We fared a lot better than the guy in the Buick simply because we were harnessed firmly to the seats and he wasn't. He banged his head smartly on the windshield, sustaining Slight Injury, which rated us all an ambulance, a fire engine, all the policemen in the world and enough spectators to stop traffic completely.

[7] Then there followed the required Great Flap about Who Was At Fault, wherein Brunhilde stood like a pillar of New Hampshire granite and told all and sundry concisely, precisely and politely that she was in the right and they could all go to hell, and finally, like the mules that drag deceased bulls from the *corrida,* the wreckers came.

[8] Just for the hell of it, I got into the Land Rover and started it. It idled quietly, with none of the sounds like the fan makes when it's stuck into the radiator, so I put it into reverse and tried backing out from within the Buick. It went backwards, alright, but the Buick wanted to come too, so I got a wrecker to sort of stand on the other car's tail and tried again. This time the Buick fell off onto the road, and I got out to inspect the damage. The Buick seemed utterly destroyed, hood buckled double, front wheels splayed out and the engine off its mounts, bathed in antifreeze.

[9] The front bumper on the Land Rover was scratched, one fender had a dent in it and there was a broken headlight. That's all.

[10] Brunhilde stood and stared in delighted disbelief, and I said, "Well, I guess that proves the factory's claim that a Land Rover can withstand the full charge of a bull rhinoceros."

[11] "Yes," she answered, "and also the charge of the cow Buick."

[12] One day I'm going to get a Land Rover, and it's going to have all the options and attachments I want, too; snow thrower, winch, mower, hydraulic mousetrap, clam digger, twin machine guns, bird call, heavy-duty traffic ram . . . and an air horn that plays "Rule Britannia!"

DISCUSSION

1. What is the main idea sentence of this essay? In what paragraph do you find it?

2. What reasons does O'Kane give to support his main idea sentence? How does he support his reasons?

3. Is O'Kane an authority on the Land Rover? How does he establish his authority?

4. In what way is the Rover different from other cars?

5. What tests does O'Kane put the Rover through to convince a buyer that the car is superior? How does he make them vivid? Does he exaggerate?

6. O'Kane says the Rover has a personality of its own. What details does he give to show that for him a Rover seems alive and not just a machine?

7. Which sales approach do you think sells more cars—humor or serious discussion of mechanics? Give the reasons for your choice.

Sheep

ingenious: cleverly invented
equanimity: calmness
recoiled: drawn back
bacteriological agents: specially produced disease germs
retaliate: to return like for like

From "Sheep" in the May 1968 edition of *The Progressive*. Copyright © 1968 *The Progressive*. Reprinted by permission.

truculent: threatening or bullying
complacent: pleased and self-satisfied

[1] Early in March, the Army conducted aerial spray and artillery tests of deadly nerve gases at the Dugway Proving Ground in Utah. The next day, sheep grazing in nearby Skull Valley began to ail. Within a week some 7,000 sheep were dead. After issuing ingenious but unconvincing alibis, military spokesmen finally conceded that the tests at Dugway might have been responsible.

[2] We grieve not so much for the sheep of Skull Valley—their days were numbered in any event, though one might wish for them a more productive end—as for the other sheep, in Congress, in the press, and in the general citizenry, who accept with equanimity the "military necessity" of the Army's massive experiments in chemical and biological warfare.

[3] Civilized nations have long recoiled in horror from such weapons. They were prohibited as long ago as 1899, when a Gas Declaration was signed at The Hague, and as recently as 1966, when a United Nations resolution called for a "strict observance" of the Geneva Protocol banning the use of poison gases and bacteriological agents. The United States voted for the resolution.

[4] But the United States, preparing, presumably, to retaliate against a barbarous and unprincipled enemy's first strike, has been engaged since World War II in extensive though secret testing, production, and stockpiling of chemical and bacteriological weapons. Nerve gases, a scientific achievement of Nazi Germany, are the mainstay of the U.S. arsenal.

[5] The Chinese, the Russians, the truculent nations of the Middle East—all these and others have their own stockpiles of gases—and they, too, are merely taking precautions against barbarous and unprincipled enemies. For them, too, it is a matter of "military necessity."

[6] For similar reasons, the Air Force until recently kept nuclear bombs airborne around the clock. But when the United States was embarrassed early this year by the second accidental dropping of such bombs on foreign soil, the Air Force found that the "military necessity" had vanished, and it discontinued the nuclear weapon flights.

[7] The death of 7,000 sheep is not, apparently, an equivalent embarrassment. It might have been, if a sufficient outcry had been raised. But sheep are notoriously complacent and so, for that matter, are people.

DISCUSSION

1. What is the main idea of this selection? Is it openly stated or implied? If openly stated, what is it? If implied, put into your own words what you think it is.

2. How does the writer's first example work in two ways? What if mountain goats had been killed by the nerve gas?

3. Are the examples typical? In dealing with the kind of problem that this writer is concerned about, is it important that the examples be typical? If the examples are out of the ordinary, would you consider such support fair persuasion? Why or why not?

4. Paragraph 3 is mostly historical background. Why does the writer include it? How is the background information connected with paragraphs 4 and 5?

5. Why is the phrase "military necessity" in quotes every time it is used (paragraphs 2, 5, and 6)? Does putting this phrase in quotations help relate it to the main idea sentence?

6. In paragraph 2, the writer makes use of a comparison. In the conclusion, he makes use of a contrast as well as a comparison. What is the connection between the conclusion and the two opening paragraphs?

Open Season

camouflaged: disguised so as to blend in with the surroundings

[1] I keep having this nightmare. I dream I'm on an island with nothing to eat but canned corned beef. I turn the key and the little metal strip starts getting narrower. And narrower. I turn it slower—and slower—and it gets narrower—and narrower—and snap! This isn't so bad as nightmares go. The only trouble is the same thing happens when I'm awake.

[2] With sardines it works the other way. As you roll up the lid it keeps getting bigger and bigger until it swallows the key. Fortunately, sardines are small and slippery, so you can get most of them out anyway.

[3] The greatest friend the packaging industry has is the sporting instinct of the American people. If you can't improve a product, make it harder to get at. If this sounds like an exaggeration, have you tried unwrapping a new shirt lately? How about a lampshade? Okay then.

[4] Take something as simple as a bag. I'm talking about the big ones that hold things such as dog food and lawn conditioner and so on. They are fastened across the top with some braided strings under which is a note saying that if you will pull the red string, or the green string, the whole top will open like magic. If you believe that, you will believe anything. Your best

bet is to put the bag in a wash tub and cut it in half like a watermelon.

[5] Milk cartons come in several styles, the most challenging being the one that comes to a peak. For the purposes of this exercise I am going to ask you to think of it as a little roof. What you're supposed to do is separate the sides so it splits along the rooftree, allowing the gable to come out and form a spout. You will find, however, that they have glued the gable to the inside of the roof and it has to be torn loose, leaving you with a crooked spout or no spout. This is particularly true of buttermilk cartons. To many people buttermilk can be unsettling at its best, and when it spurts out the side, running down the glass and across the countertop and into the drawer it is anything but at its best.

[6] To a layman the philosophy of packaging is a mystery. Light bulbs and eggs are enclosed in some of the filmsiest cardboard modern science can produce. You can crush an egg carton by putting your mail on it. On the other hand, a steel chisel designed for cutting metal comes protected by shatterproof plastic. This plastic-bubble-on-cardboard design is popular for this sort of purchase. When you want to open one, don't waste your time on the plastic—you can't dent it. Try to hack or peel away the cardboard from the back. And don't throw away any of those curled up scraps because they contain the instructions and the guarantee.

[7] The powdered-sugar and macaroni people favor the thumbnail opening. At the top of the package there is a semicircle with simulated perforations around the edge. Underneath, they have printed a little joke which says, "Press thumbnail here." Unless you have the thumbnail of a Fu Manchu, all you're going to do is cave in the side of the box—and there goes the old ball game. Better plan something else for supper. For the simple fact is that for any kind of opening purpose the thumbnail has become obsolete.

[8] Toilet paper presents a special problem. First you've got your four rolls sealed in plastic, tight as a bongo drum. That you can handle. Now you've got a single roll, wrapped or unwrapped, but again no problem. The tricky part comes because the manufacturer has carefully camouflaged the place where the paper comes to an end. If you can't find it, slide something under the outside layer—a nail file is fine—and tear it across. If you are lucky you will now be able to unroll the paper as desired. Unfortunately, I find more and more these days that the second layer is glued to the third, and so on.

[9] Food processors have a special knack for raising false hopes in their customers. Ready-sliced cheese, for instance—this sounds great. Open the package and slap together half a dozen sandwiches in a couple of minutes. Now it's true that they do slice the cheese just as they say. But what they don't tell you is that after they slice it they send it through a laminating mill where it is pressed back together like plywood. I guess that's not such a good comparison because the last time I bought plywood it got left in the rain and when I wanted to use it the layers had come apart like—well, I started to say like cheese, but I can see that's not going to clarify anything.

[10] Where is it going to end? The time may come when our cities with their

tall buildings and broad avenues will be empty. Our fur-clad descendants will be crouched over fires, gnawing on roots and bones while the fruits of our civilization lie all about them—only a thumbnail away.

DISCUSSION

1. What is the main idea sentence? Is it stated or implied? Would the effect be spoiled if it were a direct statement?

2. Do you think the examples are fair? How many are exaggerated? How many of these experiences have you had? Are they typical?

3. Pick two examples that seem to you the most effective and discuss the specific detail that helps you see it happening.

4. Is the conclusion fair? Is it far-fetched? How does it restate the main idea? Is it effective?

5. Pick some minor annoyance of daily life and make a list of examples that illustrate it.

Other Kinds of Support

Although examples are a very effective means of making a situation vivid, they are not the only way opinions can be supported. Often, in fact, they are not enough by themselves. Another very common and very effective kind of support is statistics—a collection of numbers that represent not just one example but many. For statistics to be convincing, their source must be reliable. The count must have been made, or the survey taken, by somebody we can trust—somebody who knows what he is doing, who reports his findings objectively, and who has nothing to gain or lose by what the statistics show. The sociologist who collected the figures in "Negroes and Property Values" seems to have done a careful job, and most of us assume we can trust the U. S. Census.

Quoting what some important person has said is still another way to back up reasons. What the authority says will not carry much weight, however, unless he is talking about something he really understands, and, like the people who gather reliable statistics, the expert must have no personal stake in the outcome, other than his own strong conviction. The two doctors whose opinions are quoted in "Athletes in a Turned-On World" are talking about a subject they've been trained in—medicine—and about a part of it with which they have had experience—the effect of drugs.

A third kind of support is predicting consequences—telling what undesirable things will happen if we do not adopt the writer's proposal, or what good things will happen if we do. But predictions can persuade only if they seem reasonable, if the reader's own knowledge makes him think that what the writer is predicting might really come to pass. Most readers will be inclined to agree with Gilbert's prediction, for instance, that if athletes keep searching for the "ultimate pill," there may be a big sports scandal.

Giving examples, citing statistics, referring to authorities, and predicting consequences are all sound ways by which a writer can support his reasons. Just supporting his own reasons, however, may not be enough. Wherever there is controversy, as there almost always is when someone is trying to get others to change their opinions, there are reasons on both sides. The writer who can anticipate what his opponents' reasons are, and can show why those reasons are weak, is a jump ahead of the game. Some successful arguments, in fact, consist almost entirely of demolishing the other side, as Grier and Cobbs do in persuading us that American Negroes cannot fairly be compared with other immigrant groups.

For some subjects, one kind of support will fit better than the others; on some topics, the writer can effectively use all five, as the writer does who insists that capital punishment is wrong.

An End to Capital Punishment

notorious: unfavorably well known
litigation: lawsuit
de facto: what is actually done, not what the law says should be done
adamant: completely unwilling to change
retribution: just revenge
millenium: a thousand years
Richard Speck: convicted killer of seven Chicago nurses

[1] It is two years this month since an execution took place in the U.S. Yet no fewer than 434 prisoners remain on Death Row, many of them kept alive by a series of broad legal challenges to the constitutionality of capital punishment. In a way, the executioners' grim backlog reflects widespread public uncertainty over whether to put to death even such notorious killers as Sirhan Sirhan and Richard Speck. Those asking clemency for Sirhan include Senator Edward M. Kennedy, whose late brother Robert opposed capital punishment and "would not have wanted his death to be a cause for the taking of another life."

Introduction combines interest and support:
(1) abrupt mention of 2 years startles the reader, as does the large number—*statistics*
(2) mention of names many readers will know also arouses interest—*examples*
(3) quoting from Kennedy appeals to public sympathy because of the two assassinations and is strong support since Robert Kennedy was once attorney-general—*authority*

[2] The population of Death Row probably will continue to grow, since years of litigation may be necessary before the Supreme Court decides whether to make a revolutionary decision to uphold on constitutional grounds the *de facto* moratorium on the death penalty. If it declines to, there is an even more bizarre prospect ahead. It is that U.S. justice, as one defense attorney puts it, eventually may have no choice but to "just open the gas chambers again and march 1,000 or so guys in there."

Prediction:
(a) it will take a long time for the Supreme Court to decide;
(b) if it decides to keep capital punishment, we'll have to have a lot of executions

[3] Early legislative action, state by state, on the

Transition paragraph:

question of the death penalty would obviously be preferable. The two major rationales for capital punishment no longer seem valid, and the time has come for the U.S. to move toward its abolition.

[4] First, there is the somewhat discredited assumption that capital punishment is an effective crime deterrent. Now that it has been abolished for a number of years in some jurisdictions, even its most outspoken U.S. supporter, J. Edgar Hoover, reluctantly concedes that statistics purporting to compare deterrent effect are "completely inconclusive." Of course, Hoover remains adamant on the other, entirely nonrational "argument" for the death penalty—in his words, "the savagely mutilated bodies and mentally ravaged victims of murderers, rapists and other criminal beasts."

[5] True enough, the retribution school of justice has been part of Western society ever since the Old Testament sternly demanded "an eye for an eye." But that particular decree was handed down several millenniums ago. In recent, more civilized times, more than 70 Western countries have abolished capital punishment. Now Americans may be ready to follow suit: 14 U.S. states have already abolished or drastically restricted capital punishment, and recent opinion polls showed that a national majority favored its abolition. This year, public concern about the "crime in the streets" issue has reversed the trend. Nevertheless, the arguments against the death penalty remain valid: that executions are unworthy of society and demeaning to all of us, and that the judicial process sometimes makes mistakes.

[6] A few states will doubtless retain the death penalty for some time to come. Many others probably will not want to abolish capital punishment without "protective" safeguards, such as prohibition of parole for certain offenses, or retention of the death sentence for particular crimes (*e.g.,* the killing of a prison guard by a life-termer, who otherwise would not be subject to further punishment at all). These safeguards assured, there is every reason to move faster to abolish capital punishment.

Marginal notes:

warns readers that arguments of the opposition will be gotten rid of, and states the *main idea sentence*

First opposition argument: that capital punishment keeps people from committing capital crimes; disproved by *authority*—an admission by a well-known man who favors capital punishment

Second opposition argument: criminals must "pay" for what they have done

Second opposition argument disproved: capital punishment is out-of-date and uncivilized; *statistics*—70 countries and 14 states have done away with it

Two reasons for abolishing capital punishment:
(1) it's uncivilized, supported by what has been said earlier in the paragraph;
(2) sometimes the wrong man is killed—unsupported

More prediction:
(a) some states will keep capital punishment;
(b) some will modify it

Restatement of the *main idea sentence*

DISCUSSION

1. The writer begins paragraph 3 by saying that it would be better for the states to abolish capital punishment as quickly as possible, and then moves on to the main idea sentence without discussing state legislation. When does he pick up the question of state legislation again? How does he make it work in the conclusion? Does the restated main idea in the conclusion mean that the states should abolish capital punishment or that the Supreme Court should outlaw it for all states?

2. Paragraphs 1, 2, and 4 all end with direct quotations. One reason for quoting directly, of course, is to make sure that the writer does not distort what the authority said, but there is sometimes another reason. Can you see any difference in tone between what Senator Edward M. Kennedy said and what J. Edgar Hoover said? What is the difference, and how does it affect your attitude toward the argument? What kind of people do you think of when you read the defense attorney's comment, "just open the gas chambers again and march 1,000 or so guys in there"?

3. The writer has used quotations around several other words and phrases, even though he was not quoting from anyone: "argument" in paragraph 4, "an eye for an eye" and "crime in the streets" in paragraph 5, and "protective" in paragraph 6. Why?

4. The language used in this persuasive paper is somewhat formal; most of these words would not be used in normal conversation. Do you think this formality makes the argument more or less convincing? Why?

5. Decide which of these possibilities you like better, and be prepared to defend your choice:

   a. Those asking clemency include
   or
   Some of the people who asked for mercy were   (paragraph 1)

   b. *de facto* moratorium
   or
   present practice of not giving the death penalty without changing the law   (paragraph 2)

   c. major rationales
   or
   main reasons given   (paragraph 3)

   d. executions are unworthy of society and demeaning to all of us
   or
   state killings are uncivilized and cheapen everybody in the country
   (paragraph 5)

Negroes and Property Values

credence: belief
depress: lower

[1] A seemingly indestructible myth in U.S. race relations holds that property values decline when Negroes move into a white neighborhood. It is a myth that has been shot down scores of times by university studies, in books based on scholarly surveys, and by the researches of supporters of open housing. But it stubbornly survives, and there are few Americans who have not given it some degree of credence at some time—except Negroes, especially those who have bought or rented homes in white neighborhoods at inflated prices.

[2] Now a new study has come along that provides solid evidence that Negroes not only do not depress property values, but on the contrary, their presence almost invariably results in substantially higher values for the neighborhood.

[3] Sherwood Ross, a Washington writer and urban sociologist, has painstakingly pieced together from the U.S. Census of 1950 and 1960 data concerning 1,323,762 homes in 1,810 census tracts in forty-seven major cities. He has sorted out the districts by racial composition and compared housing values over the ten-year span. Ross' research revealed that in Negro districts homes soared sixty-one per cent in value over the decade; integrated neighborhoods showed a forty-five per cent rise; in areas in the process of changing from all white to all Negro occupancy the increase in value was forty-two per cent. The most ironic finding is that in white communities that remained white, property values rose only about thirty-five per cent.

[4] "I think this should kill the myth," Ross commented, "that home values fall when Negroes move in. White homeowners talked into selling short by crooked real estate swindlers and panic-peddlers would find their homes rising steadily in value if they would only hold on to them. No white homeowner in America need lose a dollar on his house."

[5] The Ross survey is the first to measure all possible tracts in a large number of cities, and it is by far the largest study made, from impartial U. S. Census data, on the relation between race and home values. We agree with Ross that his findings "should kill the myth" of declining property values and spare the anguish of so many people who innocently believe it. But it is a myth that dies hard.

DISCUSSION

1. The word "myth" is used in several ways. How is the writer using it here? Why does he begin and end with a discussion of "myth"? What do this beginning and ending tell you about the main method the essay uses?

2. Put into your own words what the main idea of this article is. Is there a negative word in your main idea sentence? Why?

3. The writer uses two other kinds of support. What are they? How convincing do you think they are?

4. Was the sample used in the survey large enough to make the survey convincing? Discuss.

5. Who is the audience for this article? That is, what group of people is the writer trying to persuade? Back up what you say by referring to the article.

Athletes in a Turned-on World

derivative: coming from
vignette: very short descriptive story
restorative: something to repair a damaged body
emaciated: extremely thin and worn
therapeutic: healing
convulsed: doubled over in pain
dilemma: problem with two equally unsatisfactory solutions
nihilist: one who completely rejects established laws and institutions
surreptitiously: secretly; stealthily
succinctly: briefly and effectively
alchemists: early scientists who searched for the "philosopher's stone" that would change any metal into gold

[1] Among the less startling statements one could make today would be that we live in a drug culture. The vast majority of us gobble an aspirin here, gulp an antibiotic there, whiff a decongestant now or a few milligrams of nicotine then. We take a little opiate in our cough syrup, a jab of Novocain from the dentist, caffeine to start the day, alcohol to mellow it, and a sedative

Adapted by permission from *Drugs in Sport,* Part I ("Problems in a Turned-on World") by Bil Gilbert, SPORTS ILLUSTRATED, June 23, 1969. © 1969 Time Inc.

to blank it out at bedtime. However, after it has been admitted that most citizens dope themselves from time to time, there remain excellent grounds for claiming that in the matter of drug usage, athletes are different from the rest of us. In spite of being—for the most part—young, healthy and active specimens, they take an extraordinary variety and quantity of drugs. They take them for questionable purposes, they take them in a situation of debatable morality, they take them under conditions that range from dangerously experimental to hazardous to fatal. The use of drugs—legal drugs—by athletes is far from new, but the increase in drug usage in the last 10 years is startling. It could, indeed, menace the tradition and structure of sport itself.

[2] To begin, consider some examples of the role drugs have come to play in sport:

[3] "A few pills—I take all kinds—and the pain's gone," says Dennis McLain of the Detroit Tigers. McLain also takes shots, or at least took a shot of cortisone and Xylocaine (antiinflammant and painkiller) in his throwing shoulder prior to the sixth game of the 1968 World Series—the only game he won in three tries. In the same Series, which at times seemed to be a matchup between Detroit and St. Louis druggists, Cardinal Bob Gibson was gobbling muscle-relaxing pills, trying chemically to keep his arm loose. The Tigers' Series hero, Mickey Lolich, was on antibiotics.

[4] "We occasionally use Dexamyl and Dexedrine (amphetamines) . . . We also use barbiturates, Seconal, Tuinal, Nembutal . . . We also use some antidepressants, Triavil, Tofranil, Valium . . . But I don't think the use of drugs is as prevalent in the Midwest as it is on the East and West coasts," said Dr. I. C. Middleman, who, until his death last September, was team surgeon for the St. Louis baseball Cardinals.

[5] Amphetamines were among the drugs banned for use by athletes in the 1968 Olympic Games, and for which post-event testing was conducted. A U.S. weight lifter, who admitted most of his colleagues took a few amphetamines before competing in order to get that extra little lift, was asked how the Olympic ban affected performance. "What ban?" he asked blandly. "Everyone used a new one from West Germany. They couldn't pick it up in the test they were using. When they get a test for that one, we'll find something else. It's like cops and robbers."

[6] "Are anabolic steroids (a male hormone derivative that supposedly makes users bigger and stronger than they could otherwise be) widely used by Olympic weight men?" rhetorically asks Dave Maggard, who finished fifth in the shotput at Mexico and is now the University of California track coach. "Let me put it this way. If they had come into the village the day before competition and said we have just found a new test that will catch anyone who has used steroids, you would have had an awful lot of people dropping out of events because of instant muscle pulls."

[7] Dr. H. Kay Dooley, director of the Wood Memorial Clinic in Pomona, Calif., is well known among athletes as one of the few physicians who openly endorse use of anabolic steroids. "I don't think it is possible for a weight man

to compete internationally without using anabolic steroids," says Dr. Dooley. "All the weight men on the Olympic team had to take steroids. Otherwise they would not have been in the running." Dr. Dooley was one of the physicians in charge of medical services at South Lake Tahoe, the 1968 U.S. Olympic high-altitude training camp. "I did not give steroids at Tahoe," says the California physician, "but I also did not inquire what the boys were doing on their own. I did not want to be forced into a position of having to report them for use of a banned drug. A physician involved in sports must keep the respect and confidence of the athletes with whom he is working."

[8] Such a collection of drug-related vignettes can be expanded at will, but while the amount and kinds of drugs used in sports are impressive, the important difference between athletic and nonathletic drug use comes down to a matter of motive. An athlete takes—or is given by his supervisors, medical and otherwise—many drugs that he would not take or be given if he were not an athlete. And the rationale for much athletic drug use is unique, for the drugs are not taken either with the intention or effect of improving or maintaining health, or to achieve a pleasurable sensation, but rather because the athlete or those around him believe he will perform better drugged than undrugged.

[9] For example, the family of hormonal drugs, which are widely known in athletic circles as anabolic steroids, were developed as restorative aids for patients seriously weakened by age, accident, major surgery or other infirmities. As with any drug, there are risks that go with their use—in this case, disruption of certain glandular functions, particularly the sexual. However, a physician may reasonably prescribe anabolic steroids to an emaciated 70-year-old man on the assumption that if the drug helps add 10 pounds to his wasted body this advantage will outweigh the risk of decreased sperm production, testicular shrinking or prostate discomfort. On the other hand, there is no conventional medical reason for a healthy 23-year-old, 240-pound shotputter to use the drug. But many do, because they believe the drug will make them bigger and stronger than they are and because they believe they cannot become national or world-class competitors without it. It is their motivation that makes athletic anabolic steroid users unique.

[10] Another example of the same general phenomenon occurs in the case of the broken-legged hockey player. Midway through the sixth game of the 1964 Stanley Cup finals against Detroit, Bobby Baun, then of the Toronto Maple Leafs, was hit on the leg by the puck and carried from the rink on a stretcher. In the training room he received an injection of Novocain. His leg was taped, he returned to play, and he scored the winning goal in overtime. The next day it was determined Baun had a cracked right fibula. Nonetheless, he was shot with painkiller and willingly, probably eagerly, took his regular turn on the ice the following day.

[11] Numbing a broken leg and sending the patient out to play hockey is not a treatment any physician would follow with a nonathlete. It may not cause complications, but the procedure has no known therapeutic value. It is

not conceived as a method of speeding up or improving the knitting of bone. The only motive was to enable a man to play a game that he could not otherwise have played.

[12] There are abundant rumors—the wildest of which circulate within rather than outside the sporting world—about strung-out quarterbacks, hopped-up pitchers, slowed-down middleweights, convulsed half-milers and doped-to-death wrestlers. Nevertheless, it is the question of motive and morality that is the crux of the athletic drug problem. Even if none of the gossip could be reduced to provable fact, there remains ample evidence that drug use constitutes a significant dilemma, not so much for individual athletes as for sport in general. One reason is that the use of drugs in sport leads one directly to more serious and complicated questions. Is athletic integrity (and, conversely, corruption) a matter of public interest? Does it matter, as fans of sport have so long and piously claimed it does, that games be played in an atmosphere of virtue; even righteousness? If not, what is the social utility of games—why play them at all? Drug usage, even more than speculation about bribery, college recruiting, spitballs or TV commercials, raises such sticky questions about the fundamentals of sport that one can understand the instinctive reaction of the athletic Establishments: when it comes to drugs, they ignore, dismiss, deny.

[13] "Somebody should speak out on this subject, and speak out strongly," says Dr. Robert Kerlan, until recently the physician for the Los Angeles Dodgers as well as for a number of individual athletes in all sports. "I'm not a therapeutic nihilist," says Kerlan. "Situations arise where there are valid medical reasons for prescribing drugs for athletes. There are special occupational health problems in some sports. However, the excessive and secretive use of drugs is likely to become a major athletic scandal, one that will shake public confidence in many sports just as the gambling scandal tarnished the reputation of basketball. The essence of sports is matching the natural ability of men. When you start using drugs, money or anything else surreptitiously to gain an unnatural advantage, you have corrupted the purpose of sports as well as the individuals involved in the practice."

[14] The view of Dr. Dooley is quite different from that of Dr. Kerlan. In fact, the two men in many ways represent the opposite poles of medical and philosophical opinion regarding drug use in sports. Nevertheless, both the Los Angeles area physicians share the common belief that this is a serious matter and one that should be aired thoroughly in public.

[15] "I don't pretend to be a researcher or a scientist," says Dooley. "I'm a practicing physician who is interested in athletes. A lot of physicians are stuffed shirts when it comes to sports. Athletes do want to perform better, that is what it is all about. If I know of something which may improve performance, a training or rehabilitation technique, a drug that is legal and which I don't believe involves any serious health risk, I see no reason not to make it available to an athlete. I can't see any ethical difference between giving a drug to improve performance and wrapping an ankle or handing out

a salt pill for the same purpose. Athletes hear about these things and they are going to get them one way or another."

[16] Between the opposed views of the two West Coast doctors—Dr. Kerlan's that drug abuse constitutes a growing athletic crisis and Dr. Dooley's that the use of drugs is the sporting wave of the future—there are all shades of opinion and all kinds of fancy hedging and dodging. But there is also one thing that is agreed upon— a greater quantity and variety of drugs are being used now than were used a generation, a decade, or even a year ago.

[17] Generally, as Dr. Dooley says, modern athletes know a lot about drugs, or at least have a lot of opinions about them, and are willing to experiment with drugs about which no one knows very much. There are probably as many cases of athletes demanding drugs from trainers and physicians as physicians and trainers ordering athletes to take them.

[18] The whole matter has been succinctly summarized by Hal Connolly, a veteran of four U.S. Olympic teams. "My experience," says Connolly, "tells me that an athlete will use any aid to improve his performance short of killing himself."

[19] The notion that some place there is a compound, a formula or a food that will automatically convert bronze medals into gold is a general one confined to no one nation, sport or class of competitors. This conviction that there is the athletic equivalent of the philosopher's stone sought by ancient alchemists, and the terrible fear that somebody else may have already found it, is the rationale—or irrationale—behind many of the current athletic drug practices. It is used as a justification by physicians and trainers for pre-scribing drugs that cannot be justified on conventional medical grounds. It is the excuse used by coaches and trainers ("There might be something in it") for pushing pills the effectiveness and safety of which are unknown. It is the reason athletes carry their own little black drug bags, endanger their health, risk their reputations and break oaths and laws to get and use exotic drugs. It explains the ever-multiplying rumors about records being set and games being won by doped competitors. Finally, the belief in the existence of the ultimate pill, and the continuing search for it, is why many doctors share Dr. Kerlan's fear that athletic drug practices are leading to a sports scandal of major proportions.

DISCUSSION

1. The idea of associating athletes and drugs is shocking to many people. How does Gilbert use his introduction to play down this shock, yet still get smoothly into his main idea sentence?

2. Would you say the intention of this article is to *shock* or to *persuade*? Why do you say so?

3. After his introduction, Gilbert offers a series of specific examples in paragraphs 3 through 7. How widely do the examples represent the varieties of sports? How widely do the examples represent the varieties

of drugs used? How widely do the examples represent the purposes for which drugs are taken or prescribed?

4. In paragraph 8, Gilbert moves from examples to a broad consideration of the whole question. What sentence makes this transition clear?

5. Also in paragraph 8, Gilbert distinguishes between "athletic and non-athletic drug use." What is the difference? How do paragraphs 9, 10, and 11 help to clarify the difference?

6. How does paragraph 12 restate the main idea?

7. Who are the two medical experts used in this essay? Are they authorities in their field? In what ways do they differ? Do their differences make the argument more effective or less? Why?

8. In an essay that makes use of examples, authority, and prediction of consequences, why is there no use of statistics?

9. Does the conclusion summarize the main points and restate the main idea? Is it a straight repeat, or is there some variation? Explain.

Black Isolation

decimated: a great number killed
infused: filled
continuity: a sense of belonging to the past
annihilation: killing
rituals: habits and ceremonies
cohesiveness: sense of being together

[1] Because of an inattention to history, the present-day Negro is compared unfavorably with other racial and ethnic groups who have come to this country. Major differences in backgrounds are ignored. The black man was brought to this country forcibly and was completely cut off from his past. He was robbed of language and culture. He was forbidden to be an African and never allowed to be an American. After the first generation and with each new group of slaves, the black man had only his American experience to draw on. For most Negroes, the impact of the experience has been so great as to even now account for a lack of knowledge of their past.

[2] This can be contrasted with the heritage of the American Indian. He truly has known the violence of white America, but his legacies are of a

From BLACK RAGE by William H. Grier and Price M. Cobbs, Basic Books, Inc., Publishers, New York, 1968.

different sort. Now, decimated and forlorn, survivors can nevertheless tell tales of past glories. At least in reliving the time when his people ruled the land, the Indian can vicariously achieve a measure of dignity.

[3] Various groups that have come to these shores have been able to maintain some continuity of social institutions. In the process of Americanization, they have retained an identification with their homeland. The Chinese, who in many instances functioned virtually as slaves, were allowed to preserve a family structure. Other oppressed groups, notably the Irish and Italians, were never infused with the shame of color. In addition, they had the protection and support of the Roman Catholic Church. Except for the Negro, all sizable groups in America have been able to keep some old customs and traditions.

[4] The black experience in this country has been of a different kind. It began with slavery and with a rupture of continuity and an annihilation of the past. *Even now each generation grows up alone.* Many individual blacks feel a desperate aloneness not readily explained. The authors have heard stories telling of each generation's isolation from every other. Nonblack groups pass on proud traditions, conscious of the benefit they are conferring. For black people, values and rituals are shared and indeed transmitted, but with little acknowledgment of their worth. The Jew achieves a sense of ethnic cohesiveness through religion and a pride in background, while the black man stands in solitude.

DISCUSSION

1. What method of argument is being developed in this selection?

2. What other ethnic groups do Grier and Cobbs compare with the Negro? In what ways are they different?

3. The writers say individual blacks feel desperate aloneness. What reasons are given?

4. Comparisons are often made of blacks to other oppressed groups in the United States. After reading this argument, do you think such comparisons are fair? Why?

The Trees Theory of Big City Riots

rudimentary: basic; elementary
bellicose: warlike
diverge: lead away from

From Donald Bourgeois, "Recreation and the Inner City Crisis," *Journal of Health, Physical Education, and Recreation,* June 1969, pp. 21–22. Reprinted by permission of the American Association for Health, Physical Education, and Recreation.

susceptible: having a weakness for
reservoir: storage place
authentic: genuine, real
retrospect: looking backward

[1] In the summer [of 1967] 40 cities had had riots, and in the summer [of 1968] 80 cities had had riots; St. Louis remained without a scar. Does this mean that the city of St. Louis had one of the better recreation programs in the country, or does it mean that we were lucky? We were visited by writers, Ph.D. candidates, television people, and an assortment of others, all curious to know how St. Louis had avoided having a riot. I got so tired of answering their questions that I drew up a list of 16 reasons why St. Louis had not had a riot. It ranged from the fact that we had a winning baseball team to the fact that we had lots of trees . . .

[2] I'd be willing to wager, just on the basis of observation of cities I've visited, that St. Louis has more trees per capita than most cities in the United States. My research hasn't extended to this point thus far, but what I have discovered is enlightening.

[3] Two Dutch scientists, Adrian Kortlandt and J. Van Zon, of Amsterdam University, report that they have observed a rudimentary form of organized warfare among chimpanzees living on open grassland in East Africa. According to their study this demonstrates how man, the aggressor, may have diverged from more peaceful ape-like ancestors by leaving the forests for open plains. The study, based on six years of observation in East Africa, emphasizes the dramatic effects of a different environment on behavior and cultural patterns. According to Kortlandt, living in a forest encourages a more pacific and vegetarian way of life, and encourages climbing and walking on all fours. Open grassland, on the other hand, appears to encourage the development of aggressive hunting behavior and the use of weapons, which of course, demands walking on two legs to free the forelimbs. A forest environment tends to "dehumanize" apes, whereas open grassland "humanizes" them.

[4] Further transplanting the findings as they apply to humans, I feel that man's bellicose tendencies increase or decrease depending on whether he lives in a cement jungle or a forest of trees.

[5] Why do trees have this pacifying effect? First of all, men like trees. They write books, poems, and songs about trees. As boys, they climb them, and as men, they use them for fuel, shelter, and food. What is it that makes us all love trees so much?

[6] Scientists tell us now that there is a scientific basis for our feelings. These learned men have concluded that since the beginning of life on earth, there has been an increasing ratio of oxygen to hydrogen—that is, until recently . . . Trees are the greatest producers of oxygen and the greatest users of carbon-dioxide, which makes them doubly useful. Air pollution, therefore, is not caused solely through the spread of pollutants by automobiles and

industries, but also by virtue of the absence of trees. Notice how much worse the air is polluted in the downtown area than in your home community. Trees are protecting you and providing you with more of the life-giving oxygen and removing from the air you breathe, the carbon-dioxide killer air.

[7] Just as any animal thrashes about in the throes of death when the threat of suffocation approaches, so too, do ghetto dwellers in a treeless community struggle for air. Oxygen gives strength, alertness, and awareness. It wakes you up, and stimulates you. It makes you feel alive, happy, and gay. Absence of oxygen gives you the blues, makes you drowsy and more susceptible to "following orders" or "taking suggestions." Without sufficient oxygen, there's a feeling of "not being with it" and a general "I don't feel good, and don't know why" attitude.

[8] I conclude, therefore, that the absence of trees in ghettos has been a contributing factor in big city riots, because of insufficient oxygen in the atmosphere. The presence of most ghettos near the places of highly polluted air and the absence of trees, has produced a kind of permanent ghetto odor, caused not by the people who live there, but by the lack of trees, their air purifiers.

[9] Accepting these hypotheses, it becomes obvious that trees are a necessity, not a luxury. Indeed, trees are pacifiers of men and purifiers of air and one must therefore agree with the trees theory. But how did St. Louis come to have so many trees?

[10] Dick Gregory, who grew up in St. Louis, says, "Years ago when we were kids we used to celebrate Arbor Day by planting trees. Every youngster was given his own seedling to plant and we all went out and planted trees. I can take you today and show you where I used to live and 'my' tree."

[11] "I watched it grow and took care of it. Practically everybody had his own tree. It was kind of what you might call a status thing."

[12] Man has always used trees as protection from the weather. The shade is traditionally sought in summer, and the tree foliage is a wind breaker and protector from the harsher elements. Dick Gregory says, however, that the tree has an added social significance for black people. "When my people were slaves or field hands in the South," says Gregory, "they used to see the white master or boss sitting under a shade tree sipping a mint julep. All their lives they dreamed of being able to sit back and relax under some tree enjoying the shade and a cool drink. It doesn't matter whether the cat's been out working or just hanging on some corner, 'cause when early evening time comes he wants to do his thing under that tree."

[13] The analysis is borne out by an observation of ghetto neighborhoods where there are trees. When the afternoon sun starts to set and the heat of the day is at its oppressive worst, you can find the same scene repeated over and over: Transistor radios blaring, beer or lemonade handy, and folks relaxing under a tree. It's a familiar scene, but one which has great meaning.

[14] In the city of St. Louis, the so called "hot spots" are all treeless. Wherever the city fathers have taken the ax to the trees and replaced them with

brick and concrete, they've had and will continue to have trouble. The most volatile areas have only open grassland and concrete walks. The trees are gone—and with them their reservoir of benefits.

[15] I expect that some governmental agency official hearing about this will embark on a study of those cities which have had riots to determine the authenticity of the trees theory. (They've already studied the effects of a hot pennant race after it was pointed out that one year American League cities had more riots than National League towns.) Then after the trees theory is proved correct we'll have a "Trees in Town" program, and every living soul will be exhorted to solve the tensions in the cities by planting trees. Imagine slogans like "This is Brotherhood Week. Plant a tree." "Woodman, spare that tree," will become a favorite song, and letters will be signed "Very treely yours."

DISCUSSION

1. This argument is developed in a lighthearted way. How can you tell that the writer is not entirely serious in proposing it?

2. Imagine for the moment that the writer meant to be taken seriously. Would you have any objection to his argument? If so, what is it?

3. All the following ideas are used in the article:
   a. Men like trees.
   b. Trees enrich the oxygen supply.
   c. Trees have long been associated with leisure.
   d. Actual experience in St. Louis proves the trees theory.

   What support backs up each of these statements? How sound is the support? Which statements do you find acceptable? Why?

4. Prediction of consequences is used near the end to do two things. What are they?

5. Is Dick Gregory acceptable as an authority on trees? on ghetto life? on St. Louis? Why or why not?

6. An extension of this theory is the idea that environment is extremely important in determining human happiness. Can trees be taken as representative of all the material comforts that make life easier? Can you think of a part of your own surroundings that would stand for this purpose better than trees? Write a paragraph explaining it.

Introductions and Conclusions for Persuasion

In persuasive papers, more than in other kinds of writing, good introductions are very important. The first paragraph needs to be exciting enough, or interesting enough, that readers who do not share the writer's belief will want to read on. It's true that many of us like best to read arguments we already agree with, but if persuasive writing is going to have any real effect, it must appeal to people whose opinions might be changed by the reasons the writer gives.

A successful introduction can open with a lively and astonishing example, as Shearer does; it can begin with some frightening statistics, as Nader does; or it can begin, as Bagdikian does, with a flat statement so obvious that the reader wonders, "Why would anybody say that?" and keeps on reading to find out. Some writers begin with a provocative question—Why hasn't St. Louis had any riots—and assume that readers will be curious to know. Whatever the method used, a good introduction will find some way to catch the reader's interest, and once his interest is caught, he will be more receptive toward soundly supported reasons.

The ending of a persuasive paper is almost as important as the beginning. The conclusion is the writer's last chance, and he will probably want to do more than just repeat his reasons or his main idea. He may want to remind his readers forcefully, as Nader does, that we are already forty years behind; he may want to make his argument stick in the reader's mind by a neat turn of words, such as Shearer uses; or he may want to end with one final compelling example. However he does it, a good conclusion will clinch his argument.

Dishpan Hands

lubricate: oil
embellishments: extra things
gullible: easily deceived

[1] The world of cosmetics advertising is a strange one. A girl can spend her holiday on the deck of a sailboat beating into a ten-knot breeze—or so one would judge by the slant of the deck—without disturbing a hair of her well-sprayed head. A previously

First example: obviously unlikely

Second example: just as

By the editors of *Consumer Reports, The Medicine Show,* Some Plain Truths about Popular Remedies for Common Ailments; Consumers Union, Rev. 1963, pp. 187–188. Reprinted by permission of Consumers Union.

lonesome male suddenly has to fight off the feminine pursuers after he slicks down his unruly hair with a magic cream. In the commercials for another product the cream, in turn, becomes "that greasy kid stuff" in the he-man atmosphere of the locker room. In this remarkable world, you are invited to lubricate the skin with a product whose prime action removes fats and oils (*Dove* detergent bar). You can be tranquillized by a simple anti-perspirant ("Ice Blue" *Secret*). And you can cure dishpan hands by washing dishes (*Ivory Liquid*).

[2] All these exaggerations are embellishments attributed for promotional purposes to products of basically limited usefulness. Common sense says the products cannot possibly do all that is claimed for them. Why, then, does not the Federal Trade Commission step in?

[3] The answer is simple if the remedy is not. The FTC must *prove* an advertising claim to be false before banning it. With cosmetic claims this raises many problems. For one thing, most cosmetics claims cannot be proved, either true or false. What researcher would care to find proof, for example, of the claim that a cosmetic can make your body "a scented column of silken smoothness and your presence a sheer delight"?

• • •

[4] There is no ready answer to the ethical questions posed by the general acceptance of gross deception in cosmetics promotion. But there is perhaps some comfort in the thought that a mind well supplied with reliable information is less likely to be gullible.

Sidenotes:

unlikely

Third example: contradicts the second
In "this remarkable world" (an echo of the first sentence) there are open contradictions
Skin oiled with an oil remover
Dishpan hands cured by putting them in a dishpan
Interest-rousing question rests firmly on the 6 examples

Question answered

Point underlined by another example

Strong concluding sentence

DISCUSSION

1. This selection contains only the introduction and the conclusion of a somewhat longer article. Which do you think is the more effective, the introduction or the conclusion? Why? How well do the introduction and the conclusion fit together?

2. What is the "ethical question" mentioned in paragraph 4? In what sense is the problem contradictory?

3. What is the relationship between the concluding question and the sentence that follows it (paragraph 4)?

4. Using the introduction and the conclusion that are given here, find new and up-to-date examples that could be used in the body of the paper.

5. Using another group of advertisements—for washing machine detergents, headache remedies, or drinks, for instance—write an introduction and a conclusion similar to those in this article.

The Automobile Scandal

inestimable: too large to be estimated
deprivation: missing out on something good
Medea: Legendary Greek queen so bent on revenge that she killed her children
trauma: great shock
ravages: vicious attacks
viability: ability to continue and flourish
jeopardize: put in danger
gross national product: the total value of all goods and services sold in the U.S. in one year
carnage: slaughter of many people
remuneration: pay

[1] For over half a century the automobile has brought death, injury, and the most inestimable sorrow and deprivation to millions of people. With Medea-like intensity, this mass trauma began rising sharply four years ago, reflecting new and unexpected ravages by the motor vehicle. A 1959 Department of Commerce report projected that 51,000 persons would be killed by automobiles in 1975. That figure will probably be reached in 1965, a decade ahead of schedule.

[2] A transportation specialist, Wilfred Owen, wrote in 1946, "There is little question that the public will not tolerate for long an annual traffic toll of forty to fifty thousand fatalities." Time has shown Owen to be wrong. Unlike aviation, marine, or rail transportation, the highway transport system can inflict tremendous casualties and property damage without in the least affecting the viability of the system. Plane crashes, for example, jeopardize the attraction of flying for potential passengers and therefore strike at the heart

From Ralph Nader, *Unsafe at Any Speed,* Grossman Publishers, Inc. Reprinted by permission of the publisher.

of the air transport economy. They motivate preventative efforts. The situation is different on the roads.

[3] Highway accidents were estimated to have cost this country in 1964, $8.3 billion in property damage, medical expenses, lost wages, and insurance overhead expenses. Add an equivalent sum to comprise roughly the indirect costs and the total amounts to over two per cent of the gross national product. But these are not the kind of costs which fall on the builders of motor vehicles (excepting a few successful law suits for negligent construction of the vehicle) and thus do not pinch the proper foot. Instead, the costs fall to users of vehicles, who are in no position to dictate safer automobile designs.

[4] In fact, the gigantic costs of the highway carnage in this country support a service industry. A vast array of services—medical, police, administrative, legal, insurance, automotive repair, and funeral—stand equipped to handle the direct and indirect consequences of accident-injuries. Traffic accidents create economic demands for these services running into billions of dollars. It is in the post-accident response that lawyers and physicians and other specialists labor. This is where the remuneration lies and this is where the talent and energies go. Working in the area of prevention of these casualties earns few fees. Consequently our society has an intricate organization to handle direct and indirect aftermaths of collisions. But the true mark of a humane society must be what it does about *prevention* of accident injuries, not the cleaning up of them afterward . . .

[5] Decades ago legislation was passed, changing the patterns of private business investments to accommodate more fully the safety value on railroads, in factories, and more recently on ships and aircraft. In transport, apart from the motor vehicle, considerable progress has been made in recognizing the physical integrity of the individual. There was the period when railroad workers were killed by the thousands and the editor of *Harper's* could say late in the last century: "So long as brakes cost more than trainmen, we may expect the present sacrificial method of car-coupling to be continued." But injured trainmen did cause the railroads some operating dislocations; highway victims cost the automobile companies next to nothing and the companies are not obliged to make use of developments in science technology that have demonstrably opened up opportunities for greater safety than any existing safety features lying unused on the automobile companies' shelves . . .

[6] The time has not come to discipline the automobile for safety; that time came over four decades ago. But that is not cause to delay any longer what should have been accomplished in the nineteen-twenties.

DISCUSSION

1. Is the first sentence the main idea? Is the writer concerned with the extent of our highway misery? With the fact that little has been done about it? With the desperate need to make cars safer soon? Defend your answers.

2. Why does the writer offer information about airplanes and railroads? Is his point convincing? Why or why not?

3. Do the statistics and the use of authority support a set of reasons? How?

4. How does the introduction capture your interest? Does the reference to a figure in Greek mythology help or hinder for the average reader? Why?

5. The conclusion gives the fleeting impression of saying just the opposite of what the writer has been maintaining through the article. Why has this approach been taken?

6. This selection first appeared in the Preface to Nader's book, *Unsafe at Any Speed*. The book was meant to arouse the general public about car safety, and certainly it did. Much of the language Nader uses, however, is very formal. Consider these three versions of the same idea:
   a. With Medea-like intensity, this mass trauma began rising sharply four years ago, reflecting new and unexpected ravages by the motor vehicle.
   b. With fierce intensity, car accidents began rising unexpectedly four years ago, producing new and shocking levels of suffering and loss.
   c. In the last four years the number of car accidents has shot way up, killing and injuring thousands more people.

   Which sentence shocks and upsets you the most? Which do you think would have the greatest effect on people in your neighborhood? Which would have affected Congressmen the most? Why?

7. Find three other sentences in which the style seems very formal and rewrite them in simpler language. Which version do your fellow students prefer?

Detroit's Double-Talk on Safety

appalling: shocking; shameful
lavishly: with no concern for expense
adhering: sticking to
incite: stir up

[1] During the debate on the bill recently passed by Congress and signed by the President setting Federal safety standards for the production of auto-

From Jeffrey O'Connell, "Detroit's Double-Talk on Safety," in the January 1967 issue of *The Progressive*. Copyright © 1967. Reprinted by permission.

mobiles, Congress rejected a provision calling for criminal penalties against the car makers for willful failure to comply with the new standards. Denying there was any need for criminal penalties, Senator Philip A. Hart, Michigan Democrat, said, "There isn't a line in the record that points to willful misconduct [by the car makers]."

[2] In point of fact, for years there have been a great many lines of testimony in the *Congressional Record* and the record of hearings on Capitol Hill, pointing to the car makers' willful ignoring of safety . . .

[3] As appalling an example as there is of the car makers' willful misconduct with regard to safety is the manner of advertising their product to teen-agers . . .

[4] The automobile manufacturers have often, and publicly, stated that the reason for teen-agers' frightful driving records is their "aggressive personality traits, unsound and immature judgment, lack of cooperative attitude, and willingness to take undue risks." The industry has been so aware of this that it has heavily supported driver training for teen-agers and published pamphlets designed to encourage safe, courteous driving habits on the part of young people.

[5] But at the same time, while blaming the traffic carnage on reckless driving and trying to encourage safe driving habits, the car makers have also spent lavishly to encourage our worst drivers—the young—to drive recklessly. They do this by publishing glossy, glamourous advertisements designed to appeal to youngsters who read such magazines as *Road Track, Hot Rod, Motor Trend,* and *Car and Driver* . . .

[6] How the industry works both sides of the street—the "safety education" side and the sell-more-cars side—is evident from the following comparisons of messages from good-driving pamphlets distributed by car makers with those appearing in teen-age hot rod magazines.

[7] A General Motors safe driving pamphlet advises:

"For infantile motorists . . . with an unmuffled exhaust, normal driving is, of course, unthinkable. The engine must be revved up at stops, not idled. Starts must resemble a successful missile launching."

[8] But a Buick (General Motors) teen-age car advertisement offers temptation:

"Ever prodded a throttle with 445 feet of torque coiled tightly at the end of it? Do that with one of these and you can start billing yourself as the Human Cannon Ball."

[9] From a Ford safe driving manual:

"Take it easy when you pull away from a curb. Jack-rabbit starts are for Jack-rabbits or for a supervised drag strip."

[10] But from a Mercury (Ford) teen-age car advertisement:

". . . For get-away, there's a new 390 four barrel V-8 with a high lift cam. Quite a start. A console-mounted transmission. (The optional four speed manual is especially geared for a glazing get-away.)"

[11] From a Chrysler Corporation safe driving pamphlet:

"Proper driving attitudes and habits, including the adhering to the rules of the road and driving with courtesy and consideration for others, are every driver's responsibility."

[12] But from a Dodge (Chrysler) teen-age car advertisement:

"Bring on the Mustangs, Wildcats, Impalas . . . We'll even squash a few Spyders while we are at it. Dodge has made it a little harder to survive in the asphalt jungle. They just uncaged the Coronet."

[13] Unfortunately, the car makers, through their irresponsible advertisements in teen-age car magazines, are proving how the American car makers are deliberately working to make our highways *unsafe* for all Americans. For Detroit's advertising of high power and jet-like speed puts on the highways, in the hands of youths and other drivers incited to recklessness, the cars that deliver unsafe speeds and attitudes—along with death and injuries.

[14] Thus, contrary to Senator Hart's statement, there *are* items in the "record" that "point to willful misconduct" by the automobile industry.

[15] If a motorist drives carelessly and kills someone, he can be criminally prosecuted for manslaughter. But if a manufacturer purposely produces cars which violate government safety standards, he is not prosecuted, even for a misdemeanor. Not only is the car maker's offense often more serious in itself, but it is multiplied thousands of times, with every model thus produced.

[16] This double standard for treatment of the driver and treatment of the car maker should be ended by amendment of the Federal Traffic Safety Act of 1966.

DISCUSSION

1. The main point of the article is the writer's disagreement with Senator Hart of Michigan. What is O'Connell saying about Hart's opinion?

2. What method does the writer use in trying to show that Senator Hart was wrong?

3. Which seems to you to be the most "willful" misconduct on the part of the auto makers: carelessness in design and construction as emphasized by Nader, or inconsistency between officially sponsored safety programs and advertising campaigns as stressed here?

4. Can you think of ways in which power and speed built into an automobile could be coupled with an ad sincerely aimed at promoting safety on the roads? Try your hand at writing such an ad.

5. Can you think of any reason for questioning Senator Hart's objectivity? If so, what is it?

6. Check recent issues of the magazines mentioned in this article to see whether car advertising has changed. Does it emphasize safety? Speed?

Something else? Detroit advertising as it relates to the topic of safety? Report on your findings.

7. What about gasoline companies? Remember slogans such as "A Tiger in Your Tank"? Can you recall any that emphasize either speed or safety? Which kind is more common?

8. How effective do you think the conclusion of the article is? If you find it effective, what makes it so?

The Fireworks Scandal

tranquil: peaceful
holocaust: great, fiery disaster
shrouded: concealed; wrapped like a dead person
pyrotechnics: fancy name for fireworks
piously: self-righteously
exude: give off
intermittently: now and then
unscrupulous: without conscience

[1] In a wooded hollow two miles east of the tranquil little town of North East, Md., sparrows flitted from roof to roof of seven tar-paper-covered shacks, which formed a semicircle around a larger building. Suddenly the main building erupted like a massive firecracker, sending flame and smoke billowing into the azure April sky. On a nearby hillside, Mrs. Vernon Kincaid rushed to check the windows of her home. "This one didn't blow the windows out like it did a couple of years ago," she said afterward.

[2] For the second time since January, the Mid-State Fireworks Manufacturing Co. was rocked by an explosion. Several hours later, after the fire had been extinguished, 30 acres of woodland lay charred and smoking. A tangle of blackened pipes marked the spot where the main plant had stood. Three men lay in hospital beds with severe burns. Three women were in the Baltimore morgue, dead of "partial cremation."

[3] This explosion, if not as big as the one Mrs. Kincaid remembered two years earlier, was worse than the January blast which had killed only two people. Yet the seven shacks, each loaded with gunpowder, had miraculously survived the holocaust, and Mid-State continued to produce fireworks until, four days later, still another fire injured three more workers.

Reprinted from "The Fireworks Scandal," by Jack Anderson, in *Parade* (June 29, 1969), by permission of the publisher.

[4] Of course, most fireworks manufacturers operate strictly within the law and produce "safe and sane" fireworks by federal standards. These accidents are but footnotes to the sordid story of the fireworks industry, which has turned the Fourth of July, our proudest national holiday, into a national scandal. Across the country, year in and year out, fireworks users are burned, maimed, blinded and dismembered. Based on past records, the National Fire Protection Association estimates that fireworks used to celebrate Independence Day this week will cause 5000 injuries (at least four of them fatal) and 1400 fires. Most of the victims, sadly, will be children and teenagers.

[5] Yet the industry has done little to protect the public from the shady manufacturers and seedy dealers, whose operations are shrouded in acrid clouds of gunpowder smoke. They traffic in illegal and substandard fireworks, which are a hazard to the youngsters who shoot them off.

[6] Two national organizations—American Pyrotechnics Association and Pyrotechnic Distributors Association—represent most major fireworks producers and distributors. An APA spokesman piously called these the "responsible members of the industry." Yet the membership rosters of both associations are loaded with unprincipled manufacturers and dealers who violate the law or stay barely within its loopholes.

[7] The APA's statements exude an air of innocence. Compare them, however, with recent happenings.

[8] APA: "Class B fireworks (cherry bombs, M-80's, silver salutes, bulldogs, etc.) are illegal now. The situation is pretty well in hand."

[9] Fact: On Feb. 28, two teenagers climbed atop a Standard Oil tank in La Mirada, Calif., and dropped in a cherry bomb. They liked the resounding boom and dropped another. The fumes ignited, buckling the top of the tank and destroying 14,000 barrels of oil. The boys miraculously escaped injury.

[10] APA: "We operate under Food and Drug Administration regulations. They have eliminated hazardous items."

[11] Fact: On April 14, Gary Thomas, 21, of Cleveland, held a firecracker too long, lost the tips of two fingers. A few months earlier, a 14-year-old Wingate, N.C., youth was literally blown apart when 65 cherry bombs exploded on his person.

[12] APA: "Since the FDA cracked down, Class B items are hard to get. They are in short supply."

[13] Fact: Last Fourth of July, a 17-year-old Pittsburg, Kans., girl was killed and her companion seriously injured when a tossed M-80 fell back into their pickup truck into a pile of fireworks. The truck was demolished. About the same time, an automobile trunkload of heavy fireworks exploded in St. Cloud, Minn., killing an occupant of the car, age 24, and two bystanders—a girl, 4, and a boy, 19.

[14] Both the Food and Drug Administration and National Fire Protection Association claim that, despite their efforts, incidents like these are on the rise. Most of the serious accidents, incidentally, are caused by bootleg fireworks.

[15] The 1967 Hazardous Substances Act, which bans outright all fireworks except "properly labeled" Class C items, gave FDA the authority to crack down on illegal fireworks sales. Within a week after the law went into effect, the agency seized over $16,700 worth of bootlegged fireworks in South Carolina. Food and Drug officer Dale Miller told PARADE that FDA made over 50 seizures in the past year. One netted about $12,000 worth of bootleg fireworks.

[16] Still, the illegal fireworks traffic continues to increase. Why? Three loopholes in the 1967 law are big enough for the bootleggers to drive their unmarked trucks through. First, the law permits the sale of explosive items for "agricultural use." Cherry bombs or large salutes are attached at intervals to a long, slow-burning rope fuse which is then lit and left to boom intermittently—effective for keeping crows out of the cornfield. Second, "public displays" are permitted under the law and, third, the armed services use millions of fireworks each year to simulate sounds of the battlefield in training camps.

[17] These loopholes provide ready-made alibis for unscrupulous manufacturers. Thus "agricultural sales" run into the millions of dollars each year—enough to turn the nation's cornfields into a Vietnam. The FDA recently made a seizure of cherry bombs manufactured by an APA member: they were labeled "pest control bombs."

[18] Today, 18 states ban fireworks altogether, allowing only caps and pistols. Eight others allow only the popular sparkler—which, incidentally, reaches temperatures up to 2000 degrees Fahrenheit when ignited. The rest are "Class C" states; they permit the sale and use of almost all fireworks not banned by federal law. The APA, meanwhile, is working diligently but quietly to revoke or amend those state laws which forbid fireworks.

[19] Over the last 50 years, fireworks accidents have killed approximately 4000 Americans—just about as many as died in the Revolutionary War. The latter died for *independence,* most of the others died celebrating independence.

DISCUSSION

1. Why does the writer begin with a specific example? Explain how each of these words or phrases help to make the example more vivid:
   "tranquil little town"
   "tar-paper-covered shacks"
   "erupted like a massive firecracker"

2. Why does Mrs. Kincaid's comment at the end of paragraph 1 make the details given in paragraph 2 seem even worse?

3. Which of these sentences comes closest to expressing the main idea of the article?
   a. Of course, most fireworks manufacturers operate strictly within the

law and produce "safe and sane" fireworks by federal standards
(paragraph 4).

b. The fireworks industry . . . has turned the Fourth of July, our proudest
   national holiday, into a national scandal (paragraph 4).

c. The industry has done little to protect the public from the shady manufacturers and seedy dealers, whose operations are shrouded in acrid
   clouds of gunpowder smoke (paragraph 5).

d. The APA . . . is working diligently but quietly to revoke or amend
   those state laws which forbid fireworks (paragraph 18).

e. Over the last 50 years, fireworks accidents have killed approximately
   4000 Americans—just about as many as died in the Revolutionary
   War (paragraph 19).

Defend your choice by referring to the article.

4. Do you think this article is an attack on the pyrotechnic associations?
   In deciding on your answer, consider the first sentence of paragraph 4,
   paragraphs 5 through 13, and the last sentence of paragraph 18. Does
   the writer make any statement about the associations that is not supported
   by fact? If so, what?

5. According to the author, why are illegal sales increasing in spite of FDA
   seizures?

6. Is the conclusion effective? Why or why not?

Guaranteed Income

persistent: hard to get rid of
burgher: businessman
destitute: entirely without money
subsidy: grant of money
appropriated: voted money for
circumvent: get around
cumbersome: awkward and slow

[1] The poor don't have enough money. Millions of
words and countless hours of agonizing by generations of economists have gone into exquisitely com-
plicated plans to solve this problem. Maybe the time   Main idea sentence
has come to give the poor money. The most practical

way to attack poverty in America is to guarantee every family an annual income of $5,000.

[2] The idea of assuring income threatens something dear to Americans—the persistent notion that each man, armed with hoe and axe, is still master of his own livelihood. But the notion resists the harsh reality that a family in the city collapses without a certain level of cash, and so do the chances for fruitful re-employment.

[3] The notion also overlooks history. In 1914 Henry Ford shocked respectable burghers when he guaranteed five dollars a day for his workers. Solemn economists and businessmen predicted that workmen would plunge into orgies of drunkenness, crazy spending and a refusal to work a full week. Yet Henry Ford probably did more to insure growing prosperity with that act than he did with his revolution in mass production.

[4] The country, in fact, already guarantees income, not for the destitute but for the millions of comfortable Americans who quietly accept Social Security, FHA money, agricultural subsidies. Guaranteeing their prosperity has become a complicated game of self-deception. Year by year, in bits and pieces, a crazy quilt of social legislation has been crafted for them, those who have powerful lobbies—big labor, big business, big farmers. But there are few guarantees for the voiceless—the farm laborer, the unorganized worker, the small businessman.

[5] Can we afford a $5,000 minimum income? The maximum cost of the program would take a smaller proportion of the American gross national product than is appropriated for family payments in many European countries, including the most free enterprising, West Germany. It would probably not exceed the money cost of the war in Vietnam.

[6] Payments could circumvent the cumbersome welfare administration. There would be no means test, no time-consuming detective work. Families would make out income-tax forms, like the quarterly declaration of estimated income. If their income fell under the guaranteed minimum, they would receive the difference in weekly or biweekly checks. Computerized W-2 income forms made out by every employer would permit inexpensive and impersonal

First opposition argument: shown to be out-of-date

Second opposition argument: proved false by historical *example*

Reason 1: we already guarantee some incomes; brief *examples*

Reason 2: we can afford it; comparison of costs

Reason 3: it would be more efficient—*prediction;* details of how it would work

random checking to catch cheating and errors.
[7] Would America become a nation of sloths?
It might, but that is doubtful. Real striving today
comes not from those who are so poor that they
are out of the system, but from those who are inside
the system, beginning to control their income and
taste its benefits.

Third opposition argu-
ment: proved false by
prediction

[8] Some believe that such a guaranteed salary
would create masses of new jobs in services that
society needs but that are not profitable enough to
support the worker: homemakers in homes with a
sick parent, day-care workers, visitors for invalids.
Hand crafts and hand repairs are not profitable in
competition with mass-production automated machinery; but people could work at them if their
basic living were already provided. The guaranteed
income might allow us to abandon the minimum-
wage law, so that much work could be done at low
rates if the worker preferred to do it.

Reason 4: it might re-
vive hand crafts—*pre-
diction*

[9] Further, the guaranteed income might help solve
one of our economy's worst problems—getting people
to go where the jobs are. For when a family is sure
of enough to get by on, it will more readily take the
chance of moving to a place where there are jobs.

R e a s o n 5 : p e o p l e
wouldn't be afraid to
move where jobs were
—*prediction*

[10] There are fears, of course, that more money
for the poor will encourage larger families. In the
60 countries that have family allowances based on
family size, all the evidence is that the money has
not made families grow—not even in countries where
the allowance was started deliberately to encourage
child-bearing! Canada has the most generous of
family allowances, and its birth rate and ours have
risen and fallen together.

Fourth opposition ar-
gument: proved false
by *examples*

[11] Experience indicates dependable income actually encourages the poor to budget. Present poor
families never can plan. In rent, or food, or medicine, or clothes there is always an emergency. And
every purchase must first be passed upon by the welfare worker. A new coat? Ask the welfare worker.
Need eyeglasses? Ask the welfare worker. Mosquito
netting for the baby? Ask the welfare worker. How
much money next month? Next year? Ask the welfare worker. Welfare makes budgeting senseless and
impossible.

Reason 6: would en-
courage budgeting—
prediction

[12] Mrs. Louis Robinson is a 39-year-old Negro

Extended *example,*

woman in Issaquena County, Miss. She and her husband had been earning a total cash income of about
$15 a week to support their 10 children. As share-
croppers and laborers, they lived for years on credit,
plus what they could grow in a garden. Then Mrs.
Robinson got a job as a teacher's aide in a Head
Start Class, at $60 a week. It occurred to me that
not many Americans experience a 400 percent increase in income, so not long ago I looked at how
they spent their new money.

showing effects of in-
creased income:

[13] The first week the family splurged: quarts of
ice cream, gallons of orange juice, an unending flow
of milk and soft drinks. And meat.

(a) temporary splurging

[14] "Then about the third week," Mrs. Robinson
said, "we began paying back some old debts, eleven
dollars and ninety-five cents on the Deep-Freeze
we bought one year when the crops were better, and
on stores where we had accounts. My husband and
I, we plan now about clothes and what kind of
things we can do to the house.

(b) paying old debts

[15] "Funny thing. We can buy lots cheaper now.
We used to have to buy where we had credit, and
in those stores you just had to take what they had
at the price they set. When you have cash, you just
shop till you get what you want. Why, I get almost
twice as much chicken for my money as I used to.
And at a white store.

(c) saving money by
paying cash

[16] "And you know? After we leave the white
store, the owner says, 'You-all come back.' They
never said that before."

(d) gaining greater com-
munity respect

DISCUSSION

1. The idea of a guaranteed national income is controversial. How does the
   author use the introduction to get the reader on his side? Why does the
   author, right after his first paragraph, take up the arguments of the
   opposition?

2. What kind of statistical evidence would you use to support the argument
   in paragraph 5 that we can afford it? Would you think that the author
   means we can afford both the war in Vietnam *and* a guaranteed income?
   Why?

3. From your own experience, are you inclined to agree or disagree with
   paragraph 7, that real striving comes "from those who are inside the

system, beginning to control their income and taste its benefits"? Can you think of specific examples of people who do control their incomes? Of people who do not? Which individuals would you say do more "real striving"? Why?

4. Paragraph 8 suggests, "The guaranteed income might allow us to abandon the minimum wage law." Which would be easier to enforce, guaranteed income or minimum wage law? Which would do more for poor people? What do you mean by "more"? Which would you favor, or would you prefer both? Why?

5. Is Mrs. Louis Robinson a fair example? Why or why not? Does Mrs. Robinson earn $5,000 a year? Who takes care of her ten children while she works? Do you earn $5,000 a year? Are there any similarities or differences between your responsibilities and Mrs. Robinson's?

6. This argument ends with a vivid example rather than a conclusion that restates the main idea. Write a conclusion that summarizes the main points made and restates the main idea. Do you think the article is more effective with or without your conclusion? Why?

The Train Don't Stop Here Anymore

chronically: constantly
flourish: be healthy and successful
impetus: motive; encouragement

[1] If you were a regular traveler between New York and Washington, stranded at Kennedy airport for two days in February's blizzard, or a weary businessman in more ordinary weather circling over LaGuardia waiting for your turn to land at the chronically over-loaded airport, your thoughts might turn to the good old days when you made the trip by train. Trains might look even better if you anticipated that long crawl into New York City along traffic-choked highways still ahead of you. Of course trains, these days, aren't what they used to be. They don't run as often, and the service isn't very good. But even the Secretary of Transportation, John A. Volpe, is beginning to think that perhaps, especially over short distances, train service could flourish again. The Department has gone so far as to establish, with the Penn

From "Roundup Items" in *Trans*-Action, June 1969. Copyright © *Trans*-Action Magazine, New Brunswick, New Jersey.

Central Railroad, an experimental, high-speed, electric-powered train that makes the run from Washington to New York in a little less than three hours. [2] The impetus for this experiment may well be the success that Western Europeans have had with a special, high speed rail network called the Trans Europe Express. According to Albert S. Chapman, geographic attaché to the American Embassy in Bonn, Germany, the TEE is a model that we in the United States would do well to emulate. (*Economic Geography,* October 1968)

[3] Most TEE customers are businessmen traveling between major European cities. TEE offers them speed (87 miles per hour on the level), generous seating and baggage space, and scheduling for their maximum convenience.

[4] Frequent travelers choose these comfortable, weather-free trains, Chapman believes, if the overall travel time from one central city to another is about the same as by plane. To compare air travel with TEE times, Chapman has added two hours to the announced air time between two cities. This extra time includes surface travel between the downtown air terminal and the airport, time for checking in at the airport and for recovering baggage and clearing customs at the destination. Travel from Paris to Brussels (193 miles) and to Liege (228 miles) is faster by TEE than by plane. Basel, Lausanne, and Lyon, all about 300 miles from Paris, can be reached almost as quickly by TEE as by plane. TEE service is faster than plane service between Amsterdam and Brussels (147 miles) and between Amsterdam and Cologne (166 miles). Overall, Chapman found that places within 163 miles of major traffic centers were usually served more quickly by TEE than by scheduled airlines. The figures on TEE passengers also suggest that for distances up to 300 miles train service offers enough advantages to be competitive with air travel. Beyond 300 miles, the speed of air travel outweighs other factors.

[5] The implications for the United States are clear. The experimental Metroliner can cover the 227 miles between Washington and New York in just about as much time as it takes to get from downtown Washington to Manhattan by plane and cab. It costs less, too. Air and cab fare is approximately $25; cabs and a coach ticket on the Metroliner come to about $16. Similar service, with faster and more comfortable trains, could be successful, Chapman predicts, between New York and Boston (230 miles), Chicago and Detroit (284 miles), Houston and San Antonio (206 miles), Chicago and St. Louis (286 miles), etc.

DISCUSSION

1. What specific details does the writer use in the introduction to help the reader see the situation more vividly?

2. What two comparisons are made in paragraph 1? What is the purpose of the first comparison? How does the second comparison anticipate the arguments of the opposition and get rid of them?

3. What authorities are used in this essay? What is there in their backgrounds that make them authorities?

4. What main example does the writer use? What reason is supported by this example?

5. What statistics does he use? What reasons are supported by these statistics?

6. What prediction does he make? What reasons are supported by this prediction?

7. What is the main idea of this article? Is it implied or stated? Write a concluding paragraph for the essay, making sure that your conclusion does state (or restate) the main idea clearly.

Two Ways To Get There: Serious and Satirical

In some of the earlier essays, writers have used a startling approach—an example, some appalling statistics, a frightening prediction—to shock their readers into paying attention. Such startling introductions often make the reader curious enough that he is prepared for the serious, carefully supported, reasons that the writer gives. For most beliefs, this method of persuading readers is probably the best: it is straightforward, orderly, and fair.

Occasionally, however, a writer doesn't give any serious reasons at all. Instead, he shows his readers how ridiculous the present situation is, or he offers some solution so absurd that we are obliged to see the absurdity in our own position. By poking fun at the way things are, by extending an accepted argument to the point of obvious silliness, he can deal with the other side more effectively than if he argued all day. When the reader laughs, his defenses are down; satire can be a devastating weapon.

In each pair of selections in the next group, one writer offers a carefully reasoned, well supported argument; another writer, whose conviction is very much the same, uses satire to make a similar point.

"It's Vicious, Undemocratic, Immoral"

arbitrarily: according to somebody's whim or fancy
grossly: extremely
self-concept: a person's idea of his own importance and ability
recourse: a way to find help
warp: turn or twist out of shape
subvert: destroy; undermine
ignoble: inferior; dishonorable

[1] Comparing one child with another and reporting this comparison in terms of letters, percentages or numerals is a vicious, undemocratic and immoral practice.

[2] As a nation we take great pride in fair play, sportsmanship, in our consideration for others, respect for the individual, taking up the battle for the underdog or the deprived because we truly care about people. We make certain that a heavyweight is matched with a heavyweight, that all of our ball-teams play in leagues that allow them a reasonable chance for success,

From John Munden, "It's Vicious, Undemocratic, Immoral," *Washington Education,* May 1968. Reprinted by permission of the author and the publisher.

even that racing cars meet certain specifications in order to compete. [3] When it comes to our public schools, though, we set aside all rules of fair play and return to the philosophy of the dark ages when one man was pitted against the other in a life or death struggle for survival. We don't bother to weigh, measure or even look at our contestants as they enter our system of education. We simply sort them off in groups, herd them into over-crowded classrooms of 30 or 40 and begin the competition for the misleading reward of a grade . . . We continue to pigeonhole children arbitrarily with an outmoded, outdated system of grading that is grossly out of tune with the needs of children and society.

[4] The system is not only unfair; it is vicious, undemocratic and immoral. It's vicious because of what it does to innocent children. By law, it forces children to attend school, it puts many or most of them in curricula where their chances for success are limited (and in some cases nonexistent), and it penalizes the children for not succeeding. The children are provided with daily evidence of the degree of their failure, and at each report period, their failures are presented in concrete form to their parents. (I say that failures are reported, knowing full well that all children don't fail, but the end-all of our education system at present seems to be the "grade.") It's sort of a competition between children and teachers who use a system of curriculum, testing, and grading as a means of categorizing those children. This, if you please, when the job of the teacher should be to teach, not to test, grade and categorize. Such categorizing has little, if anything, to do with meeting individual differences, respecting individual dignity, and leading each child to the maximum of his capacity to learn.

[5] The sad and vicious aspect of this is that after we penalize the child for not fitting our curriculum, he in turn penalizes himself for being dumb and each day his self-concept is lowered and his chance for becoming the kind of truly positive, creative and responsible citizen needed in our society is lessened . . .

[6] Our traditional comparative system of dealing with children is undemocratic because it has no regard for individual dignity. In fact, it tends to offend the dignity of most of our children, yet we live in a society which has as one of its basic tenets that of respect for the individual. It's undemocratic because a child has no recourse even when he finds a situation in school to be intolerable. He is a captive who has neither the maturity to understand nor the right to leave when he is psychologically mistreated by a system of testing and grading that is wrong. It's undemocratic simply because it denies most children the rights to happiness and success which are basic to the development of the rational, good citizen.

[7] Such a system is immoral for several reasons. It's immoral because it warps the moral values of children. It may force them to cheat, to lie, to forge names on papers, and worse, often to be dishonest with themselves in order to answer a question in the way they think the teacher wants it answered and not the way they truly feel. It subverts their basic honesty by

forcing them to seek ways of pleasing someone else rather than seeking the truth for themselves.

[8] It is time that teachers and parents look for practical ways of communicating more effectively about the progress of a child in school. We are beginning to get more and more equipment which could make the regular parent-teacher conference more effective. We could be using tape recordings made at a youngster's desk or, in some cases, television kinescopes of the child in action in the classroom so that parents might really see how their child acts and reacts. There are many other possibilities if we would simply take time to explore them.

[9] At any rate, it's time that we abolished a system described this way by John Holt in his book, *How Children Fail.*

[10] "We destroy the love of learning in children, which is so strong when they are small, by encouraging and compelling them to work for petty and contemptible rewards—gold stars, or papers marked 100 and tacked on a wall, or A's on report cards, or honor rolls, or dean's lists, Phi Beta Kappa keys—in short, for the ignoble satisfaction of feeling that they are better than someone else. We encourage them to feel the end and aim of all they do in school is nothing more than to get a good mark on a test, or to impress someone with what they seem to know. We kill not only their curiosity but their feeling that it is a good and admirable thing to be curious, so that by the age of ten most of them will not ask questions, and will show a good deal of scorn for the few who do."

[11] In its stead we should institute practices in tune with the present world, practices that more factually and accurately report the progress of a child in school, but most important, practices that respect children.

DISCUSSION

1. How does Munden use the idea of sportsmanship and fair play to introduce his argument against grades? Do you think his comparison with sports is sound? Give reasons.

2. Do you agree that the present system of grading is "out of tune" with the needs of children and society? In what way is it out of tune?

3. What specific examples from your own experience or the experience of others support the writer's idea that students are put in situations where it is difficult or impossible for them to succeed?

4. Can you think of examples that demonstrate the writer's point in paragraph 7 that the present grading system forces students to be dishonest? If so, what are they?

5. If students were not competing for grades, do you think they would continue to be interested in learning? Why or why not?

6. Munden suggests one possible substitution for grading so that parents may know about a child's progress. What would you suggest?

7. Would you like to have grades done away with in this class? Give reasons to support your answer.

8. How does Munden keep the contract made in his main idea sentence? What would be the effect of changing the order—putting paragraph 7 before paragraph 4 or 6, for instance?

The Chitling Test

concepts: ideas; ways of looking at something
topical: having to do with a certain time, and thus easily out of date

[1] It doesn't take a high IQ to recognize that intelligence tests have a built-in cultural bias that discriminates against black children. Tests designed to measure how logically a child can reason often use concepts foreign to the ghetto: a Harlem child who has never handled money or seen a farm animal, for example, might be asked a question that assumes knowledge of quarters and cows.

[2] Adrian Dove, a sociologist and a Negro, for one, knows that black children have their own culture and language that "white" tests don't take into account. He saw this clearly when he worked with white civic and business leaders after the Watts riots. "I was talking Watts language by day," he says, "and then translating it so the guys in the corporations could understand it at night." Dove then designed his own exam, the Dove Counterbalance General Intelligence Test (the "Chitling Test") with 30 multiple-choice questions, "as a half-serious idea to show that we're just not talking the same language." The test has appeared in the Negro weekly *Jet* as well as in white newspapers, but mostly, says the 38-year-old Dove, "it has been floating around underground." Some samples (see end of story for the correct answers):

    1. A "handkerchief head" is: (a) a cool cat, (b) a porter, (c) an Uncle Tom, (d) a hoddi, (e) a preacher.

    2. Which word is most out of place here? (a) splib, (b) blood, (c) gray, (d) spook, (e) black.

3. A "gas head" is a person who has a: (a) fast-moving car, (b) stable of "lace," (c) "process," (d) habit of stealing cars, (e) long jail record for arson.

4. "Down-home" (the South) today, for the average "soul brother" who is picking cotton from sunup until sundown, what is the average earning (take home) for one full day? (a) $.75, (b) $1.65, (c) $3.50, (d) $5.00, (e) $12.

5. "Bo Diddley" is a: (a) game for children, (b) down-home cheap wine, (c) down-home singer, (d) new dance, (e) Moejoe call.

6. If a pimp is up tight with a woman who gets state aid, what does he mean when he talks about "Mother's Day"? (a) second Sunday in May, (b) third Sunday in June, (c) first of every month, (d) none of these, (e) first and fifteenth of every month.

7. "Hully Gully" came from: (a) East Oakland, (b) Fillmore, (c) Watts, (d) Harlem, (e) Motor City.

8. If a man is called a "blood," then he is a (a) fighter, (b) Mexican-American, (c) Negro, (d) hungry hemophile, (e) Redman or Indian.

9. Cheap chitlings (not the kind you purchase at a frozen food counter) will taste rubbery unless they are cooked long enough. How soon can you quit cooking them to eat and enjoy them? (a) 45 minutes, (b) two hours, (c) 24 hours, (d) one week (on a low flame), (e) one hour.

10. What are the "Dixie Humming birds"? (a) part of the KKK, (b) a swamp disease, (c) a modern gospel group, (d) a Mississippi Negro paramilitary group, (e) Deacons.

11. If you throw the dice and seven is showing on the top, what is facing down? (a) seven, (b) snake eyes, (c) boxcars, (d) little Joes, (e) 11.

12. "Jet" is: (a) an East Oakland motorcycle club, (b) one of the gangs in "West Side Story," (c) a news and gossip magazine, (d) a way of life for the very rich.

13. T-Bone Walker got famous for playing what? (a) trombone, (b) piano, (c) "T-flute," (d) guitar, (e) "Hambone."*

[3] Dove, now a human-resources analyst with the Federal Bureau of the Budget in Washington, is not sure what to do next with his Chitling Test. Topical questions have to be revised and, says Dove, "working in the government I have to hustle to keep in touch with the language of the ghetto. This is an unreal world."

DISCUSSION

1. How does Dove's "intelligence" test relate to what Munden says about tests in the earlier article? What does Dove think a so-called intelligence test actually measures?

---

*Those who are not "culturally deprived" will recognize the correct answers are 1. (c), 2. (c), 3. (c), 4. (d), 5. (c), 6. (e), 7. (c), 8. (c), 9. (c), 10. (c), 11. (a), 12. (c), 13. (d).

2. Why does Dove call his test a *"counterbalance* intelligence test"?

3. When you tried your own skill on this part of the test, how many questions did you get right? What does the score you made on this test have to do with Dove's main point?

4. Which do you find more convincing, Munden's straightforward argument that the tests by which we place children are unfair, or Dove's "half-serious" example? Why does Dove say it is "half-serious"?

5. Dove himself says that ghetto language goes out of date very quickly. If you were familiar with any of these terms, which of them seem to you out-of-date?

6. Construct a five-question "intelligence test" made up of slang items in your vocabulary, to be given to people over fifty, and try the test on some of your friends. How well do people your own age do? How well do your parents do?

A World to Win

profound: deep
allege: claim
Nuremberg trials: trials conducted by the Allies at the end of World War II in which Nazi leaders were found guilty of crimes against humanity
military-industrial complex: cooperation between armed forces and business for the benefit of both
beleaguered: under attack
semantics: word meanings related to a particular subject
circumvent: get around
apocalyptic: having to do with the end of the world
ideological: according to a set of beliefs or doctrine
sufferance: permission

[1] In the last couple of years there has been student unrest in many parts of the world, in many parts of this country. Unless we are to assume that students have gone crazy, there must be some common meaning.
[2] I don't need to go far afield to look for that meaning. I am a teacher, and

From George Wald, "A World to Win" in the May 1969 issue of *The Progressive*. Copyright © 1969. Reprinted by permission of the publisher.

at Harvard I have a class of about 350 men and women—most of them freshmen and sophomores. Over these past few years I have felt increasingly that something is terribly wrong—and this year ever so much more than last. Something has gone sour, in teaching and learning. It's almost as though there were a widespread feeling that education has become irrelevant.

[3] I think I know what's the matter. This whole generation of students is beset with a profound uneasiness. What is more, I share their uneasiness.

[4] What's bothering those students? Some of them tell you it's the Vietnam War. I think the Vietnam War is the most shameful episode in the whole of American history. The concept of war crimes is an American invention. We've committed many war crimes in Vietnam; but I'll tell you something interesting about that. We were committing war crimes in World War II, even before the Nuremburg trials were held and the principle of war crimes started. The saturation bombing of German cities was a war crime, and if we had lost the war, some of our leaders might have had to answer for it. I've gone through all of that history lately, and I find that there's a gimmick in it. It isn't written out, but I think we established it by precedent. That gimmick is that if one can allege one is repelling or retaliating against an *aggression*—after that everything goes. And you see we are living in a world in which all wars are wars of defense. All War Departments are now Defense Departments. This is all part of the double talk of our time. The aggressor is always on the other side.

[5] I think we've lost in Vietnam, as a lot of other people think, too. The Vietnamese have a secret weapon. It's their willingness to die, beyond our willingness to kill. In effect they've been saying you can kill us, but you'll have to kill a lot of us, you may have to kill all of us. And thank heavens, we are not yet ready to do that. Yet we have come a long way—far enough to sicken many Americans, far enough even to sicken our fighting men.

[6] But that Vietnam War, shameful and terrible as it is, seems to me only an immediate incident in a much larger and more stubborn situation. Just after World War II, a series of new and abnormal procedures came into American life. We regarded them at the time as temporary. But those procedures have stayed with us for more than twenty years, and those students of mine have never known anything else. They think we've always had a Pentagon, a big army, a draft. But those are all new things in American life; they are incompatible with what America meant before. How many of you realize that just before World War II the entire American army including the Air Force numbered 139,000 men? Now we have 3,500,000 men under arms. I say the Vietnam War is just an immediate incident, because so long as we keep that big army, it will always find things to do. If the Vietnam War stopped tomorrow, the chances are we would be in another adventure abroad or at home before you knew it.

[7] As for the draft: Don't reform the draft—get rid of it. A peacetime draft is the most un-American thing I know. All the time I was growing up I was told about oppressive Central European countries and Russia, where

young men were forced into the army. We sympathized, and were glad to welcome them here. Now by present estimates 4,000 to 6,000 Americans of draft age have left the country for Canada, another 2,000 or 3,000 have gone to Europe, and it looks as though many more are preparing to emigrate. We must cut back the size of the armed forces. In peacetime, a total of 1,000,000 men is surely enough.

[8] There is another thing being said closely connected with this: that to keep an adequate volunteer army, one would have to raise the pay considerably. That's said so positively that people believe it; I don't think it is true. The great bulk of our armed forces are genuine volunteers. Only twenty-one per cent are draftees. Whole services are composed entirely of volunteers: the Air Force, Submarine Service, Marines. That seems like proof that pay rates are adequate. It seems plain we can get all the armed forces we need as volunteers, at present rates of pay.

[9] But there is something much more important than the draft. The bigger thing, of course, is what [the late] President Eisenhower warned us of, calling it the military-industrial complex. We must begin to think of it now as the military-industrial-labor union complex. What happened under the plea of the Cold War was not alone that we built up the first big peacetime army in our history, but we institutionalized it.

[10] I don't think we can live with the present military establishment and its $80 billion-to-$100 billion-a-year budget, and keep America anything like we have known it in the past. It is corrupting the life of the whole country. It is buying up everything in sight: industries, banks, investors, universities; and lately it seems also to have bought up the labor unions.

[11] The Defense Department is always broke; but some of the things they do with that $80 billion a year would make Buck Rogers envious. For example: the Rocky Mountain Arsenal on the outskirts of Denver was manufacturing a deadly nerve poison on such a scale that there was a problem of waste disposal. Nothing daunted, they dug a tunnel two miles deep under Denver, into which they have injected so much poisoned water that beginning a couple of years ago Denver began to experience a series of earth tremors of increasing severity. Now there is a grave fear of a major earthquake. An interesting debate is in progress as to whether Denver will be safer if that lake of poisoned water is removed or left in place.

[12] Perhaps you have read also of those 6,000 sheep that suddenly died in Skull Valley, Utah, killed by another nerve poison—a strange and, I believe, still unexplained accident, since the nearest testing seems to have been thirty miles away.

[13] As for Vietnam, the expenditure of fire power has been frightening. Some of you may remember Khe Sanh, a hamlet where a force of U.S. Marines was beleaguered. During that period, we dropped on the perimeter of Khe Sanh more explosives than fell on Japan throughout World War II, and more than fell on Europe during 1942 and 1943. One of the officers there was quoted as having said afterward, "It looks like the world caught smallpox and died."

[14] The only point of government is to safeguard and foster life. Our government has become preoccupied with death, with the business of killing and being killed. So-called defense now absorbs sixty per cent of the national budget, and about twelve per cent of the gross national product.

[15] A lively debate is beginning again on whether we should deploy anti-ballistic missiles, the ABM. An ABM is a nuclear weapon. It takes a nuclear weapon to stop a nuclear weapon. And our concern must be with the whole issue of nuclear weapons.

[16] There is an entire semantics ready to deal with the sort of thing I am about to say. It involves such phrases as "Those are the facts of life." No— these are the facts of death. I don't accept them, and I advise you not to accept them.

[17] We are under repeated pressures to accept things that are presented to us as settled—decisions that have been made. Always there is the thought: Let's go on from there! But this time we don't see how to go on. We still have to stick with those issues. We are told that the United States and Russia between them have stockpiles in nuclear weapons with approximately the explosive power of fifteen tons of TNT for every man, woman, and child on earth. And now it is suggested that we must make more. All very regrettable, of course; but those are "the facts of life."

[18] I think all of you know there is no adequate defense against massive nuclear attack. It is both easier and cheaper to circumvent any known nuclear defense system than to provide it. It's all pretty crazy. At the very moment we talk of deploying ABMs, we are also building the MIRV, the weapon to circumvent ABMs. So far as I know, with everything working as well as can be hoped, the most conservative estimates of Americans killed in a major nuclear attack run to about 50,000,000. We have become callous to gruesome statistics. You think, Bang!—and next morning, if you're still there, you read in the newspapers that 50,000,000 people were killed.

[19] But that isn't the way it happens. When we killed close to 200,000 people with those old-fashioned uranium bombs we dropped on Hiroshima and Nagasaki, about the same number of persons was maimed, blinded, burned, poisoned, and otherwise doomed. A lot of them took a long time to die. That's the way it would be. Not a bang, and a certain number of corpses to bury; but a nation filled with millions of helpless, maimed, tortured and doomed survivors huddled with their families in shelters, with guns ready to fight off their neighbors, trying to get some uncontaminated food and water.

[20] A few months ago Senator Richard Russell of Georgia ended a speech in the Senate with the words: "If we have to start over again with another Adam and Eve, I want them to be Americans; and I want them on this continent and not in Europe." That was a U.S. Senator giving a patriotic speech. Well, here is a Nobel laureate who thinks that those words are criminally insane.

[21] How real is the threat of full-scale nuclear war? I asked a distinguished professor of government at Harvard. "Oh," he said comfortably, "I estimate the probability, provided that the situation remains about as it is now, at

two per cent per year." That means that the chance of having that war by 1990 is about one in three, and by 2000 it is fifty-fifty.

[22] I think I know what is bothering the students. What we are up against is a generation that is by no means sure it has a future. I am growing old, and my future so to speak is already behind me. But there are those students of mine, there are my children whose future is infinitely more precious to me than my own. So it isn't just their generation; it's mine, too. We're all in it together. Are we to have a chance to live? We ask only for a reasonable chance to work out our destiny in peace and decency. Not to go down in history as the apocalyptic generation.

[23] And it isn't only nuclear war. Another overwhelming threat is in the population explosion. That has not yet even begun to come under control. There is every indication that the world population will double before the year 2000; and there is a widespread expectation of famine on an unprecedented scale in many parts of the world. The experts tend to differ only in their estimates of when those famines will begin. Some think by 1980, others think they can be staved off until 1990, very few expect that they will not occur by the year 2000.

[24] That is the problem. Unless we can be surer than we now are that this generation has a future, nothing else matters. It's not good enough to give it tender loving care, to supply it with breakfast foods, to buy it expensive educations. Those things don't mean anything unless this generation has a future. And we're not sure it does.

[25] I don't think that there are problems of youth, or student problems. All the real problems I know are grown-up problems.

[26] Perhaps you will think me absurd, or "academic," or hopelessly innocent—that is, until you think of the alternatives—if I say as I do now: We have to get rid of those nuclear weapons. There is nothing worth having that can be obtained by nuclear war: nothing material or ideological, no tradition that it can defend. It is utterly self-defeating. Those atom bombs represent an unusable weapon. The only use for an atom bomb is to keep somebody else from using it. It can give us no protection, but only the doubtful satisfaction of retaliation. Nuclear weapons offer us nothing but a still terror. We have to get rid of those atomic weapons, here and everywhere. We cannot live with them.

[27] We've reached a point of great decision. I tell my students, with a feeling of pride, that the carbon, nitrogen, and oxygen that make up ninety-nine per cent of our living substance were cooked in the deep interiors of earlier generations of dying stars. Gathered up from the ends of the universe, over billions of years, eventually they came to form in part the substance of our sun, its planets, and ourselves. Three billion years ago life arose upon earth. It is the only life in the solar system. Many a star has since been born and died.

[28] About two million years ago, man appeared. He has become the dominant species on the earth. All other living things, animal and plant, live by his

sufferance. He is the custodian of life on earth, and in the solar system. It's a big responsibility. The thought that we're in competition with Russians or with Chinese is all a mistake, and trivial. We are one species, with a world to win. There's life all over this universe, but the only life in the solar system is on earth; and in the whole universe, we are the only men.

[29] Our business is with life, not death. Our challenge is to give what account we can of what becomes of life in the solar system, this corner of the universe that is our home and, most of all, what becomes of men—all men of all nations, colors and creeds. It has become one world, a world for all men. It is only such a world that now can offer us life and the chance to go on.

DISCUSSION

1. In which paragraph does Wald state his main idea sentence? What is it? Why does he wait so long?

2. How many reasons does Wald give to support the main idea? What are they? How are the reasons connected?

3. How does Wald use suspense in developing his argument? Why does he begin paragraph 6 with "But that is only . . ." and paragraph 9 with "But there is something much more important . . ."?

4. The statement in paragraph 3, "I think I know what's the matter," leads the reader to expect an explanation. Where is the explanation given? What is it?

5. How does that explanation relate to the question asked at the beginning of paragraph 4? Where is that question answered? What is the answer?

6. How does Wald's comment at the end of paragraph 4, "All War Departments are now Defense Departments," relate to the point he makes in the earlier part of that paragraph? In what sense is "Defense Department" a slanted term?

7. What comparison does Wald make in paragraph 6? How well does the comparison support the point he is making?

8. Wald gives some statistics in paragraph 6. How does he use the statistics to support the prediction made at the end of the paragraph? How sound do you think the prediction is? Why?

9. What is the comparison in paragraph 7? How is the comparison supported by the statistics Wald gives?

10. What argument of the opposition is discussed in paragraph 8? What method does Wald use to weaken that argument?

11. What cause and effect relationship does Wald mention in paragraph 8? How sound is it?

12. Do you agree with Wald that the sheep incident is "still unexplained"? Why or why not?

13. In paragraphs 16 and 17 Wald mentions another opposition point of view: "These are the facts of life." How would the opposition define "facts of life"? How does Wald define it?

14. What words used in paragraph 19 give the reader a vivid picture of what happens after a nuclear attack? Are these words slanted? If you think they are, rewrite the paragraph, describing what would happen in what seems to you more objective language.

15. Why does Wald say, in paragraph 20, that Senator Russell's words are "criminally insane"? Which man do you agree with, Wald or Russell? Why?

16. What kind of authority is used in paragraph 23? Is he speaking in his own field? What is the source of the statistics given in paragraph 23? How reliable are they? Why does Wald quote this authority and these statistics without any further comment?

17. Where does the conclusion begin? How effective is it? Why?

18. Trace the connection between each sentence of paragraph 29 and something Wald has said earlier in the essay.

19. Would you consider that Wald's presentation is subjective or objective? Support what you say by referring to specific things in the essay. How might Wald's audience (college students and faculty) affect his presentation?

20. How does the fact that Wald received the Nobel prize (1968) in physiology and medicine affect your reaction to this article?

21. *The Boston Globe* said of this article, "It may be the most important speech given in our time." Explain what the newspaper meant by that comment. Do you agree or disagree? Why?

Go Forth—and Shut Up

cloistered: sheltered; shut away from the real world
complacently: pleased with themselves
subsequent: done afterwards

From "Go Forth—and Shut Up," by Art Hoppe in the *San Francisco Chronicle* (June 18, 1968). Reprinted by permission.

[1] Of all the thousands of commencement addresses delivered across the land in the past few weeks, one is of interest. It was delivered by that noted professional commencement speaker, Dr. E. A. Farnsby Murd, H.S.G., B.A., D.V.M. (hon.).

[2] Dr. Murd had planned to give for the 373d time his well-known address, "Your Future Lies Ahead," which has so pleased boards of trustees and faculty deans, if not students, across the country.

[3] But whether it was "a touch of the sun," as Murd said later in his official apology, or, as several students put it at the time, "Man, is he ever shnockered!" the address took a different turn.

[4] "As you go forth from these cloistered halls," began Murd, as the dignitaries settled complacently in their chairs, "you represent the greatest hope of our society: we hope you won't rock the boat.

[5] "As I look over your acne-ridden faces, I can only pray that you will somehow meet this challenge. Although for the life of me, I can't see how. You look like nothing but trouble to me.

[6] "But at least you've had the benefit of a college education. Now I know that some of you may have wondered during the past four years what good it was to study Etruscan funeral orations or the derivation of Urdu dog calls.

[7] "Well, the answer to that is it kept you out of trouble. And there's nothing that's more trouble than a pack of adolescents with time on their hands.

[8] "Also, never forget that you are not the same snotty-nosed kids who entered this great institution four year ago. You are four years older.

[9] "This may help you to realize that you're going to go right on growing older until you're as old as I am. And then you're not going to want a bunch of long-haired, know-nothing young kooks rocking the boat either.

[10] "So it's in your long-range interest to keep your mouths shut and not go around asking a lot of fool questions about war, poverty or how come there aren't any Negroes on your firm's board of directors. Believe you me, these problems are a sight easier to live with if you ignore them.

[11] "So go along with the system. Get a good job in a growth industry, like missiles. Join a decent golf club where you can tell dialect jokes without offending any of the other members. Show a lot of respect for any leader or institution that's respected, so that others will respect you. And, for God's sake go to church on Sunday. It's a great place to make business contacts.

[12] "If you can thus apply what you have learned in college—namely that it doesn't matter what you do as long as you stay out of trouble—you will soon be a respected member of the community knocking down twenty grand a year.

[13] "To sum up with the basic message of every commencement speaker— if you can only somehow manage to follow my advice, you can wind up like me."

[14] In his subsequent letter of apology, Murd declined to take responsibility for the students shedding their caps and gowns and marching off to burn down the Administration Building.

[15] "Although my language may have been a bit unusual," he said quite truthfully, "I didn't say a thing I haven't said 372 times before."

DISCUSSION

1. How far into this article did you read before you discovered that this "report" was a hoax? What was there in the article that let you know?

2. What phrases does Murd use in paragraphs 4, 5, 6, and 8 that might appear in a conventional commencement address?

3. What phrases does he use that you would not expect to hear?

4. What specific pieces of advice, in paragraphs 10 and 11, urge the graduates to conform to the existing situation? How much of this advice might have appeared in a real speech? If it had appeared there, what would be the difference in the way it was said?

5. What comment about colleges is being made in paragraph 12?

6. How does what Murd said in paragraph 13 relate to what the students did in paragraph 14?

7. What does Hoppe mean when he uses the phrase "quite truthfully" in paragraph 15?

8. What is Hoppe actually attacking in this satirical article? Be prepared to defend your answer.

9. Can you see any relationship between the main idea underlying Hoppe's article and any of the points Wald made? What is the relationship?

A Serviceman's Servitude

status: standing; position
allot: give or assign a place to
defer: put off; delay
dominate: have power over; rule
inequity: unfair act or condition

[1] A few years ago a stranger might have wandered onto any college campus in America and found no more than a handful of male students who questioned the justness of their own academic careers. The families and friends of these young men expected them to go to college, and, having passed their entrance requirements, they wasted no time in asking just how it was they

Used by permission of S. S. Raymond.

now found themselves playing out the role of the serious student while others were undergoing basic training or trying to stay alive in Viet Nam. Their status as "students" was a familiar classification assigned to them by the government and not one in a hundred was reflective enough to challenge the system that had sorted them out for the campus. They were, after all, doing what came naturally.

[2] But things have changed. Recently, many students have begun to realize that the Selective Service System which allots the classification leading to the relative shelter of college is essentially unfair.

[3] This new conviction comes from the awareness that several reasons stand squarely against a sympathetic view of the draft. In the first place, large groups are discriminated against from the outset. If college is important enough to hold off even temporarily the demands of the military, then anyone who finds his way into college blocked by some barrier is excluded from the "protection" which college affords. There are families without the money for college, Black students whose life styles have not prepared them for the culturally biased entrance exams, and vocational trainees whose interests take them into industry, only some of which is considered deferable. The young Negro, drafted from the street corner in Cleveland and sent to the Mekong Delta *in place of* a future accountant in Beverly Hills is almost certainly being trained in a bitterness that will one day explode.

[4] Another reason that the present system strikes many as lacking in fair play is the absence of jobs available to those just below the current drafting age. Employers are understandably unwilling to give expensive job training to men who are no sooner trained than drafted. Yet through no fault of their own, these men can find no worthwhile work. Many, in desperation, enlist in order to get the "obligation" over with. Representative Taft of Ohio has said that the unemployment rate of those awaiting the draft is "double" that of "the entire . . . labor force." The draft would not be the sole cause of this shocking figure, but it is obviously a major consideration.

[5] A third point, and one not widely appreciated, is that the classification system at the heart of the draft controls the lives of even those not called, since it directs or pressures individuals into occupations that they would not otherwise have chosen. By setting aside certain classes of manpower as being free from military service, people are practically forced to accept second choices; they often want to prepare for one occupation, but end up training for a different one in order to escape the army. This kind of indirect planning of a person's life, in taking away the freedom of choice, smacks all too loudly of total domination by the State. The example of Hitler's Germany serves as the most vivid reminder of the great dangers which lie in this direction; and as with all great dangers in political life, lack of timely protest plays a part in allowing the full grown evil.

[6] So far we have been considering inequities of the system seen from the standpoint of those who succeed in escaping the armed services. But seen from the "hindsight" of those actually inducted, even more serious flaws can be

counted. A fighting man, like any other man, would earn a certain wage if competing in a free market, or better yet, if protected by some sort of collective bargaining arrangement. Not only are members of the army or navy not allowed to form a union, they actually face quite the opposite situation in labor-management terms. The draft might well be described as an officially imposed method of providing scab labor for the fighting forces. No sooner is one set of trainees available than a new "catch" of unskilled manpower is on the scene, competing unfairly, because they are artificially driving down the bargaining position that skilled laborers normally have, namely, the withholding of their services in time of need. Thus what is ordinarily a free man's privilege, the resort to the strike, is translated into a traitorous act: "insubordination" or "mutiny." The result is that the military "worker" is grossly underpaid. By undercutting the supply and demand balance, the draft imposes one more built-in miscarriage of justice.

[7] Finally, recruitment based on a threat is perhaps the most decisive reason for resenting and opposing the entire system. In normal human arrangements we assume that the appeal to good will rather than to fear will produce more long term social good. Yet here, a man is threatened with what will happen to him unless he submits to conscription. Furthermore, a citizen ordinarily faces the "confiscation" of his person by the State only after the commission of a crime. But under Selective Service, a man's body is appropriated without his consent and he is, oddly enough, expected to consider it an honor. Only because we have become conditioned by more than a generation of official propaganda do we fail to see the harsh nature of the draft and the extent to which it contradicts the values of the Founding Fathers. Free men, in time of real national peril, could be expected to volunteer in defense of their homeland. But how long has it been since our national leaders were willing to entrust that decision to the people?

[8] These five reasons, if carefully weighed, should raise serious questions as to the basic justice of our method of guaranteeing military manpower. Without in any way denying a need for armed forces capable of protecting against aggression, it is nevertheless apparent that too much inequality exists in the present system for the American people to tolerate it much longer. Military servitude, an existence only slightly better than the penitentiary term awaiting as the alternative, must somehow be turned back into true service: an option freely chosen on the behalf of others.

DISCUSSION

1. Which of these sentences comes closest to expressing the main idea of this article?
   (a) Their status as "students" was a familiar classification assigned to them by the government [and they did not] challenge the system that had sorted them out for the campus.

(b) Recently, many students have begun to realize that the Selective Service System which allots the classification leading to . . . college life is essentially unfair.

(c) The Selective Service System is . . . essentially unfair.

(d) Military servitude must somehow be turned back into true service.
Support your choice by referring to the essay.

2. How do the transitions between paragraphs help you identify the reasons supporting the main idea? What are the reasons?

3. What kinds of support are used for the reasons?

4. Some of the reasons support the idea that the present draft is unfair. Some of the reasons suggest that *any* draft would be unfair. How does the writer pull these two different points together? Discuss whether this shift in point of view might be one way of meeting the opposition's argument.

5. Would the argument be more effective if it gave statistics about how many students have chosen prison rather than the draft? Why or why not?

6. Would examples taken from the writer's own experience have strengthened the argument? Why or why not? If you think an example would help, where should it be used?

7. On what issues do you think Raymond would agree with Wald? Where would he disagree? How can you tell?

Let's Draft Only Men over 40

negligible: so minor it's not worth considering
encumbrance: a nuisance or burden
formidable: feared and dreaded
invariably: always
instituting: putting into effect
passé: out of date
melancholia: permanent sadness

[1] The trouble with the new plans for changing the draft law is that they do not take into account the changed nature of society and modern warfare. Both the President's plan and that of the House Committee on Armed

Services cling to the out of date theory that an army has to be young.
[2] This is typical of the military establishment's habit of gearing up to fight
the last war. What this country needs today is not a young army but a middle-
aged army. Let us consider the benefits that would follow from raising to 40
the minimum age at which a man becomes eligible for the draft.

[3] First, it would solve the problem of education deferments. By the time
they reach 40, most men have finished their educations.

[4] Moreover, once they became accustomed to the idea, they would
undoubtedly look forward with considerable pleasure to the prospect of two
years in uniform. For most, it would offer a welcome release from the
humdrum of rush-hour traffic, expense account swindling, and fixed smiles
that make up so much middle-aged living.

[5] Their wives might miss a few of them, but a patriotically forced separation would surely give many couples a welcome opportunity to reassess the
value of their relationships.

[6] Absence, says the old saw, makes the heart grow fonder. Can we not
expect that drafting at age 40 will restore life to wilting marriages?

[7] The parenthood problem is negligible. At 40, most men find their children
moving into adolescence, an age when most children find parents an encumbrance. And, for that matter, when most parents find the children an encumbrance, too. Financially, of course, the government would have to raise the
family allotment for the middle-aged draftee to match his civilian income, but
this would be a minor budget item.

[8] There is, then, no practical argument against the middle-aged draft. (We
need not linger over the wheezing military argument that combat requires
youthful muscularity. As we have seen with the astronauts and many of the
combat pilots in Vietnam, a well-conditioned 40-year-old can be a formidable
fellow. Practically all our generals are well over 40, and if their magazine
clippings can be believed, they are invariably tigers.)

[9] But the more important consideration is that the whole concept of the
young army no longer satisfies contemporary needs. Up through World
War II, war was essentially an activity for the enthusiastically immature. In
Korea and now in Vietnam it has evolved into a mature political form.
Practicality demands that it should be fought by mature draftees.

[10] By instituting the middle-aged draft, for example, we would surely
eliminate most of the immature harassment of the Administration by youngsters who feel that they have had no hand in determining national policy.

[11] A 40-year-old has 19 voting years behind him. In 19 years he acquires
plenty of responsibility for what the government does.

[12] When one of these mature wars comes along, you will not hear the
40-year-old sulking that "old men make the wars and young men fight them."
(And of course that always embarrassing cry of the young, "Too young to vote
but not too young to die," will happily become passé.)

[13] The politicians need not worry that the political weight of men approach-
ing 40 will make it more difficult to begin a mature war. Just as the over-40

population now can comfortably support a war policy, knowing that they will be exempt from the inconveniences of bullets, so the under-30 population of the future will be able, with the 40-year-old draft, to support war policies on the assumption that it will be better to get it over with before they reach draft age.

[14] The sociological arguments for the middle-aged draft are even more compelling than the political. As the population becomes ever younger, the civilian future of the 40-year-old becomes correspondingly bleaker. Today the man who has not won his vice presidency by 40 has little to look forward to until retirement.

[15] The prospect of being drafted would undoubtedly relieve the melancholia of early middle age. The draftee would look forward to meeting new people, discovering new cities, mastering firearms, and traveling abroad, perhaps to savor the fleshpots of Asia or the restaurants of Europe. After discharge, instead of returning to his corporation's retirement waiting room, he might tell his wife, "Hey, there's a hell of a good world all around here. Let's cut out."

DISCUSSION

1. What is the main idea sentence?

2. List the reasons given to support the main idea sentence.

3. Which of these reasons are supported by predictions?

4. What examples does Baker use? Do the examples seem typical?

5. What statistics does Baker give? How convincing are they?

6. Does Baker cite any authorities? If so, who?

7. Does Baker deal with the arguments of the other side? Where and how?

8. Do you find Baker's argument convincing? Do you think he intends you to be convinced? Find words and phrases in the essay to support your answer.

9. If you think Baker didn't mean to convince you, why did he write the article? What point is he really trying to make?

10. Do you think Baker would agree with Raymond? With Wald? Why?

11. Whose argument do you think is more effective, Raymond's or Baker's? Why?

WRITING TOPICS
FOR PERSUASION

The following list represents topics on which you probably already have
some specific convictions. If you select any of these topics, you will need
to be for or against something that the topic suggests to you. You can praise
or blame ("Eating snails is a good thing" or "Eating snails is disgusting")
or you can urge or oppose some action ("The use of marijuana should be
made legal" or "The penalties for smoking marijuana should be made
stiffer"). Some of these topics will obviously need to be narrowed.

electoral reform
gun laws
the use of drugs
automobile regulations
restrictions on travel
the value of travel

slum clearance
guaranteed income
euthanasia
compulsory composition courses for
   all freshmen
exercise (jogging, push-ups, etc.)

*"Classrooms! Classrooms! Do the Russians worry about classrooms?
Mr. Chairman, I, for one, want to know what our children are going
to learn in all those fancy classrooms."*

Drawing by Saxon, Copyright © 1958, The New Yorker Magazine, Inc.

industrial wastes
conservation
segregated schools
grading practices in schools
discipline of children
divorce laws
traffic violators
the jury system
taxation
the use of alcohol
women's clothes
men's clothes
compulsory school attendance
separation of church and state
need for dental care
rapid transit systems
limited access highways

academic freedom for faculty
academic freedom for students
student participation in
    college government
women's liberation
the generation gap
the plight of American Indians
dog laws
hunting and fishing regulations
underground magazines
government control of television
pornographic books
dirty movies
overpopulation
birth control
sexual relations outside of marriage

persuasion— fair and unfair 9

PERSUASION—FAIR
AND UNFAIR

Probably the main difference between fair and unfair persuasion is the difference between "I think" and "I feel"—between rational attitudes and emotional binges. Fair persuasion is always supported; it avoids *glittering generalities*—those carefully cushioned, pleasant sounding statements that never offend anybody because they never mean anything definite. A classic example is the expression, "a man of the people." Fair persuasion avoids *name-calling,* and instead of labeling its opponents "sniveling cowards" or "fascist dogs" or "loathsome perverts," it substitutes facts and figures and the weight of authority. Although fair persuasion may use opinion words freely, it does not depend on *slanted language* to prove its point. When we persuade fairly in our own writing, or are fairly persuaded by what we read, we are reacting rationally, not emotionally.

This does not mean, of course, that reason and emotion cannot exist together. In an honest argument, however, the emotion is created by the situation, by the specific detail, sometimes by the very calmness with which the writer states his conviction. There is nothing at all unfair about the following brief statement, one of the finest speeches in American history, yet almost nobody can read it unmoved:

> I am tired of fighting. Our chiefs are killed. Looking Glass is dead. The old men are all dead. It is the young men who say yes or no. He who led the young men is dead.
>
> It is cold and we have no blankets. The little children are freezing to death. My people, some of them, have run away to the hills and have no blankets, no food. No one knows where they are—perhaps freezing to death.
>
> I want to have time to look for my children and see how many of them I can find. Maybe I shall find them among the dead.
>
> Hear me, my chiefs. I am tired; my heart is sick and sad. From where the sun now stands I will fight no more, forever. (From the speech of Joseph, Chief of the Nez Perce, at Bear's Paw Battlefield, Montana, October 5, 1877.)

The emotion that results is created in the reader; it is not spewed out by the writer's hatred or his uncontrolled enthusiasm. What Chief Joseph has done is far different from what happens in the next selection:

> If you love the little children sleeping innocently in their cradles; if you do not want to break your dear old mother's faithful heart that has beat so loyally for you since you were a helpless babe in arms; if you would not sell out that beloved country over which the stars and stripes wave so gallantly, resist with every ounce of your manly strength the treacherous, foreign-inspired

agitators who want to deny your sacred rights as a brave American. Every
true man has an inalienable and God-given right to defend his homefires and
his loved ones from the rabble that seeks to defile them. Every real patriot
will refuse to register his guns. (From a letter protesting restrictions on the
sale of mail order guns.)

Honest argument gives reasons for its beliefs and backs up those reasons
with reasonable proof. When it gives specific *examples,* it uses them to make
the meaning clearer or the situation more vivid; and it uses typical examples,
not those that are rare or unusual. When it gives *statistics,* it makes sure
that the figures are honest. The surveys it reports are based on large samples,
representative of the whole group, and the results are stated in specific,
objective language, by someone who is not being paid for finding anything
special. It quotes from *authorities* who are speaking on subjects they are
well informed about, and who have nothing to gain by spreading their
opinions. Honest persuasion avoids "everybody knows" or "It's always
been . . ." When it makes a *prediction,* it remembers that what we say
about the future must rest on what we know about the past.

Honest persuasion does not recklessly claim that one thing *caused* another
without remembering that most events have many causes and that we are
never safe in saying that apple blossoms *caused* the baseball season to open,
just because they happened at the same time. When honest persuasion
supports its point by a *comparison,* it makes sure that the things being
compared are alike in important ways, and that the differences have nothing
to do with the comparison.

And honest persuasion avoids *guilt by association*—the kind of pigeonholing that assumes that because Jake eats lunch with a man who's been in
jail, Jake must be a jailbird too.

The next group of writings deal with what we do to our environment—
how we pollute it and how we work, occasionally, to improve it. Some of
the persuasion is fair, some unfair.

The Physical Environment

equated: two different things treated as though they were the same
boondoggle: like *pork barrel,* refers to private citizens making money
                 out of public funds
unsavory: bad-smelling, bad-tasting

Peter Matthiessen, "The Decent Society: The Physical Environment." Reproduced by special
permission of *Playboy* magazine (January 1969), copyright © 1968 by HMH Publishing Co., Inc.

bureaucracy: a large group of administrators, often thought to be as much interested in keeping their jobs, and thus making work for themselves, as in doing their jobs

contaminating: making dirty and unhealthy

aesthetic: beautiful or pleasing

defame: to attack a person's reputation unfairly

pervasive: found all over

[1] As long as Government indulges the commercial notion that growth of any kind means progress, as long as this blind "progress" is equated with the public good, its own agencies will compete in the cavalcade of development, led by the highway and construction engineers, that dooms a million acres of green land each year to asphalt or worse. The nation will lose much more than money in huge land-consuming boondoggles like the useless Arkansas River Navigation Project and the very unsavory Central and Southern Florida Flood Control District, which has made millions for a few speculators and big farmers at the expense of the public investment in Everglades National Park.

[2] As long as greed is glossed over—and it usually is—as an expression of "the free-enterprise system that made America great," we will witness such monumental idiocies as the proposed Rampart Dam, designed to drown a Yukon wildlife area larger than Lake Erie to furnish hydroelectric power *that nobody needs*. Government agencies, especially Interior's Bureau of Reclamation and the headless Monster called the Army Corps of Engineers, must play in the pork barrel with politicians and special-interest groups to find new make-work, for their bureaucracies have grown as huge and as obsolete as dinosaurs. The Corps of Engineers, for example, has recommended the nuclear blasting of a new canal across Central America, without troubling to ascertain the effects of such a series of contaminating explosions on the oceans and atmosphere of the whole world.

[3] The Corps still claims the strong support of politicians, but from the public it is meeting resistance; conservation education—the first step toward a decent environment—is beginning to pay off. Today, people look hard at the word "progress," and their skepticism must be encouraged.

[4] When told of United States concern for the world's poor, remember the fish-flour episode; this cheap, high-protein concentrate made from whole fish, a true source of hope to famine-haunted nations, was suppressed for years by the FDA on "aesthetic" grounds, due to pressure, it is said, from food interests fearing domestic competition. When informed of the chemical companies' dedication to "America's future," remember the great Mississippi River fish kill caused by dumped poisonous wastes, and the campaign to defame *Silent Spring*. When shown the merry chipmunk at play on the pretty stumps of reseeded forests, remember the orgy of cutting staged by lumber interests before new bills to save the vanishing redwoods could be passed. When introduced to the folks down at the utility companies and their

tradition of public service, remember the plentiful recent evidence that the public has been grossly overcharged for this service. Ask why these excess profits can't be spent, not on tax-deductible propaganda designed to con us but on replacing with stormproof underground cable the utility poles that rank with the billboards and garish gas stations as the most pervasive and unnecessary eruptions on our blighted landscape.

DISCUSSION

1. Obviously Matthiessen believes strongly in conservation, and he uses a good many opinion words intended to make his readers share his disapproval of what government agencies and businesses are doing. For instance, in the first sentence of this article, he uses *indulges* (what a parent does to spoil his children); *blind* (can't see where it's going); *cavalcade* (a parade for show, not usefulness); *dooms* (associated both with a death sentence and with the Judgment Day); and *worse* (as though paving green meadows weren't bad enough, there are other activities too dreadful to mention). What other opinion words can you find in the article? Do you consider the emotional language justified?

2. What is the effect of calling the people who manage utility companies *folks* instead of *a bureaucracy?* Why do you think Matthiessen chooses *folks?*

3. Are the examples Matthiessen uses in paragraphs 1 and 2 fair? Why or why not?

4. What is your definition of "progress"? After you have worked out a general definition, make it more specific by listing 4 or 5 definite things you would use to finish each of these sentences:
   a. Progress in city government means . . .
   b. I would expect a *progressive* government to . . .

5. *Silent Spring* is a book by naturalist Rachel Carson, in which she points out that chemical sprays used to kill farm pests have killed millions of birds and fish, often in areas far removed from where the actual spraying was done. How does knowing what *Silent Spring* is about help you see why Matthiessen mentions a chipmunk in the next sentence?

6. How does the mention of "conservation education" serve as a transition between Matthiessen's attack on government agencies and his attack on advertisements? Why does he attack advertisers at all? What support does he give for his attack? Do you think the support is fair?

7. Does Matthiessen believe that big business has a big conscience? Do you know any big businesses that have big consciences? Explain your answer by giving examples.

8. What would Matthiessen think of the five advertisements that follow this article? Try writing "When" sentences, similar to those Matthiessen uses in paragraph 4, for each of these ads.

PHOTO BY JAY MAISEL

"I'm sorry—but it's none of my business."

You've seen it happen.

Our anguished cities teeter on collapse, and the suburbs turn their backs.

A man falls down in the street, and no one stops to help.

There's a cry in the night, and everybody assumes "somebody else" will take care of it.

It seems that everywhere relationships have broken down. Starting with our broken relationship with God. Resulting in our broken faith with ourselves. And ending in our growing disregard for the other fellow.

It's true that maybe you, personally, can't change the whole world. But it's remarkable what one person can do, when he makes up his mind to start to mend a broken world.

Why not start today, in your church or synagogue? A visit in the place where the rule of the house is "Love thy neighbor as thyself" is always a great place to start great endeavors.

And who knows, you might even feel like spreading The Word.

How can you help? Write for free booklet, The Turning Point, Religion In American Life, 184 Fifth Avenue, New York, N. Y. 10010.

Advertising contributed for the public good

anguished: full of terrible pain and suffering
endeavor: a strong attempt

DISCUSSION

1. The Advertising Council, which paid for this ad, says the ad was "contributed for the public good." Is the Advertising Council's definition of *public good* the same as Matthiessen says the government's definition is? How do the two differ? What is Matthiessen's own definition? What is yours?

2. This advertisement begins with three situations in which, according to the ad, most people say, "I'm sorry, but it's none of my business." Does the advertisement give any specific examples of people minding their own business? Can you think of any? What is the relationship between the situations mentioned in the ad and the "broken world" that the ad asks its readers to "mend"?

3. More specifically, what does the ad try to get readers to do? What is the cause-and-effect relationship implied here? In your own experience, is this a sound cause-and-effect relationship? Why or why not?

4. Why does the ad use "our" instead of "your" or "people's"? Do you, as a reader, object to being told that you have broken faith with yourself, or, when you read the ad, did you think that comment referred to "those other people" and not to you?

5. Do you know any advertisers or businessmen who pay for advertisements? Are they more willing than other people to investigate cries in the night? Do the people you know who go to church regularly stop to pick up strangers who have fallen in the street? Do you do it yourself? Why or why not?

When you invest a billion dollars to help the cities, you learn some things.

Like hope.

Troubled minds: Back some 18 months ago, there were a lot of troubled minds all over this country. Including many in our business.The life insurance business. And what troubled everyone was the cities. There was poverty and frustration and decay and much ugliness all the way around.

In that atmosphere, when there was precious little hope anyplace, a lot of companies from our business got together to do something about it. To give it a try. You can't ride out the ups and downs of business without a certain inherent strain of optimism.

The life insurance business decided to invest a billion dollars worth of loan funds in the city core areas. Money that would create more jobs. More housing. Hopefully, more hope. And we made a public pledge of this investment.

You may say, this was just business as usual.

Because historically, life insurance companies invest in housing and in enterprise that makes jobs.

But this was different.

This was a new and special case of investment.

It went to an area—the inner cities—where capital was not readily available on reasonable terms, because of risk and location. Our business felt this special commitment was essential.

After all, our business is totally bound up with the health and safety of people. And people live in the cities. You could say people are the cities.

If those cities crumble, people are going to crumble, and business—ours, yours, anyone's—is apt to crumble right along with them.

In a businesslike way, our business was investing in its own future.

Due to the nature of the problem, the life insurance companies would need the closest cooperation of government and responsible leaders of the community. And they're getting it. With the result that the billion is now almost completely committed.

What we learned, was people.

By our very involvement in the core areas, we of the life insurance business found ourselves getting a lot closer to where people live.

We found that despite all the talk of backlash and Blacklash, there's an

A social services center grows in Bedford-Stuyvesant, being built with mortgage money provided by the life insurance investment. One of hundreds of projects in 227 cities.

even greater drive to work together. A drive to create, not to hate.

We confirmed a deep feeling. That the problem of the cities needs people—people in government, business, and labor, working together—to help solve it. And we discovered we weren't trying alone; other businesses were making special efforts.

The life insurance companies are re-learning a basic truth. Let everyone do what he does best. We ourselves know investment in housing and enterprise. Local planners, developers, and agencies know their communities and know their needs.

Our business has learned that its hope was justified.

Sure, minds are still troubled today. The situation won't "just go away." But...

The life insurance business has so much hope that it's taking another step.

A second billion.

A second billion devoted to the same aims.

While knowing that it doesn't nearly fill the whole need, the life insurance business regards this, like the first billion, as an investment in its own future.

Isn't it your future, too?

If you would like some suggestions on what you can do, write for the booklet "The cities...your challenge, too."

Institute of Life Insurance
On behalf of the life insurance companies in America
277 Park Avenue
New York, N.Y. 10017

invest: put money into a business in the hope of making a profit
enterprise: a project or plan

DISCUSSION

1. Words such as *involved, committed, commitment,* and *devoted* have picked up some associations from being used by activists in student movements and black groups. Can you explain why this advertisement says *commitment* instead of "investment," and *involvement* instead of "investing"? What other similar words does the advertisement use?

2. What is the "nature of the problem" mentioned at the top of the second column? Why doesn't the ad discuss the problem more specifically? Why is the ad writer careful to talk about "poverty and frustration and decay and much ugliness" rather than about riots, vandalism, and crime-in-the-streets? Since the people who live in the "core areas" of most large American cities are black, why doesn't the ad use the word *Negro*?

3. What is meant by saying "closer to where *people* live?" Don't "people" live in the kind of housing the insurance companies used to invest in?

4. How does this advertisement fit with the idea held by most black leaders that black people want a voice in planning and controlling their own communities?

5. What is meant by, "We ourselves know investment in housing and enterprise"? Does "investment in housing" mean the insurance companies know how to make a profit? Does "know . . . enterprise" mean that local people don't know how to make plans?

6. Bedford-Stuyvesant is a heavily black New York slum where one of the country's worst riots occurred a few years ago. That a social services center is being built there is definite enough, but what is meant by "being built with mortgage money provided by the life insurance investment"? Whose mortgage money? Is the Institute of Life Insurance donating the social services center from the interest it has collected on other mortgages? Is the Institute holding a mortgage on the social services building and will the people of the community pay interest to the Institute?

7. What does the "hope" in the title of this ad refer to? Who does the *hoping*? What do they hope for?

8. According to the list of the six wealthiest businesses in the United States in the *1967 Information Please Almanac,* three of these businesses are insurance companies. How did these insurance companies become wealthy? How much "risk" does an insurance company take when it issues a policy?

organic: from living creatures
despite: in spite of
pollutant: anything that contaminates

DISCUSSION

1. Unlike the two earlier ads, the Monsanto advertisement is doing two things: convincing its readers that Monsanto has a social conscience (it cares about water pollution) and trying to sell Biodize control systems. Which words in the ad are directed toward the first aim? Which part of the ad is directed toward the second purpose? Which part is more specific?

2. Except for the heading, all of this advertisement is written in conventional sentences instead of the fragments used in the earlier two. Explain why.

3. Although the advertisement is careful to say that "many wastes" cause pollution and that organic waste (human sewage) is only one cause, the ad avoids talking about the "poisonous wastes" that Matthiessen mentions. Monsanto is a big chemical company near the Mississippi River, manufacturing many more things than sewage disposal systems; why doesn't the ad talk about other kinds of pollution?

4. Why is the last sentence of the third paragraph in italics? Does the sentence mean that if the Monsanto Biodize system is installed, the surrounding rivers will be 99% unpolluted? If not, what does it mean?

It's your picnic.

Water conservation, recreation, forest management . . .

Electricity abundant, reliable, low-priced . . .

Protection of wildlife, aquatic life, plant life . . .

More than $100 million for cleaner air last year alone

And we electric light and power companies are glad to have a part. We've opened up thousands of acres of land so people can enjoy them.

Camping grounds, recreation areas, wildlife preserves, better environment—they're a way of life with us, and have been for many years.

We do our best to preserve this land we all live in—to share it with you as we work constantly to keep electricity plentiful, reliable, low in price.

That's one of the great things about free enterprise in the electric light and power industry: we know that the best way to make business better for ourselves is to keep making life better for you.

The people at your Investor-Owned Electric Light and Power Companies*

*For names of sponsoring companies, write to: Power Companies, 1345 Ave. of the Americas, N.Y., N.Y. 10019.

environment: everything that surrounds us
preserve: keep unchanged and unspoiled

DISCUSSION

1. What is the connection between going on picnics and paying your electricity bill? Why doesn't this advertisement make any attempt to sell electricity? What is it "selling"?

2, On the West Coast, many hydroelectric dams are built on public land, leased from the Forest Service. Why do the power companies need to "preserve" the land? In what sense do they "share it" with us if it already belongs to the public? What is meant by "opened up"?

3. What is the connection between the use of "The people" in the acknowledgment and Matthiessen's use of "folks down at the utility companies"? Between "wildlife preserves" and Matthiessen's comment about the dam that would "drown . . . a wildlife area larger than Lake Erie"? Between "keep electricity plentiful, reliable, low in price" and Matthiessen's "plentiful recent evidence that the public has been grossly overcharged"? Can you be grossly overcharged for something that's still fairly cheap?

4. Why does the acknowledgment say "*your* Investor-Owned Electric Light and Power Companies"? In what sense are the companies "ours"? Since all companies are owned by the people who have invested money in them, why doesn't the ad say "owner-owned"? Why is "Investor-Owned" capitalized?

5. The phrase "free enterprise" in the last paragraph contrasts owner-owned utilities with "public utilities"—that is, those owned and operated by the cities or areas they serve and thus supposedly selling electricity at cost. Is the ad suggesting that PUD's don't want to make "life better" for people? Why or why not?

George Washington Wept Here

WHY THE PEOPLE OF ANNAPOLIS
FOUGHT TO SAVE
THEIR HISTORIC BUILDINGS

[1] The nearly unbearable struggle, the almost impossible victory, the Revolution itself was over . . . and the Leader was going home. In the domed building at the left, Washington resigned his commission. "There wasn't a dry eye in the chamber," one witness wrote.

[2] The Continental Congress sat in that building. It was the Nation's Capitol for a while. Today it is still making history—as Maryland's bustling Capitol building.

[3] No other American community has such a concentration of *original* historic structures, most of them still doing a good day's work. Among them Reynold's Tavern, built in 1737, houses a public library office. The home of Charles Carroll, signer of the Declaration of Independence, is now a church building. Even the oyster dredging fleet—the last workboat sailing vessels in the U.S.—still brings its catch to the harbor.

[4] Time and events nearly erased these symbols of our heritage. But a citizens' group—Historic Annapolis, Inc.—fought to save them. Forward-thinking Mayor Roger Moyer gave his support because he foresaw economic benefits. The Maryland Historical Trust joined in. The State of Maryland created a Capitol City Commission. The National Trust for Historic Preservation rallied. The press rolled up its sleeves, and soon all Maryland echoed Secretary Udall's words, "Unless we understand and prize our past, we can't become a great and lasting civilization."

[5] Sinclair believes that everyone has a stake in preserving our scenic beauty and historic landmarks. We publish these true stories of private citizens—such as those in Annapolis—in the hope that *other* Americans will be inspired to action in their *own* communities. Visit Annapolis—see what the people there saved for you. Let us help you plan this trip, one to *any* of America's historic places, or to any vacationland in the U.S.A. Write Sinclair Tour Bureau, 600 Fifth Avenue, New York, N.Y. 10020. Dept. G.

concentration: collected in one place
heritage: something that belongs to people from, or because of, their
birth
rally: draw together for joint action

DISCUSSION

1. How is glamor by association used in this advertisement? What associations does the ad writer want his readers to make?

2. Although the advertisement mentions several groups who worked to save the historic buildings in Annapolis, he says the mayor supported the project because he "foresaw economic benefits." What are the economic benefits? Who would profit from them? Was that his only possible reason? If so, how "forward-thinking" is he really?

3. Even though there is nothing in the ad to tell you so, you may already know that Sinclair is an oil company, selling gasoline. How might Sinclair share in the economic benefits the mayor mentioned? What is the secondary purpose of the ad?

4. Is there a difference between "preserving" buildings dating from the Revolutionary War and "preserving the land we all live in" as the Power Companies' ad promises? Explain the difference.

5. The last paragraph of this advertisement says Sinclair believes in preserving "scenic beauty" too. Does Matthiessen believe that the "garish gas stations" help to preserve scenic beauty? What do gas stations do to beautify the landscape in your area?

6. Matthiessen's article mentions the fish killed in the Mississippi River by poisonous wastes; he does not mention the oil leak off the California coast in 1969 that ruined beaches for many miles and killed sea-life in an area more than a hundred miles square. Would you consider the oil company (not Sinclair) whose well caused the leak responsible for the wildlife damage? Why or why not? If you do think it responsible, who should be compensated for the damage?

Pollution

sturgeon: a very large fish, nearly wiped out

[1] If you visit American city
You will find it very pretty.
Just two things of which you must beware:
Don't drink the water and don't breathe the air.
Pollution, pollution.
They got smog and sewage and mud.
Turn on your tap and get hot and cold running crud.
[2] See the pollywogs and the sturgeons
Being wiped out by detergents.
Fish gotta swim and birds gotta fly,
But they don't last long if they try.
Pollution, pollution.
You can use the latest toothpaste
And then rinse your mouth with industrial waste.
[3] Just go out for a breath of air
And you'll be ready for Medicare.
The city streets are really quite a thrill:
If the hoods don't get you, the monoxide will.
Pollution, pollution.
Wear a gas mask and a veil.
Then you can breathe as long as you don't inhale.
[4] Lots of things there that you can drink,
But stay away from the kitchen sink.
Throw out your breakfast garbage and I've got a hunch,
That the folks downstream will drink it for lunch.
So go to the city, see the crazy people there.
Like lambs to the slaughter,
They're drinking the water and breathing the air.

DISCUSSION

1. When Tom Lehrer sang this song, he pretended he was a foreign visitor
   reporting on a visit to America. What specific details did he use to make
   his hearers see the situation through the eyes of a stranger?

2. How effective are his comparisons? How fair?

3. If you live in a large city, pretend that you are a visitor from another part of the country and list specific details about some definite city problem the way the visitor might see it. If you live in a farm area or a very small town, try to see some local problem from the viewpoint of a visitor from the city.

Chug Chug

vulnerability: openness to attack (by disease, an army, an argument, etc.)
susceptibility: likelihood of catching a disease
inhibit: interfere with

[1] Unless you drive a brand new Detroit made machine with its engine modified to discharge only modest amounts of pollution, you are contributing to the main source of smog in Portland.

[2] In 1968 it is estimated that our emitted exhaust added to Portland's air:

$$
\begin{array}{l}
\text{559 tons of carbon monoxide} \\
\text{51 tons of hydrocarbons} \\
\text{33 tons of nitrogen oxides} \\
\text{3 tons of sulfur dioxide} \\
\text{3 tons of particulate matter} \\
\underline{\text{3 tons of acid, inorganics, aldehydes}} \\
\text{652 tons per day} = \text{238,000 tons per year}
\end{array}
$$

[3] The carbon monoxide level inside your car in traffic is sufficient to impair the ability of the driver to react quickly. Sulfur dioxide aggravates existing respiratory diseases and contributes to their development. The hydrocarbons released from car exhausts react with the air to produce oxidants which cause eye irritation, fatigue, difficulty in breathing, and headaches. Nitrogen oxides affect lungs and increase vulnerability to infections. These chemicals are not definite causes of disease in humans, but they increase our susceptibility to diseases ranging from lung cancer and chronic bronchitis to the common cold and headaches. The air in an average city, like Portland, is equivalent to smoking seven cigarettes a day . . .

From "Shill" in *Willamette Bridge,* August 15, 1969. Reprinted by permission of the publisher.

[4] The best alternative is to use your car much less, use your legs a lot more, buy a bike, encourage a more adequate transit system in Portland, and arrange car pools for going to work. Car pools may inhibit your ability to get up and go but you will be able to get up and go longer. "Walk today, live a day; walk today, live a day"—say this as you trundle down the street.

[5] We must realize each time we step into a car that we are part of the main source of pollution in Portland. We cannot complain about the smog that makes it hard to see the West Hills and at the same time worship our second or third car. If you go to work with three other people, you decrease your contribution to pollution by ¼. Much thought should be given to a new cheap transit in Portland that would encourage people to leave their foul cars at rest in their garages. The change begins with each individual recognizing that he becomes a dirty animal in the car and that he is dependent upon machines at the expense of the air and his health.

DISCUSSION

1. What is this writer trying to persuade his readers to do? What reasons does he give for thinking they should do it?

2. What kind of support does he give in paragraph 2? In paragraph 3? Is the support fair?

3. What kind of questions would you need to ask before you knew whether or not to accept the statistics?

4. What cause-and-effect does the writer use? How sound is it?

5. What prediction is the writer making in paragraph 5, in the sentence beginning "If you go to work . . ."? How sound is the prediction?

6. Do you think the conclusion is slanted? Why or why not?

Senator Whiffenpouf Speaks Out

> **conservationist:**   a person who wants to save the natural beauty, wild-life, and resources of the country
> **nationalize:**   bring under control of the federal government

[1] My good friends and fellow taxpayers, before I begin my talk I want to ask you for your patience while I say something that is in my heart. I don't

Reprinted by permission of the author, Sheila Simonson.

have the gift of gab that some of these college men have. I'm just a plain-spoken man, a small-town boy like yourselves, but I want to thank the honest home folks who first gave a country boy a chance to serve in politics. [2] For the past two months my opponent has been mounting a vicious attack on the sacred institution of private property. His tactics are particularly vicious because they are disguised in a program to preserve the natural beauty of this state. He calls himself a conservationist. But do not be deceived. My opponent's plot to turn the beaches of our fair state into public domain is nothing more than an attempt to deprive property owners of what is rightfully theirs.

[3] Let me tell you a little story about my opponent. When he was at the University back in 1941, my opponent was a roommate of Joe Blough. I guess you all know about Joe Blough; he's over at the state pen serving time for bank robbery. That's the kind of people my opponent has associated with—convicted thieves. Well, this new public beaches project is thievery, too. It's robbing men of their private property so that a lot of riffraff can lie around on the sand. We don't need that kind of robbery any more than we need bank robbery.

[4] My opponent wants all the beaches to be public land—*public* land. That means he's against private property, and where I come from, a man is either for private property or he's for socialism. Do you want a socialist in the state senate? That's not all. He wants us to give away our ocean beaches to the Federal government. For a national park, he says. What if they turn those beaches into a rocket testing site? Look at what they did at Cape Kennedy. That was a public beach, wasn't it?

[5] My opponent favors nationalizing the ocean beaches. Nationalizing the ocean beaches is like nationalizing medicine. All you get is a big headache.

[6] Now in the past my opponent's program as a so-called conservationist has included an attack on billboards in recreational areas. Everybody knows that billboards are an old American institution, as traditional as turkey on Thanksgiving and trick-or-treating on Halloween. Billboards have been praised as an authentic form of pop art by leading art authorities.

[7] Let's take a look at some facts. In the five years after the residents of the Shenandoah Valley had wisely encouraged the erection of billboards, automobile death rates fell 25%. Clearly, such displays of attractive outdoor art had a beneficial effect on driving.

[8] Thank you for turning out to hear me in this hour of crisis. As I look at you here, all clean, hardworking honest taxpayers, I know in my heart that you are with me in my cause. A man's home is his castle and private property is the bulwark of freedom. Remember that, my friends, and remember that a vote for Whiffenpouf is a blow against socialism. Thank you, and God bless you every one.

DISCUSSION

1. Obviously, the main idea of this speech is "Vote for Whiffenpouf." What reasons are given to support the belief? How are the reasons supported?

2. What is the senator doing in the introduction and the conclusion? Do you consider it fair persuasion? If you had heard the speech, what would be the effect on you?

3. Does the senator use any glittering generalities? If so, where?

4. Does he do any name-calling? If so, where?

5. Does he give any examples? Are they fair? Why or why not?

6. Does he offer any statistics? Are they reliable? Why or why not?

7. Does he make any predictions? Are they sound? Why or why not?

8. Does he use any authority? Is it sound? Why or why not?

9. Does he use any cause-and-effect relationships? If so, what are they? Are they fair? Why or why not?

10. Does he make any comparisons? If so, what are they? Are they fair? Why or why not?

11. Does he use any guilt by association? If so, what is it?

On subjects everybody gets excited about, such as violence at home or abroad, all of us are inclined to fall back on slogans that soon become as meaningless as the glittering generalities they closely resemble. Recently such slogans as "law and order," "crime in the streets," and "peace in Vietnam" have become very familiar. In talking or writing about the bomb and the war, or about law and order, it is especially easy to rely on emotion instead of reason.

Three on Law and Order

obscurity: being little-known or unimportant
surveillance: watch
turmoil: great confusion
ideology: set of political convictions

[1] "The streets of our country are in turmoil. The universities are filled with students rebelling and rioting. Communists are seeking to destroy our country.

Russia is threatening us with her might, and the republic is in danger. Yes, danger from within and from without. We need law and order. Yes, without law and order our nation cannot survive. Elect us and we shall restore law and order. We shall by law and order be respected among the nations of the world. Without law and order our republic shall fall."

[2] "Our constitution favors the many instead of the few; this is why it is called a democracy. If we look at the laws, we see that they afford equal justice to all; if we look at social standing, we see that advancement in public life depends on a reputation for ability, and class considerations are not allowed to interfere with merit. Nor does poverty bar the way, for if a man is able to serve his country, he is not hindered by the obscurity of his condition. The freedom which we enjoy in our government exists also in our ordinary life. Far from keeping a jealous surveillance over each other, we are not angry with our neighbors for doing what they like. But all this ease in our private relations does not make us lawless citizens."

[3] "We hope you are taking sufficient precaution to prevent your being murdered by Nazi assassins. We think it is deplorable that those who profess the foreign ideology of National Socialism have taken it upon themselves to threaten the lives and wreck the property of our local Communists.

"We feel that if Communists are to be slaughtered here, that is the duty and privilege of real patriots. Already the crosshairs are on the backs of your necks."

DISCUSSION

1. These three statements about law and order were written by different people in different countries at widely separated periods of time. One of them is from a letter circulated in the American Midwest in the summer of 1969; one of them is from a speech attributed to Hitler when he was a candidate for office in 1932; and one is from a speech delivered in Greece in 404 B.C. Can you tell which is which? On what evidence in the statements is your guess based?

2. Which of these statements seems to you the most accurate description of the kind of conditions you are used to? Why? Which writer expresses the most reasonable attitude? Why?

3. Which of these statements seems the most upsetting or frightening? Why?

4. How does the writer of the first statement define "law and order"? What kind of laws would you expect him to want? What do you think he would do to maintain order? What is there in the statement that helps you answer these questions?

5. How does the writer of the second statement define "lawless"? What is there in the statement that helps you answer this question?

6. How does the writer of the third statement define "patriotism"? What is there in the statement that helps you answer the question?

7. Would the writer of the first statement consider the writer of the third statement to be acting according to "law and order"? What makes you think so?

8. Would the writer of the second statement consider the writer of the third statement to be a "lawful" or a "lawless" citizen? What makes you think so?

9. Which of these statements gives specific examples that support or illustrate the generalizations?

10. What is your own definition of "law"? Of "order"? Of "lawless"? Give specific examples that illustrate what you mean.

We Seem To Be Turning Our Backs on Everything That Made America Great

jeopardy: danger
solvent: out of debt with money left over

[1] We pamper criminals and hamper police, when the police are all that save us from anarchy.

[2] We spend billions to pay people not to work—when we need the workers, and haven't got the billions.

[3] Devoted men in uniform spend their lives, underpaid and in jeopardy, fighting to keep our nation safe. Then, for political advantage, we sweep aside their gravest advice.

[4] Companies which provide millions of the best-paying jobs in the world were built out of profits made by ambitious men who plowed those profits back, to make more. Now Government and unions call such men selfish, and tax and destroy the profits vital to tomorrow's jobs.

[5] We spend billions to get to the moon, for some ridiculous "prestige", instead of using those billions to reduce our debt and make us safe and solvent again.

An advertisement paid for by The Warner & Swasey Company. Reprinted by permission.

[6] For voters at home we placate our enemies abroad and attack our friends (and *how* we need those friends!).

[7] We concentrate more and more power in a central government (too often of little people) and so weaken the local governments—which are the very essence of democracy and freedom.

[8] We spend billions for foreign aid and let prosperous foreigners who owe us billions spend *our* money to deprive us of *our* dangerously-needed gold.

[9] *Common sense* used to be the outstanding trait of Americans. In Heaven's name, *what has happened to it?*

DISCUSSION

1. What is the main idea of this selection? What reasons are given to support the main idea?

2. How are the reasons supported—by examples? By statistics? By authorities? By prediction? If any of these methods is used is it fairly handled?

3. Does the writer use glittering generalities? Slanted language? Cause and effect? Comparison? Glory or guilt by association? If you think he does, explain where.

4. For each interpretation given in this article, first, find the factual statement on which it is based and, second, rewrite the interpretation to give a different view. For instance, paragraph 1 might be handled this way:
   Factual statement: The Supreme Court recently ruled that confessions obtained by force would not be admitted as evidence in the trial.
   Different interpretation: We are finally beginning to protect the rights of helpless citizens against the brutal tactics used by the police.

President Johnson's Baltimore Speech of April 7, 1965

infirmities: weaknesses

[1] I have come here to review once again with my own people the views of the American Government.

[2] Tonight Americans and Asians are dying for a world where each people may choose its own path to change. This is the principle for which our ancestors fought in the valleys of Pennsylvania. It is a

From Department of State *Bulletin*, Washington, April 26, 1965.

principle for which our sons fight tonight in the jungles of Vietnam . . .
[3] Why must we take this painful road? Why must this nation hazard its
ease, its interest, and its power for the sake of a people so far away?
[4] We fight because we must fight if we are to live in a world where every
country can shape its own destiny, and only in such a world will our own
freedom be finally secure.
[5] This kind of world will never be built by bombs or bullets. Yet the
infirmities of man are such that force must often precede reason and the
waste of war, the works of peace. We wish that this were not so. But we
must deal with the world as it is, if it is ever to be as we wish.
[6] The world as it is in Asia is not a serene or peaceful place . . .
[7] It is a war of unparalleled brutality. Simple farmers are the targets of
assassination and kidnapping. Women and children are strangled in the
night because their men are loyal to their government. And helpless villages
are ravaged by sneak attacks. Large-scale raids are conducted on towns, and
terror strikes in the heart of cities . . .
[8] In recent months attacks on South Vietnam were stepped up. Thus it
became necessary for us to increase our response and to make attacks by air.
This is not a change of purpose. It is a change in what we believe the purpose
requires.
[9] We do this in order to slow down aggression.
[10] We do this to increase the confidence of the brave people of South
Vietnam who have bravely borne this brutal battle for so many years with
so many casualties.
[11] And we do this to convince the leaders of North Vietnam—and all who
seek to share their conquest—of a simple fact:
[12] We will not be defeated.
[13] We will not grow tired.
[14] We will not withdraw, either openly or under the cloak of a meaningless
agreement.
[15] We know that air attacks alone will not accomplish all of these purposes. But it is our best and prayerful judgment that they are a necessary part
of the surest road to peace.

DISCUSSION

1. What is President Johnson doing in the introduction and the conclusion?
   If you had heard the speech, what would be the effect on you?

2. Does President Johnson use any glittering generalities? If so, where?

3. Does he do any name-calling? If so, where?

4. Does he give any examples? Are they fair? Why or why not?

5. Does he offer any statistics? Are they reliable? Why or why not?

6. Does he make any predictions? Are they sound? Why or why not?

7. Does he use any authority, other than himself? Is it sound? Why or why not?

8. Does he use any cause-and-effect relationships? If so, what are they? Are they fair? Why or why not?

9. Does he make any comparisons? If so, what are they? Are they fair? Why or why not?

10. Does he use any guilt by association? If so, what is it?

11. Put into your own words, as simply as you can, what President Johnson says in paragraph 8. Do the same for paragraph 9. What is the relationship between the two? What is the relationship with the last sentence of paragraph 15?

12. Compare what President Johnson says in paragraph 5 with what Wald says about "the facts of life" on page 379.

13. Compare what President Johnson says in paragraph 7 with what is said in "A Raid on a Fishing Village," page 313.

14. Is what President Johnson says in paragraphs 12, 13, and 14 a fact or a prediction? Why?

15. Is the language President Johnson uses suitable for his audience? Be specific in your comments.

Three on Nuclear Warfare

jingoistic: super patriotic
proliferation: rapid increase
euphoria: senseless happiness

I. BOOM,
EVERYBODY'S DEAD

[1] After a couple of decades in the nuclear age, we're reconciled to living with the Bombs—as long as we can keep on living.

[2] It's just as well that we don't get entirely accustomed to them; and there

From *The Herblock Gallery,* Simon & Schuster, 1968. Reprinted by permission.

are occasional new developments and reminders to keep us from feeling too comfortable. China's nuclear explosion in 1965 put the world under a new cloud; and that nation's membership in the Nuclear Club provided something to think about for people who wouldn't consider admitting it to membership in the U.N.

[3] There is also just enough loose talk from some military men and jingoistic politicians about getting tough with China and Russia, and making them back down, or showing them who's boss, to make us realize that all our dangers don't come from abroad.

[4] The bombs have grown up, but some of our politicians have not.

II. WHO'S NEXT?

[1] First we got the bomb and that was good
'Cause we love peace and motherhood.
Then Russia got the bomb, but that's okay,
'Cause the balance of power's maintained that way.
Who's next?

[2] France got the bomb, but don't you grieve,
'Cause they're on our side—I believe.
China got the bomb, but have no fears.
They can't wipe us out for at least five years.
Who's next?

[3] Then Indonesia claimed that they
Were gonna get one any day.
South Africa wants two—that's right,
One for the black and one for the white.
Who's next?

[4] Egypt's gonna get one too
Just to use on you know who.
So Israel's getting tense.
They want one—in self defense.
"The Lord's our shepherd" says the psalm,
But just in case—we better get a bomb.
Who's next?

[5] Luxembourg is next to go
And who knows, maybe Monaco.

We'll try to stay serene and calm
When Alabama gets the bomb.
Who's next, who's next, who's next?

III. THE ATTACK-PROOF
ABM

[1] Right Guard is a spray deodorant that sells for seventy-nine cents in the small size. Safeguard is an anti-ballistic missile system that would cost six or seven billion dollars in the early stages. Right Guard comes in a large economy size and Safeguard comes in a large futility size; the bigger it is and the more our country pays for it the less protection it provides as the Soviet escalates its ABM's and offensive missiles in response.

[2] The similarity of the names struck us as soon as President Nixon announced his Safeguard ABM program. Somewhere in the Pentagon or the White House, we suspect, someone with a flair for merchandising was hunting for a name for the new ABM system that would inspire a feeling of confidence and security. And there on a shelf stood Right Guard. A slight change and the name Safeguard emerged.

[3] We have had Sentinel; next came Safeguard, and there are reports of another ABM system to be called Defender. What we are waiting for is the ultimate euphoria in ABM nomenclature, the nuclear anti-missile system so happily named that no Senator, no Representative, no editor, no citizen, and probably not even the Russians or the Chinese will dare attack it:

[4] That ABM system will be called *Motherhood*.

DISCUSSION

1. Put into your own words, as briefly as you can, what you think the main idea of each of these brief selections is. How are these main idea sentences alike? How are they different?

2. What method of support is used in selection I? In selection II? In selection III?

3. What point is Block (selection I) making in the second sentence of paragraph 2? How does he make the point effective?

4. What point is Lehrer (selection II) making in lines 3 and 4 of paragraph 4? In lines 3 and 4 of paragraph 6? Do you think these comments are off the subject? Why or why not?

5. Is the writer of selection III serious in the comment he makes in the last sentence of paragraph 3? What is the difference between the four groups mentioned in the first part of the list and the two mentioned in the last part?

6. Are any of the methods of persuasion used unfair? Which ones? Why?

7. Which of the three articles seems to you the most effective? Why?

Maximum Security

enclave: territory belonging to one country, mostly surrounded by territory belonging to another country
sensors: detectors
prospectus: descriptive advertisement
labyrinth: a confusing system of enclosed paths, with the only exit hidden
almshouse: a poorhouse, where people live on charity
mausoleum: building for housing the dead
amended: added to or changed

[1] Specifications for a maximum-security residential development to be built in Potomac, Maryland, call for wire-mesh fencing around the entire hundred-and-sixty-seven-acre, sixty-seven-home enclave; for two guardhouses at each of the two entrances, where residents will show identification cards to gain admittance; and for electronic sensors installed in the shrubbery to set off an alarm on the arrival of unbidden guests.
[2] We are going to give people safety—something they can't get anyplace else," said a spokesman for the developers. "We will make it as burglary-proof, as trespass-proof, and as vandalism-proof as possible. Security is the thrust and theme of the development."
[3] Once inside this security, residents of the development will live on streets called circles and named, according to the prospectus, after various literary figures, including Frost, Hemingway, Melville, Thoreau, and Whitman. Frost

is, we believe, the poet who said, "Something there is that doesn't love a wall." Hemingway referred to one of his characters as being "just a coward, and that was the worst luck any man could have." Melville wrote of "The Nantucketer," who, "out of sight of land, furls his sails and lays him to his rest, while under his very pillow rush herds of walruses and whales." Whitman wrote a line that went, "For my enemy is dead, a man divine as myself is dead." And if there is to be a Thoreau Circle in the Maryland development, it should be marked by a plaque reproducing the advice of that expert in maximum security, who dealt with the problem this way: "However, if one designs to construct a dwelling house, it behooves him to exercise a little Yankee shrewdness, lest after all he find himself in a workhouse, a labyrinth without a clue, a museum, an almshouse, a prison, or a splendid mausoleum instead." [4] We hope that preliminary plans can be amended to include a Franklin Circle, in honor of Poor Richard, who once observed, "He that's secure is not safe." But, however the prospectus is adjusted and the maximum-security community is finally built, it seems fated to provide, in plan and spirit, one more dreary example of what happens to us when we function without the "Yankee shrewdness" Thoreau specified. We ought, somehow, to be able to outwit that kind of planning which seeks freedom from danger and finds that it has erected prison walls, or which, in its quest for peace and safety, shapes us a mausoleum world.

DISCUSSION

1. What kind of structure is suggested by the words "maximum-security," "wire-mesh fencing," "enclave," "guardhouses," "identification cards," "electronic sensors," and "alarm"? If the words "residential," "home," and "guests" were removed, what would you think the first sentence was describing?

2. What is the transition used between paragraphs 2 and 3? How does this transition relate to the point that is made in paragraph 3?

3. Probably the people who planned the development intended to give a touch of culture to the area by naming streets after well-known American writers. How does the author of this article show that these names are ironic, that there is a contrast between what these writers really stand for and what the builders hoped their names would mean?

4. The quotation from Robert Frost comes from a poem called "Mending Wall," in which one of the characters says, "Good fences make good neighbors"; the poet, however, thinks that fences are barriers between people. Which point of view would the developers agree with? Which do you agree with?

5. In what sense are the people who will live in the development "cowards"? Does the writer *say* they are cowards? Does he think they are? How can you tell? Do you think "cowards" is a fair term to apply to them?

6. How does the quotation from Melville fit with the main point the writer is making? Would Melville's Nantucketer have wanted to live in the new development? Why or why not?

7. How does the line from Whitman fit?

8. Why does the writer save the quotation from Thoreau for the last? In what sense could a dwelling house become a workhouse? A labyrinth? A museum? A prison? A mausoleum?

9. Is the author being fair when he includes the quotation from Benjamin Franklin, even though the prospectus does not include a "Franklin Circle"? Why or why not?

10. What is the main idea sentence of this article? What reasons does the writer give for his belief? How are the reasons supported?

11. How does the "prison walls" in the last sentence relate to the introduction?

Another highly controversial topic is the way young people behave, especially those who go to college. Public indignation has been aroused by everything from beads to bomb protests, from short skirts to sit-ins. The next group of readings all deal, in one way or another, with the ways people react to college students.

C. S. Rott and the Taxi Driver

C. S. Rott has been visiting some friends in Chicago between semesters. When we focus in on him he is in a taxi on his way to O'Hare Field to catch a plane back to college. C. S. feels ill at ease because several times the taxi driver has turned around in his seat to sneer at him.

TAXI DRIVER (*watching* C. S. *through the rear-view mirror*): You're a college
          kid, aren't you?

C. S. ROTT (*nervously*): Eh . . . Yeah.

TAXI DRIVER (*smugly*): I knew it. I can spot 'em every time.

C. S. ROTT (*inching his hand toward the door handle in case he has to get out*
          fast. "Roll when you hit the pavement," he remembers having read
          somewhere.): Really? How interesting.

TAXI DRIVER (*grunts, shrugs his shoulders, picks up a folded newspaper lying*
          on the front seat, and jabs it in the general direction of C. S.):
          You see this?

C. S. ROTT (*ducking back to avoid being swatted by the newspaper*): Uh . . .
          what?

TAXI DRIVER (*waving the newspaper in front of* C. S.'s *face*): This!

    (C. S. *takes the newspaper and makes out the item the driver means. It's*
about a college student of twenty-three who refused to be inducted into the
armed services.)

TAXI DRIVER (*who has been observing* C. S. *in the mirror again*): You finished
          reading it?

C. S. ROTT (*laying the paper on the seat*): Yes.

TAXI DRIVER: I hope he gets the full five years in the pen that he deserves.

C. S. ROTT: Why?

TAXI DRIVER (*getting more and more worked up as he talks*): Unpatriotic peo-
          ple like that *should be* locked up. He's shirking his responsibil-

ity. He refuses to serve his country. He's not willing to do his duty. He's a dirty un-American peacenik. In fact, he should lose his citizenship. He's a disgrace to our country. A lousy draft dodger!

Apparently the taxi driver has actually said something. *Apparently* he has said what he thinks about the young man. *Apparently* he has communicated his opinions to C. S.

Actually he has communicated nothing except an *attitude,* a *moral judgment.* He has said nothing.

C. S. wants to pin him down, but he isn't going to have much luck.

c. s. ROTT: What do you mean when you say he's "unpatriotic"?

TAXI DRIVER (*with conviction*): He's un-American.

c. s. ROTT: Why?

TAXI DRIVER: He won't do his duty.

c. s. ROTT: What's his duty?

TAXI DRIVER (*decisively*): To support America.

c. s. ROTT: How should he support America?

TAXI DRIVER: By doing the honorable thing.

c. s. ROTT: What would be the honorable thing to do?

TAXI DRIVER (*glaring meaningfully at* c.s. *in the mirror*): Joining the Army.

c. s. ROTT: Why?

TAXI DRIVER: Because that's the patriotic thing to do.

c. s. ROTT: Why?

TAXI DRIVER (*banging the steering wheel with his fist*): Because a *real* American wants to support his country!

c. s. ROTT: Why?

TAXI DRIVER: Because he loves his country.

c. s. ROTT: How do you know this man doesn't love America?

TAXI DRIVER: Because he won't do his duty.

c. s. ROTT: What's his duty?

TAXI DRIVER (*waving his fist at* c. s.): I already told you! To support his country! If there's one thing I hate more than lousy draft dodgers, it's punk kids who think they know everything! In my day . . .

(*For the rest of the trip* c. s. *endures a lecture on punk kids.*)

DISCUSSION

1. Which of these tactics does the taxi driver use?
    glittering generalities
    name-calling
    slanted language
    unfair examples

        unfair statistics
        misuse of authority
        unsound prediction
        poor cause-and-effect relationship
        unfair comparison
        guilt by association
  Point out the place where you think they are used.

2. What support does the taxi driver give for his point of view?

3. What is C. S. Rott trying to do by the questions he asks? Why doesn't he succeed?

Letter to the Editor: Creep-Coddling Sickens Citizens

treason: giving assistance to the enemies of your country
incite: urge or arouse
permissive: allowing people to make their own decisions
gratification: getting what one wants
perspective: point of view

To the editor:

[1] As a loyal American citizen, I want to know whether the leaders of the recent Chicago riots are in jail. Is Stokeley Carmichael behind bars? Have we locked up H. Rap Brown and countless others? Why not?

[2] Thank God this country has laws against treason, and against disregarding the law. Why don't we enforce these laws?

[3] Respectable citizens who work hard and pay their taxes are sick and tired of dirty, unshaven, straggly-haired protesters. We love our country. Why can't they clean themselves up and show some respect?

[4] Honest, hardworking citizens are disgusted with the disloyal agitators who incite riots. We're fed up with the spoiled, mindless teen-agers who demand immediate gratification of all their hare-brained desires. Pampered by permissive parents and permissive schools, they think they can get their way by sit-ins, demonstrations, and riots. Honest Americans do not use such methods. Civilized people keep their protests for the voting booth.

[5] If television programs paid less attention to these mini-brained, shaggy-haired creatures, maybe they would stop showing off. Why can't news coverage show clean, decent American youth who show how much they care by doing constructive works?

[6] We should also thank God for the wonderful, patriotic, dedicated law officers in Chicago and other places. Without them, where would we be? [7] Now these addle-brained agitators are going to harass free Americans when they go to vote. But free Americans have civil rights, too, and we are going to vote for candidates who see things from the right perspective. We will vote for people who promise to stop coddling creeps. We're in favor of civil rights that benefit the majority of honest, God-loving, patriotic American citizens.

Mrs. L. T. Smead, a Law-Abiding Citizen

DISCUSSION

1. The riots referred to in this letter occurred during the Democratic National Convention of 1968. According to *Rights in Conflict,* the Walker Report to the National Commission on the Causes and Prevention of Violence, blame for the violence that occurred in Chicago should be shared by both the Chicago Police and the demonstrators. Who does Mrs. Smead think was responsible? Support your answer by referring to the letter.

2. Does the introductory paragraph give the impression that any of the demonstrators were arrested? The Walker Report lists and analyzes 668 arrests. What does ignoring these statistics suggest about the completeness and reliability of the writer's argument?

3. What "laws" were being broken by the Chicago demonstrations? What definition of "treason" does Mrs. Smead seem to be using? What kind of actions would you say constitute "treason"?

4. According to paragraph 3, how does the writer think love of country is shown? Would you agree with her definition? What is the connection between shaves, haircuts, and good grooming on one hand and love of country on the other?

5. What examples of name-calling are found in this letter?

6. What does Mrs. Smead mean by "constructive works"? By "decent"? How do you know?

7. In paragraph 6, what does the "also" refer to? What do the police have to do with Mrs. Smead's point?

8. Peaceful demonstrations and nonviolent sit-ins are not against the law; they are, in fact, rights guaranteed by the Constitution. Would Mrs. Smead agree or disagree with the writer of "Rights *Are* for Rats"? (See page 330.)

9. What is your definition of "civil rights"? Who has the greater need for the protection of civil rights, those in the majority or those in the minority? Why?

Good, Clean Fun

manhandled: treated roughly
habitually: usually; regularly
quivered: shook
provocation: an action that angers, or irritates

[1] A city relatively free of civil disorders finally erupted into a major riot on the weekend before last. Over 6,000 citizens of Columbus, Ohio, took to the streets in a demonstration that lasted more than nine hours before it was rained out. Traffic on the city's main street was stopped; motorists had their cars walked on, painted, overturned. Store windows were broken. Police officers were manhandled by young rioters; bystanders were hit by flying bottles and bricks. And the mayor, who habitually responds to peaceful protests by sending in his club-swinging D-platoon, joined the festivities. Columbus newspapers, whose editorials quivered with outrage after hippies marched in Chicago, reported property damage without concern and pronounced the whole affair delightful. The police joyfully escorted the demonstrators. Governor Rhodes, who calls out the national guard at the slightest provocation, felt it had been a great day for Ohio.

[2] In short, this was a good riot. Well-scrubbed young Americans were celebrating the football victory of Ohio State over Michigan.

DISCUSSION

1. Why is it effective to begin this article as if it were the usual report of a "bad" riot? How far in the article did you read before you realized that something different was going on? What was the first clue?

2. Which makes the greater use of specific detail—this short article or Mrs. Smead's longer letter? Give examples of the specific detail you find.

3. Which of the two articles makes the greater use of name-calling?

4. The writer of this article depends on the comparison to make his main point clear. In your own words, what is the main idea sentence that underlies the article? Would the article be more or less effective if the writer had said openly what his belief is? Why?

Reprinted by permission of *The New Republic*, © 1968, Harrison-Blaine of New Jersey, Inc.

5. Would Mrs. Smead consider this a "good" riot or a "bad" riot? Defend your answer.

6. Is there any connection between "well-scrubbed young Americans" and the "clean and decent" youth mentioned in the Smead letter? If there is a connection, what is it? Could this "good riot" be an example of "constructive works"? Why or why not?

Smash-the-ROTC Drive Gains Momentum

devious: shifty; crooked
deferential: polite and respectful
academician: anyone professionally connected with education
diligence: earnest effort
PMS and T: Professor of Military Science and Tactics
factotum: a person who does all kinds of odd jobs for someone else
millennial: referring to a state of general perfection, far in the future
philophastering: a made-up word, giving the impression of false philosophy
unadulterated: pure; not weakened by anything
authoritarianism: control by the person in charge, without consulting or listening to the people being controlled
servility: slave-like behavior
inconsistent: not fitting with
candid: open and honest

[1] To Simple Simons who believe peace can be made by wishing hard enough, the faculties of Yale and Harvard must have endeared themselves lately by striking a body blow against the ROTC system.
[2] The manner of doing it was more devious than honest, and more deferential to the Students for a Democratic Society than to a national tradition begun at Lexington and Concord.
[3] The professors decided that training for possible military service rates no university credits and that professional officers detailed to such training duty are not to be accorded the dignity of professorship. That is exactly what the SDS says, so there must be a meeting of great minds.
[4] It is all too easy and natural for an academician, who shunned war

Reprinted from an article by Brig. Gen. (Ret.) S.L.A. Marshall by permission of the Los Angeles Times Syndicate.

service though he had the youth and physique that would qualify him, to draw the conclusion that acceptance of a commission is proof only of the individual's dim-wittedness. Still, I have served with professors out of the Ivy League in wartime who could not do one piece of assigned work properly because they lacked both horse sense and diligence.

[5] Since, due to kind Providence, there is something to the nation other than Harvard and Yale, it is scarce time to cry aloud: "Flee to the walls, all ye free men, everything is in collapse around us." Some of the commentators are doing that, professing they smell out a trend.

[6] Out over the country there are lesser halls of learning which are getting with the ROTC program for the first time this year. Administrators worry about a growing undiscipline on campuses elsewhere. They believe a cadet corps might become a counter-force for stability. There also are faculties and presidents rallying to strong support of the ROTC for the first time, and for much the same reasons. So it is not yet time to despair. The ROTC and God Bless America probably will be able to survive the blow.

[7] But if the SDS (Sudden Death Syndicate) is to get its way, along with an assist from Harvard and Yale, what is now called a trend could become an avalanche. This is not to say a national conspiracy exists among a minority of students and their helpers from the outside to smash the universities. It is to remark that the SDS has the ROTC in its sights and will gun it down wherever possible.

[8] The heat is on at Michigan University, not as yet a very big heat, but enough to give the PMs and T's the feeling that their backs shortly will be against the wall.

[9] The tactics are the same as those used against the system at Harvard and Yale, first to deny any credit to students who volunteer for training, next to refuse status to the trainers.

[10] The student factotum of this smash-the-military hoorah on the Ann Arbor campus is one Ron Landsman, from Oak Park, Mich., who spins out editorials for the Michigan Daily. He is categorized as a history major. The lesson he appears to draw from history, as deduced from his writings, is that all war can be ended tomorrow and we can turn on the millenial dawn, provided the world is made safe for hippyocracy. This daring approach to the baffling problems of our day has won him the managing editorship of the campus bugle. If Landsman knows any more about the military than did P. T. Barnum's Ooofty Goofty, such knowledge eludes him when he sits down to write.

[11] That would still make him a whizz kid alongside the mouthiest anti-military voice on the faculty, one Carl Cohen, who is rated as a professor of philosophy, and is beyond challenge a master of philophastering when he tilts against all things military, past and present.

[12] Prof. Cohen's thesis is that all who have served with the U. S. military are by reason of their service disqualified for effective citizenship. None but the unadulterated civilian is worthy of democracy in our day. He only is

able to think clearly and decide firmly; his strength is as the strength of 10 because his heart is pure. The ex-service person has been contaminated for life.

[13] How? Let me quote directly from Cohen. In these passages the philosopher sets forth to describe the brutalization and brainwashing of the U.S. recruit "torn out of the fabric in which his life has been lived, frightened, weak, defenseless, the hard and relentless rule to which he is now subject is impressed upon him in every possible way."

[14] "He is not forbidden to read or think, but he is given little time."

[15] "He is harassed, belittled, humiliated, not incidentally but as a part of the training program."

[16] "Not until he has really forgotten how to think seriously . . . not until then is he a soldier."

[17] The trouble with a soldier, says Cohen, is that he learns to be obedient. Sure enough, that could have been where Washington, Lincoln, Andy Jackson, Garfield and Teddy Roosevelt went wrong. The poor fellows had disciplined minds which is death to democracy, or so writes Cohen in this passage: "Obedience is the keystone not of democracy but of authoritarianism, of which the military is the perfect example. Obedience encourages, if it does not demand, a servility of manner inconsistent with candid expression of opinion."

[18] Cohen reminds me of the man who came to dinner. The show opens with some such lines as, "I think I have to vomit."

DISCUSSION

1. The way this article begins (referring to people who believe in the possibility of making peace as "simple Simons") is often called *name-calling*. It works, not by offering reasons that show why the other side is wrong, but by saying they are stupid to think as they do. What other examples of name-calling can you find in the article?

2. Explain the guilt by association used in paragraph 3.

3. How does Marshall answer the professors' argument?

4. Does the generalization implied in the first half of paragraph 4 include too much? How many professors that you know have served in the armed forces? Among those who have not, what evidence is there that they "shunned" military service?

5. In the last half of paragraph 4, Marshall mentions some professors who did serve in the war. Does this apparent contradiction weaken what he said in the first half of the paragraph? Why or why not?

6. Does Marshall give any definition, or example, of what he means by "do one piece of assigned work properly"? If so, what is it? Even if he had

been more specific, how sound would the cause-and-effect relationship be?

7. In Paragraph 6, Marshall says that there are some "faculties and presidents rallying to strong support of the ROTC and for much the same reasons." What are these reasons? How are they supported?

8. What justification does Marshall give for calling SDS a "Sudden Death Syndicate"? What are the connotations of "syndicate"? Whose death does Marshall mean? Which is more likely to cause "sudden death"—a trained soldier or a peace supporter? Why?

9. Can you find any sign of "It has always been that way so we can't change now" kind of authority in paragraph 10? What is it?

10. Why doesn't Marshall say that Landsman *is* a history major or that Cohen *is* a philosophy professor?

11. In paragraph 12, Marshall interprets what Cohen has said; in paragraphs 13 through 16, he quotes Cohen exactly. Does the quoted material support Marshall's interpretation? Why or why not?

12. If you have had any military experience, compare what happened to you in basic training with Cohen's description. How accurate is Cohen?

13. In the first sentence of paragraph 17, is Marshall quoting or interpreting? Is what he says supported by the quotations from Cohen in paragraphs 13 through 16? Why or why not?

14. Can you find any examples of glory by association in this article? What are they?

15. Is the "disciplined mind" Marshall mentions in paragraph 17 the same as the unquestioning obedience that Cohen says military training develops? Why or why not?

16. Express in your own words what you think Marshall's main idea is. What reasons has he given for his belief? What support has he given for his reasons?

17. How effective is Marshall's conclusion? Why?

Rock Event Ends Without Violence

exodus: departure
adverse: bad, unfavorable

[1] WHITE LAKE, N.Y. (AP)—The great rock festival ended today in the same spirit of peace and sharing that enabled 400,000 young people to gather for three days of music, marijuana and mod living without a major incident.
[2] "There has been no violence whatsoever, which is remarkable for a crowd of this size," said Dr. William Abruzzi, the festival's chief medical officer. "These people are really beautiful."
[3] As the great exodus of tired, thirsty, hungry youths began Sunday, security officials reported three deaths and close to 5,000 persons treated for injuries, illness or adverse drug reactions during the three-day span.
[4] A late afternoon thunderstorm speeded departures. But thousands of determined fans remained and huddled around flickering campfires through the chill night to hear the final concert.
[5] Despite the rain that turned the farm fields of the festival site into seas of mud again, despite the shortages of water and food and the lack of sanitary facilities, the spirits of the audience remained high at the end.
[6] Everything from drugs, to rides, to sandwiches donated by local residents and merchants was being shared. Volunteer doctors and nurses were treating the sick in hurriedly set up clinics to keep the hospitals free for emergencies.
[7] "Today," said Michael Lang, 24, one of the festival organizers, "is a time to think about what happened here—the youth culture came out of the alleys and streets. This generation was brought together and showed it was beautiful." "The peace they were screaming about is what they really want—they're living it. They value each other more than material things," said Lang, who had anticipated an attendance of only about 50,000 each day.
[8] The extraordinary response created traffic jams, health problems and material shortages beyond anyone's expectation.
[9] One man who worked to alleviate the problems was Max Yasgur, the dairy farmer who rented his 600-acre spread to the festival for a reported $50,000. He sold or gave away quantities of milk, butter and cheese.
[10] He also put up a big sign saying "Free Water" on his barn after he heard that some residents were selling water to the youths. "How can anyone ask money for water?" he asked angrily of his friends.
[11] "I never expected this festival to be this big," he told an acquaintance.

Reprinted by permission of The Associated Press.

"But if the generation gap is to be closed, we older people have to do more than we have done."

[12] And there was some evidence of understanding and appreciation between the old and young.

[13] "Notwithstanding their personality, their dress and their ideas, they were and they are the most courteous, considerate and well-behaved group of kids I have ever been in contact with in my 24 years of police work," said Lou Yank, head of the constabulary in nearby Monticello.

[14] Laura Glazer, an 18-year-old from Fort Lee, N.J., stopping in Monticello on her way home, commented, "Like wow, these people are really beautiful, the cops, the storekeepers, the Army, everybody."

[15] State police and deputies from the Sullivan County sheriff's office reported no disturbances or even arguments. They arrested about 80 persons on drug charges but there was widespread use of marijuana . . .

[16] Many of the remaining youths planned to camp at the festival site for a few days before moving on. "Some of them might decide to live here permanently," said one state trooper.

DISCUSSION

1. Is the headline of this article slanted? If you think it is, how—by the words it uses or by what it picks out to emphasize?

2. Does the writer himself use slanted words (not including the quoted material)? If you think he does, where?

3. What "authorities" does the writer quote? Are they all acceptable as authorities? Why or why not?

4. What statistics does the writer give? How reliable are the statistics?

5. What is the similarity between what Dr. Abruzzi says (paragraph 1), what the chief of police says (paragraph 13), and what Laura Glazer says (paragraph 14)? Why are all these statements unexpected or unusual?

6. Although this article appeared in newspapers as a straight news report, obviously what the reporter decided to omit reflects his own attitude and influences the attitude his readers have. What do you think the writer's attitude is? How might the readers' attitudes be changed?

7. Of all the police, neighbors, and young people who were involved in the festival, probably the writer could have found some whose comments would have been different from those he quotes. Write a brief sentence or two quoting what might have been said by
   (a) one of the neighbors who was selling water
   (b) some other policeman who was upset by "their personality, their dress, and their ideas"

(c) one of the 80 young people who were arrested.
What difference would there be in the general effect of the news story if these quotations were substituted in paragraphs 10 and 11, paragraph 13, and paragraph 14?

Puke Ethics

portfolios: collection of stocks owned by an individual or a corporation

[1] Early this year, students at Cornell demonstrated that since Cornell owned stock in the Chase Manhattan Bank, and Chase owned a piece of some foreign banks that made loans in South Africa, Cornell was committed to the monstrous policy of apartheid. So effective was the student analysis that Cornell sold its Chase stock and apartheid vanished from the earth forever. Most American colleges have yet to undertake the moral purification of their portfolios. The policies of a few major colleges, based on their most recent available financial reports, are here exposed; the rest are just as bad.

[2] *Harvard:* 340,658 shares of Gulf Oil, worth $26,311,764. Gulf Oil is in the process of producing natural gas in the Bolivian jungle. Bolivia killed Che. Therefore, Harvard killed Che.

[3] *Dartmouth:* 26,214 shares of Bulova Watch Company, worth $811,409. Bulova is the largest manufacturer of jeweled-movement watches in Switzerland. Women cannot vote on national issues in Switzerland. Therefore, Dartmouth is guilty of the subjection in which Swiss women are held.

[4] *Stanford:* 36,573 shares of Royal Dutch Petroleum, worth $1,828,650. Royal Dutch owns sixty per cent of Shell Oil Company in Oman, which has producing wells in Oman. Oman is one of the world's last havens of human slavery. Therefore, Stanford is one of the world's last slaveholders.

[5] *Princeton:* 92,509 shares of Litton Industries, worth $7,127,813. Litton is under contract to the Greek government to find development capital and perform economic studies. Therefore, Princeton is an accomplice of the colonels who have subverted popular government in the birthplace of democracy.

DISCUSSION

1. Does the writer of this article agree with the Cornell students? How can you tell? Does the title help?

2. What does the writer mean by "have yet to undertake the moral purification of their portfolios"?

3. What is wrong with the reasoning used in paragraphs 2 through 5?

4. Is the comparison between what the Cornell students were protesting and the examples given in paragraphs 2 through 5 a fair one? What are the likenesses? What are the differences?

5. Here are some other comparisons that might have been made to Cornell's investment policy and the students' attitude toward it. Which ones do you think are fair? Why? Which are not? Why?
   (a) If a man owns a parked automobile whose brakes give way so that it crashes into and damages a store, is the man (or his insurance company) responsible?
   (b) If a man owns a dog which bites a neighbor's child, should the man be held responsible?
   (c) If a church owns slum property where the roof leaks, the windows are broken, and the plumbing doesn't work, although the flats rent for more than five-room houses in the suburbs, is the church responsible?

6. Put into your own words the point the writer of this article is trying to make. Do you agree with it? Why or why not?

The problems of the poor are somewhat less controversial than crime and colleges, but any argument about how to get rid of poverty, or even whether we should get rid of it, can still create considerable excitement. A discussion on the problems of the poor and how to solve them may produce less name-calling and less guilt by association than a discussion of riots and revolution will, but it can lead to just as much unfair persuasion. On topics which can be measured statistically, as poverty can, it is especially important to decide whether the statistics are honest.

Not By Bread Alone

impact: noticeable effect
capricious: according to whim; irrational
thwart: keep something from being done
benighted: ignorant; unenlightened

[1] Encouraging though it is that the Senate Agriculture Committee has recommended increasing the appropriation for food programs for the hungry from $340,000,000 to $750,000,000, the desired impact will be blunted if significant reform in the administration of the food programs is not undertaken simultaneously. An Agriculture Department study found that on the average only 22 per cent of the poor are reached in those counties with surplus food distribution programs and only 16 per cent in those counties with food stamp programs.

[2] There are a number of reasons why some 20,000,000 poor Americans are not being helped in any way by either the surplus commodities or the food stamp programs. Foremost among them are unreasonable and capricious eligibility requirements. An example, cited not because it is typical but because it illustrates the absurd heights to which an obsession for regulations can be carried, is the dog-in-the-house rule in Cass County, Indiana. A poor family that owns a dog cannot get food aid in Cass County, presumably because a pet is regarded as a luxury. A widespread practice in farm communities is to deny food aid during periods when farm labor is needed, even though the pay for such work may be so low that a family cannot make ends meet on it.

[3] Obviously the most generously-funded food program can be thwarted by spiteful or benighted administrators. For that reason Congress ought to make sure that simplicity, reasonableness and flexibility are characteristics of the certification for food aid.

Reprinted from the *St. Louis Post-Dispatch* (July 2, 1969), by permission of the publisher.

DISCUSSION

1. The statistics given in paragraph 1 were gathered by the Department of Agriculture. Do you think these are honest statistics? Why or why not?

2. What is being illustrated by the dog-in-the-house rule used in Indiana? Do you think this is a fair example? Why or why not? Do you think it is a fair ruling? Why or why not?

3. Does the writer think denying food aid when farm labor is needed is a fair practice? How can you tell?

4. What is the main idea sentence of this article?

5. Would the article be more convincing if the writer gave examples of what he meant by "simplicity, reasonableness and flexibility"? Why or why not?

6. If you were administering a food program, what rules would you make to insure that the poor in your area were fed by the program? Give examples of how your rules would work. Do you consider your rules simple, reasonable, and flexible? Can you imagine anyone calling his own rules complicated, unreasonable, and inflexible? Why not?

Food: The Poor Still Pay More

disclosure: revealing something not widely known
devised: worked out
staple: a basic food item people need regularly, such as flour, salt, and potatoes
consistent: fitting with something else
mass media: method of communication (newspapers, radio, television) which reaches almost all the people in an area

[1] In the heart of the breadbasket of America—St. Louis, Missouri—food prices in 1967 were the third highest in the nation, according to the Bureau of Labor Statistics. This disclosure was made in the *Post-Dispatch* in October, 1967, by Eugene Bryerton, who suggested that lack of competition was the major reason groceries here cost so much. Mr. Bryerton's article led to the

Reprinted, with changes, from an article by Alberta Slavin and Jo Ann Budde in the *Mill Creek Valley Intelligencer* (June 1969) by permission of the authors and the publisher.

formation of a women's organization called H.E.L.P. (Housewives Elect Lower Prices).

[2] HELP devised a 65 item food price survey of food items basic to the homemaker's cupboard. HELP thought that if prices on these staple items were similar from store to store and from chain to chain, it would show there was little or no competition. The original HELP group surveyed 20 stores, 5 of which were in the low income areas. The comparison of four stores in the Kroger chain, two in Black neighborhoods in the inner city and two in upper middle-class white suburbs, is used as an example.

[3] Here are the results of the first survey, made in late October:

	GHETTO STORE A	GHETTO STORE B	SUBURBAN STORE A	SUBURBAN STORE B
Produce	$ .97	$ .99	$ 1.05	$ .89
Staples	7.35	7.29	7.05	6.78
Meat	4.00	3.98	3.44	3.70
Dairy	2.49	2.56	2.31	2.31
	$14.81	$14.82	$13.85	$13.68

[4] About two weeks after this survey was made, the results of two other surveys, one by the Human Development Corporation and the other by two *Post* reporters, were published. Both showed much the same price differences HELP had found.

[5] The third week of the survey showed how quickly prices could be adjusted by chain managers when differences were published. Of the sixty some items on the HELP list, well over half were more expensive for the ghetto shopper in the first studies. In less than two weeks, however, local concern had affected prices in the inner city, but only in the inner city. Prices which had been higher were reduced to a level fairly consistent with similar items in other stores of the same chain. Two pounds of Maxwell House coffee which sold for $1.69 in a ghetto store and $1.51 in a suburban store had been changed to $1.51 in both by the third week of the survey. A name brand of tuna dropped from $0.41 to $0.35 a can, a small box of Jello from $0.16 to $0.11, and an 8 ounce package of cream cheese from $0.39 to $0.35.

[6] By January, a dramatic change had occurred in some poverty area food prices since the original October survey:

	GHETTO STORE A	GHETTO STORE B	SUBURBAN STORE A	SUBURBAN STORE B
Produce	$ 1.09	$ 1.05	$ .95	$ 1.09
Staples	6.77	6.86	6.80	6.77
Meat	3.76	3.76	3.84	3.86
Dairy	2.25	2.25	2.32	2.21
	$13.87	$13.92	$13.91	$13.93

[7] The same items costing the poverty area housewife $14.81 at one store and $14.82 at another in October could be purchased at these same stores for $13.87 and $13.92 in January. Obviously the "human errors" the store managers blamed, errors which had been penalizing some poverty area shoppers in October, had been corrected. This 6% savings occurred at a time when the Bureau of Labor Statistics report showed a final quarter increase of 1.4% for food prices in the St. Louis area.

[8] By March, 1968, however, discriminatory pricing in some poverty stores was again evident. The same items cost $13.89 at ghetto store A, $14.56 at ghetto store B, $13.90 at suburban store A, and $13.97 at suburban store B.

[9] These results, along with results of previous surveys, were presented to a hearing conducted by the Better Business Bureau in March. The Bureau presented an 87 page report at the Press Club in June, 1968, which declared that no discriminatory pricing was practiced or being practiced by any St. Louis chain!

[10] "Human error" is not the only factor in pricing differences. Competition among chains in one area produced price drops while other area prices remained constant or increased. Prices also drop when community pressure is applied to individual stores within a chain. Note the results of selective picketing by members of the Tandy Area Council which, during January, distributed 5,000 leaflets listing all area stores for the purpose of consumer buying education:

	JANUARY	FEBRUARY	PRICE DROP
National	$11.78	$11.05	− .73
I.G.A.	11.74	11.39	− .35
Bettendorf	11.79	11.48	− .31
A & P	11.88	11.69	− .19
Fairlane	12.54	11.98	− .56
Gill's Market	12.57	11.37	−1.20

[11] So where have we come? It seems evident that the Better Business Bureau, an organization of businessmen designed to protect businessmen, is going to render no assistance and still wishes to maintain the fiction that there is no price discrimination. The Mayor's Committee for Development of Consumer Values has never existed in actuality. The two major newspapers in St. Louis depend a great deal on advertisements from grocery stores for their livelihood and are not willing to risk the displeasure of these supporters by publishing HELP results. So the problem becomes one of public pressure and publicity where there is no support from the mass media. Shopping for and buying food is a necessity. We must feed our families. We must buy food on a regular weekly or bi-weekly basis. We can wear clothes that are out of fashion, we can avoid the local movie theaters, but we cannot avoid the food market. And for regular shopping we cannot avoid the neighborhood store and travel frantically from store to store to shop the "specials."

[12] Meantime, HELP needs help. We need a better method of getting survey results published, or at least distributed to interested consumers. The ghetto housewife deserves a yardstick by which she can measure comparative prices, and she needs some means of making sure she is being offered competitive prices.

DISCUSSION

1. What is the main idea of this article? What are the writers' reasons for holding this belief? What kinds of support do they use to back up their reasons?

2. The introduction reports that Bryerton thought a main reason for such high prices was a lack of competition. How did HELP's survey show that Bryerton was partly right? What other reasons for higher prices are suggested in the article? Which of these reasons are given factual support and which are not?

3. Why did HELP include 65 items on its survey list and 20 stores in its survey? Do you think this was enough? Too much? Why or why not?

4. This article mentions a number of statistical surveys made or reported by various people: the Bureau of Labor Statistics; Bryerton, a reporter for the *Post-Dispatch;* HELP, a group of concerned housewives; the Human Development Corporation, a government agency; two other newspaper reporters; the Better Business Bureau of St. Louis; and the Tandy Area Council, another community group of concerned citizens. Which of these people or groups had something to gain by the outcome of the survey? What was it? How much would you consider their own interest in the outcome would affect the results they found?

5. What kind of language do the writers of this article use in reporting HELP's survey—objective or slanted? Support your answer by referring to the article.

6. What specific examples of changed food prices does this article give? Do you think these are fair examples? Why or why not?

7. Paragraph 11 begins with a prediction of what the Better Business Bureau is likely to do. How sound do you think this prediction is? Why?

8. Paragraph 11 also suggests a cause for the newspapers' failure to publish the results of HELP's surveys. How sound do you think this cause-and-effect relationship is? Why?

9. If you were going to make an honest survey of comparative prices on something sold by several merchants in your own area (washing machines, cars, textbooks, toothpaste—whatever interests you), how would you go about it? Be specific in outlining your plan.

Is the U.S. Really Filled with Poverty? A Look at the Facts

cult: a group brought together by worship of the same thing
diffusion: spreading
acute deprivation: sharp or intense condition of being without things
others have
per se: as such
adequate: enough
erroneous: in error, wrong
constitute: make up
affluent: comfortably wealthy
longitudinal: extended along a line; as Parrish uses it, extended in time
cumulative: building up over a period of time
malnutrition: not getting enough food

[1] When future historians write the history of the 1960s, there will be no more extraordinary episode in their accounts than the rise of America's "new poverty" cult. Intellectuals from every social-science discipline, every religious denomination, every political and social institution have climbed aboard the poverty bandwagon.

[2] Does the evidence on diffusion of economic well-being support the "new poverty" cult? Has diffusion mysteriously slowed to a halt, leaving millions "hopelessly trapped"? Are 30 to 80 million suffering acute deprivation in today's America? The plain truth is there is no basis in fact for the "new poverty" thesis. The high priests of the poverty religion have been exchanging each other's misinformation.

[3] The "new poverty" cult has built much of its case on family-income statistics. Some technical matters aside, there is nothing wrong with these statistics, per se. But there is something wrong, very much wrong, with their use. It is impossible for anyone adequately to interpret them in terms of average family economic well-being.

[4] Poverty fallacy No. 1 got its big push from the 1964 report on "The Problem of Poverty in America" by the Council of Economic Advisers. CEA determined that households with less than $3,000 annual income were in poverty. Using this income yardstick, it was determined that 20 per cent of

Reprinted by permission from a copyrighted article, "Is the U.S. Really Filled With Poverty?" by John B. Parrish, Professor of Economics, The University of Illinois, in *U.S. News and World Report* (September 4, 1967).

U.S. households containing 30 million persons were in the poverty class. [5] This report provided a wonderful takeoff point for poverty statisticians. With 30 million to build on, it was not difficult to find millions of additional families who should be added to the poverty population. The poverty numbers game became quite exciting. Who could count the most? Honors so far have gone to those claiming nearly 80 million. A majority of cult members have settled for a more modest 40 to 50 million.

[6] The truth about poverty-income statistics is this: Under no reasonable assumptions does income below $3,000 indicate poverty status. It may or may not, and to say otherwise is not only erroneous but absurd.

[7] Let's take as an example a young married couple, the Smiths. They are attending college. They constitute a statistical household. Their annual income is $1,500 a year. They are not being "hopelessly" shut out from the good things of life. They are, along with other American youth, enjoying a rate of access to higher education greater than the youth of any country, any time, any place. They enjoy electric lighting, refrigeration, adequate if not fancy food, and a second-hand automobile or motorcycle. They would like a new Cadillac, but will manage without one. They aren't "poor" and need no crocodile tears shed in their behalf.

[8] At the other end of the life cycle are the Joneses. Mr. Jones has been a machinist all his life. He and Mrs. Jones had always wanted to visit the country's great national parks after the children had grown up and left. So he has opted to retire at age 60. The retirement income will come to only $2,000 a year. Are they poor? The poverty cult says, "Yes," these people are suffering from deprivation. They have been "hopelessly" cast aside. Yet the truth is they have a small home paid for, a modest automobile paid for. They enjoy refrigeration, automatic cooking equipment, inside plumbing, TV, enough clothes to last for years—the accumulation of a lifetime. And now they propose to enjoy more leisure, in more comfort, for more years than similar working-class families of any country, any time. The Joneses think the Council of Economic Advisers is statistically wacky.

[9] And take the Browns. They are in the middle years. Both Mr. and Mrs. Brown work. Their three children are in school. They have a modest new home, partially paid for, some savings, some insurance, good clothes—yes, and a paid-for refrigerator and TV set. They have a new car and six install-ments still outstanding. Mr. Brown becomes ill. Mrs. Brown quits work to take care of him. Their income drops to below $3,000 for the year. Are they in trouble? Yes. Are they in desperate consumer poverty? Are they "hopelessly trapped"? By no means. After a tough year they will resume as members of the affluent society even by CEA's definition.

[10] These illustrations could be multiplied many times. Cross-section household-income statistics are a very inappropriate yardstick with which to measure economic well-being, which is a longitudinal and cumulative process.

[11] Let's return for a moment to the telephone as a luxury—or at least a semiluxury—consumer good. Now take the desperately poor on whom the

doors of affluency have presumably been "slammed shut." Now take the "poorest of the poor"—those at the very rock bottom of the income scale, those desperately deprived households earning less than $500 a year. You just can't get much poorer than that.

[12] Now observe that nearly 60 per cent of these poorest of the poor had telephone service in 1965. How could this be? Why would families presumably facing the grim miseries of malnutrition order telephone service? And, if we make allowance for the availability factor and the "can afford but don't want" factor, then it is reasonable to conclude that 70 to 80 per cent of America's poorest poor had telephones in 1965.

[13] If this is the "new poverty," it is apparently not too severe. How to explain this paradox of income poverty, consumer-goods affluence? The answer is quite simple. Income data are a very bad measure of economic well-being. The Smiths, the Joneses, the Browns, all had telephone service even though the CEA's income statistics put them in the "poverty class."

[14] The number of low-cost food programs has been growing rapidly. For example, the national school-lunch program provided low-cost noon meals for nearly 20 million children in 1967. The food-stamp plan provided low-cost food for 1 million persons in 1966, and was scheduled to rise to 2 million in 1967. The low-cost milk plan—along with school lunch—accounted for 5 per cent of total U.S. nonfarm fluid-milk consumption in 1966, and would have expanded even more in 1967 had not cutbacks been ordered because of Vietnam.

[15] The total number of low-income persons reached by various food-subsidy programs came to nearly 30 million in 1966, or precisely the number of persons classified as poor in 1964 by the Council of Economic Advisers. Since many of CEA's 30 million didn't belong in the poverty classification in the first place, some questions may well be raised as to who and how many poor have been "forgotten."

[16] The poverty intellectuals say they are building a great new society. Perhaps they are. But phony statistics are hardly convincing proof. Perhaps they should take a second look. They may well be rushing us pell-mell toward social chaos. The dogmas of the poverty cult may not prove as effective as expected.

DISCUSSION

1. In the first paragraph Parrish says that future historians will find the 1960s' concern about poverty an "extraordinary episode." Do you agree that it is "extraordinary"? If you do, are your reasons the same as Parrish's? Do you agree that it is just an "episode"? Why or why not?

2. "Cult" usually refers to people who hold the same odd or radical religious faith. What effect does Parrish gain by applying the word "cult" to people who are concerned about poverty?

3. What happens to the word "poverty" when Parrish keeps repeating it in *poverty cult, poverty bandwagon, poverty religion,* and *poverty intellectuals?*

4. In paragraph 4, Parrish says that it is impossible to tell how well-off a family is simply by looking at income; yet, though he does not agree with CEA's definition, he doesn't offer a definition of his own. What does this omission indicate about his purpose?

5. Does Parrish suggest that any of the consumer goods owned by the Smiths, Joneses, and Browns will wear out? Why or why not? How much can each family spend each week? Will their expenses each week stay the same? How much travelling can two people do on $38.46 a week? What kind of travel will it be?

6. What does Parrish mean by "automatic cooking equipment"? Which is likely to be the more expensive method of cooking in a large American city today, "automatic cooking equipment" or an old-fashioned wood stove?

7. What does Parrish mean by "telephone service"? Can this term be interpreted in more than one way? How?

8. In paragraph 8, Parrish includes "inside plumbing" among the list of things showing the Browns are not really poor. What does "indoor plumbing" mean? Is indoor plumbing something that everyone should have or is it a luxury? Are outhouses legal inside the city limits of most American cities or towns? Are they legal in the area in which you live? If they are illegal, why?

9. In paragraph 11, Parrish refers to "those desperately deprived households earning less than $500 a year. You just can't get much poorer than that." Is he being serious or sarcastic in the last sentence? Defend your answer by referring to other parts of the article.

10. In paragraph 12, Parrish uses two terms that are not very clearly defined. By "availability factor," he probably means that in some areas there are no telephone lines, and thus telephones are not available. What does he mean by "can afford but don't want"? Is "afford" an objective or a subjective word? What is the maximum income of those households which he says "can afford but don't want"?

11. If 60 out of 100 people have telephones, and some of the others can't get them and some others don't want them, does that mean that 70 or 80 people have telephones? Is that what Parrish says it is "reasonable to conclude"? Why or why not?

12. What is the source of these statistics on telephones? What is the source of the statistics on food and milk given in paragraph 14? There are other statistics given in this article; for which ones does Parrish give a source?

13. Is the information given in the last sentence of paragraph 14 a point for or against Parrish's belief? Explain.

14. Is the point of paragraph 15 that all 30 million poor people in the U.S. were "reached by various food-subsidy programs"? Or is the point that some people got help who didn't need it while others who needed help were "forgotten"? Does he mean both? Explain your answer. Would more precise statistics and definitions help to make this point clearer? Why or why not?

15. From the information given and implied in this article, write a definition of poverty according to the way Parrish sees it. How does your definition compare with the two definitions in Chapter 2?

16. Do you agree with Parrish's statement in paragraph 16 that "phony statistics are hardly convincing proof"? Has Parrish used any statistics that you would consider "phony"? Which ones? Do they make his article less convincing?

17. How much of Parrish's reasoning is sound? How much is unfair?

We've Been Brainwashed!

omnibus: including everything
idyllic: charmingly simple
leavening: lightening, as yeast does bread
asperity: sharpness; annoyance
allegation: claim
mortality: death
preposterous: outlandish; too silly to believe

[1] It seems there's no poverty problem in America after all. This wonderfully heartening news is inserted in the *Congressional Record* by Congressman Ashbrook (R., Ohio) from an article that we have just got around to reading from the *US News & World Report*. It's by John B. Parrish, and he's a University of Illinois economics professor.

[2] It seems we've been brainwashed by a new "poverty cult" which is trying to scare us with fancy statistics. Parrish uses the word "hogwash," and

Reprinted from "TRB from Washington," in *The New Republic* (October 7, 1967), by permission of The New Republic, © 1968, Harrison-Blaine of New Jersey, Inc.

the USN&WR, owned by millionaire David Lawrence, is delighted to spread the good word just as Congress debates the omnibus Social Security bill. It certainly is fine to know that young people are going out from the University of Illinois knowing that poverty doesn't exist. Oh well, maybe *some* exists; Professor Parrish agrees that there is a little—by "consumer-goods yardsticks" it covers "less than 5 per cent of U.S. households."

[3] Take the Smiths, the good prof says. They're a fine young college couple with annual income of $1,500 a year. Are they poor? Goodness, no! They have "adequate if not fancy food, and a secondhand automobile or motor-cycle." They "aren't poor, and need no crocodile tears shed on their behalf."

[4] Or the Joneses. They are in an almost idyllic situation. Professor Parrish explains that Mr. Jones has opted to retire at 60 in order to spend the leisurely autumn of his life visiting his children and "the country's great national parks." They own a small home and a modest automobile, both paid for, and have an income of $2,000 a year ($38.46 a week). Are they "poor," asks the professor? Nonsense, he replies.

[5] It's nice to think of such splendid families as these leavening the dis-content of our times with their solid satisfaction. Imagine the Joneses sitting down to their evening meal in Illinois. "Not chili con carne again, Mary?" says Mr. Jones with a trace of asperity.

[6] "It's wonderfully nutritious," she explains, "and we had some left over from lunch and breakfast."

[7] "Why, of course, dear," he answers, opening the mail. "Here's the elec-tric bill and the fuel bill and the telephone bill and the gas bill, and the real estate tax on our splendid little home has gone up $50."

[8] "It's so nice we own our own home," coos Mrs. Jones. "Have some more chili, dear—that way you won't have it for breakfast again."

[9] "I've been thinking," he replies, "how about a little trip. We have just paid the last installment, you remember, on our sturdy 1954 Studebaker and it's all ours now, free and clear." He opens the dentist's bill. "We might drop in on a national park. Or perhaps on one of the children."

[10] "I prefer the children, darling. The last time we went to Yosemite in winter they had to get us out with a snow-plough."

[11] "You're the practical one!" laughs her husband. "Which child shall it be?"

[12] Just then a tremendous racket is heard outside, and the doorbell rings. "It's that fine, free-enterprise young couple, the Smiths," says Mr. Jones, "on their motorcycle. They are doing famously on $28.84 a week; no need to shed crocodile tears for them, Mary. They do look a little thin. Always hungry, these young people! Perhaps you might put away the chili."

[13] We can imagine what a merry, merry evening the Joneses and Smiths made of it, and how they roared with laughter at the concept of the govern-ment that an individual is poor whose income falls below $1,570, or a family of four under $3,400. By this criteria, one-fifth of the US population, or upward of 30 million people are "poor."

[14] But the affluent stockbrokers and businessmen who read David Lawrence's comfortable magazine know better, and so no doubt do the bright-eyed students of Professor Parrish. The lower classes have not found "the doors to medical service slammed shut. Almost every urban community has free or very low-cost medical service for low-income families."

[15] I missed the professor's article when it came out September 4 because I was down in the Negro quarters of Belzoni, Miss., looking at the sordid shacks from behind whose cracked windows the hungry children peered out in wonder at a Whitey who wasn't a landlord, a cop, or an inspector. A family of four on ADC (Aid to Dependent Children) receives an average of $380 a year in relief in Mississippi.

[16] The infant mortality rate for Negroes in Mississippi is about double that of whites and is rising, while that of whites is declining.

[17] "We do not want to quibble over words, but 'malnutrition' is not quite what we found," said a panel of doctors of the Delta last summer. "The boys and girls we saw were hungry—weak, in pain, sick . . . They are suffering from hunger and disease and directly or indirectly, they are dying from them —which is exactly what 'starvation' means."

[18] Well, it's nice to find it's not so. In some mellow big city club a well-heeled broker will tap the ash off his expensive cigar and hand David Lawrence's magazine across the arm of his leather chair to his friend from First National. "Excellent piece, Charles," he says.

[19] Other statistics must be in error, too. That allegation that the world's richest country has been steadily dropping behind in reducing infant mortality, for instance. In 1950, the US ranked 6th among nations in conquering it; in '60, 11th; in '64 it was down to 14th.

[20] Then there was that preposterous allegation of President Johnson that 60 per cent of all poor people had never seen a dentist. Bah: humbug!

[21] . . . When I was a child at my grandfather's farm they used to kill the pigs in the fall. They tied them up by their hind legs, shrieking and squealing before they slit their throats. Once we children protested bitterly. But the hired man was reassuring.

[22] "They like it," he said firmly. We couldn't believe it. Their squeals, their heart-rending cries!

[23] "They like it," said the hired man.

[24] Today he's in Congress, voting against the poverty program.

DISCUSSION

1. As the introduction says, this article is obviously a reaction to Parrish's earlier essay. Does the author expect you to believe the first sentence? How can you tell? If you think he does not mean what he says, find other instances of statements readers are not supposed to take seriously.

2. Nearly a third of this article is an imaginary scene between two of the families Parrish mentions in his article. Does TRB treat Parrish's examples fairly? Give reasons for your answer.

3. What is the effect of the frequent short quotations from the Parrish article?

4. The conversation between Mr. and Mrs. Jones is written like the script for a television soap opera. What qualities that we usually associate with soap operas does TRB use? Why are they effective or ineffective here?

5. Why does TRB break Parrish's (actually the government's) yearly income figures down into weekly income? How does he use what Mr. Jones says in paragraph 7 to make this weekly income more meaningful?

6. The Parrish article does a lot of name-calling; for instance, Parrish says openly that the members of the "poverty cult" have deliberately distorted their statistics for their own purposes. How does TRB suggest that the motives of Parrish and USN&WR may not be completely honest? How does he suggest that USN&WR may be biased?

7. Which of the two men would you be more willing to accept as an authority on poverty? Why?

8. In paragraph 17, why does TRB quote from the doctors' report? Is this a fair use of authority? Why or why not?

9. TRB mentions four brief statistics related to poverty in the U.S. (See paragraphs 13, 15, 16, and 19.) What sources does he give for these statistics? If you doubted their accuracy, how could you check them?

10. One way TRB makes his point is by emphasizing the contrast between the children in Mississippi (paragraphs 15–17) and the readers of USN&WR (paragraph 18). Which words and statements point out these contrasts?

11. Paragraph 18 begins with a very quiet, ordinary statement, in natural conversational language. Would it have been more or less effective if TRB had accused Parrish of not knowing what he was talking about? Why?

12. In the comparison with which TRB ends his article, what is being compared to what? Do you think this is a fair analogy? Why or why not? Is it effective? Why or why not?

13. How satisfactory is the single-line conclusion? If you think it is satisfactory, explain why.

14. What does the title of this article refer to? Who is brainwashing whom?

Cartoons As Persuaders

In daily life we are "persuaded" by almost everything we experience. Not just editorials and advertisements, but also popular songs, movies, news reports, conversations, class discussions, television comedians all influence our attitudes and therefore our convictions. Among the most prominent of these "persuaders" are the cartoon strips that all of us read, often before we are old enough to fully understand what is funny about them.

Writing Exercises

For each of these cartoons
1. construct a main idea sentence that seems to represent the point;
2. analyze how the cartoon "supports" the point—what assumptions the cartoonist makes, what ready-made attitudes he expects his readers to have;
3. write a persuasive paper based on the cartoon, agreeing with the cartoonist and offering other kinds of support; disagreeing, attacking his argument, and offering reasons of your own; or taking off on some related conviction, suggested to you by something in the cartoon.

From Florida to Oregon . . . every man his own gun!

Drawing by Behrendt. Reprinted with permission of the Ben Roth
Agency.

FEIFFER

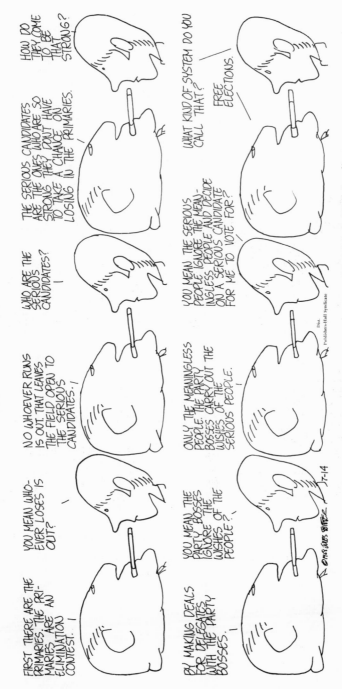

FIRST THERE ARE THE PRIMARIES. THE PRIMARIES ARE AN ELIMINATION CONTEST.

YOU MEAN WHO-EVER LOSES IS OUT?

NO. WHOEVER RUNS IS OUT. THAT LEAVES THE FIELD OPEN TO THE SERIOUS CANDIDATES.

WHO ARE THE SERIOUS CANDIDATES?

THE SERIOUS CANDIDATES ARE THE ONES WHO ARE SO STRONG THEY DON'T HAVE TO TAKE A CHANCE ON LOSING IN THE PRIMARIES.

HOW DO THEY COME TO BE THAT STRONG?

BY MAKING DEALS FOR DELEGATES WITH THE PARTY BOSSES.

YOU MEAN THE PARTY BOSSES IGNORE THE WISHES OF THE PEOPLE?

ONLY THE MEANINGLESS PEOPLE. THE PARTY BOSSES CARRY OUT THE WISHES OF THE SERIOUS PEOPLE.

YOU MEAN THE SERIOUS PEOPLE IGNORE THE MEAN-INGLESS PEOPLE AND DECIDE ON A SERIOUS CANDIDATE FOR ME TO VOTE FOR?

WHAT KIND OF SYSTEM DO YOU CALL THAT?

FREE ELECTIONS.

Drawing by Dan O'Neill. Reprinted with permission of The Chronicle Publishing Co.

MUTT AND JEFF — 'THAT'S A BLAST!

Created by BUD FISHER

Copyright © 1969. AEdita S. de Beaumont. All World Rights Reserved. Trade Mark Registered. A Bell-McClure Syndicate Feature.

SOME SUGGESTED
PROJECTS

1. Make a survey of campus opinion on
    some current controversial topic, either local or national:
    attitudes toward the draft
    faculty participation in political issues
    student participation in planning curriculum
    the discussion of controversial issues in the classroom
    improvement (or deterioration) of counseling services
    of cafeteria food
    of physical education facilities
    of convocation speakers
    of social life

2. Make a survey showing something about college backgrounds:
    areas of the country represented in the college
    education and previous experience of the faculty
    religious affiliations represented
    foreign students attending
    ratio of cars to students
    number of married students

3. Use the results of your survey in two ways: first as an accurate, objective
    report; second, to back up one of your reasons in a paper of persuasion.

4. Write two reports of the same controversial event, slanting one of the
    reports so that readers will sympathize with the main participants,
    one so that the readers will feel distaste or disgust.

5. Write an advertisement for any product that appeals to you; then write
    a "social service" ad that might be sponsored by the same company.

6. Write two persuasive papers taking the same stand on the same topic.
    Make one of them a straightforward argument, supported by the best
    methods you can find; make the other a satirical attack.